*Edward Ilsley*

*Yours faithfully*

*+ Edward Bp of Birmingham*

*Bishop Ilsley at the time of his silver jubilee. The archives of the Archbishop Ilsley School.*

# Edward Ilsley

## Bishop of Birmingham
## 1888–1911

## Archbishop
## 1911–1921

MARY McINALLY

With a Foreword by
BISHOP PHILIP PARGETER
*Apostolic Administrator of the Archdiocese of Birmingham*

BURNS & OATES
London and New York

First published in Great Britain in 2002 by
BURNS & OATES
*A Continuum imprint*
The Tower Building
11 York Road, London SE1 7NX

© 2002 Mary McInally

ISBN 0 86012 3154

Typeset by BookEns Ltd, Royston, Herts
Printed and bound in Great Britain by Biddles,
Guildford and King's Lynn

# Contents

List of Illustrations       vii

Foreword by Bishop Philip Pargeter       xi

Preface and Acknowledgements       xiii

Family Tree       xvi

Biographical Notes       xvii

Abbreviations       xxiii

1. Early Years       1

2. Missionary Priest       16

3. The Formation of St Bernard's Seminary       37

4. Father Rector       63

5. Auxiliary Bishop       81

6. The Succession       99

7. The Closure of St Bernard's       118

8. A Return to Oscott       137

9. The Central Seminary       151

10. The New Order of Things       173

11. Policies Reversed       187

12. Rescue, Emigration and Welfare       207

13. The Struggle for Catholic Education       230

14. Diocesan Bishop       249

15. Cotton College       276

16. A Transformation Scene       292

# CONTENTS

| | | |
|---|---|---|
| 17. | Archbishop and Metropolitan | 309 |
| 18. | The Great War | 330 |
| 19. | Besford Court | 350 |
| 20. | Retirement | 362 |
| 21. | Final Years | 377 |
| | Epilogue | 396 |
| | Bibliography | 402 |
| | Index | 406 |

# *Illustrations*

Frontispiece   Bishop Ilsley at the tiime of his silver jubilee

1.1   Charles and Mary, the father and mother of Edward Ilsley   2
1.2   A view of Harvington Hall after its restoration in the 1930s   3
1.3   The graves of Joseph and Isabella Ilsley   4
1.4   Sedgley Park in 1826, from a drawing by Robert Noyes   7

2.1   The six pottery towns of North Staffordshire   17
2.2   Drawing made from a postcard of Longton *c*. 1900   19
2.3   Drawing of women brushing down their houses in
        Heathcote Road, Longton   20
2.4   St Gregory's Church, Longton   24
2.5   Edward Ilsley elected as a member of the first school
        board formed at Longton in 1871   28
2.6   James Massam and his curate Edward Ilsley outside
        St Gregory's Longton   31

3.1   Cardinal Nicholas Wiseman, Archbishop of Westminster   38
3.2   Elevation of St Bernard's Seminary   41
3.3   St Bernard's Seminary, Olton   42
3.4   William Bernard Ullathorne, Bishop of Birmingham   51

4.1   Edward Ilsley when Rector of St Bernard's   62
4.2   Henry Parkinson as a student at St Bernard's   64
4.3   The Grace Cup   66
4.4   Henry Parkinson, Vice Rector of St Bernard's   71
4.5   Memorial card, Charles Ilsley   73
4.6   John Henry Newman   74

5.1   The pectoral cross and chain presented to Edward Ilsley
        in 1879   86
5.2   Edward Ilsley, Bishop Auxiliary   89

6.1   Cardinal Henry Edward Manning, Archbishop of
      Westminster                                                    106
6.2   Admission card for the enthronement of Bishop Ilsley           107
6.3   Edward Ilsley, Bishop of Birmingham                            112

7.1   Canon James O'Hanlon, the rector of St Bernard's, with
      a group of students in 1888                                    122

8.1   A view of Oscott College, *c*. 1880                            139
8.2   Mgr Henry Parkinson, Vice Rector of Oscott College             141

9.1   Cardinal Herbert Vaughan, Archbishop of Westminster            152
9.2   Victor J. Schobel, St Bernard's Seminary                       161

10.1  Bishop Ilsley with a group of servants                         175
10.2  John McIntyre on the steps of the entrance to Oscott
      College                                                        179

11.1  Cardinal Francis Bourne, Archbishop of Westminster             188
11.2  Archbishop Ilsley's Arms                                       205

12.1  Edward Ilsley, Bishop of Birmingham                            206
12.2  From the archives of the Father Hudson's Homes                 215
12.3  Father George Hudson in 1898, aged 25                          215

13.1  Growth of expenditure on maintenance                           232

14.1  Pope Leo XIII                                                  255
14.2  Title page of a Jubilee Song                                   268
14.3  'Familiar Figures' 637, from the *Evening Dispatch*            270
14.4  Postcard from Edward Ilsley to his sister Ellen Brindley       271

15.1  James Dey                                                      280
15.2  A drawing of John Hopwood                                      282
15.3  Walter Ireland                                                 285

16.1  Revd Michael Glancey                                           298

17.1  Edward Ilsley at the time of his investiture as first
      Archbishop of Birmingham                                       308
17.2  Dioceses in England and Wales                                  310
17.3  Investiture booklet cover                                      313
17.4  Right Reverend Peter Amigo                                     317
17.5  Cover of the *Official Catholic Directory of the Province of
      Birmingham*                                                    325

18.1  John McIntyre                                                  332
18.2  Bishop James Dey                                               337

18.3  Invitation to a Pontifical High Mass                    346

19.1  Thomas Newsome standing outside the stables at
      Besford Court                                           354
20.1  Souvenir programme cover of the first procession of
      St Chad                                                 363
20.2  Published route of the procession of St Chad, 1921      363
20.3  Gilded casket containing the relics of St Chad          363
20.4  Archbishop Ilsley walking in the procession of St Chad  363
20.5  Antonio and Mary de Navarro                             373

21.1  Archbishop Ilsley in his later years                    379
21.2  A distant view across the fields                        382
21.3  Stained glass windows by Donald B. Taunton              386
21.4  Front view of St Chad's                                 387
21.5  A portrait of Alice Holden                              391
21.6  A last sketch of Archbishop Ilsley from *The Universe*  393
21.7  Death certificate                                       394

E.1   Archbishop Ilsley's coffin lying before the high altar
      in St Chad's Cathedral                                  397
E.2   Edward Ilsley's memorial card                           399

*In memory of Father Peter Dennison*
*with gratitude for his unfailing help and encouragement*

# *Foreword*

In the 1927 *Birmingham Directory* the author of Archbishop Ilsley's obituary wrote: 'To so many of us in this archdiocese, the memory of the late Archbishop Ilsley is so inseparably interwoven with our own Catholic life that it is most difficult to realise that he has gone. Through the long years of our childhood, and on to adolescence and manhood, he was always "the Bishop", the revered supreme spiritual authority who confirmed us, visited at regular intervals our respective missions, and appeared as our leader at various diocesan functions. There are tens of thousands who, as long as they live, will cherish pleasant recollections of their venerable father in God, their personal contact with him on some occasion and the gentle dignity of his manner when among them.'

For the 47 years of his episcopate, from 1879 until 1926, Edward Ilsley was involved in almost everything that happened in this huge diocese of ours, and from 1888 until 1921 he was its chief shepherd. In her new book, Mary McInally tells both stories, of the Birmingham diocese and of its bishop. Almost three quarters of a century have passed since his death, so she is telling a story that is long overdue. As such, it is a memorial that is to be warmly welcomed, one that I hope will be of interest not just to people living in our diocese but elsewhere.

Much of the story is about Oscott and the training of future priests, for this was probably Archbishop Ilsley's main concern. That in itself is a reminder that in our very different age, the preparation of priests for ministry is not only important but essential if the work of the Church in our diocese is to continue. But because our times are different, with lay people already playing a much bigger part in the Church's mission, the need for vocations to every ministry has become apparent. Perhaps it is not too much to hope that the readers of this story will be moved to offer their own services to the Church so that her mission of evangelization will continue. This would surely be a fitting tribute to one 'who never spared himself or rested at the oar'.

† Philip Pargeter
Apostolic Administrator of the Archdiocese of Birmingham

# Preface and Acknowledgements

In 1988, when it was nearing the centenary of Edward Ilsley's appointment as Bishop of Birmingham, I began to explore his life and work. He had always remained a rather distant figure to me because of the general lack of information about him. But a footnote in Father Philip Hughes's essay published in 1950, entitled 'Bishops of the Century', conveyed an impelling message. It ran: 'If local patriotism in various sees has not been sufficiently interested, who shall preserve their memory?' His memory has been well preserved inside the chapel of St Edward, in St Chad's Cathedral, but there was surely more to be said about him.

He held high office in the Church for 42 years, from 1879 until 1921, and looking back over his life it can be seen that he was involved in that broad area of church history in Britain, stretching from mid-Victorian times until well past the turn of the century. It was this remarkable staying-power throughout the years that establishes him as the secure bridge between the nineteenth and twentieth centuries in the history of the Diocese of Birmingham.

Much of the interest of his story lies in the details of his association with those personalities who shared the stage with him at different times during his long life. Many of these have since become well known while others have dropped from view. Among the most notable was Bishop William Bernard Ullathorne, who ordained him in 1861, and whom he subsequently succeeded as Bishop of Birmingham in 1888.

His life spanned the pontificates of four Archbishops of Westminster – Nicholas Wiseman, Henry Manning, Herbert Vaughan and Francis Bourne, and he was the Ordinary of Cardinal John Henry Newman, who for much of his time lived and worked in the diocese. So Edward Ilsley had the unique experience of having worked alongside many of those great churchmen of his time who had been instrumental in re-establishing the restored Catholic Church. The part he played was to consolidate and take forward what they had won – long after many of his contemporaries had left the scene.

While recognized for the firmness of his views, he was also known for the gentleness of his character. His deepest concerns were in the training of his priests and the pastoral care and welfare of his people. In spite of his elevated position in an age when archbishops were regarded with reverential awe by their subjects, he endeared himself to both clergy and laity alike by his ready accessibility and the kindly interest he always showed toward them.

A great deal that Archbishop Edward Ilsley initiated has stood the test of time as the following pages will show.

I wish to thank the following:

The Archdiocese of Birmingham, and particularly the Metropolitan Cathedral Chapter, who have made this publication possible.

Canon Francis Grady, who has read through my manuscript and made valuable comments on certain sections. Frs Petroc Howell and John Sharp, Birmingham Archdiocesan Archivists, for their guidance on many occasions, and Dr Judith Champ and all those who have made materials available to me from the Oscott College Archives. Fr Ian Dickie, Archivist to the Archdiocese of Westminster, and Fr Michael Clifton, Archivist to the Diocese of Southwark, who have provided me with letters and information. Fr William Mol, St Joseph's College, Mill Hill, for his assistance with various references concerning Cardinal Vaughan, and Margaret Osborne for the use of archives held at Northampton. Neil Henshaw of Stonyhurst College, who has furnished me with the history and records of Sedgley Park School and Cotton College, and the Very Reverend C. J. Gregory Winterton of the Birmingham Oratory, for information regarding Cardinal Newman. Kevin Caffrey for the use of photographs and archive material in connection with Father Hudson's Society. Michael Hodgett for assistance with the history of Harvington Hall, and the late Fr Geoffrey Tucker, who supplied records of St Mary's, Harvington. The Sacred Heart Fathers for allowing me to explore the buildings and grounds of Olton Friary, and making available early plans and drawings. Dr R. O'Connell for providing details of St Gregory's, Longton. Dr Percy Young for supplying Elgar's letters and details of his work. Also Fathers of the Institute of Charity, who have filled in portions of family history for me. The Sisters of St Dominic's Convent, Stone, for their assistance with papers and documents held in their archives relating to Bishop Ullathorne. The Sisters at Oulton for letters from St Mary's Abbey archives. To the following Headmasters: T. P. Quigley, formerly of Besford Court School, for details he has given about its early history, and J. McEwen, of St Edmund's College, Old Hall, Ware, for information on the past history and development of the college. For engravings and journals supplied by S. M. O'Donnell of the Archbishop Ilsley School, and the records and references from P. J. Jones, of Cobridge RC Primary School. Also Richard Cunningham for his valued opinions on Catholic education.

I would also like to thank members of my family, not only for the memories they have shared and the anecdotes they have told, but also for lending me their precious photographs, books and documents, and for their interest and support. Particularly my cousins Cyril Ashmore, for the material he has made available connected with Harvington Hall, and Bob Brindley, for the use of his family archives and the practical help given me with the reading and checking of early manuscripts. Also my son David for the assistance he has given me with the technical production, all of which has been greatly appreciated.

Mary McInally
*September 2001*

# *Family Tree*

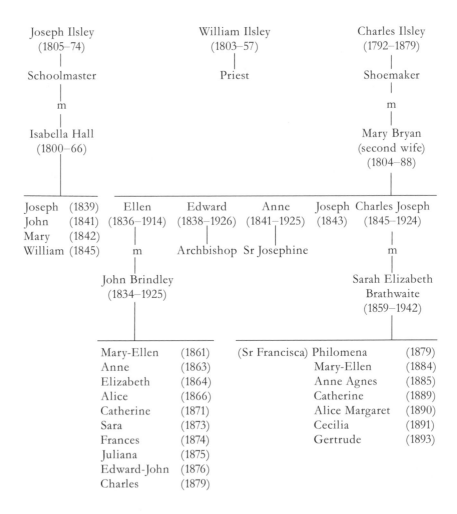

| Joseph Ilsley (1805–74) | William Ilsley (1803–57) | Charles Ilsley (1792–1879) |
|---|---|---|
| Schoolmaster | Priest | Shoemaker |
| m | | m |
| Isabella Hall (1800–66) | | Mary Bryan (second wife) (1804–88) |

| Joseph | (1839) | Ellen | Edward | Anne | Joseph | Charles Joseph |
|---|---|---|---|---|---|---|
| John | (1841) | (1836–1914) | (1838–1926) | (1841–1925) | (1843) | (1845–1924) |
| Mary | (1842) | | | | | |
| William | (1845) | m | Archbishop | Sr Josephine | | m |

John Brindley (1834–1925)

Sarah Elizabeth Brathwaite (1859–1942)

| Mary-Ellen | (1861) | (Sr Francisca) Philomena | (1879) |
|---|---|---|---|
| Anne | (1863) | Mary-Ellen | (1884) |
| Elizabeth | (1864) | Anne Agnes | (1885) |
| Alice | (1866) | Catherine | (1889) |
| Catherine | (1871) | Alice Margaret | (1890) |
| Sara | (1873) | Cecilia | (1891) |
| Frances | (1874) | Gertrude | (1893) |
| Juliana | (1875) | | |
| Edward-John | (1876) | | |
| Charles | (1879) | | |

# Biographical Notes

**Bishop Peter Amigo**: Born Gibraltar 26 May 1864. Educated St Edmund's, Ware, 1878–85 and St Thomas's, Hammersmith. Ordained 1888. Bishop of Southwark 1904. Died 1 October 1949 aged 85.

**Mgr William Barry**: Born London 21 April 1849. Educated Sedgley Park 1863–5. Entered Oscott College 1865–8. English College and Gregorian University Rome (DD) 1868–73. Ordained 1873. Vice Rector St Bernard's 1873. Professor of Divinity Oscott 1877–80. St Mary's, Harvington, 1880–1. Snowhill, Wolverhampton, 1882. Dorchester, Oxfordshire, 1883. Leamington, 1908. Writer and lecturer. Died 15 December 1930 aged 81.

**Cardinal-Archbishop Francis Bourne**: Born Clapham, London, 23 March 1861. Educated Ushaw and St Edmund's, Ware. St Sulpice, Paris, and University of Louvain. Ordained 1884. Rector of Wonersh 1889. Bishop of Southwark 1897. Archbishop of Westminster 1903. Cardinal 1911. Died 1 January 1935 aged 73.

**Revd John Brownlow**: Born Harley, nr Lincoln, 2 April 1795. Educated Lincoln Grammar School and Cambridge. Received into the Church and then attended Old Oscott. Ordained 1820. Stourbridge 1821. Harvington 1824–75. Died 4 March 1888 aged 92.

**Canon Willibrord Buscot**: Born 1863. Educated Cotton College 1885. Ordained 1889. Vice President of Cotton College 1899 under Walter Ireland. Wrote *The History of Cotton College*, 1940. Died 1941 aged 78.

**Revd John Caswell**: Born Dudley, Worcestershire, 8 May 1846. Entered Oscott August 1862. Ordained Oscott 1870. Vice President of Cotton College under Canon Souter 1884–5. Vice Rector of Oscott

College 1888–9. Prefect of studies Cotton 1889. Died 11 November 1912 aged 66.

**Mgr Charles Cronin**: Born Stafford 1872. Educated Cotton College and St Bernard's 1888. Transferred to Oscott 1889. English College, Rome, 1891. Ordained 1894. Vice Rector English College, Rome, 1898–1913. Rector Oscott College 1924–9. Vicar General 1929–42. Died 9 January 1942 aged 70.

**Bishop James Dey**: Born Walsall 14 November 1869. Entered St Bernard's 1889 and transferred to Oscott College. Ordained 1894. Joined staff of Cotton College 1894–1900. Staff of St Edmund's College, Ware, 1901–2. Vice Rector of Cotton 1902–3. Army chaplain 1903–29. Rector of Oscott 1929–35. Army bishop 1935–46. Died 8 June 1946 aged 77.

**Canon Estcourt**: Born Newtown, Wiltshire, 7 February 1816. Studied Oxford 1834. Ordained in the Anglican Church. Later came under the influence of the Tractarian movement and was received into the Catholic Church in 1845 at the same time as Newman, aged 29. Ordained 1848. Financial adviser to diocese 1850. Died at Leamington 1884 aged 68.

**Bishop Michael Glancey**: Born Wolverhampton 25 October 1854. Entered St Bernard's 1873. Ordained 1877. Staff of Oscott 1877–88. Diocesan Inspector of Schools 1888–97. Canon 1905. Vicar General 1922–25. Consecrated Auxiliary Bishop 1924. Died 16 October 1925 aged 70.

**Bishop Thomas Grant**: Born Ligny-les-Aires, France, 5 November 1816. Educated Ushaw 1829 and English College, Rome (DD), 1836. Ordained Rome 1841. Rector of the English College 1844. Bishop of Southwark 1851. Died 1 June 1870 aged 53.

**Canon John Hawksford**: Born Wolverhampton 1833. Educated Sedgley Park 1844–50. Entered Oscott 1850. Ordained 1859. Oscott staff 1860–8. President of Oscott 1877–80. President of Cotton 1885–97. Died 1904 aged 80 and buried in Cotton churchyard.

**Revd John Hopwood**: Born nr Birmingham January 1859. Educated St Chad's Grammar School, under Revd James O'Hanlon. Cotton College 1873. St Bernard's 1877–82. Ordained 1882. Professor at Oscott for 17 years. President of Cotton 1902–3. Rector of SS Peter and Paul, Wolverhampton. Died 1913 aged 54.

**Mgr Vincent George Hudson**: Born Kinsham, Worcestershire, 27 September 1873. Entered Oscott 1891. Ordained 1898. Chaplain St Paul's Home, Coleshill. Secretary to the Birmingham Rescue Society 1901. Domestic Prelate 1920. Canon of the Cathedral Chapter 1927. Made 30 journeys to Canada in the interest of poor and destitute children. Retired 1934. Died 25 October 1936 aged 63.

**Archbishop Edward Ilsley**: Born Stafford 11 May 1838. Educated Sedgley Park 1848–52. Entered Oscott 1852. Ordained 1861. Curate at Longton 1861. Rector of St Bernard's 1873–83. Canon of the Cathedral Chapter 1876. Auxiliary Bishop 1879. Bishop of Birmingham 1888. Archbishop and Metropolitan 1911. Retired 1921. Died 1 December 1926 aged 88.

**Father Walter Ireland**: Born Doncaster, Yorkshire, 1850. English College, Lisbon. Staff of Cotton College 1873. Yvetôt Seminary, Normandy. Ordained 1878. Staff of Cotton 1878. Vice President of Cotton College under Canon Hawksford 1884–97. President of Cotton 1897–1902. Appointed Handsworth 1903, Tamworth 1904. Died 1906 aged 56. Buried Cotton churchyard.

**Pope Leo XIII**: Reigned February 1878 until July 1903. Died aged 93.

**Bishop Frederick William Keating**: Born Birmingham 13 June 1859. Educated St Chad's Grammar School and Sedgley Park. St Bernard's 1877. Ordained 1882. Vice Rector of St Bernard's 1888. Consecrated Bishop of Northampton 1908. Translated to Liverpool as Archbishop and Metropolitan 13 June 1921. Died 7 February 1928 aged 68.

**Cardinal-Archbishop Henry Edward Manning**: Born Totteridge, Hertfordshire, 15 July 1808. Educated Harrow and Oxford. Ordained in the Anglican Church 1832. Received into the Catholic Church and ordained 1851. Archbishop of Westminster 1866. Cardinal that year. Died 14 January 1892 aged 83.

**Revd James Massam**: Born Scarisbrick nr Ormskirk, Lancashire, 28 October 1812. Attended Newborough day school, near Wrightington.

Began his studies at English College, Lisbon, 1826. Ordained Lisbon 1837. Longton, Staffordshire, 1837. Died 1893 aged 81.

**Canon James McCave**: Born Wolverhampton 1 December 1837. Educated Sedgley Park 1850–1853. Oscott College 1853–8. English College, Rome (DD), Ordained 1862. Rector of St Bernard's 1883. Canon in 1884. Retired 1888. Appointed to Solihull 1892. Died 24 October 1899 aged 61.

**Archbishop John McIntyre**: Born Birmingham 1 January 1855. Educated St Chad's Grammar School and Sedgley Park. St Bernard's 1874. English College, Rome, 1875. Ordained 1877. Staff of Oscott College and Olton 1880–7. Ilsley's secretary 1889–1914. Auxiliary to Archbishop Ilsley 1912. Rector of the English College, Rome, 1913–17. Re-appointed auxiliary 1917, also Vicar General and Titular Archbishop. Archbishop of Birmingham 1921. Retired 1928. Died 21 November 1934 aged 79.

**Revd Samuel Myerscough, SJ**: Born Rochdale 2 April 1879. Music Degree, Oxford. Received into the Church 1905. Entered Oscott College 1908. Ordained 1912. Curate at Longton 1913. Became a Jesuit 1919. St Francis Xavier's, Liverpool, 1920. Leeds. Manchester. Died 5 August 1954 aged 75.

**Cardinal John Henry Newman**: Born London 21 February 1801. Ordained in the Anglican Church 1824. Received into the Catholic Church and ordained 1846. Cardinal 12 May 1879. Died August 1890 aged 89.

**Mgr Thomas Newsome**: Born Burnley 25 May 1880. Entered Oscott 1899. Ordained 1905. St Joseph's, Chasetown, Wallsall, 1915. Appointed administrator to Besford Court 1916. Died 1942 aged 62.

**Canon James Spencer Northcote**: Born Feniton Court, Devonshire, 26 May 1821. Corpus Christi, Oxford, 1837–41. Received into the Church 1846. Studied for the priesthood at the Oratory, Edgbaston, and at the *Collegio Pio*, Rome. Ordained at St Dominic's, Stone, 1855. President of Oscott 1860–77. Founded the Oscotian Society. Provost of the Chapter 1884. Died 3 March 1908 aged 86. Buried at Oscott.

**Canon James O'Hanlon**: Born Ballymoyer, Armagh, 15 June 1839. Entered Oscott 1860. Ordained 1865. Headmaster of St Chad's

Grammar School. Professor of Theology at Oscott 1872. Rector of St Bernard's 1888–9. Vicar General 1888. Died 21 February 1921 aged 81. Buried at St Bernard's, Olton.

**Revd Joseph Parker**: Born Stafford 1851. Educated Sedgley Park and the English College, Lisbon. Ordained 1875. Secretary to Bishop Ullathorne 1875–88. Mission of Woodlane 1888. Died 19 May 1935 aged 83.

**Mgr Henry Parkinson**: Born Cheadle, Staffordshire, 1852. Educated Sedgley Park and St Edmund's. Entered St Bernard's 1873. English College, Rome, 1874. Ordained 1877. Vice Rector to Edward Ilsley at St Bernard's 1877–83. Senior curate and choirmaster St Chad's 1887–9. Vice Rector of Oscott 1889. Rector of Oscott 1897. Domestic Prelate 1897. President of the Catholic Social Guild 1909. Died 22 June 1924 aged 72.

**Dr Victor Schobel**: Bavarian. Born Rottweil, Black Forest, 18 September 1848. English Seminary, Bruges, and the Gregorian University (DD). Ordained Rome 1871. Professor at the English College, Bruges, and at the *Grand Séminaire*, Bruges. Staff of St Bernard's Seminary 1873. Vice Rector 1884–5. Professor of Theology at Oscott 1886–95. Chaplain to the Benedictine Community, Oulton 1895. Died 18 July 1915 aged 66.

**Mgr Joseph Henry Souter**: Born Birmingham 15 August 1827. Educated St Augustine's Priory, Newton Abbot. Entered Oscott 1838. Ordained 1852. Founded St Chad's Grammar School 1858. Cathedral Parish and St John's, Banbury, 1864. Professor at Oscott. President of Cotton College 1873. Canon 1881. President of Oscott 1885–9. Kenilworth and Leamington. Retired 1900. Died 29 September 1911 aged 84.

**Revd Percy Styche**: Born Burton-on-Trent 1887. Educated Douai. Ordained 1911. Secretary to Archbishop Ilsley 1914–22. Later Southwark Archivist. Died 4 October 1961 aged 74.

**Bishop William Bernard Ullathorne, OSB**: Born Pocklington, Yorkshire, 7 May 1806. Downside 1823–31. Ordained Ushaw 1832. Australian Mission 1832–40. Coventry 1841–6. Vicar Apostolic of Central District 1846–50. Bishop of Birmingham 1850. Retired 1888. Died 21 March 1889 aged 82.

**Cardinal-Archbishop Herbert Vaughan**: Born Courtfield nr Ross 15 April 1832. Stonyhurst 1841–7. Downside 1849–51. *Academia Ecclesiastica*, Rome, 1852. Ordained 1854. Vice President of St Edmund's College, Ware, 1854–61. Foreign missions 1863–72. Established Mill Hill College 1866. Bought *The Tablet* 1868. Bishop of Salford 1872 Archbishop of Westminster and Cardinal 1892. Died 19 June 1903 aged 71.

**Canon Arthur H. Villiers**: Born Derby 1857. Educated St Edmund's. Entered St Bernard's 1877. Ordained 1882. Rector St Anne's, Birmingham. Diocesan Inspector of Schools 1899. Canon 1916. A controversial correspondent in the press from 1885 known as 'A. H. V.' Canon of the Cathedral Chapter 1916. Died October 1938 aged 81. Buried at St Bernard's, Olton.

**Bishop Bernard Ward**: Born St Edmund's College, Ware, 4 February 1857. Son of W. G. Ward one of the leaders of the Oxford Movement. Educated St Edmund's 1868–75. Entered Oscott College 1879. Ordained 1882. Staff of St Edmund's 1882–5. Began a new mission at Willesden, North London, 1886. Staff of Oscott College 1888–90. Vice President of St Edmund's 1890. President 1893–1916. Bishop of Brentwood 1917–20. Died 21 January 1920 aged 62.

**Archbishop Thomas Leighton Williams**: Born Birmingham 20 March 1877. Educated Cotton College. Christ's College, Cambridge. Entered Oscott 1893. Ordained 1900. Cotton College 1903. St Edmund's College 1903. Army chaplain 1916–20. Principal of St Charles House, Oxford, 1920. Headmaster of Cotton College 1922. Archbishop of Birmingham 1929. Died 1 April 1946 aged 69.

**Archbishop Nicholas Wiseman**: Born Seville 2 August 1802. Educated Ushaw 1810. English College, Rome, 1818. Ordained 1825. Vice Rector of the English College, Rome, 1827. Rector 1828. President of Oscott 1840. Cardinal-Archbishop of Westminster 1850. Died 15 February 1865 aged 62.

# Abbreviations

| | |
|---|---|
| B.A. | Birmingham Archdiocesan Archives |
| Barry | Mgr William Barry, *Memories and Opinions*, London and New York, 1926 |
| Beck | Bishop Andrew Beck (ed.), *The English Catholics, 1850–1950*, London, 1950 |
| Bellenger | Don Aidan Bellenger, OSB, *The Normal State of the Church: William Bernard Ullathorne, First Bishop of Birmingham*, The Catholic Record Society, 2000. |
| B.P. | *Birmingham Faces and Places,* vol. iii, 2 February 1891 |
| Briggs | J. H. Briggs, *A History of Longton: The Birth of a Community*, Dept of Adult Education, University of Keele, Staffordshire, 1983 |
| Brookes | D. Brookes, *Reminiscences of St Gregory's, Longton, Staffordshire*, Manuscript, 1954, Birmingham Archdiocesan Archives |
| Buscot | Canon W. Buscot, *The History of Cotton College*, London, 1940 |
| Butler | Dom Cuthbert Butler, *The Life and Times of Bishop Ullathorne, 1806–1889*, 2 vols, London, 1926 |
| Chadwick | Owen Chadwick, *The Victorian Church*, 2 vols, London, 1970 |
| Clifton | Revd M. Clifton, *Amigo: Friend of the Poor*, Leominster, 1987 |
| D.B. | Revd Patrick O'Toole, 'Diocesan Bishop', *The Oscotian*, New Series, 1 (1927) |
| Dey | Bishop James Dey, 'The Presidency of Dr Hopwood', *The Cottonian*, 1940 |
| Diary | The Seminary Diary, St Bernard's Seminary, Olton, Warwickshire, July 1873–August 1888, Birmingham Archdiocesan Archives |

| | |
|---|---|
| *Essays* | Judith Champ (ed.), *Oscott College 1838–1988: A Volume of Commemorative Essays,* Stafford, 1988 |
| Fitzgerald | Percy Fitzgerald, *Fifty Years of Catholic Life and Social Progress*, 4 vols, London, 1901 |
| F.R. | Mgr Arthur H. Villiers, 'The Father Rector', *The Oscotian*, New Series, 1 (1927) |
| Glancey | Mgr Michael Glancey, *Characteristics from the Writings of Archbishop Ullathorne*, London, 1889 |
| Gray | Robert Gray, *Cardinal Manning: A Biography,* London, 1985 |
| Greenslade | Michael Greenslade *St. Austin's Stafford*, Stafford, 1962 |
| J. | A seminary student's journal, St Bernard's, Olton, 1878–1882, no name, Oscott College Archives |
| J.F.C. | Judith F. Champ, *Oscott*, The Archdiocese of Birmingham Historical Commission, 1987 |
| Kiernan | R. H. Kiernan, *The Story of the Archdiocese of Birmingham*, Birmingham, S. J. Wones, 1950 |
| *Letters* | The nuns of St Dominic's Convent, Stone (ed.), *Letters of Archbishop Ullathorne*, London and New York, 1892 |
| *Longton* | *A Short History of St Gregory's, Longton*, Longton, 1894, Birmingham Archdiocesan Archives |
| McClelland | Alan McClelland, B*ourne, Norfolk and the Irish Parliamentarians: Roman Catholics and the Education Bill of 1906*, The Catholic Record Society, 1996 |
| McCormack | Revd Arthur McCormack, MHM, *Cardinal Vaughan*, London, 1966 |
| McIntyre | Archbishop McIntyre, obituary, *The Oscotian*, 5th Series, no. 1 (Shrovetide 1935) |
| Myerscough | Revd Samuel Myerscough, *The Official Catholic Directory of the Archdiocese of Birmingham*, 1927 |
| Norman | Edward Norman, *The English Catholic Church in the Nineteenth Century*, Oxford, 1984 |
| Northampton | Northampton Diocesan Archives |
| O.C.A. | Oscott College Archives |
| Oldmeadow | Ernest Oldmeadow, *Francis Cardinal Bourne*, 2 vols, London, 1944 |
| O'Neil | Revd Robert O'Neil, MHM, *Cardinal Herbert Vaughan*, Tunbridge Wells, 1995 |
| *Oscotian 24* | *The Oscotian*, 5th Series, 24/3, no. 72 (Autumn 1924) |
| Parkinson | Henry Parkinson, *A Brief Sketch of the History of St. Bernard's Seminary, Olton*, manuscript, 1900, Oscott College Archives |

Roberts      Frank Roberts, *A History of Sedgley Park and Cotton College*, ed. Neil Henshaw, Preston, 1995. ('Frank Roberts' refers to the original manuscript of above.)

*S.A.*      *The Staffordshire Advertiser*

Schobel      Mgr Victor Januarius Schobel, obituary, 'The Right Reverend Monsignor Schobel, D. D', *The Oscotian*, 3rd Series, 16 (December 1915)

Snead-Cox      J. G. Snead-Cox, *The Life of Cardinal Vaughan*, 2 vols., London, 1912

Southwark      Southwark Diocesan Archives

*St Chad's*      *A History of St Chad's Cathedral, Birmingham, 1841–1904*

Thomson      Revd John Henry Thomson, 'The History of Oscott College', *The Oscotian*, 5th Series, 8 (1938)

Toplass      Canon D. Toplass, 'Archbishop Ilsley, Priest and Oscotian', *The Oscotian*, Centenary Number, vol. 8/2 (1938)

*Victoria*      Michael Greenslade (ed.), *The Victoria History of the County of Stafford*, vol. viii

Westminster      Westminster Archdiocesan Archives

## CHAPTER ONE

# Early Years

Born on 11 May 1838, in the first year of Queen Victoria's reign, Edward Ilsley came from an ordinary working family. His father Charles, by then middle-aged, was a shoemaker in the county-town of Stafford, working in a trade that had thrived there since medieval times.[1] His mother, formerly Mary Bryan, was Charles's second wife. She was a young woman whose family came from Waterford with earlier Irish immigrants,[2] and Charles originally lived in Hyde Lea, a village just outside Stafford. Edward had stepbrothers and -sisters living and working in the town who had already left home by the time he was born.[3]

They lived in a small lane named 'Appleyard Court' lying just inside the remains of the old 'Far Back Walls' which once enclosed the town at that part.[4] Beyond these walls lay the open countryside[5] and at the end of their little court, Tipping Street led into the main street which was alive with the bustle of people and the noise and clatter of horse-drawn vehicles. Other shoemakers and their apprentices lived in the same court,[6] as they were mainly outworkers working from their homes.[7] Trade was good during those years, so although their home was simple, the Ilsley family would not have gone short of anything they needed.

## Family

Mary and Charles had four children. Ellen was the eldest, then Edward was followed by Anne, and the youngest was Charles. Joseph, who had been born two years before Charles, died at birth. They attended daily Mass at St Austin's, reached by crossing the river at Green Bridge and going outside the town along the Wolverhampton Road. In those early years St Austin's was a small chapel which had originally been unobtrusively erected on the simplest lines behind the

Figure 1.1 *Charles and Mary, the father and mother of Edward Ilsley. From a photograph in a private collection.*

priest's house in 1791, and had virtually been rebuilt in 1817–18.[8] It did not compare in any way with the solidly built, old Anglican church of St Chad lying only a few steps from their home, with its splendid Norman carvings seemingly untouched by the passage of time, or with the parish church of St Mary across Greengate Street, described as being 'almost cathedral-like in its dimensions'.[9]

Edward's younger sister Anne, later to become a Sister of Mercy at St Mary's Convent in Handsworth, writing to him when their brother Charles died many years later, remembered those early years with fondness: 'It seems to me only a few months since he and I used to kneel either side of Mother at daily Mass in the old chapel, while you were at Sedgley Park,' she wrote.[10] A school was built behind this chapel in 1818, in the form of one long room where all the children were taught together.[11] The young Ilsleys probably received their early education there. Beyond the playground there was a large unused plot of land, where in later years later a fine new church was built to E. W. Pugin's design.

Stafford, a busy and prosperous market town, was probably by this time at the finest stage of its development.[12] Its size and shape had remained almost unaltered throughout the years, being built virtually on an island, with a loop of the river on one side, and a marsh on the other, so everything was ideally placed within easy distance in any direction across the town. There was a cobbled marketplace, 'many well-stocked shops', lawcourts and inns, and streets lined with picturesque old half-timbered houses with their characteristic high-pitched roofs. Here Edward spent his childhood, until he was sent away to school at Sedgley Park, near Wolverhampton, aged 9.

One of his uncles, Joseph Ilsley, was schoolmaster for 48 years at the village school attached to the old moated hall of Harvington, in Worcestershire. After the opening of the church of St Mary at Harvington by Father John Brownlow on Trinity Sunday in 1825, Sir George Throckmorton, the owner of the hall who built the church, set up a school for the children of the village and neighbourhood in the old disused chapel a few months later, and he continued to maintain the school at his own expense. Edward's uncle became schoolmaster there when he was 21, and continued in the position until he died at the age of 69 in 1874. He married Isabella Hall in 1837 when he was 31

Figure 1.2 *A view of Harvington Hall after its restoration in the 1930s.*

Figure 1.3 *The graves of Joseph and Isabella Ilsley in St Mary's churchyard, Harvington.*

and they had four children, Joseph, John, Mary and William, all similar in age to their cousins.[13] It is very likely that Edward's family visited them there because his father and mother, Charles and Mary, had their photographs taken at Harrison's when they were in Kidderminster, which was the nearest town of any size. Also in the obituary of Father Brownlow, who was in charge of St Mary's for some 64 years, it says that he knew Edward Ilsley when he was a boy. The graves of Joseph and his wife lie side-by-side near the wall of the graveyard of the little church which is not far from the Hall. Another of Edward's uncles, William Ilsley, was a priest, who was ordained at Oscott College in 1836.[14]

## A Church Student at Sedgley Park

In January 1848 Edward was sent to Sedgley Park School near Wolverhampton as a church student. The church students gained special places at the school by way of scholarships provided by the diocese. The boys were all treated the same as regards tuition, but the so-called 'parlour boarders', who paid a higher fee, had their meals in the Little Parlour with the masters, away from the other boys.[15] The origins of this school were begun at the instigation of Bishop Challoner in January 1761, in a house at Betley, a village on the

4

Shropshire border of Staffordshire, by William Errington, who was then his chaplain.[16] The following year, in order to provide premises more suitable for the numbers that Bishop Challoner had in mind, the boys were transferred from there to a mansion at Sedgley Park, rented out by a Protestant nobleman, Lord Ward. Realizing the desperate need at that time, Challoner's purpose in founding the school was to provide a complete secondary education for the sons of those middle-class parents working in trade or commerce who either did not wish to follow the custom of sending them abroad or could not afford to do so. The establishment of the school at Sedgley Park, which he initiated in 1762, gave training to many of the clergy and laity from all parts of the country for years to come.

Although the routine there became typical of any mid-Victorian boarding school, there were some differences in the courses provided that were due to the conditions prevailing in the country at the time. Because many careers were closed to Catholics, a more 'modern' course of studies was substituted. The original intention had been to continue the study of classics as at Douai, but the classical course later became optional and a modified system of higher mathematics and English subjects was substituted. This was unusual for the eighteenth century, but it showed that those in charge were alive to the needs of the time.

There was opposition to Bishop Challoner's plans from some of the Catholic gentry who were against the foundation of this type of school because they feared that an establishment so completely different from those already existing (which were mainly for the sons of nobility and gentry) would provoke the Government to further repressive measures. They were also concerned that the foundation of Sedgley Park was conceived on a larger scale than Standon Lordship, a preparatory school which had been founded in Hertfordshire by Bishop Challoner in 1749 and was limited to 25 boys under 12 years of age. But they were met with a firm reply from the Bishop: 'Whether you patronise it or not, it will be undertaken, and moreover, blessing of God be upon it, it will prosper.'[17]

English colleges originally settled abroad owing to the situation that developed for Catholics in Britain from the mid-sixteenth century. As priests were no longer tolerated in Britain, it had become a virtual impossibility to educate Catholics in their own religion here, and for this reason colleges for English boys began to be established on the Continent, the first being Douai in Flanders, founded by William Allen in Elizabeth's reign, in 1568. Each successive reign brought with it the imposition of heavy penal laws against Catholics, with the exception of that of James II between 1685 and 1688 when four vicars apostolic were appointed to the districts of London, the Midlands, the North and the West. The following years were ones of considerable unrest, and Catholic property was liable to be attacked and damaged. 'The fact that this first period of the school's existence passed under the shadow of the penal laws, meant it had to lie very low,' and although the Catholic Relief Act of 1778 improved things, it did not legalize Sedgley Park, and as a school it was subject to penalties of the law, so it continued quietly on its course.[18] Finally the Relief Act of 1791, which exempted Catholics from existing laws was passed, and 'thus Sedgley Park became protected by law, both as a Catholic institution, and a school; and this was an important point affecting its continuity'.[19]

Before the turn of the century the situation was altered by the French Revolution of 1789–93, which forced English schools to leave the Continent and attempt to become re-established back on their native soil. Sedgley Park flourished alongside these in its own right, and although the Catholic Relief Act of 1791 actually prohibited the foundation of Catholic Schools, this was interpreted as applying only to schools concerned exclusively with the training of Catholic priests.[20] Bishop Milner, a former pupil there himself who always had the school's interests at heart, liked to visit it frequently, and called it 'that nursery of the English Priesthood'.[21]

The school lay in the countryside just south of Wolverhampton, and when Edward Ilsley came there the encroachments of the Black Country had already begun to take their hold on the surrounding districts. William Barry later described himself as gazing out of the dormitory window on 'that spectacle of some 2,000 fires blazing up or seeming to die down under dark wintry skies',[22] and 'occasionally there would be a "long walk" on which the boys were taken to places of interest in the neighbourhood, one of the most popular being the "big furnace" where iron was smelted all day long'.[23]

## School Years

An early print shows Sedgley Park much as it would have been in Ilsley's time, a tall three-storey building with basements, built in the Queen Anne style, with additional rather plain-looking classrooms and other accommodation set on each side. All this overlooked 'the Bounds', a large playground sloping down and away from the

Figure 1.4 *Sedgley Park in 1826, from a drawing by Robert Noyes.*

building.[24] There was a row of great old beech trees along one side of this area and an avenue of smaller ones on the other, planted outside the railings and stretching for about half a mile in the direction of Wolverhampton. William Barry, who went there in 1863, described the classrooms as 'a ramshackle addition to Lord Ward's Mansion, without comfort or beauty', but the fact that the lease had run out some years earlier, in 1857, in Mr Bowdon's time, made it inadvisable to spend any more money to improve the buildings at that stage. In 1871 the wells were found to be contaminated and this was a contributory factor to the school being moved out in 1873 to cleaner air among the hills and moorlands of north Staffordshire, when it became known as Cotton College after the local hamlet – or officially, 'St Wilfrid's'.[25]

The Revd James Brown had just become President when Edward arrived.[26] Two years later, in 1850, on the re-establishment of the hierarchy, he was appointed the first bishop of the new See of Shrewsbury, and the Revd Thomas Flanagan took his place. Dr Brown's main influence was spiritual and he introduced the annual three-day retreat during Holy Week which continued on through the years at Cotton College. With the setting-up of religious houses there were now more priests available for such services.[27] Dr Brown also introduced plainchant in the chapel, replacing the music of Mozart and Haydn; this was to be a lasting tradition, and it was performed so well that later, as Bishop, he was to write to them, 'Your plainchant was so delightful last time, that I long to hear it again.' Edward retained these early influences he gained at Sedgley Park, using his talents in music and choral work later with considerable ability as both organist and choirmaster.

The new president, Thomas Flanagan, was described as a man 'not without humour and commonsense', who endeavoured 'to soften the roughness of the Park boys'. He improved the evening supervision of the dormitories by always having a master on duty and eased the prevailing rowdy situation during winter evenings in the playroom, where all the boys came together for recreation in a large area with brick floors and whitewashed walls, forming the basements of two buildings. Observing the rougher, noisier element tending to dominate the situation, while the quieter boys had to seek refuge to pursue their games in any available corner, 'he established the boys' reading room in the lobby, which was found a great relief to the overcrowded playroom on the long winter nights'.[28] But, as in most public schools, the routine was designed to instil self-discipline and independence in the boys, and it is recorded that in 1800 they had an early call at 6 every morning throughout the year and after dressing would go downstairs to wash in the pumproom and then out for a run round the 'Bounds'. As part of the old stabling, this washroom was originally open to all weathers on one side, where the farm horses used to come in and drink from the lead-lined trough, but it was walled and roofed over by Mr Brown during Ilsley's stay.[29] On returning to the dormitory they would kneel by their beds to say their morning prayers aloud and then recite their catechism to the master of their own study from 6.45 until it was time to go to Mass at 7.30. Although this is an earlier account and some adjustments would probably have been made over the years, the first part of their day would in essence have been much the same when Edward Ilsley was at 'The Park'. Meals were simple but substantial and were taken in silence except when permission was granted for conversation on certain feast days. In later years readings were introduced according to the old Douai custom.

There were two holidays in the year, at Christmas and midsummer. There were about 140 boys in the school when Ilsley was there, but few of them went home at Christmas, and only about half departed in the summer. Even when the coming of the railways made travelling home much easier, the bishops who had students at the school 'set their faces sternly against' allowing them to go home for Christmas when the matter was raised, and it was not until many years later, long after the move to Cotton, that they were allowed any such innovation. William Barry, who went there at the age of 14, mentioned that 'the Diocese of Birmingham offered free scholarships open to competition, among eligible candidates whom the clergy recommended'.[30] The fact that numbers of boys were assisted in this way meant that the bishops considered they had particular jurisdiction over them, and Edward Ilsley was one of these. But life at 'The Park' had its compensations, because in their spare time the boys were allowed to occupy themselves with a variety of hobbies, and during vacations they were taken out on visits to various places of interest.[31]

## William Bernard Ullathorne

It was during Edward's stay at Sedgley Park that William Ullathorne was appointed, in May 1848, to assist in the organization being carried out in Rome to restore the Catholic hierarchy in Britain.[32] Ullathorne, then aged 43, was Vicar Apostolic of the Central District, and he later became the first Bishop of Birmingham in 1850. During those years at Sedgley Park, links began to be forged in a chain of events destined finally to lead to the future association of the two. The annual synods of the Midland clergy, over which he presided, had been held at Sedgley Park since 1822 and the general decision was against their transfer to Oscott College,[33] so his visits there probably gave Ullathorne a special interest both in the school and in its students. It was during this time that he confirmed Edward Ilsley, who later, when he was at Oscott College, received Holy Orders from him.[34] So in both places the young Ilsley would have come to his notice.

Things could have worked out very differently, as in his early years Ullathorne seemed destined for the hierarchy in Australia, a destiny he resisted partly on the grounds of ill-health. Later he might well have left Birmingham for the See of Westminster, as the choice of Archbishop of Westminster in 1865 was a close-run thing between himself and Henry Manning, but this was not to be either.[35] At one time Ullathorne sought to resign as Bishop of Birmingham in order to return to the cloister at Downside,[36] but this was not accepted because he was considered indispensable and was prevailed upon to continue his work as bishop of the diocese. This he did, for nearly forty years, far into his old age, by which time Edward Ilsley was working closely at his side.

In January 1853, at the age of 14, Edward transferred to St Mary's College, Oscott, to begin his training for the priesthood. By then the

Church was moving away from 'the old Church' of his early childhood, in which priests still dressed as laymen in public places for fear of giving offence.[37] In those days they would wear a suit of brown or grey material, with open collar and cravat, as in this way they could pass unnoticed, and they were also addressed as 'Mister', as any other layman.[38] The term 'Father', later used by the poorer people, was possibly introduced by the Irish immigrants, or influenced by the French *Père*. Said to have been 'pushed' by Manning to enhance the standing of the clergy, it was beginning to be in wider use by mid-century, so Ilsley was known as 'Father Ilsley' when he was curate at Longton.[39] While he was at Sedgley Park the restoration of the hierarchy furthered the move away from the 'old hidden ways' of the Church into the new system of ecclesiastical administration, which brought with it a considerable flowering of the liturgy. As the 'Romanizing effect' was strengthened, priests everywhere reflected this image by wearing the Roman collar and Roman style soutane with its short cape.[40]

## Preparation for the Priesthood

It was at this time of change and development that Edward Ilsley began his preparation for the priesthood. Six months before he came there, the first synod of the Province of Westminster took place at Oscott in the summer of 1852, when the new hierarchy came together to formalize the administration of English Catholicism. One of the most memorable aspects of this occasion was Newman's celebrated sermon 'The Second Spring'. His words were said to 'still linger round the walls of the college' for many months after.[41] *The Times* was later to comment that Ilsley was also at the College at a time when 'the genius and inspiration of Nicholas Wiseman had given it new status', but the image of Nicholas Wiseman in this connection has since been questioned, and Owen Chadwick says of him: 'Eminent as a public figure, he was capable of superb appearances and telling gestures' but 'details of diocesan or collegiate administration bored him; the college at Oscott sank under his rule'.[42]

There are some later references to this period of Ilsley's life in newspapers and periodicals after he became Bishop of Birmingham, and later Archbishop. The correspondents had very likely interviewed some of his former tutors or fellow students at Oscott. A profile which appeared in the local magazine, *Birmingham Faces and Places*, in February 1891, added: 'Those who knew him in his student days describe him as remarkable for his cheerfulness and amiability and also for his religious zeal and piety. He had a natural taste for music and excelled as an organist. While at Oscott we believe he for some time acted as organist.' Samuel Myerscough, who went to Longton as curate in 1913, wrote in his obituary in *The Official Catholic Directory*, that Edward Ilsley's college acquaintances described his character as being, 'gentle, unassuming and amiable, of solid practical piety and edifying those with whom he came in contact'.[43] Myerscough's description is carefully restrained, but even so it might be possible to deduce something more from them than his words immediately suggest.

One is struck by a certain sense of timing and things falling into place for Edward Ilsley. There was a tide of change flowing, and a feeling of urgency in the affairs of the Church at that time. Newman's words were to give much of the necessary guidance and inspiration needed by those who were leading the way. Speaking of the order of things, and the constant renewal of them, he said of the Church: 'It is like an image on the waters, which is ever the same, though the waters flow.'[44] Later, when Ilsley was Rector of St Bernard's Seminary the guiding voice of the old cardinal was still there, and it was as Bishop of Birmingham that Ilsley was to be with him when he was dying.

Ilsley remained a student at St Mary's College for eight years until 1861, first coming under the directorship of Monsignor Weedall, who died in office in 1859. He then spent his final year during the presidency of James Spencer Northcote, who was previously Vice President. Northcote took over at the age of 39, after the brief and unsuccessful installation for seven months of George Morgan, and he remained there until 1877. As a convert there was originally some prejudice against Northcote's appointment from some of the 'old Catholics', but over the coming years he introduced a series of enlightened reforms there under the guidance of his friend Thomas Arnold, the founder of Rugby School, which gave him the reputation of being the most able of all the presidents of the college.[45] William Barry on first arriving as a student at Oscott in 1865, four years after Ilsley left, described Northcote as 'a remarkable-looking man, with a fine presence and the air of a schoolmaster'.[46]

In those years English Catholicism took on an increasingly Roman flavour,[47] and the old restrained traditions were superseded as Italian influences were adopted and became part of the new liturgy.[48] Canon Buscot, writing *The History of Cotton College*, included Ilsley's name among his associates and contemporaries in a fitting tribute. He described them as 'that fine type of cleric that Oscott was sending forth – men of deep piety, of wide erudition and distinguished by unfailing courtesy toward all with whom they came in contact'.[49]

## Notes

1   Public Records Office, London.
2   *Ibid.*: Charles Ilsley's first wife was named Catherine. The fact that Mary Bryan came from Waterford was family knowledge. She and Charles were married in 1835.
3   Staffordshire Record Office, census returns.
4   Plan of Stafford 1835, J. Wood. It was formally called 'Diglake Place', and older inhabitants used to refer to Tipping Street as 'up the Diglake' long after the name was changed. This area is now built over with the new court building and probation office.
5   Education Dept, Source Book L 40, *Stafford Remembered*, p. 11.
6   Staffordshire Record Office.
7   Vivian Bird, *Staffordshire*, p. 131: 'shoemakers in those days were mainly outworkers supplied with materials and lasts by the manufacturers'. Also Roy Lewis and Joan Anslow, *Stafford in Old Picture Postcards*, p. 31: The supplier in that area was 'Jen's Shoe Factors' and his store was among the workers' cottages behind St Chad's Church. The system was that leather was collected by the workers on Monday mornings and the made-up shoes returned the following week.
8   Greenslade, pp. 16, 17. Also p. 4, 'With the coming of quieter times in the 18th century Mass was again said regularly in the town itself, and at the end of the century a small church was built. This first St. Austin's was much enlarged a few years later, and some forty-five years after that, in 1862, the present church was opened.' See further details in Archdiocese Historical Commission, publication no. 8, *Saint Austin's Stafford*, p. 11.
9   Arthur Mee, *Staffordshire*, p. 155.
10  B.A. Letter from Sister Josephine to Edward Ilsley, 29 July 1924. Edward was seven years older than his brother Charles.
11  Greenslade, pp. 27, 28. This building, measuring 30ft by 15ft, is still standing today.
12  Michael Greenslade (ed.), *The Victoria History of the County of Stafford*, vol. vi, p. 215.
13  H. R. Hodgkinson, *Further Notes on Harvington Hall*, p. 95. This is a supplement to *Recent Discoveries at Harvington Hall*, an earlier paper read to the local historical society in 1938. The school was still in existence in 1913. See also *The Tablet*, Saturday 31 March 1885, obituary John Brownlow.
   The 1851 Census recorded:
   Joseph Ilsley, head, age 45, Isabella, wife, age 50,

Joseph, son, age 11, John, son, age 9, Mary, daughter, age 8, William, son, age 5.

Isabella died in 1866 and Joseph in 1873.

14 Cotton College Archives (now in the Birmingham Diocesan Archives), Index Cards; and O.C.A., Students' Registers, 13 January 1853.

15 Roberts, p. 23.

16 Roberts, p. 9. Richard Challoner received his early training from John Gother and went to Douai in 1705 at the age of 14. Later he became Vice President there. On resigning he returned to England in 1730. After acting as coadjutor to Bishop Petre, he became Vicar Apostolic for the London District in 1761.

17 Roberts, p. 8.

18 Roberts, p. 13. Bishop Challoner died in 1781, an old man of 89. He had fled from his home in London at the time of the Gordon Riots, where he had been in hiding from a mob who were searching for him with the intention of dragging him through the streets. But he died a few months later in Finchley having never fully recovered from the effects of the shock and fear of being hunted in that way.

19 Buscot, p. 51. See also Roberts, pp. 24, 25.

20 Buscot, pp. 63–4. Norman, p. 178.

21 Roberts, p. 51. Also M. N. L. Couve de Murville, *John Milner*, p. 1.

22 Barry, p. 38. He came to the school fifteen years after Ilsley in 1858. Roberts, p. 74.

23 Frank Roberts's original manuscript.

24 Buscot, p. 118 and Roberts pp. 71, 20. The date of the building seems to have been 1707: 'this date used to be visible on a leaden spout at back of the house'. It is the present Park Hall Hotel, Wolverhampton. The term 'Bounds' was carried on at Cotton.

25 Buscot, ch. 24 and pp. 251–5. Also Roberts, pp. 108–9. They moved to Cotton Hall, which Bishop Ullathorne had set up as a preparatory school for Sedgley Park in 1865.

26 Roberts, ch. 8, 'The School in the Mid-Nineteenth Century'.

27 Roberts, p. 82. As early as 1848, Father Clough, SJ, began the long series of annual retreats. The following year the retreat was given by a Passionist, Father Gaudentius, who was soon in charge of the Passionist monastery at Cotton Hall. One of the 'retreat fathers' was Father Robert Coffin, an Oratorian, who had been with Newman and Father Faber at Cotton.

28 School Annals. Also Roberts, p. 84.

29 Roberts, p. 21.

30 Barry, p. 26.

31 Roberts, p. 90. Also, ch. 5, 'Life and Work at Sedgley Park'. Expeditions to Dudley Castle would be arranged, or the caverns, and on some days they would visit Oscott College.

32  Beck, p. 90. He worked with Dr Grant, Rector of the English College, and later described this undertaking as 'the most important and most eventful of the labours of his episcopal life'.

33  Buscot, p. 139, and Kiernan, p. 22. The first Provincial Synod was at Oscott in 1852.

34  Ilsley later thanked Ullathorne for all his guidance over the years, at the dinner given after his consecration in 1879.

35  Butler, ch. 10. The fact that Ullathorne had testified against the transportation of convicts to Australia told against him in the eyes of the Government. But there were many other factors affecting the decision in favour of Manning. See Gray, ch. 8, p. 200: 'Happily Father Coffin, the Vice-Principal of the Redemptorists in England, was in Rome to offer the authorities more correct representations, possibly the only occasion on which one old Harrovian has been able to do a good turn for another at the Vatican.' Both men were converts. There was a feeling at this time that Manning, as a convert, would assist in bringing more converts into the Church if he were appointed to the position of Archbishop of Westminster. But according to Dom Aidan Bellenger: 'Many considered Ullathorne the safer man for the job.' He added the thought that, 'Perhaps it was institutionalised snobbery.' See also Bellenger, p. 332.

36  *Ibid.*, p. 233.

37  Norman, p. 28.

38  *Ibid.*, p. 12. Also, Chadwick, vol. i, p. 281: 'The old traditions of Roman Catholics were slowly being superseded ... they were being swamped partly by Irish labourers who knew nothing of these traditions, and partly by converts who joined the Church of Rome because it was *not* like the Church of England ...'

39  Fitzgerald, p. 9. Also Roberts, p. 7. Some changes were slow to take place and a 'Garden of the Soul' attitude persisted. Right up to early days at Cotton, the priests on the staff were always referred to as 'Mr', and this later became 'Sir' and not 'Father'.

40  Beck, p. 128. Provincial councils: 'The first two councils dealt with important points in English Catholic life. The xxivth decree is concerned with the clergy and there are laid down principles that have governed clerical dress and behaviour ever since.'

41  P. O'Toole, 'Archbishop Ilsley, A Memoir', *The Tablet*, 11 December 1926, p. 11.

42  *The Times*, 2 December 1926. Wiseman was President of Oscott from 1840 until 1847. Also R. S. Schiefen, 'Wiseman's Oscott', in *Essays*, p. 75: 'It was already apparent that Wiseman's activities and interests led to administrative neglect within the college ... Wiseman, it seems, was overly indulgent with the younger boys and, according to some, tended to ignore the needs of the divines.'

43 Myerscough, p. 162. Samuel Myerscough SJ, was received into the Church at the age of 26, having first taken a music degree at Oxford. He entered Oscott in 1908, so his information could have come from some of Ilsley's contemporaries with whom he was acquainted there. Ordained in 1912, he became a Jesuit in 1919. Also *The Birmingham Mail*, 6 December 1926.

44 John Henry Newman, *Sermons Preached on Various Occasions*, p. 164.

45 J.F.C., pp. 13, 14. Also *The Oscotian* (1907), pp. 111–70. The Bishop of Shrewsbury opposed his appointment. He took over in July 1860 and retired in July 1877.

46 Barry, p. 45.

47 Chadwick, vol. i, p. 283.

48 Roberts, p. 7. Canon Burton describes the attitude of the old type of Catholics, 'and their reluctance to receive with enthusiasm practices unfamiliar to them'.

49 Buscot, p. 259.

CHAPTER TWO

# *Missionary Priest*

## Ordination 1861

Edward Ilsley was ordained by Bishop Ullathorne in St Chad's Cathedral, Birmingham, on the Feast of SS Peter and Paul, in 1861. He was then just six weeks past the age of 23 and although the requirement for the ordination of a priest at that time was for the candidate to have completed his twenty-fourth year, bishops generally received the power of dispensation for one year, and Bishop Ullathorne would have exercised it in this case.

He was about to take up his duties as curate to James Massam at Longton, which lies in the south-east of the Potteries area, in the northern part of the town then known as 'Lane End'.[1] Something of the personality of the young priest can be gathered from the Bishop's words in a letter to the Revd Massam when he notified him of the appointment: 'I am just going to the Cathedral to ordain a priest who will be a consolation to you,' he wrote.[2] Edward said his first Mass the following morning in his native town of Stafford, in the little chapel in the mission of St Austin where his parents were married, and he and his brother and sisters had been baptized. Two weeks earlier a foundation stone for the new church had been laid by Bishop Ullathorne on the plot of land adjoining the old chapel, and it was to be this newly ordained priest who returned fifty years later, at the time of his golden jubilee, when he was about to become Archbishop of Birmingham, to consecrate the church about to be built there.[3]

## Edward, Charles and Anne

The years 1860 and 1861 were memorable ones for the Ilsley family. On 23 January 1860, at the age of 20, Edward's sister Anne took the habit as a lay sister with the Sisters of Mercy, in St Mary's Convent at

16

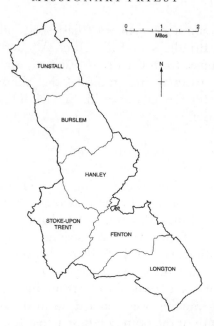

Figure 2.1 *The six pottery towns of North Staffordshire.*

Handsworth, assuming the name of Josephine. On 29 June 1861 Edward was ordained to the priesthood, and on the feast of the Immaculate Conception on 8 December, his brother Charles, then aged 16, took final vows as a Rosminian at the congregation's house at Rugby.[4] Charles, however, fifteen years later in 1876 decided to leave the Institute of Charity. He went first to Rugby and then to St Etheldreda's in London and left the Institute from there shortly after.

Two years after this, when he was 33, he married Sarah Brathwaite, then 19, in a civil ceremony[5] and from then on the couple lived in Norwood in the London area, and Charles never returned home to see his parents again. On his marriage certificate he described himself as a musician, but he took any job that came to hand in the following years in the struggle to make ends meet. So the lives of the two brothers went in very different directions, and looking back, Charles apparently always suffered remorse and never really came to terms with the path he had taken. On the other hand, a close relationship existed between Edward and his sister Anne. He often visited her, and she wrote to him regularly, especially on his birthdays and on religious feast days, telling him any news of his family. Charles visited his sister Ellen and her family in later years with Sarah. In 1889 Ellen's daughter Catherine, then 19, was godmother to Charles's daughter Catherine, and when they were older, some of Charles's daughters occasionally stayed with the Brindleys at Erdington. An undated note in the Birmingham archives from Charles to Edward, thanking him for his good wishes at Christmas time, indicates that although Charles lived away from his family for the rest of his life, he did keep in touch with them, however briefly.

## Life in Longton

Edward Ilsley's life in Longton, serving as a young priest, presents an interesting social document. In the mission of St Gregory where he assisted the elderly James Massam, he was hard-working and uncomplaining in some of the worst conditions brought about by the Industrial Revolution. His uncle William also served there for a few months in 1836 with its first priest Father Daniel, so Edward would have heard about Lane End already from his descriptions.[6] Coal-mining and iron-smelting were carried on in the district, but it was through the growth of the pottery industry that Longton had become a busy market town by the turn of the century, with trade notably increasing when improved roads and the coming of railways made it possible for china and pottery to be supplied further afield to many other parts of the country.[7] The subsequent development of the community where Ilsley came to work represented a microcosm of much that was happening in many other industrial areas in Victorian England at the time. From a population of around five thousand at the beginning of the century, it had risen to some twenty thousand in Ilsley's time. A local description reveals, 'as the century proceeded, the town became more solidly built up and the earlier courts and terraces, hemmed in by later streets, soon degenerated into slums'.[8]

At least Longton had the advantage of not having developed from an old town, so the main streets were reasonably wide and they were well-lit with gas lamps. The centre of the town reflected an air of prosperity, and a fine town hall designed in the classical style was completed in 1863, two years after Ilsley came there. A large covered market was built at the same time, and there was a court house, bank buildings and a variety of shops. In the vicinity of Lane End, although the dwellings in general were small, space was not a problem and some roads were lined with the newly built houses of tradesmen. In Ilsley's time, many self-made men in trade or manufacturing still lived locally in order to be near their work, and they were the ones looked on as the leaders of the community.[9]

Figure 2.2 *Drawing made from a postcard of Longton* c. *1900 titled 'Firing a Potter's Oven'. From the Warrillow Collection, Keele University Library.*

But less was done by way of general improvement because there was no public body responsible for ordering the town's common life and development during the time of its rapid expansion. As local industry tended to spring up where the workers lived, those worst affected were the poorer people living in the back-alleys and crowded courts. Some of their cottages on the higher ground were in terraces built in such a way that the rows were balanced at odd angles to one another. This prompted a local man to say they looked as though they had been 'discharged from a mighty volcano and dropped haphazard upon land ready-built'.[10] Small pottery works were wedged in every available space there, so they were almost indistinguishable from the surrounding dwellings and became part of the same scene. There were as many as 65 of these in the town in the mid-1860s, and factories even lined some of the main streets as well.

So closely did industry encroach on the people's lives that deep, waterlogged 'marlholes', from which the local clay had been dug, presented a terrifying picture by lying dangerously near their dwellings in many places. The women would try to brush the thick grime caused by the oven fires from the fronts of their houses with their rough brooms, before attempting to whiten their doorsteps and lintels. The town lay in a hollow, which made it the most polluted of all the Potteries towns, so the only time photographs could be taken of

Figure 2.3 *Drawing of women brushing down their houses in Heathcote Road, Longton. From a photograph in the Warrillow Collection, Keele University Library.*

the area was on the general workers' holiday when the great chimneys stopped smoking for a day or two, allowing the air to clear sufficiently.[11]

So Edward Ilsley found himself working for a Catholic community where a great deal of poverty and deprivation prevailed. When work became scarce in mines or foundries, they were the first ones to be laid off, and even when it was available, notices often carried the footnote, 'No Catholics need apply', because of the bigotry and fear nurtured at this time.[12] If Catholics were employed at all, it was merely to fill a situation that no other workers would take on, and a newspaper correspondent visiting the Irish colonies in the Midlands in 1856, and seeing their dreadful working conditions, wrote, 'It is lives that are bought and sold in the furnaces and forges of South Staffordshire.'[13]

## Working among the Poor

Ilsley proved himself an indefatigable worker, particularly among the very poorest. 'As assistant to Father Massam he had constantly and assiduously visited the sick, attended the distressed, sympathised with those who suffered in body or in mind.'[14] It was realized among the clergy in those days that a great deal of practical help was needed from them towards those in their care, as well as their spiritual guidance, so it would fall directly into his hands as their priest to help guide them forward to something better in life, by working for them through the schools and various guilds and confraternities at St Gregory's. Samuel Myerscough, who went to Longton as a curate in 1913, when later describing the everyday lives of Ilsley and his rector, said they paid whatever they could out of their own pockets at times to help some poor parishioner in need. Ilsley was called to work there for the next twelve years, and coming there forty years later, Myerscough still found what he termed 'Abundant evidence of good work done by Father Ilsley, as the old folk who remember him well, call him. His health, they said was far from robust.'[15]

This was very probably very true, as he gave himself little comfort in life. Indeed when the time came for him to move on to his new appointment as Rector of Olton Seminary, his successor, John Stringfellow, who received a somewhat abrupt summons to serve at Longton from Bishop Ullathorne, was quite dismayed when he saw the poor room Edward had occupied in the old presbytery for the last twelve years.[16] 'How can a man live in a place like this?' he exclaimed. 'Do as I have done,' was Ilsley's forthright reply, 'Live out of it!'[17] This came almost like a command, meaning the pressing circumstances allowed no time for such considerations, as more often than not he needed to be out, working among his people.

The young priest came to know a community with various sides to it. There were the workers, a close-knit group, many of whom were earnestly striving to improve their lot. 'Longton cleaves to its own and its own cleave to it', was a good description of them.[18] They were resilient and cheerful, in spite of the fact that life had little to offer them in the way of comfort through the long working hours. Another side of life was portrayed by the prospering industrialists, whose prospects were very different. But the young curate realized the pottery works owners and mine managers did not maintain only a narrow interest in their own world of trade and commerce. It was part of their *alter ego* to encourage the spiritual and cultural welfare of their fellow men, so they acted generously towards their own community, and it was through their good offices the town came to have many of its amenities.[19] These self-made men were in sympathy with those from whose humble origins they had themselves sprung, and both master and men were alike in recognizing their mutual dependence on each other and sharing in local pride.[20] So when Ilsley looked for help in building the proposed new church many of them were ready to come forward and take part in it.

A parishioner of St Gregory's, giving his name as 'D. Brookes', was born in 1867. He served as an altar boy there until he was 17, when in 1884 he took over as choirmaster, and he retained that position until just after the consecration of the church in 1887, when he went to teach in London. A book he wrote later, *Reminiscences of St. Gregory's, Longton, Staffordshire*, has a number of passages in it that give first-hand information about Edward Ilsley's time spent there. Brookes finished writing it when he was 87, and it is still in manuscript form. Suggestions that Ilsley worked quietly and unobtrusively while in Longton, before being chosen by Bishop Ullathorne as rector for his seminary, are not entirely borne out by the facts because in his *Reminiscences* D. Brookes described him as being 'an active and energetic priest', and this was demonstrated by his many pastoral activities which brought him in contact, not only with all the parishioners, but also with many other townsfolk. His work, it seems, benefited everyone, from the poorest and neediest to those in more prosperous circumstances, and 'he won not only the affections of the Catholics but also the respect of notable non-Catholics'. The same writer described these years as 'St. Gregory's golden age of advancement', and he summed it all up by saying, that it was the case in those days of 'all hands to the pump, and right well vigorously pursued'.

By the time Edward Ilsley arrived in Longton, the congregation attending the Lane End Mission had been steadily increasing, especially in the previous two decades, and the small chapel of St Gregory, built in Bishop Milner's time in 1818, was soon barely accommodating the needs of their rapidly growing numbers.[21] The situation was pressing because when the chapel was first built, there were about twenty people hearing Mass there on a Sunday, and those had now risen to about 260. Bishop Ullathorne is quoted as saying to James Massam, when on a visit in 1856, 'You must put your congregation in order for a new church.' On this occasion Father Massam inferred this was not yet necessary, but undeterred, Bishop Ullathorne greeted him shortly afterwards with, 'Well, when are you going to begin your new church?' When a mission was given later and a number were left standing outside, Father Massam at last started to give the matter some serious thought.[22] Passages in the *Reminiscences* mention that on Ilsley's arrival in 1861 to assist him, 'the ageing Father Massam was pleased to let his new curate go ahead with the plans for building a larger church'. Ullathorne probably foresaw things would work in that direction when he made the appointment, and Brookes also recorded that 'Father Ilsley was largely instrumental in the building of the new church at Longton.' He played a leading part in the fundraising, in the negotiations for the purchase of the site and the general overseeing of the building of the church which began seven years after his arrival in Longton. He must have gained some first-hand experience on how to go about things when visiting his home in Stafford, as the new St Austin's was completed just a year after his ordination.[23]

## The New St Gregory's

It is in his neat, legible hand that all the details concerning the new building are entered into St Gregory's Church Book. On 12 November 1863 there is a record of the negotiations for the purchase of the land, and in the following March another entry stating the sum of £2,025 was paid over to complete the purchase. The way in which he helped to tackle the organization and planning of it all was a foretaste of the systematic way Ilsley would go about things in the future. He obviously worked tirelessly and applied himself with great determination to achieve such a result in his first years as curate. It was later written of him: 'This work would perhaps have staggered an older and more experienced man, but the devotedness with which he applied himself to the task overcame all obstacles.'[24]

As well as providing schools, the problem of building new churches at this time for the rapidly expanding Catholic population was one which the bishops of the newly restored hierarchy recognized must be dealt with without delay. They realized that if adequate provision was not made promptly for their people to congregate for worship, there would be a falling away from the faith, and the revival of Catholicism would begin to decline. In some places small churches were quickly and cheaply erected with corrugated roofs and plain deal altars. But there was another school of thought which adhered to the principle that a suitable place must be provided for worship, fitting for the humblest man to make his devotions beside the highest in the land. The revivalist Gothic style was favoured for these buildings, which were to be set in prominent positions on main streets to declare to all the Catholicism which had returned after being hidden for nearly three hundred years.[25]

This more expansive view was subscribed to at Longton with the hope that this new church would contribute to all their lives in many ways. On laying the foundation stone on 13 September 1868, Bishop Ullathorne expressed himself in extraordinarily strong terms when he declared that it should prove 'a great boon to the poor Catholics in this dreary town of sin and mud'.[26] The rather plainly worded discourse he delivered on this occasion was the subject of considerable criticism in the *Birmingham Post*, but nevertheless the church was to prove to be all that he said and much more, because by the 1920s St Gregory's was the largest parish in the Potteries, with 4,000 parishioners.[27] One hundred years earlier in the first little chapel there had been only sixteen people in all attending Mass.

There was a twofold interest in the minds of the wealthier Catholics in Longton who not only wished to support the church directly but also hoped to see Longton develop into a town with good provision for those who lived and worked in it. So the idea of a new, well-built, imposing Catholic church was well received, and pledges of financial help were given by some whose firms are still flourishing today.[28]

Figure 2.4 *St Gregory's Church, Longton, designed by E. W. Pugin and opened in 1869. From a photograph taken in 1900.*

24

Father Ilsley enlisted the help of a committee of interested men, and a site was chosen for the proposed building in Heathcote Road near the centre of the town. Edward Welby Pugin was the architect selected to design the new St Gregory's, and Ilsley's entry in the Church Book on 15 September 1866 reads as follows: 'The Bishop and E. W. Pugin consult about the general plan of the new Church and Presbytery.'[29]

*The Staffordshire Advertiser* reported at the opening on 18 July 1869: 'The church is one of the most spacious and beautiful in the Roman Catholic Diocese of Birmingham.' The descriptions of the church given in the newspaper at this time are impressive, particularly the design of the interior with its lofty clerestoried nave and high-vaulted chancel, terminating in a five-sided apse whose stained-glass windows rose to roof height. All this was typical of Edward Pugin's exuberant style.[30] Photographs taken at the opening also show the decorative brilliance of the elaborate carved tracery on the high altar, also the west front set with a magnificent rose window, characteristic of his finest work. On the opening day, Pontifical High Mass celebrated by Bishop Ullathorne was attended by a large congregation which included a number of Protestants. Admission for all seats was by ticket, the custom for church openings in those days, with fundraising in mind. On this occasion the seats were graded into 'the best reserved seats five shillings, the second half a crown and unreserved, one shilling'. Some churches regularly charged for 'sittings' so that the well-dressed people did not have to mix with the poorer ones when hearing Mass, but this went against the philosophy behind this kind of 'big church building' which openly embraced all levels of the community without let or favour.[31]

At the dinner given later at the town hall for all the dignitaries, and those who had come forward and made the building of the church possible by their generosity, Bishop Ullathorne said that no act had gratified him more than, 'the erection of this church of Longton with all that accompanied it – the example is worthy of imitation by the whole diocese'. He went on to say, 'The building of this fine church at Longton demonstrated to him the revival of the Catholic spirit of mediaeval times' – and he concluded (in spite of the mixed company as regards religion) by asserting all this had been achieved with the help of God 'notwithstanding the boasted Protestantism in this country'. James Massam spoke of 'the steady devotion of Father Ilsley who has worked with unswerving zeal and energy', while Ilsley's toast was for 'The health of the collectors'. To show the spirit in which the Catholics at Longton had acted with respect to their new church, he said that when the scheme was first mooted one lady said to him, 'I will give you £500: Go on with it!' While another friend had said, 'I will give you £100 now and another hundred as soon as I can,' and he kept his word. 'Another gave £300, some £100 each, others £50 each, others £10 each, and so on down to shillings and sixpences, which the humblest members had regularly subscribed from the beginning of the undertaking.' It was the small regular donations, he said, that made the sum grow.[32]

Once work on the new building began, an onus fell on the people to contribute to the church debt-fund, and alongside all the other Catholics in Longton the poorest of the poor gave of their scant earnings. A notable feature of these times was the unflagging support of the working classes by putting any small sum they could find into the collecting boxes of those going round the houses making the weekly outdoor collection. Every Sunday after Mass the collectors went round to receive these weekly contributions 'and Mr Tams for 40 years was one of the collectors, and never missed a collection, except during his holiday each year'. Mr Tams was a well-known pottery manufacturer in the town. He died in 1919 when he was 83.[33] These small sums provided whatever personal income the priests could count on, and they in their turn always guaranteed 'that the interest on the money borrowed was paid out of their meagre savings'.[34] Debts involving large financial repayments were of course carried on the shoulders of wealthy patrons, and the situation was relieved through the generosity of those who individually subscribed toward such expensive details as the stained-glass windows, the richly carved altars and other major items.[35] By such means, and through a great deal of dedicated effort toward fundraising, the debt was lifted only eighteen years later in 1887 when the consecration took place.[36]

## Talented Organist and Choirmaster

Ilsley's most notable talent and cultural interest was in music, and he became widely known in the surrounding districts as an able organist and choirmaster. Brookes mentions that Father Daniel's sisters were in charge of the organ and the choir 'in the old Marsh chapel, until Father Ilsley came on the scene'. He continues, 'He was a capable musician, and by reason of his talent St. Gregory's choir of that period, and for many years after, was noted for its choral work for the Church. It was probably the best Catholic choir in the Potteries, and non-Catholics were often attracted to the church to listen to the music.' When he was later appointed Auxiliary Bishop and was working at Bishop's House in Birmingham, St Chad's Cathedral was acclaimed for giving a beautiful interpretation of the liturgy, and his influence surely played a part in this.[37] On special occasions in Longton, such as at Easter or Christmas, an orchestra assisted in performances of Masses by Mozart, Beethoven, Weber or Schubert. By coincidence a fine stone-faced theatre called 'The Royal Victoria' was being erected in Stafford Street in 1867 at the same time as the church, and whenever there was a visiting opera Father Ilsley would take the opportunity to make arrangements for the cast to augment the church choir or for solo performances to be given. The church would be well-filled on these occasions, which were used for fund-raising to reduce the debt.[38]

During his stay there Edward Ilsley also developed an abiding interest in the education of the poorer Catholic children in the area. He was made responsible for the mission schools soon after his arrival which meant he became 'school manager' whose job it was to supervise details in the running of the schools, including the appointment of staff. He taught the children singing during the week, examined them on their catechism and also kept a check on their attendance at Sunday Mass.[39] The mission schools were housed in a two-storey building opposite the church. The first St Gregory's was often called the 'Old Marsh Lane Chapel' by local people in those days, because it lay on land between Marsh Lane, which is now called 'Griffin Street', and St Gregory Street. By the time Father Ilsley took over as manager, the schools had been considerably enlarged and reorganized, the girls' and infants' departments being on the ground floor, while the boys were on the upper floor.[40] A communicating door had been made through between the school and presbytery some five years earlier when these additions were being made. There were nearly 100 boys and girls there at this time, and they would remain there throughout all their school years.[41]

When stricter regulations in education were introduced by the Act of 1870, Father Ilsley stood as a member for the first school board formed in the town in January 1871. Brookes mentions: 'He was a successful candidate, being placed third on the list.' There were nine candidates altogether. Bishop Ullathorne said he considered the presence of Catholics on these school boards 'the only securities we possess for the safety of our Catholic children'.[42] Father Patrick O'Toole later wrote of Edward Ilsley, 'If there was one other department of his arduous duties, beside the building of St. Gregory's that distinguished

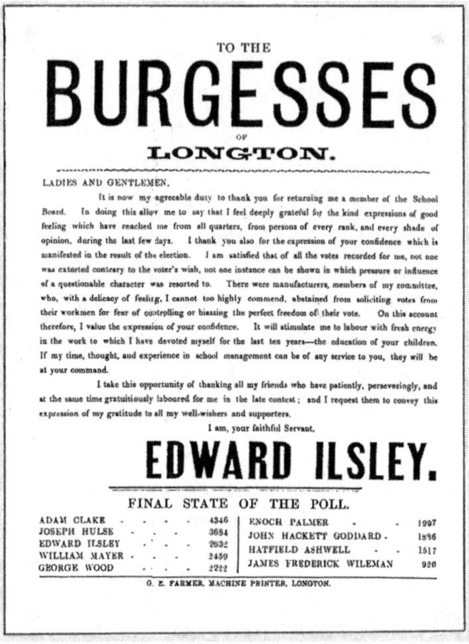

TO THE

# BURGESSES

OF

## LONGTON.

LADIES AND GENTLEMEN,

It is now my agreeable duty to thank you for returning me a member of the School Board. In doing this allow me to say that I feel deeply grateful for the kind expressions of good feeling which have reached me from all quarters, from persons of every rank, and every shade of opinion, during the last few days. I thank you also for the expression of your confidence which is manifested in the result of the election. I am satisfied that of all the votes recorded for me, not one was extorted contrary to the voter's wish, not one instance can be shown in which pressure or influence of a questionable character was resorted to. There were manufacturers, members of my committee, who, with a delicacy of feeling, I cannot too highly commend, abstained from soliciting votes from their workmen for fear of controlling or biassing the perfect freedom of their vote. On this account therefore, I value the expression of your confidence. It will stimulate me to labour with fresh energy in the work to which I have devoted myself for the last ten years—the education of your children. If my time, thought, and experience in school management can be of any service to you, they will be at your command.

I take this opportunity of thanking all my friends who have patiently, perseveringly, and at the same time gratuitously laboured for me in the late contest; and I request them to convey this expression of my gratitude to all my well-wishers and supporters.

I am, your faithful Servant,

## EDWARD ILSLEY.

### FINAL STATE OF THE POLL.

| | | | | | |
|---|---|---|---|---|---|
| ADAM CLARK | . . . . | 4346 | ENOCH PALMER | . . | 1997 |
| JOSEPH HULSE | . . . | 3684 | JOHN HACKETT GODDARD | . | 1836 |
| EDWARD ILSLEY | . . . | 2632 | HATFIELD ASHWELL | . . | 1517 |
| WILLIAM MAYER | . . . | 2459 | JAMES FREDERICK WILEMAN | | 920 |
| GEORGE WOOD | . . . | 2222 | | | |

O. E. FARMER, MACHINE PRINTER, LONGTON.

Figure 2.5 *Edward Ilsley elected as a member of the first school board formed at Longton in 1871. Private collection.*

him more than the others, it was the care he took of the children of the parish. He laboured in season and out of season for the educational and spiritual welfare of the young.'[43] The log book of the boys' school gives some idea of the interest he had in his young parishioners: Friday 20 June 1873, 'Father Ilsley has given us a nice framed picture of Our Blessed Lady and Child.' Friday 27 June, 'Father Ilsley has promised a picture showing each of the fifteen mysteries of the Rosary to the boy who knows his Catechism and understands the Rosary best.'

During these busy years he also found time to help the mission schools in the neighbouring district in need of extra funds. On 17 September 1866 it is recorded in *The Records of the Mission of St Peter's, Cobridge, 1866–73*, 'Father Ilsley of Longton kindly preached in the evening, on behalf of the schools to procure funds for the payment of the rent. This is now the third time Cobridge had been indebted to him for similar charity – about the same time of the year.' A visiting preacher was a great draw in those days, and people would walk several miles to another district to attend such an evening service.

## Appointment to St Bernard's 1873

Twelve years later, in the summer of 1873 when he was 35, the course of Father Ilsley's life was suddenly changed when he received a letter from Bishop Ullathorne telling him he was appointed Rector of St Bernard's Seminary in Olton. An entry in the school logbook indicated he was about to leave Longton: 'A subscription has been made by the children in order that, in union with the other children of these schools, they may present their dear and loved manager, Father Ilsley, with a present, on the occasion of his leaving Longton to become Rector of the new diocesan College at Olton near Birmingham.' He received confirmation of the appointment the week before, when Bishop Ullathorne wrote on 9 July, 'I will no longer keep you in the inconvenient state of being burdened with a secret, I write then to enable you to state publicly that you are appointed Rector of St Bernard's Seminary. As soon as I can, I will free you from your present position. It would be well if after Sunday you could come over for a day or two here that we may talk over matters.'[44] Two weeks later there is a simple statement in the school diary with no further comment: 'Father Ilsley has finally left us today.' There would have been many heavy hearts that day, for the dedicated priest would be missed by young and old.

The following April there is another entry in the school logbook, 'Father Ilsley, from the Diocesan Seminary, near Birmingham, the late Manager came to see the children today.' Ilsley always remembered his 'little flock' at Longton, the place where he spent many hard-working and fruitful years, and he made no secret in the future that the happiest period in his life had been spent there among them.[45] It was a tribute to his general popularity among all the people of the district that the non-Catholics requested to be included in the presentation of a crozier to him as Bishop Elect in 1879. This took place in the Longton Town Hall on 18 November, two weeks before his consecration in St Chad's Cathedral. The Protestant Mayor of Longton, Mr G. Bennion, presided over the ceremony, and the teachers and children gave him a silver casket, a chrismatory for the holy oils, also to be used at his consecration service. On the day of his consecration he had a section of the cathedral specially reserved for a number of his old parishioners who had travelled from Longton to Birmingham for the occasion.[46]

As auxiliary bishop, Ilsley returned to Longton on 18 July 1887 to consecrate his own church of St Gregory, and to celebrate High Mass the following day. Having finally cleared the debt, the parishioners made further efforts to have everything complete and well-furnished for that day. A marble slab was procured for the high altar, crosses and brackets for the walls, chairs for the priests, a new sanctuary lamp, a lectern and extra cassocks, so that everything was at its best.[47] Brookes takes up the narrative again: 'When the new St. Gregory's Church was consecrated by Dr. Ilsley in 1887, Longton choir was augmented by members of Stoke and Hanley Catholic choristers to sing '*Missa Papae Marcelli*', a famous composition by Pierre Luigi (usually known as Palestrina). It was a Mass for seven different voices, sung without accompaniment. The Mass was known to be a favourite of the Bishop.' Luncheon was held in the town hall, and later, having boarded the train with his secretary, ready for his return journey to Birmingham, he was heard to make this joking remark by way of praising the young conductor (the 20-year-old Brookes), who was standing there on the platform. Leaning forward he said through the carriage window, 'In my day we never got beyond the *Kyrie*!'

## James Massam

After leaving Longton, Edward Ilsley would occasionally take time to escape his many arduous duties to pay a courtesy visit to his old parish priest, Father Massam, who finally retired in 1882, but continued to live in the new presbytery which had been built in 1880. As soon as the church was free from debt the parishioners resolved to build this new presbytery, having in mind 'the need to provide accommodation for their new bishop should he visit Longton'. Brookes described how the two would be seen walking along arm in arm engrossed in conversation, 'Naturally people concluded in their own minds they were like Father and Son together', he said. This was because Father Massam always trained the boys in his care on the principle 'like father, like children'. The two men obviously always had very much in common, especially as James Massam, who received his training at the English College at Lisbon, was originally intended on his return to be one of the professors at Oscott College. However, when he returned from Lisbon, having first visited his home in Lancashire, he arrived at Oscott only to be told by Dr Weedall, who was then president of the college, that because of the shortage of priests at that time, and because of the poor health of the Revd Edward Daniel, he would have to go to Longton instead.

An unusual photograph, taken after the new church was built,

Figure 2.6  *James Massam and his curate Edward Ilsley outside St Gregory's, Longton.*
*Drawing made from a photograph in Oscott College archives.*

shows the elderly James Massam seated, with the young curate standing by his side evidently engrossed in a book.[48] It portrays Father
Ilsley in his thirties wearing the Roman-style cassock and biretta. The
photograph might have been taken when his duties as curate at
Longton were nearly completed and he was about to move on to further responsibilities. Father Massam on the other hand, ordained fifty
years earlier in Lisbon, was part of 'the old Church', and is dressed in
an earlier style. As Father Daniel's curate at the age of 25 in 1837 (the
year before Edward Ilsley was born), he used to cover the area between
Longton and Newcastle,[49] walking along rough country lanes,
accompanied by his faithful dog Dash, visiting isolated farms and
villages, and usually saying Mass in a wayside barn or house. He would
often feel dejected as he travelled through those scattered communities seeing the disadvantages suffered by the Catholics because of the
suspicion and bigotry that still existed in those days. The picture was
taken outside the side door of St Gregory's commonly known as 'the
people's door' because it was used most often by the parishioners.

James Massam finally left Longton in 1892, to be cared for by the
Alexian Brothers in Manchester, and he died the following year at the
age of 81. 'The body was brought to Longton and met at the station.
Dense crowds thronged the Market Place, and lined the streets as the
procession moved to the church.'[50] Bishop Ilsley offered a solemn
Requiem Mass for his old friend the following day, and delivered the
panegyric. A special vault in the local cemetery, reserved for the
interment of their Catholic priests, was provided at the time by his
parishioners.

## Notes

1  *Victoria*. In 1848 the name of this part had officially been changed to
   Longton as a postal district and for government purposes, but the old
   name was still in use in Ilsley's time.

2  Myerscough, Obituary Notice, p. 162. Under the *Corpus Iuris Canonici* –
   which preceded the first *Codex Iuris Canonici* of 1917 – the age for ordination as a priest was 24. It was common practice for a bishop to dis-
   pense a candidate for one year.

3  Greenslade, p. 23. It was consecrated on 26 July 1911. Edward Ilsley
   became Archbishop and Metropolitan on 8 December that year.

4  This would seem an inordinately young age to be taking final vows,
   but these facts are recorded in the Institute of Charity archives, Wonersh. Charles Ilsley was born on 25 March 1845. After 1918 no perpe-
   tual vows were allowed to be taken before the age of 21.

5  Sarah Brathwaite came from a Protestant family. She and Charles were married in Brentford Register Office in Ealing in May 1878. The ceremony was witnessed by Sarah's father and mother. Sarah was never received into the Catholic Church.

6  Longton, p. 7. After a short stay William Ilsley went on to St Augustine's, Solihull. He died in 1857, aged 54. His death is recorded in vol. i of the registers of St Mary's, The Mount, Walsall. His early years spent on the staff of Oscott College are described in Mary Roskell, *Francis Kerril Amherst D.D.*, pp. 92, 106–7.

7  Briggs, ch. 1, p. 8. Fine clays were also imported from the south-west of the country, pp. 2 and 3.

8  *Victoria*, pp. 229–30. The population of Longton numbered 10,000 in 1831. By Ilsley's time in 1870 it had nearly doubled itself again by reaching over 19,000. During the nineteenth century the population of the borough was estimated at nearly 39,000.

9  Briggs, p. 52. They later moved out to such parts as Blythe Bridge or Barlaston.

10  Briggs, p. 51. T. H. Hawley, a member of a distinguished family in Longton, writing as an old man, recalling the world of 1842.

11  Briggs., pp. 62, 22, 23. J. Blake took a series of dramatic pictures of Longton in the 1900s.

12  Brookes, p. 5. Also Norman, p. 203: 'In areas of heavy Irish immigration there was the addition of antipathy to an Irish labour force.'

13  Beck, p. 267. Mr A. M. Sullivan, writing for the Irish *Nation*.

14  *B.P.*, 2 February 1891, p. 146.

15  Myerscough, p. 162.

16  O.C.A., Letter dated 14 July 1873.

17  Myerscough, p. 162.

18  Bevis Hillier, *Master Potters of the Industrial Revolution*, p. 9.

19  Briggs, ch. 9, 'Selected Biographies, Longton People', pp. 107–11. They greatly assisted in the provision of a local hospital, working men's libraries and other educational facilities, with help from the local patron and landowner, the duke of Sutherland. The amenity of one of the earliest public parks, The Queen's Park, was also provided for the people of Longton in this way, to commemorate Queen Victoria's Jubilee.

20  Briggs, ch. 2, 'Town Hall and Mayoral Chain', p. 18. The town secured the Borough Charter in 1865. This meant that local government began to become more democratic instead of being in the hands of a wealthy and influential oligarchy.

21  William White, *History, Gazetteer and Directory of Stafford*, p. 235 and B. W. Kelly, *Historical Notes on English Catholic Missions*, p. 259: 'A brick tower was added by Bishop Milner and in 1850 it had the addition of a Lady Chapel.'

22  Longton, pp. 11, 12. St Gregory's became a rectory in 1858.

23  Greenslade, p. 23. The opening of St Austin's was in July 1862.

24  *B.P.*, pp. 146, 274.

25  Chadwick, part i, pp. 273–4. 'Between the different tugs Catholic bishops found it vexatious to decide how to spend the money which they had not got.'

26  B. W. Kelly, *Historical Notes on English Catholic Missions*, p. 259. Also reported in *The Birmingham Post*, 16 May 1868.

27  The parish then included the areas comprising three neighbouring parishes, Meir, Bucknall and Blurton.

28  *Victoria*, pp. 219–20. John Tam's Crown Potteries, James Kent's Old Foley Pottery and the Moore Brothers.

29  Edward Welby Pugin followed in the tradition of his famous father, Augustus Welby Pugin, the leading Catholic Gothic Revivalist in Britain. Sharing Bishop Milner's belief that a link existed between Gothic architecture and the true principles of the Catholic religion, Augustus Welby Pugin insisted on using the Gothic style rather than the prevailing Classical. In this way he attempted to recreate and restore some of the fervour of the old medieval Church throughout his architectural designs. He carried his ideas through in church furnishings and wall decorations, and even redesigned the priest's vestments in a Gothic style. The same spirit was captured in the development of an inspiring liturgy which continued into the twentieth century. Although much of Pugin's thesis has since been rejected by architects and churchmen alike, because it is considered too narrow in concept, his dogmatism is reflected in later stylistic interpretations. R. O'Donnell, 'Pugin as a church architect', pp. 62–89, and 'The later Pugin', pp. 258–71, in Paul Atterbury and Clive Wainwright (eds), *Pugin as a Gothic Passion*.

30  *S.A.*, 24 July 1869. Owing to subsidence, the church was demolished in March 1968, and a third St Gregory's was built in 1970. The cost of necessary repair work on the old building was estimated at £40,000, and the new church erected in its place cost well over £80,000, 'Axe to fall on 100 year old church in March' was the headline in the *Evening Sentinel'* on 2 November 1967. 'In Pugin's oeuvre this was an important example and a regrettable loss,' commented Dr R. O'Donnell of English Heritage, letter 16 August 1988.

31  R. O'Donnell, 'The Architecture of the London Oratory Churches', Michael Napier and Alistair Laing (eds), in *The London Oratory Centenary 1884–1984*, pp. 21–47. One of the exceptions was the Oratory in London which continued to charge for seats at services such as High Mass and went so far as to provide a separate chapel for the wealthier parishioners. Although Father Faber's mission was to the Irish and less well-off, there was always the risk otherwise of losing wealthy patrons who objected to mixing with the unkempt poor. See also Chadwick, part i, p. 330.

32  *S.A.*, 24 July 1869. Brookes, p. 6: 'Prominent Catholic laymen at the opening of the church were Dr Dawes and Messrs. Tams, Kent, Boardman, Collis, Moore Brothers.'

33  Obituary of Mr John Tams, pottery manufacturer, extract from *The Staffordshire Sentinel.*

34  Myerscough, p. 162. See also Morgan V. Sweeny, 'Diocesan Organisation and Administration', in Beck, pp. 137–8.

35  Fitzgerald, pp. 227–8. Large bequests were often given un-ostentatiously by donors not giving their name. Also Longton: The stained-glass window over the high altar was the gift of Mrs Moore. That over the Sacred Heart altar was given by Mr John Tams. Also B.A., B1162: 'In 1898 Mrs Caroline Boardman arranged for the conveyance of "The Meir House," for the benefit of keeping the church in repair.' (The Meir House is no longer standing.)

36  *The Builder*, 4 July 1868 and *ibid.*, 7 August 1869: The cost of the work for St Gregory's was originally contracted by the builders to be basically '£5,000 excluding fittings in 1868, before the cornerstone was laid, but by August 1869 after the building was opened a further estimate was given as £7,000'. This sum was bound to soar higher when such details as the carved tracery to the high altar, the pulpit and the Lady Altar were added, especially as those were carried out by master craftsmen of the day from London.

37  Chadwick, part ii, p. 410. Article by G. J. Mivart, *The Dublin Review*, 1884.

38  *Victoria*, p. 246. The theatre was completed in 1867. It was burnt down in 1996.

39  School Logbook for 1872.

40  *Longton*. In 1822, Father Daniel built the lower storey of the first school, and also a small presbytery. He saved the money for these by lodging with a family with the name of Brassington.

41  P. Jones, *The Records of the Mission of St Peter's, Cobridge, 1866–73*, and letter: 6 January 1985. The Sisters of Mercy were initially responsible for the teaching and welfare of the girls and infants, and the boys were always taught by secular teachers.

42  St Dominic's Convent, Stone, Archives. Box G/ULL/V1/17. Bishop Ullathorne was against the Act and did not trust the school boards. Cardinal Manning on the other hand supported the Education Act, which he used as a stepping-stone to further negotiation with the government on the Catholic schools question. See Norman, p. 166, also B.A., B4854 : *A Pastoral Letter to the Faithful of the Diocese on the Education Bill*, given on 27 October 1870, by Bishop Ullathorne.

43  *B.P.*, February 1891.

44  O.C.A., Letter from Bishop Ullathorne to Edward Ilsley.

45  *B.P.*, p. 147.

46  *Ibid.*, pp. 7, 8. Also *S.A.*, 22 November 1879: 'Presentation to a Roman

Catholic Bishop at Longton'. Also, *B.P.*, p. 146, Mr Dawes actually made the presentation.

47 *Longton*, p. 19.
48 O.C.A., Letter from Revd D. Donnelly, 2 November 1984: 'Part of the Wall shown is still intact.'
49 Brookes, p. 5. This town was Newcastle under Lyme, Staffs.
50 *Longton*, p. 22.

## CHAPTER THREE

# The Formation of St Bernard's Seminary

## The Organization of Seminaries

The organization of seminaries was an important matter of debate among the bishops during the years following the restoration of the Catholic hierarchy. Bishop Thomas Grant of Southwark initially put forward the idea of separate education for church students at the First Diocesan Synod which was held at Oscott College in 1852, and although this was generally approved, it was not acted upon, because it would have thrown the colleges into debt, relying as they did on the lay students' fees to help cover their running costs.[1] By the time of the Third Diocesan Synod in 1859, two quite differing views concerning their future organization and administration had emerged among the bishops.

The seminaries in question were St Edmund's College, Ware, for the London District, Ushaw for the North and St Mary's College, Oscott, for the Midlands. It was argued by some that although founded on the same lines as Douai, they were not strictly seminaries in the terms of the Council of Trent, as all these colleges were also secular schools, taking in lay boys who mixed freely with the church students. At Oscott, for instance, the lay boys and church boys were brought up together until they had finished their 'Humanities', which completed the lay boys' course. The intended clerics lived from then on under 'seminary' regulations and were called 'divines'.[2]

While the need for separate 'Tridentine' seminaries became a major consideration in some minds, others considered the prevailing 'dual' system of mixed lay and church students to be wholly acceptable, because they had seen it working well over the years and they had no wish for change. No one bishop had sole authority over any of these establishments because students were sent to them by several bishops, who collectively contributed to the upkeep. The bishop of the diocese by the very nature of his position had more immediate control over his own college than the other bishops, but major issues concerning policy would ultimately be resolved through a group decision. They now sought to reinforce their jurisdiction through the formation of a 'board of bishops' to decide the future policies of the particular colleges they supported, even though the amount of influence any bishop would have under these circumstances would naturally depend on the number of students he supplied.

## Wiseman, Manning and Ullathorne

Cardinal Wiseman, then Archbishop of Westminster, at this synod of 1859 added his own interpretation of the decrees of the Council of Trent. Strongly backed by Manning, he said that by their provision each individual diocese should set up a seminary solely for the training of their own ecclesiastical students under the control of the bishop.[3] Bishop Ullathorne's wish to 'regularize' the workings of ecclesiastical education through a more definite application of canon law caused him to support this policy. For some time he had seen

Figure 3.1 *Cardinal Nicholas Wiseman, President of Oscott (1840–47), first Archbishop of Westminster (1850–65). Taken from a portrait in the London Oratory albums.*

grave disadvantages in the dual system, whereby church students were constantly mixing with the more leisured lay students whose future lives were to be so different from their own. The fact that the divines were used in the capacity of supervising and teaching in the college was another underlying cause of dissatisfaction. It was regarded by those who opposed the system as calculated to bring about a lowering of standards. Ullathorne reported to Rome that the dual system led to a 'secular tone'. His report to the Cardinal Prefect of Propaganda concerning the Third Synod of Westminster forcibly stated that 'the Church in England will not be in a normal state until higher ecclesiastical studies, at least, are conducted in seminaries exclusively devoted to ecclesiastical training'.[4]

Since becoming Bishop of Birmingham in 1850 he made his preferences clear regarding his own church students by declaring his earnest wish to institute a separate seminary of his own. In his own diocese the College of St Mary's, Oscott, was housed in a magnificently well-endowed building standing on high ground and distantly looking out over the city. As a testimony to the Catholic revival no expense had been spared when it was completed by A. W. Pugin in 1838, and it was sufficiently spacious to accommodate ecclesiastical students as well as running as a public school of some standing. But despite the facilities the building offered, Ullathorne did not at any time consider altering the role of the college and converting it, ideal as it would be, to the needs of his diocesan seminary. It would have been unwise for him to attempt to make any unfavourable changes in the lay section of the school just then, because his present financial circumstances would not allow him to make any radical alterations to the system. Burdened by debt, he could not risk breaking relations with the wealthy aristocracy on whom he depended and who largely represented the lay element at that time. Weighing the cost, he had once considered making a clear-cut division between the church and lay students while under one roof by separating their recreational areas.[5] But he recognized that in its present form the college lacked the true ecclesiastical character he sought, and realizing that there could be no other satisfactory solution, he determined to remedy the matter by going along the path of separate clerical education on his own elsewhere.

## Ullathorne's Problems

Even when this was achieved later his problems were only partially solved because the new seminary could not absorb all the students from Oscott. Another difficulty he encountered, and that proved to be a considerable stumbling-block, was through the attitude of his three bordering bishops – James Brown of Shrewsbury, Richard Roskell of Nottingham and Francis Kerril Amherst of Northampton. They had no wish for change, and were against any move threatening what they considered to be their rightful interests, and when the new seminary was built they continued to send their students to Oscott. So the policies regarding Oscott College became a bone of contention between them and Ullathorne throughout the years.[6] Bishop Amherst, who had attended both Old Oscott and the new college, was staying there at one time in the company of Ullathorne, when the question came up in conversation 'as to how far the Church benefited from the mixture of lay and clerical students, which was then the custom'. Amherst, and others present, were able to supply strong arguments in its support, saying it favoured the priesthood because, 'on looking through lists of old students, the names of fifty-two were found (then living), who had gone through the whole college course as lay students, and were at the moment Bishops, priests and religious'. This account was given by Edmund Knight, later Bishop of Shrewsbury, who continued: 'and of these, eight were bishops; no inconsiderable addition to the ranks of our clergy and some testimony to the spirit and influence of their *Alma Mater*'.[7]

Ullathorne remained unmoved by these assertions. His strong motives in making these moves can be well understood as a man with a monastic background. Although he had a natural aptitude for dealing with people he at the same time had a tendency to seek seclusion for himself, which was probably strengthened through his time spent at Downside. Aware that the mood of the developing 'Roman' Church was one concerned with the removal of her future clergy away from the world into a more secluded sphere of their own,[8] he renewed his firm intention of building his own independent establishment for this purpose. But Manning's unrealistic plan for the setting-up of numerous small diocesan seminaries did not last very far beyond his period in office because this policy, coupled with prohibiting Catholics to attend university, did not find favour with more percipient churchmen of the day who felt this was not the way forward.

## Plans for the New Seminary

'The seminary is the question which now occupies my thoughts more than anything,' Ullathorne wrote in January 1867, and his vision came nearer reality the same year through a legacy of £600 which was left by Canon Richmond, specifically for the purpose of starting a seminary fund.[9] Things progressed still further for him that summer, when a decision was taken by the clergy in his absence at a meeting held by them at Oscott, to make him a presentation toward the seminary fund on his return from Rome, in gratitude for all he had done for the diocese over the years and specifically towards 'the establishment of a seminary in which the future clergy of the diocese may be trained in the fulness of the ecclesiastical spirit, discipline and learning'.[10] The considerable sum of £2,200 was collected for this purpose, and when news of it reached him in Rome, Ullathorne said he felt 'a glow of happiness beyond description'. In his reply to them after the presentation ceremony at Oscott he outlined his vision for a seminary 'freed from all secular intermixture' which he hoped would spring forth 'a spectacle to angels and to men'.[11]

In 1871, having purchased 40 acres of land at Olton on the outskirts of Birmingham, in what was described as 'a very rural and picturesque district of Warwickshire', he drew up plans for his new establishment with the architect, Edward Joseph Hansom.[12] Having got this far, Ullathorne appeared to be moving cautiously by not embarking on anything over-ambitious that might run him seriously into debt again having only recovered in recent years from those incurred by his predecessors. So he decided the initial building stage should consist of only half the architect's original plan, in order to produce something 'plain and substantial' and suited to the purposes of a small diocesan

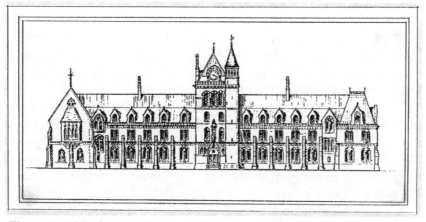

Figure 3.2 *The elevation of St Bernard's Seminary designed by the architect Edward Hansom. Edward Hansom's original drawing of St Bernard's Seminary is reproduced by permission of the priests of the Sacred Heart (SCJ), Olton, Solihull.*

Figure 3.3 *St Bernard's Seminary, Olton, built to half the size of the original plan.*

seminary. He announced at the outset, 'I have long held the maxim that an institution destined to become solid and permanent should have a humble and unpretentious beginning.' It is significant that the committee of the seminary fund at that time reported that 'they were pleased to be able to announce the completion of the work for which they were appointed – or at least the completion of so much of it as has enabled the Bishop to collect a certain number of students under a Rector and Professors, and so has placed his Lordship for the first time in a position to carry out what his heart has so long been set upon'.[13] But sadly enough, it was his concept of this small and modest beginning that limited its practical usefulness in the long run, and his over-cautious attitude ultimately brought an end to its functioning in that capacity altogether. This happened sixteen years later, when it finally returned to Oscott College in 1889.

Ullathorne said he hoped that what had for so long been to him little better than a distant vision would now become 'The crowning work of my episcopate'. Since laying the foundation stone at Olton in 1872, he had been carefully sifting over in his mind whom he should most suitably select from among his clergy to be the rector of the new seminary, which was to be called 'St Bernard's' after the patron saint of its founder. He had a particular method for making such decisions: 'It is well,' he said 'after thinking over persons and things, to let them rest altogether for a while, you then come back to them, fresh and untangled with fixed ideas ... A solution always comes if you are willing to wait for it.' Having discussed the matter with his chapter, he finally made the choice of Edward Ilsley. Why Ilsley was chosen for this position is summed up simply in Dom Cuthbert Butler's words: 'Ullathorne had for rector Father Ilsley who enjoyed his full confidence as a priest after his own heart, to whom was entrusted the religious and spiritual formation of the seminarists.'[14]

The appointment came as a surprise to many who had only seen Ilsley as buried in unobtrusive work 'in the heart of the Potteries, at Longton, amid the smoke and toil of a busy district'[15] right away from the centre of things. But Ullathorne probably shrewdly perceived something similar to his own approach in the way in which Ilsley tackled 'the job in hand'. Ullathorne's vision was for proper ecclesiastical organization, and there was a great deal for him to do in this field. 'His objective was to see the diocese as the Church in miniature.'[16] While he saw the other bishops surrounding him not knowing properly how to proceed in these matters because they were still covering unfamiliar ground, he must have at the same time recognized Ilsley as just the man to be trained to protect and carry forward his work. Dom Cuthbert Butler saw Ullathorne as 'reserved, orderly, businesslike, a born organiser', and Ilsley had already proved himself to be all of these during his time at Longton.

At 35 he had been working at St Gregory's for twelve years when he received a letter on 9 July 1873 setting a seal on a completely new period of his life, taking him away from his former busy and varied experience in the industrial community at Lane End to an interval marked in contrast by quiet routine and order, and far removed from the type of everyday cares that as a young curate he had to deal with previously. The Bishop's letter confirming Ilsley's appointment as rector of the new seminary at Olton suggested an early meeting between the two the following week, 'as the Synod will soon occupy me'. At the same time Bishop Ullathorne wrote to John Stringfellow at Caverswall, giving him brief notice of his transfer: 'I wish you to take the place vacated by Mr Ilsley at Longton, and if you can manage to move by the end of next week it would be convenient.'[17]

## Ilsley at Olton

The seminary building was not ready when Ilsley arrived at Olton a fortnight later on 22 July. He noted the fact in the seminary diary: 'Arrival of Edward Ilsley first Rector. As the building was not complete he was entertained by Canon Estcourt at Olton Grange.' This was a large house lying within sight of the seminary building, as part of the same estate. Canon Edgar Edmund Estcourt handled many of the legal and financial affairs of the diocese, being experienced in matters concerning property law. Previously an Anglican clergyman, he came under the influence of the Tractarian Movement during his time at Oxford in the 1830s, and this finally led him to Catholicism. He was received into the Church in 1845 when he was 29, in the same year as John Henry Newman. He was close friend and mentor of Bishop Ullathorne, who said of him that he was a particularly kindly man with a sympathetic ear, always ready with his help and advice when needed.[18]

It was during his stay at the Grange that Ilsley began a meticulously presented diary in which he later recorded the day-to-day routine of the students and the activities of the staff at the seminary. He occasionally included small vignettes containing details of their personal everyday lives and made notes of the domestic staff or described the laying-out of the grounds and what was planted there – all of which otherwise would have been lost to view.

## Victor Schobel and William Barry

On 11 September 1873 Bishop Ullathorne and the two principal professors met with Edward Ilsley at St Bernard's to plan the future running of the seminary. They were Dr Victor J. Schobel, then aged 25, a Bavarian, and Dr William Barry, who had been transferred there after a brief stay in St Chad's Mission. Barry was appointed professor of philosophy, and was also to be Ilsley's vice rector. At the age of 24, he had just completed his studies at the English College in Rome. He had been ordained there three months previously and had gained his DD at the Gregorian University. He developed a considerable talent for writing over the years which he cultivated seriously once he was appointed to the mission of Dorchester-on-Thames ten years later at the age of 34. Over the following years he became a literary figure not only in London but on the Continent and in America – travelling widely in both places. Principally known for his contributions to articles in the leading Catholic publications of his day such as *The Tablet* and *The Dublin Review*, he wrote books and essays on a wide range of subjects, and his work also included novels and biography. Victor Schobel received his training at the Belgian College in Rome and the Gregorian University, and 'he gained a gold medal for dogmatic theology, obtained his doctor's degree and received the sacred priesthood at a private ordination in Rome on August 20th, 1871'. On his return 'he taught philosophy at the English College in Bruges and at the same time occupied the chair of theology at the *Grand Seminaire*'.[19] Dr J. Verres, a Frenchman, joined the staff two years later as professor of moral theology and canon law.

Together they planned how the seminary day was to be divided into the *Horarium*, and Ilsley set it out in the diary:

| | | |
|---|---|---|
| 6 a.m | Rise. | |
| 6½ | Meditation. | On Sundays and Holy days of |
| 7 | Mass. | Obligation, half an hour Spiritual |
| | | Reading before breakfast. |
| 7½ | Study. | The Chant to be practised at 9. |
| 8½ | Breakfast | High Mass at 10. |
| 9 | Study. | After High Mass Free time till 1¼. |
| 10 | Lecture. | After dinner Free time till 5 the |
| | | hour for Vespers. |
| 11 | Recreation. | 5½ Study. |
| 11½ | Study. | 9. Night prayers and Benediction. |
| 12¾ | Spiritual Reading. | |
| 1¼ | Wash hands, *examen*, and | |
| | visit to the B. Sacrament. | |
| 1½ | Dinner. | |
| 3½ | Study. | On Tuesdays and Thursdays. |
| 5 | Recreation. | Free time till 6p.m. |
| 5½ | Study. | |
| 7½ | Supper. | |
| 9 | Night prayers – After which retire to rooms. | |
| 10 | Rest. With Special permission at 10½. | |

Bishop Ullathorne next discussed what he had in mind for the general conduct of the students: 'I insist much on manners,' he said, 'even the manner of doing the commonest things, such as going in and out of a room, saluting superiors and doing some manual work such as keeping the walks in order; all that will develop sense and conduct.'[20] He took the closest interest in how everything was to be laid down and carried out, many of his ideas being similar to those used in his own training at Downside which he wrote about in his autobiography. 'Our work was not all study, manual labour was sometimes added in the old Benedictine spirit; and there is no doubt that a man who can handle a spade, or do some mechanical work, will have more practical sense than he who can only handle books.'

## Schobel's Plan of Studies

Ilsley's diary continues: 'The following day a second conference, having reference principally to studies was held, the Bishop presiding.' It was at this conference that Victor Schobel made his first valuable contribution. As a student in Rome he attended the lectures at the Gregorian University of men of such eminence as Cardinal Johann Baptiste Franzeline, and the Jesuit theologian, Clement Schrader, so he was 'very much alive to the issues of the day that affected the Church and society as a whole', and he approached things in a very scholarly way, using methods ahead of his time. The carefully prepared plan of studies he devised for that day in many ways opened up paths of new thought that had already transformed ways of learning on the Continent, so it was largely through his influence that the new seminary came to be considered unparalleled in its approach in Britain.[21]

A list of textbooks was drawn up, and Ilsley gave an account in the diary of the decisions they made regarding the future programme of studies: 'It was decided to adopt Jungman's Textbook for Dogmatic Theology, and San Severino the Textbook for Philosophy.[22] Scripture to be taken in the evening by Dr Schobel alternately with Church History by Dr Barry. Public Examinations to be held before Christmas and before Summer vacation. Lectures in Theology and Philosophy in Latin.' 'As to its spirit and rules,' the Bishop decided to use *The Rules of Seminaries and Secular Priests living in Community without Vows*, by Bartholomew Holzhauser. 'I have seen such a volume in Oscott library bound in thick vellum,' he said. 'The Bishop of Orleans has just had these rules printed anew, together with a copious life of its author. Its object is to give those who conduct a seminary not only the spirit of the Priesthood, but also that of a common life, and to inspire the priests of the mission with the love of preparing youths for the seminary.'[23]

The Bishop seemed pleased with their two days' work, and on the evening of 12 September, after leaving, he wrote to a friend, 'I have been engaged these two days at St Bernard's with the little staff of the seminary, settling rules and regulations. I am more than satisfied with their spirit. It will be a common life and family life between superiors and students. They all feel, as I do, that this is one of the most important germs that can be planted in England, and they are not at all afraid to do the work.'[24]

On that day, eleven students, the majority from St Edmund's, Ware, were admitted ready for the opening. At this time the style of clothing for seminary students was clearly defined. For daily wear they had long black cassocks, with the use of a white cotta for services and other special occasions. When outside they wore birettas, and a long clerical coat, and the Roman collar was always worn. Photographs among the seminary archives which were taken out in the grounds show that even in more relaxed moments during their times of recreation, this strict formal dress was always adhered to. This reflected the attitude of the Church toward her clergy as being professional. The clothes they wore were an outward manifestation of this. The albums show the same mode of dress worn by the divines at Oscott College. Their pictures were in sharp contrast to those of their fellow lay students wearing individually styled, hand-tailored clothes.[25]

## Administrative Opportunities

As the new rector of St Bernard's, Edward Ilsley was now able to use administrative skills of a kind given few outlets before. In a discourse given at his consecration as assistant bishop, Bishop John Hedley said of him: 'In his new sphere he speedily displayed qualities of mind and heart that had not had the opportunity of being exercised at Longton. Firmness of character, tact and intellectual grasp were the first necessity for Rectorship. All these qualities he displayed in no small measure.' Ilsley also needed a good grasp of how best to deal with people, and Bishop Hedley mentioned that all this was more than evident, 'to an eminent degree, by the great progress of this institution over which he presided'.

A few months before, he had unquestioningly closed the door on his former life as a missionary priest, and turned his mind instead to the responsibility of training young seminarians to be the future priests of the diocese. 'We lived a very happy family life. Three professors and never more than twenty students and rarely that,' wrote Canon Arthur Villiers, who had been one of the seminarists in Ilsley's time.[26] The 'Father Rector', as they liked to call him, was looked on very differently from the three professors in the house, because they were men of learning, but he was the model they wished to emulate. His approach to their training was not so much through formal channels of academic knowledge, as through his own example. He left their dogmatic studies to the professors, and the spiritual books on which Villiers said 'he really brought us up', were the Old Testament, the Gospels, *The Imitation* and *The Devout Life* of Francis de Sales – 'he placed before us the Holy Spirit and the Sacred Heart'. Ilsley trod a middle path in his attitude to their training. While promoting the beauty of the 'Romanized' liturgy and encouraging devotions to the Sacred Heart and the Blessed Virgin, he still handled things in careful moderation where his students were concerned, being in no hurry for them to adopt some of the new Continental ways being followed. Although they attended daily Mass, Villiers observed: 'in fact we were never invited, still less urged, to daily Communion'. So although Ilsley was in many ways immersed in the developing ways of the Church, he was nevertheless looked on by his former student as 'of the old-fashioned school of Gother, Challoner and Ullathorne'.[27]

As the professors, with the exception of Dr Barry, were foreigners, Ilsley always corrected the English in the students' sermons and gave criticisms of their delivery. Not a gifted orator himself, he nevertheless 'knew what should be done', and his appraisals were valuable, if at times a little hard. Because he was well and widely read, 'he had the faculty of hitting on the right word ... and his style was vigorous though simple'. But the young Villiers considered him 'unduly severe' at times, especially when 'called over the coals' for 'unintelligible' handwriting or poor spelling, but Ilsley's handwriting was always impeccably clear and well-formed and his spelling unfailingly accurate, so Villiers could have expected nothing less from his tutor. Ilsley was obviously well-loved by the students though, and an interesting insight into his character and the impression he made on them is again given by Arthur Villiers: 'The ideal of our seminary life and our model of what we hoped to be in the future was the Father Rector. Nor do I think, looking back on those days, that in our youthful estimate we were in any way wrong.' Describing the occasions when the Rector gave his weekly lecture in theology, he said how much they benefited from his thoughts on the priestly life and office. 'In these lectures you felt that all he said was the revelation of his own life, his own aims and ideals, the outcome of much thought and many prayers.' Ilsley's strict sense of duty towards his calling is shown by this further observation: 'If any of us showed any aptitude towards music, oral or instrumental, he was always anxious to encourage us, though he himself, because it distracted his mind from more important things, rarely, if ever touched any musical instruments in the house.'[28]

## Training his Students

In those years he always followed a strict routine. His life had been hard up to this point and he seemed determined to keep it so. He never allowed himself the comfort of a soft armchair and chose, whenever possible, to walk to his destination rather than ride. In church, however long the service, he was always observed to be kneeling very upright in his stall; he also made fasting and abstinence a regular part of his life. His early training had taken place at Oscott, 'under the lofty traditions of Weedall, Wiseman and Northcote', and it was these same traditions he would now seek to instil into his young seminarians as well as his own edict, handed down to this day by his own family, that 'a gentleman should only be conspicuous by his absence'.

The key to Ilsley's method of training those in his care is perhaps contained in Villiers' statement: 'Strict with himself he did not suffer laxity in others', and he went on to say, 'and no one of us when we reached the fasting age dreamt of asking for a dispensation, which we knew we were not likely to obtain.' But although a disciplinarian, he was also said to be 'never blustering nor bullying, always candid and never sarcastic',[29] and Villiers said he found that, because they had been disciplined resolutely at this stage, and 'having borne the burden in our youth', when they came on the Mission, exercising self-discipline later in life 'was in no way burdensome'. However, Ilsley's concern was not confined only to spiritual matters, as he was also noted for his 'kind solicitude', whether for someone who had a racking cough or if they were just seeking helpful advice on some ordinary everyday problem.[30]

'He loved the plain chant,' wrote Canon Villiers, 'and he himself conducted our weekly practice. He had a very accurate ear and was a musician of no mean skill, and though we never, in my time at least, rendered the chant as he would have liked it, it was not his fault if we failed, because his ideals were so high, and his knowledge of the subject so thorough. I well remember a little trick he had of humming preludes in the mode of the piece to be sung before he would let us attack it, in order that we might not only be attuned to the scale of the mode, but its spirit and characteristics.'

The general opinion of staff and students was that Ilsley was in every way ideally suited to the position of Rector. To any verbal instructions he gave, 'he added the example of his daily life', wrote Villiers. 'He never missed any public religious exercises in the house, nor was he ever late ... with him no detail was slight, no action profane, no word slurred or broken ... and the scrupulous carefulness he displayed in all the details of his Mass, awoke in our young souls a reverence and love for the sacred things of the altar which in most of us never died.'[31]

## Arthur Villiers

Arthur Villiers was obviously a devoted student who had a great deal of respect for Ilsley. His recollections of him which he wrote in an article in *The Oscotian* entitled 'The Father Rector', many years later at the age of 70 when he was a canon of the cathedral chapter, express an obvious fondness for the memory of Ilsley in those early days. This was endorsed by his request to be buried in the grounds of St Bernard's, a place he must have loved.

As one of the few men close to him who wrote about Ilsley so fully, Villiers' portrayal of him bears some scrutiny. At the time he was a student he saw Ilsley as a man who allowed himself little in his own life by way of creature comforts. On becoming Rector he had even set aside his music in order to devote all his time to the important demands of the office without being distracted from his purpose in any way. Villiers also described how Ilsley appeared to offer the example of his daily life for his students to follow. He remarked that for this reason during religious services he would be seen to display almost scrupulous carefulness in all he did before them, particularly during the community Mass which he said every morning.

He accepted Ilsley's right to strictly discipline his students because he was so unfailingly strict with himself. Something of the same situation prevailed throughout Ilsley's time in office. He was considered a disciplinarian by his clergy but was respected as one who did not rest at the oar himself, so he was well-liked among them. Seen as an idealist by his young student, Villiers describes how, on the occasions when he was giving them his lectures concerning the priestly life and office, their attention was riveted as Ilsley always spoke 'with a humility and reverence which awed us, his eyes for the most part closed, and his hands joined as if in prayer'. It was his habit all his life to put across his ideas and ideals within a deeply spiritual context, acknowledging his own involvement merely as an instrument within God's plan. In the same way Arthur Villiers said that although they were trained and moulded by Ilsley, because he always seemed to shrink from putting himself forward and was invariably self-effacing,

Figure 3.4 *William Bernard Ullathorne, the first Bishop of Birmingham (1850–88).*

it was almost impossible to be able to give in so many words an exact analysis later of what he had presented to them. Even so, he came to realise later that it must have been a revelation of the aims and ideals within Ilsley's own life that he was describing to them.

On becoming Rector of St Bernard's Ilsley may have then been aware that further demands might be made on him as regards future promotion. This possibly may have caused him to maintain the carefully reserved attitude that was always to remain with him, coupled at the same time with a discreet sense of co-operative service towards Bishop Ullathorne. The Bishop had watched Ilsley's progress since he was a young boy at Sedgley Park, and the knowledge that he was being observed may have contributed to Ilsley's very punctilious attitude, conscientiously keeping himself in line with William Ullathorne's scheme of things and having to take a firmer approach at times with his students than he would have otherwise. Added to this he was a naturally hard worker, was physically strong and capable of considerable endurance. All this fitted into the life of measured self-discipline he had chosen for himself.

But there was another side to Ilsley's nature. It would seem he could take a kindly view of things and be lenient with others at times, and the lighter side of life did not escape him. Although the boy who

51

cleaned the boots at the seminary neglected his job one evening, everyone found their boots perfectly polished the next morning. The secret somehow leaked out that the Father Rector had acted as 'auxiliary to the boot boy'. The writer who told this anecdote was Father Patrick O'Toole, who came to St Bernard's as a student in 1882. He also gave an account of how during their times of relaxation in the evening Ilsley did not in any way distance himself from those around him: 'Students in those days will recall the figure of an amiable superior sitting of an evening in the common room, joining in the conversation, listening, arguing, sometimes earnestly but always in good humour, taking part in their concerts and occasionally in the games, making them all feel that he was almost one of themselves by his quiet and unobtrusive manner.'[32] This description of Ilsley would come in line with the more natural side of his nature in contrast to the retiring, formal side he had adopted. The following year he was to leave the seminary to take up his duties as auxiliary bishop, and this more relaxed attitude of allowing himself to come closer to the students in a far more human way would have been part of a realization that such an opportunity would not come again in quite the same way. Later, as bishop of the diocese, he was noted for the personal interest he always took in the welfare of his priests, and he knew them well either because they had trained under him or because of his close interest in their parish work.

As supper at the seminary was at 7.30 and night prayers at 9.00 there was a half hour after supper which the students were anxious to turn to greater advantage. They devised a system whereby lots were drawn and those involved had to stand in readiness to entertain the rest 'by a Lecture, Reading or Other Intellectual Amusement'. Whatever was presented was in turn 'subject to the audience and freely criticised'. The Rector's obvious appreciation of those brief periods is contained in a letter to Henry Parkinson just after Christmas 1874: 'Our fellows appear to enjoy their evenings in the Common Room: they quite cheer me with their hearty laugh and innocent mirth' was his comment.[33] As his room adjoined the common room he could easily hear them, but when James McCave became Rector in 1883, he acted without any delay the following day by deciding to have the library moved from upstairs 'from the place it had occupied for ten years' down to the room used by the Rector adjoining the common room. He then moved upstairs into the quieter position.

## Inauguration Ceremony attended by Newman

An important landmark in the life of St Bernard's was the inauguration ceremony held in early October 1873. Bishop Ullathorne and the cathedral chapter were there, also James Northcote, the president of Oscott, together with a gathering of clergy and laity. As the chapel was not yet ready, the Rector celebrated Mass in the library, and the presence of Dr John Henry Newman, who gave the discourse, marked the importance of the occasion. He was said to speak in a 'kindly and familiar tone', taking for his theme the words of St Peter, 'You are the chosen people, a kingly priesthood'. William Barry later described how 'Dr. Newman preached in front of the Altar. He had neither notes nor manuscript, but held a small bible in his hand, where he sought in a curiously eager fashion the texts he was about to recite. His voice sounded low and clear, with exquisite modulations, as though he was thinking aloud.'[34]

Both the seminary diary and *The Brief History of St Bernard's Seminary at Olton*, written in 1900 by Henry Parkinson, indicate that in those early days Bishop Ullathorne continued taking a close personal interest in forming many of the policies, not only concerning the spiritual side of things but in directing practical everyday details of the students' lives as well. He liked to impress on them that his visitations were a 'fatherly office', and this expression aptly described his attitude toward them. He told them he was looking for a 'spirit of unity and charity' among them. To pass someone over during recreation was a slight, so no cliques must be formed. He urged a rejection of 'faddiness' either about themselves or for their belongings, and urged 'manliness' upon them, saying they were not to be particular about any kind of work they did. Referring to 'smoking on the sly', he said they must forego smoking altogether during their training. He said he noticed that, though diligent in their studies, 'they were wanting in taste for reading and general intellectual culture in their lives', and recommended the use of the library, but not to the point of curtailing their outdoor recreation.[35]

The diary describes how it had became part of the tradition to celebrate the Rector's feast day of Edward the Confessor on 13 October, with a dinner and invited guests. The story is told in the history of the seminary, however, that on Ilsley's birthday on 11 May 1881, 'The senior student went and congratulated him, who quietly deprecated the celebration of a birthday.' It continues: 'By a strange coincidence, the following words occurred this morning in the

Dogma lecture concerning Martyrology *"sed illum non celebramus etsi nos-cemus"*.[36] Whereupon there was a spontaneous burst of laughter.' The students would be quick to pick up the gist of such a passage, however subtle, as they were well-versed in the language. Lectures in theology and philosophy were in Latin, so were their disputations; also certain mornings were selected throughout the year for 'Latin to be spoken until dinner'.

Although set out in the Warwickshire countryside, the seminary was well-served by the local railway station, less than a mile away. This ease of access contributed to a fairly constant flow of visitors 'coming up' to St Bernard's, and there is a note in the diary about Father Massam arriving from Longton to make a retreat there in the first summer of 1873. The seminary was a great source of pleasure and satisfaction to Bishop Ullathorne, and he frequently brought people to see it, one of the most important of these being Henry Manning, the Archbishop of Westminster who came the following summer accompanied by Herbert Vaughan the Bishop of Salford and Francis Mostyn the Bishop of Newport. St Bernard's would be of considerable interest to the Cardinal-Archbishop as he had set his seal of approval on such diocesan seminaries, having established his own seminary of St Thomas in Hammersmith four years earlier in 1869.[37]

## Sister Josephine

There is also a record of a visit to Olton of 'four Sisters of Mercy from Handsworth' in August 1874, and it is very probable Edward Ilsley's sister Anne might have been among them. A close bond existed throughout the years between Edward and his sister, who was three years younger. When she wrote to him she would keep him in touch with the family by sharing the latest news, and she dealt with even the simplest details in life in a spiritual way: 'I had begun to think that the stockings had got stuck fast to the loom,' she wrote when sending a gift, 'but they have come at last. I hope they will fit you and may the Holy Spirit keep whispering to you all the time you have them on. Yes, and at every other time besides, for there's no getting on without Him.'[38]

Her niece Cecilia said it was suggested by Sister Josephine's mother superior, Mother Juliana Hardman, that it was no longer suitable for her to remain as a lay sister once her brother became auxiliary bishop, especially as he would often visit her at the convent. The lay sisters carried out the domestic duties of the convent, doing the laundry work and general cleaning; whereas the 'choir' sisters were engaged in teaching, nursing and visiting, and they chanted the Office of Our Lady. This was a social division depending on the amount of the dowry the nun brought with her into the community. In contrast to the choir sisters' habit of fine serge, the lay sister's was made of heavy, coarse material. The division between them also meant that the lay sisters lived in a different area in the house from the choir sisters. However, Anne had no wish to be elevated in the community and so continued in her humble position.

The seminary's first year moved on into November, with the first of the annual retreats being given by Bishop Ullathorne. Toward the end of term a disputation was held, for which twelve theses were drawn up by Dr Schobel, and the whole day's proceedings were conducted in Latin. Ilsley noted in the diary that 'the theologians acquitted themselves very creditably in the presence of the whole house'.[39] These public disputations were usually held two or three times a year and widely varying subjects were chosen, such as 'The Trinity', 'The Infallibility of the Pope', 'The Eucharist', 'The Creation', 'The Incarnation', and so on.

By now the seminary had settled down to an ordered way of life, and as part of their daily occupation the seminarists were encouraged to keep their own journals. One of these is preserved which is in the form of a four-year diary written between September 1878 and August 1882, through which it is possible to see how the traditions of St Bernard's were gradually built up. It is beautifully presented, but unfortunately the name of the student is not included. There is another record book of the students' meetings and debates and the pages are written up in the handwriting of several different students. One page, signed 'W. Sutherland Senior' and dated November 1873, is of particular interest because it sets out why certain resolutions have been written down: 'through a desire that the first Traditions of the Seminary should be preserved whole and entire ... further that those who come after us will have little or no difficulty on tracing the history of many of the Customs and Traditions they may find in existence in St. Bernard's. Whilst the one object and wish of all has been to establish in us, as the first Students and foundation of our Diocesan Seminary, a real Ecclesiastical Spirit.' Another page deals with a meeting held at the special request of the Father Rector to consider the desirability of securing a uniform pronunciation of Latin: 'Are we to retain the classical one in use at St. Edmund's College Douai, or do we adopt the ecclesiastical one in use at Rome?' A tradition regarding

mutual correction and improvement was also discussed and the outcome was that the nature of the substance of the rules they sought was
the same as of those that 'generally rule the conduct of gentlemen,
with the exception of a few minor points which the object of the
seminary required'.

At the beginning of December 1873 Bishop Ullathorne demonstrated he intended keeping a tight rein on the students. He continued
taking an active part in the running of things, and it appears Ilsley
complied with the old Bishop's wishes without question, so the following episode and Ilsley's written comment are not unexpected. On
5 December there is an entry in the diary saying that there was a
communication from the Bishop: 'I prohibit Ecclesiastics in the
seminary from performing plays or farces.' A quiet footnote added by
the Rector follows, 'A rumour, for which there was very scanty foundation, had been whispered about the fact that the students were
going to play a farce.' In contrast to this, J. S. Northcote mentioned in
the Oscott College diary for mid-February 1875 that a farce was going
to be performed because, 'the weather being so wretched the boys were
without means of enjoyment'. Later in the year another theatrical
performance was mentioned by Northcote: 'The farce especially
seemed to meet with favour,' he recorded, 'the pieces were got up by
the Rev. S. Sole at a very short notice.' Samuel Sole was one of the
church students at this time, so it would seem Bishop Ullathorne's
dictum did not apply to the group of divines at Oscott College, whose
activities were not so curtailed as the students at St Bernard's. This
was apparently where the idea originated, and it was an influence the
Bishop wished to break with. After this any entertainment given by
the students at St Bernard's was to be either in the form of operettas
taken from Gilbert and Sullivan, or musical pieces they had written
themselves.[40] Ilsley's habit of unquestioning compliance with
Ullathorne's wishes may have coloured his own expectations of others
later, on becoming Ullathorne's successor. On several occasions his
own lack of consultation was to cause untoward difficulties with those
not so ready to co-operate with him as he himself had been in relation
to Ullathorne.

## Christmas at St Bernard's

The following spring 1874 the last details of the building were completed and trees and shrubs were planted along the drive and in the
plantation. By the end of the same year as Christmas approached the

old Bishop directed that 'the Christmas vacation begin on Christmas Eve and terminate with the Epiphany'. But the period over Christmas and the New Year was not to be a time for homecoming for the students, all of whom remained at the seminary. Of the staff, Dr Schobel left early for the Continent, and Dr Verres and the Vice Rector went off immediately after Christmas Day. The students filled in their remaining time visiting places of interest, and Ilsley made the following note in the diary: 'No-one left the Seminary for a day during the whole vacation.'

It would seem from the way Ullathorne continued to closely supervise the running of the seminary that he had chosen Ilsley not only for his spiritual calibre but because he knew him to be thoroughly cooperative and pliable as far as his wishes were concerned. So it is interesting to note that Ilsley appeared to have introduced a sympathetic change of his own choice regarding this vacation, the year after he became auxiliary bishop. In December 1880 he allowed his students to go home on 27 December for a ten-day break, and this proved so beneficial in every way that it became part of the tradition. A student noted it in his diary that year as 'this important innovation'.[41]

Christmas Eve was always spent decorating the chapel, and the midnight Mass of Christmas 1874 was the first High Mass sung at St Bernard's. The atmosphere of the occasion is captured in a letter written by Ilsley to Henry Parkinson in Rome two days after. 'Our midnight office was perhaps more solemn and beautiful than last Christmas,' he wrote, 'the chanting of the office was beautifully subdued, we could hear one another and caught more of the spirit. We have a little crib this year, i.e. only a Bambino – but a little Bambino without Our Lady won't do at all. She must come next year with St Joseph.' Describing their Christmas Day in the common room, he continued: 'We had our family gathering much the same as last year, only we missed you and Dr Schobel, and some thought it dull but I didn't – I have had far duller Christmases before now.'[42]

Bishop Ullathorne joined the students for Christmas dinner the year Edward Ilsley became his auxiliary, in 1879. He was 74 then, and Arthur Villiers described how hard it could be 'to keep sedate and well behaved when the old man with his silver-rimmed spectacles and his slow deep-toned utterance delivered to us his words on Christian Patience and Humility without an 'H,' and spoke of Saint 'Ilary, the 'oly 'ermit'. But Villiers described how they would become quite spellbound when the old Bishop later regaled them with stories of his early pioneering days working with the convicts in Australia: 'With what wonder did we gather round him, by the fire in the Common Room, and listen to his stories of adventures in Botany Bay and the Australian Penal Settlements, of long rides through orange groves and primaeval forests, of sermons prepared as he lay on his back resting and preached in wayside camps and roadside houses; of condemned men visited in solitary confinement or ministered to upon the scaffold.' More than just a narrative for the festive season, this was the remarkable story of a young priest who played a great part in putting an end to the transportation of convicts to Australia, and who helped alleviate the injustices of the system.[43]

In 1874 the Rector established the tradition of an annual outing for 'the whole house' on the feast of St Stephen to a performance of *The Messiah* held in Birmingham Town Hall. He paid for it out of the interest gained from a gift of money given to him by his congregation when he left Longton. Canon Villiers described their experience on these occasions: 'Every Feast of Stephen saw us sitting in a row in the gallery of the Hall, and though as far as I can remember the choir never sang, "And great was the company of the preachers", we all looked very sheepish when the leading soprano broke out into the aria, "How beautiful are the feet of those that preach the Gospel of Peace", and we felt the eyes of the whole audience were turned in our direction, which of course they were not.'

Notes in a student's journal describing the Rector's sermon about 'The Finding of the Child Jesus in the Temple' portray the closeness between members of the seminary in those years. Ilsley suggests that at the time they were 'living in the temple' and supposedly, 'sitting at the feet of the doctors, and what is said of study may also be applied to prayer and the general round of duties'.[44] The same feeling is conveyed by him in a brief but descriptive passage taken from a letter he wrote to Henry Parkinson on 2 July 1875, giving a picture of the group of students gathered at the end of the seminary day: 'Our Sacred Heart picture is framed at last and we have had our devotions during the month of June at night prayers. It shows up well by candle light – I fancy the artist must have painted it in his over time by gas light.' Bishop Ullathorne consecrated the seminary to the Sacred Heart when it was founded.

From all accounts there was a feeling of positive fulfilment of purpose in everything that was being undertaken in those first years at St Bernard's, and Bishop Ullathorne wrote to a friend in 1873, 'The spirit of all, both priests and students, is beyond all I could have hoped for. The place seems under a benediction. There is not only the right spirit, but solid learning and zeal to inculcate it.' He summed up his feelings again in a letter written in 1878: 'In short the Seminary, thank God, is going well and is my consolation. All the good in it I attribute to Dr Ilsley.' [45]

## Notes

1   McCormack, p. 138.
2   Barry, p. 46. Mgr William Barry's description. He said the 'Humanities' were termed 'Poetry, Rhetoric, Philosophy'. He went to Oscott in January 1865 at the age of 15.
3   Beck, p. 128, and also Norman, p. 134.
4   B.A., B3915. Also Norman, pp. 180–1.
5   *Essays*, 'The Crown of the Diocesan Structure', p. 95.
6   *Ibid.*, pp. 97–8. Edward Bagshawe of Nottingham also followed this policy.
7   Mary Roskell, *Francis Kerrill Amherst, D.D.* Preface by Edmund Knight, pp. x, xi. Bishop Amherst wrote a very full article entitled 'Oscott's Influence on Catholic Education' for the Jubilee Edition of *The Oscotian*, brought out in 1888.
8   *Essays*, p. 95.
9   *Letters*, pp. 178, 179.
10  B.A., B4993.
11  Butler, vol. ii, p. 183.
12  The plan was drawn up by Dunn and Hansom Architects, Newcastle upon Tyne. Archibald Matthias Dunn and E. J. Hansom formed a partnership between 1871 and 1900. *The Tablet*, 11 October 1873, p. 467. Also, Thomas E. Muir, 'The Making of a Victorian Architect: Edward Hansom's work at Stonyhurst and Downside, 1868–1900', the Annual Conference, Plater College, Oxford 1994.
13  Parkinson, ch. 2, 'The Formation of the Seminary'. Committee Report. Also Butler, vol. i, pp. 171–4: In 1853 Ullathorne went bankrupt through inherited debts and spent ten days in Warwick Gaol before his release. He considered this a salutary way to learn prudence in money matters regarding church-building. When he was previously Vicar Apostolic for the Western District in 1846 he had begun to deal with the debts left behind by Bishop Baines when he died, but he was transferred to the Central District two years later before he had time to resolve the problem.
14  Butler, vol. ii, p. 185. Also Fitzgerald, p. 237.
15  *The Oscotian, Literary Gazette of St Mary's College, Oscott, The Jubilee of Oscott, 1888*, p. 172.
16  Bellenger, p. 330: 'His was a clerical vision, with his three principal priorities being the refinement and definition of episcopal power and

responsibility, the restoration of the cathedral chapters and the place of the cathedral at the centre of the diocese, and, perhaps most crucially the establishment of an ecclesiastical seminary.' Also Butler, vol. 1, p. 40.

17  O.C.A., Letter from Bishop Ullathorne to Edward Ilsley, 9 July 1873, and to John Stringfellow, 14 July 1873. He addresses both priests as 'Mr'.

18  Obituary, *The Tablet*, Saturday 26 April, 1884, p. 670. Edgar Edmund Estcourt helped resolve Ullathorne's financial difficulties in the Western District when he was Vicar Apostolic, and the bishop subsequently brought him to Birmingham for this purpose.

19  Barry refers to his own writing throughout *Memories and Opinions*. Also Schobel, p. 2.

20  Parkinson, ch. 2, 'The Formation of a Seminary'. Also Butler, vol. i, p. 18.

21  M. Tower, 'A missing Link: Oscott's Bavarian Connection, Victor Schobel 1848–1915', in *Essays*, p. 14. Also, *The Oscotian*, 16/1, p. 3.

22  Bouquillon's textbook *Institutiones Theologiae Moralis Fundamentalis* was used for moral theology and San Severino's *Philosophia Christiana in compendium redacta* was appointed for philosophy.

23  *Letters*, p. 190. *Constitutiones Clericorum Saecularum in Communi Viventium*. There is a second edition, Rome, 1684, at Oscott, which was on the shelves of the library at the time, so this would be the copy Ullathorne was referring to. The book was revised and corrected, and reprinted in Paris and Lyons in 1861, so it is likely he would have used that edition. G. F. Pullin, *Recusant Books at Oscott*, part 2, Innocent XI, p. 2114. Information given by George Every, Oscott, January 1989.

T. A. Birrel wrote in a letter 1 July 1988: 'In the late 17 Century several groups of English priests, including some in the Midland District had been using *Constitutiones Clericorum Saecularum in Communi Viventium* and it was printed in England in 1697 by the Catholic Publisher Thomas Metcalfe who was prosecuted for it.'

Holzhauser, parish priest, ecclesiastical writer and founder of a religious community, was born in 1613 in Bavaria and died in 1658.

24  *Letters*, p. 255.

25  There would be a contrast between them generally. See Norman, p. 180. Henry Parkinson and Michael Glancey were among the new arrivals.

26  The word 'seminarist' was still being used. It came into the language as a pejorative term in penal times when seminaries abroad were deemed traitorous. The word 'seminarian' gradually came into use later on.

27  F.R., pp. 1, 7, 6. In his youth he had come to know about the Italian influences, as Dominic Barberi gave a mission in Stafford in 1846.

28  *Ibid.*, pp. 2, 3.

29  Obituary, Archbishop Frederick Keating, *The Birmingham Mail*, 6 December 1926.

30  F.R., p. 4. Also *The Oscotian, Literary Gazette of St Mary's College, Oscott, The Jubilee of Oscott, 1888*, p. 172.

31  F.R., p. 3.

32  P. O'Toole, 'Archbishop Ilsley, a Memoir', *The Tablet*, 11 December 1926, p. 810. 33

    O.C.A., 27 December 1874. 'Fellows' was the word in common usage in those days to describe the students. It was also used by the students when talking of themselves as a group.

34  Barry, p. 109. Text taken from 1 Peter 5.9.

35  Parkinson, episcopal visitations on 18 September 1883 and 4 July 1886. His visitation included an inspection not only of the chapel, but of the professors' and students' rooms as well.

36  Parkinson, 1881, Hurter, vol. ii, p. 387. *'Quando natus est ignoramus; et quia hodie passus est, natalem ejus celebramus, sed illum non celebramus etsi noscemus.'* Meaning: 'We ignore the day of his birth; but today, the date of his death, we celebrate his entry into heaven *(dies natalis)*, but not his birthday on earth, even if we knew it.'

37  Beck, Hughes, p. 36. Diary, 12 August 1874: 'Visit of the Bishop accompanied by the Archbishop of Westminster.'

38  B.A., Letter from Sister Josephine to Edward Ilsley, 1 August 1886.

39  Diary. The disputation was held on 22 December 1873.

40  Parkinson, ch. 9, section 6, 'Operettas performed by students'.

41  J., Diary, December 1873: 'During the Christmas vacation several excursions were made to places of interest in the neighbourhood, such as Henley-in-Arden, Hampton Lapworth, King's Norton, Yardley, Knowle.'

42  O.C.A., Letter from Edward Ilsley to Henry Parkinson, 27 December 1874. Parkinson's history records: 'The Midnight Mass was the first High Mass ever sung at St Bernard's. The Rector officiated as Priest; the Vice Rector, Dr Barry as Deacon and Mr William Sutherland, the newly-ordained, being subdeacon. Matins commenced at 10.30. Midnight Mass at 12.00 followed by Lauds.'

43  F.R., p. 6. Also Butler, vol. i., ch. 4, 'The Convicts'. Ullathorne was Vicar General in New South Wales in 1832 when aged 27. He wrote forcefully on his return of their dreadful treatment and exposed the inherent evils of the system in his pamphlet on 'Horrors of Transportation'.

44  J., January 1880.

45  Letters, pp. 255, 378.

Figure 4.1 *Edward Ilsley when Rector of St Bernard's Seminary, Olton (1873–1883).*
*Taken from a photograph in Oscott College Archives.*

## CHAPTER FOUR

# *Father Rector*

From the time Edward Ilsley became the rector of St Bernard's, the first of his letters have been preserved. Written in a fine, flowing style and in a beautifully legible hand, they show the detailed interest he took in the supervision of the seminary and those within it, and they help to reveal the type of man he was through the advice he gave to others, which in turn reflected his own direct and simple trust in God.

## The Parkinson Correspondence

On 9 October 1874 he wrote in the diary, 'Mr Parkinson left Seminary for the English College in Rome. He has been a model student in every way.' From the time Parkinson left for Rome Ilsley took it upon himself to write to him every few weeks with detailed news of life at the seminary, and Parkinson must have preserved these letters over the following four years. The collection later became known as 'The Parkinson Correspondence', and they show the continuing guidance of the Father Rector toward his student. One of the earliest of these letters was written that year on 27 December and Ilsley starts with an apology: 'I feel I have been treating you shamefully by delaying so long to acknowledge your letters – the only excuse I can offer is that I am a very slow writer; as for pressure of work why I might have done as you have done, make a commencement & get through it piecemeal.' He continues, 'I have to thank you for your letters & to say every word of them was interesting to me & the good fellows you have left behind you at St Bernard's . . . Of course it doesn't matter much to whom you address the letter; it will always be common property. Write just what you feel inclined to say & leave us to make the distribution of the spoils when it reaches St Bernard's.'

As regards Parkinson's future work at the seminary, Ilsley's advice to him the following summer was sound: 'Much as I would wish you to be able to devote more time to philosophy, I would much prefer for you a year at the mission. It is of vast importance that Superiors of the Seminary should realise what is in store for our students, what is the life, what the duties, difficulties, dangers etc. for which the Seminary Course is a preparation. I won't venture to promise you an easy mission that would leave you much leisure for your studies – nor would you desire it probably – but having done your duty in proposing the matter, you may fairly leave it in God's hands, in full reliance that He will prepare you for the work He is going to employ you about, for His own honour and glory, and that what He will dispose for you will be better than you could propose for yourself.'[1] Certainly the extraordinary years of service Henry Parkinson was about to give are borne out by this – first at St Bernard's as Vice Rector, and then from 1889, as Vice Rector and later Rector, of Oscott College, until he died there in 1924. But for one reason or another Ilsley changed his mind about first placing him 'at the mission', and four years were to pass before Parkinson was moved to the cathedral parish for two years. It was the

Figure 4.2 *Henry Parkinson as a student at St Bernard's Seminary. Oscott college albums.*

extreme poverty he saw there among the working people that led him to engage in a lifelong commitment to social reform.

Writing in similar vein to Parkinson when he was anxious about his future work, Ilsley said, 'Be prepared to tackle anything you may be called upon to teach ... We must leave ourselves in God's hands and do our best – he won't ask us to do impossibilities.'[2] And again: 'I haven't time to write all I would wish to say about the preparations for preaching. I hope you read scripture regularly. You will find there the doctrine you have to preach, the illustrations you want to make it plain to the people. The rest will soon be acquired and practice will perfect your method. So don't be alarmed about that.'[3] A letter written two years later in 1877 to congratulate Parkinson on his ordination, and at the same time to allay any further apprehensions about preaching, demonstrates the complete trust Edward Ilsley placed in the Holy Spirit: 'The truth is the H. Spirit has a good deal to do with sermons when preachers allow Him to guide them both as to what to speak about and how to say it.'[4] His advice was always practical, when dealing with either spiritual matters or everyday realities: 'Don't let your studies ever become an obstacle with your union with God – take care to sanctify them with pure intention, and they will keep you in God's presence. But you know that as well as I do. Don't deprive yourself of recreation to write long letters to us or anyone else; we can afford to wait till you have the leisure.'[5]

When Henry Parkinson first went to Rome, Edward Ilsley asked him to try to obtain an autographed photograph of Pope Pius IX for the seminary. An entry in the diary for Easter Monday 1875 – obviously added later at the bottom of the page – tells of the success of the venture: 'The Holy Father on this day (as we afterwards learned) at the instance of Cardinal Manning, gave his blessing to the Seminary, written in his autograph in the margin of a portrait presented for the purpose by Mr. Parkinson.' In early July Ilsley wrote enthusiastically to Parkinson, 'I must say you managed the matter of the blessing superbly. The picture is a gem, the autograph a treasure and the array of circumstances in connection with the procuring of it gorgeous – to crown all, the Bishop brought it from London to Birmingham. It hangs now in a good gilt frame in the cloister.'[6] The array of circumstances in connection with the picture was that Manning was in Rome to be created Cardinal by Pope Pius IX on 31 March and he apparently had a hand in procuring the blessing. Ullathorne was present at the ceremony. Pope Pius died three years later in February 1878, and there was a Requiem Mass at the seminary.

The students also attended the *Missa coram Episcopo* at St Chad's Cathedral, when the solemn dirge was sung and the grand catafalque, known as the Shrewsbury Catafalque, was erected for the occasion.[7] Cardinal Pecci was the new Pope, his title, Leo XIII.

## The Feast of St Aloysius

Bishop Ullathorne instituted an unusual tradition for the seminary in 1875, on 21 June, the feast of St Aloysius.[8] He chose this date in lieu of his own feast of St Bernard, which fell during the summer vacation, and from then on it became the special feast day of the seminary. Ilsley wrote a description in the diary of how things were carried out on this first occasion, which was attended by the Birmingham chapter.[9] 'High Mass sung by the Rector at 11. After dinner the Bishop presented an ivory grace cup to the Seminary which was the gift to His Lordship of

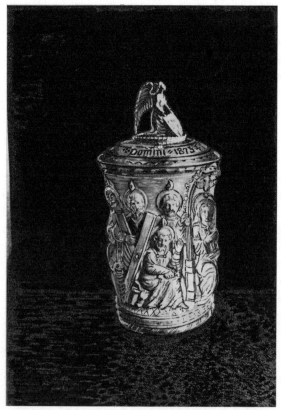

Figure 4.3 *The Grace Cup presented by Bishop Ullathorne to Olton in 1875. The Grace Cup is in the museum at Oscott College.*

Messrs. Hardman & Co.' The cup was over two hundred years old and it was formed all in one piece from an elephant's tusk which had been richly mounted in silver gilt. The lining and mounting of the cup was carried out by Hardman's craftsmen and there were figures carved all round it depicting the coming of the Holy Ghost on the apostles and Our Lady.[10] On the lid, which was circumscribed with alternating bands of gold and silver, knelt an angel cast in gold, holding the Bishop's arms. The inscription round the lid was *Fundatoris Poculum Caritatis Anno Domini 1873*, meaning: 'The Grace Cup of the Founder the year of the Lord 1873'.[11]

A month later he described the event to Henry Parkinson – 'The Bishop inaugurated the grace cup,' he wrote. 'The ivory is all one piece, the cup holds a quart, so you may guess the size. After explaining the origin of the grace cup, the Bishop took a sip & passed it on to his neighbour saying *"poculum charitatis"*,[12] & so it was passed all round for the first time. It was intended as a surprise for our fellows and they remarked afterwards that they ought to have practised the ceremony a few times previously!' The tradition flourished over the years, and it was simply referred to as 'The Feast', or 'The Great Feast'. From then on the students always decorated 'the chapel, refectory and cloister, to give a festive appearance to the seminary', and ornate menu cards, each individually drawn in pen and ink, were done for the luncheon guests.

## A Canon of the Chapter 1876

On 16 November 1876 Ilsley received a document appointing him to a stall in the cathedral, and this was accompanied by a note from the Bishop, part of which he copied into the seminary diary. Ullathorne explained that the appointment was essentially fulfilling the requirements of the Tridentine provisions: 'Considering the importance of having the Diocesan Seminary represented in the Chapter, as was always the case when the Episcopal Seminary was in earlier days under the charge of the Archdeacon; considering the importance of placing the Rector of the Seminary as the fountain of the Diocese in the Episcopal Senate, on these grounds of ecclesiastical policy, I have appointed you to the vacant stall.' (The stall had been left vacant by the sudden death of Canon Jefferies.) It was a crucial part of Bishop Ullathorne's vision to regularize the organization of the diocese in this way, at the same time being aware of the value of associating Ilsley more closely with the cathedral chapter, which would smooth his path should he take higher office later on.[13]

The installation took place in the cathedral on 5 December with all the seminarians present. Henry Parkinson mentions in the seminary history that the day before, they presented the Rector with a congratulatory address and gave him a full set of canonicals. There is also a note written by Ilsley in the diary for 6 December saying, 'Playday on occasion of Installation'. The granting of a 'play day', as it was termed, was a feature woven throughout seminary life during those early years. It was often obtained by the students because someone important had visited, or it was given by the Rector for such a simple reason as the day being fine, or even for an exceptionally cold one. In the January 1879, which was one of the coldest winters on record, a student wrote in his diary 'Frost during the night. Fellows asked for play all day. Rector gave the whole afternoon. They went to skate on the Warwick canal and reached as far as Lapworth where they found the ice was broken up for 3 miles.'

The students obviously enjoyed this outlet for their energies, but Arthur Villiers, writing later in *The Oscotian*, reviewed the whole question of the insufficient exercise taken by them: 'Though the majority of students were Douai men and brought with them the love of manly games, few if any opportunities presented themselves for any strenuous form of exercise, other than long walks ... One day that we grouped together on the New Street platform waiting for a train for Oscott where the Ordinations were to be held, a bystander casually remarked to his friend, but in the hearing of the Rector that we were wanting in physique. This evidently set the Rector thinking, for he at once took the matter up.' Suddenly aware that in comparison with the students at Oscott, who had excellent recreational facilities, those at St Bernard's had none, Ilsley decided to put matters right straight away: 'A pitch was levelled for cricket, outdoor parallel bars were erected, and a tennis net was stretched across the lawn and the duty of games was duly pressed upon us. Moreover a bathing pond was excavated in the lower field which already was watered by a constant stream.' Henry Parkinson described all this in his seminary history, written later at Oscott, and gave the date as September 1882.[14] According to Arthur Villiers, the Rector's plans were too late. He may have meant that this was because no tradition had been built up, or that by this time Ilsley was too busy to see it all through properly. At this time he was often away from the seminary for weeks at a time working as Ullathorne's assistant at Bishop's House, and he resigned his rectorship the following summer of 1883. Villiers wrote, 'The gymnasium was a nine-days' wonder, a horse let loose in the cricket field galloped over the pitch before it was well set and pitted it with holes, whilst weeds grew up so rapidly in the pond that it was choked in no time.'[15]

In a letter written in November 1876, Ilsley told Henry Parkinson about what had happened when he and one of his students, Charles Wheatley, were travelling with other pilgrims through Italy on his way to Rome to offer the homage of the seminary to the Holy Father. He allows his narrative to stray on to the everyday sort of details not usually touched on in his other letters, and in this case a spirit of quiet determination is revealed. 'By the by, we recovered 31s/6 from the *Alta Italia* railway through Cook – they had chiselled us out of it on the ground of a flaw in our circular tickets. They tried to levy another fine for another technical flaw when we were travelling from Naples to Loretto – I resisted and was determined to go before the magistrates sooner than pay. They made three or four attempts to extort between 8 o'clock at night and 2 the following morning; one of them was a regular Court Martial before the *Capo Stazione* & his officers; but they got no lire out of us. I showed them an empty purse & said, 'I can't pay' – so after my final victory I had four quiet hours to prepare for Mass at the *Santa Casa*; the first part of the journey was passed in a mood not altogether congenial to pilgrims.'

## Disagreement between Ilsley and Barry

The earlier decision made in 1874 for Henry Parkinson to work for a year 'on the mission' when he returned from Rome was altered when the time came, because by then it was Ilsley's wish to replace Barry with Parkinson. William Barry, who had been Vice Rector since the opening of the seminary in 1873, was now appointed to the chair of divinity at Oscott College for September 1877 under the presidency of the Revd John Hawksford. This changeover was bound to come about, because Ilsley found Barry's manner too informal with the students at the seminary and he had written to Parkinson as early as November 1875: 'There is no confidence between Dr. Barry and myself, nor do I see any prospect of restoring that happy understanding that worked so well at the commencement.' Regarding Barry's attitude he continued: 'This cannot but fail to prove disastrous to the position and influence of the superior and the family of the community. I am sorry that neither I nor the Bishop can bring Barry to see it.'[16]

After spending four years at St Bernard's, Barry seemed well-pleased with his move to Oscott, where he discovered much greater freedoms for himself than he had previously. No mention was made in his memoirs of any disagreement with Ilsley; instead he was full of enthusiasm with his changed circumstances: 'This was a position of unrivalled authority in which I could arrange my Lectures as I pleased,' he wrote. 'My appointment suited me exceedingly well. I had a larger class of divines than Olton Seminary possessed. My studies pleased me, my scholars became speedily interested, and I felt altogether at home among this new generation.' He found the college had other benefits to his liking that were lacking at St Bernard's: 'The Oscott library was of course open to me. At Olton I had often wanted books; here there was no lack.' He undoubtedly preferred the more liberal atmosphere of Oscott, where he remained on the staff for the following three years and which he later described as 'more like an Oxford College presided over by clergymen'.[17] Later described as 'a man of almost amazing energy and mental application', he was among those who very much regretted the changeover that took place there twelve years later when the lay school was closed by Bishop Ilsley and the college became the diocesan seminary.

Ilsley wrote to Parkinson in Rome on 10 July 1877 making some suggestions about Parkinson's forthcoming meeting with Bishop Ullathorne: 'The last interview that I had with the Bishop he said he shouldn't decide what to do with you till he had seen you. He has a dislike of Doctors' degrees because he thinks they turn people's heads – I shouldn't have told you this, only I know that when you come into his presence you won't be disposed to act a part or even take into account the prejudice he might entertain against DDs in general.' He continued, 'I know in your case it will be a meeting of Father and Son & that you will be the good boy you always were.'

Following this interview with Ullathorne, Ilsley wrote again to Parkinson, who was then staying at St Edmund's College, and this letter conveys the idea that Parkinson would have preferred an appointment at Oscott: 'After all it seems the Bishop has made up his mind and appointed you, at my request, not to Oscott but to St Bernard's. Dr Barry is to profess Dogma and Philosophy at Oscott and you are to teach Philosophy here and be Vice Rector ... Don't say impossible and wait till we meet and then you'll understand the why and wherefore of the motives of the change that is now taking place. All that we can go into when we meet.'[18] From the style in which this letter is written there is a clear indication that this was an occasion when Ilsley failed to have a fair consultation with the person he was dealing with. He was not always given to discussion even with those he counted among his closest friends, if he had set his mind on a certain policy he wished to carry out. From this attitude, coupled with a tendency not to delegate sufficiently, it can be seen that at times he forfeited the benefits he could have gained by acting on the advice of his friends and colleagues, rather than going ahead and determinedly acting on his own.

## Henry Parkinson Vice Rector

So after spending four years at the English College, Henry Parkinson returned to the seminary in August 1877 to start the academic year as Vice Rector and Professor of Philosophy. He evidently fitted in well with the Rector's scheme of things, and Ilsley must have initially seen the situation between them somewhat resembling his own relations with Ullathorne. Parkinson applied himself to the task with an intense dedication, and the fact he merited Ilsley's wholehearted approval was shown when he commented to Bishop Ullathorne two years later, 'I cannot speak too highly of Dr. Parkinson's devotedness to his class work, and I rejoice that he has some good material to work on. I am satisfied that he has made the most of all his pupils – but he is the

Figure 4.4  *Henry Parkinson, Vice Rector of St Bernard's Seminary (1877–83). Oscott College albums.*

same throughout whatever he undertakes.'[19] The students however sometimes viewed Parkinson's assiduity in a different light. Frederick Keating, who entered the seminary in 1877, writing an article later in *The Oscotian* in 1924 when he was Archbishop of Liverpool, gives a remarkably illuminating picture of the Vice Rector's character from the student's point of view: 'Our professor was, then as always, the model of the perfect seminarian, and his example an unfailing stimulus to work. He lived by a time-table which left no moment of the day unaccounted for, and would have found it as irksome to break his routine as most people would have found it impossible to adopt. He exacted unhesitating submission to authority and meticulous observance of rules. He was slow to recognise compensating qualities in someone who could not be squeezed into his mould, and occasionally failed in his diagnoses of character.'[20] Barry and Parkinson seemed almost two opposites in character, Barry was fearless and outspoken in his views, whereas Parkinson's approach was considered 'rigid' by Keating. But in spite of all this, Keating finally had to acknowledge, 'that if he erred, he erred on the side of the angels. He lived up to his own ideal; and as he lived it, it seemed to be a very fine ideal indeed.'

Edward's younger brother Charles got married on 9 May 1878. Like Edward his interest was also in music. After becoming a Rosminian in 1861 he first worked as a choirmaster, and was appointed to teach at Ratcliffe College in 1864, and in 1869 he was sent to Ireland to teach at Upton in County Cork. Seven years later, in 1876, he spent six months in Rugby, where he had received his early training, beginning his noviciate there at the age of 14. Then he came to London in the July, and stayed for some weeks at Ely Place before finally deciding that after fifteen years he would leave the Rosminian Order for good, and he was married two years later at the age of 33. Although he never went back to his family home in Stafford, he certainly stayed with his wife at his sister Ellen Brindley's house in Erdington, and his daughters also kept in touch with their cousins over the years.[21] As Edward was a frequent visitor to the Brindley household the two brothers may have met on these family occasions. Charles's family remained staunchly Catholic, although his wife Sarah was never received into the Church. They had seven daughters, and the first, Philomena, born in March 1879, became a nun, Sister Francisca, in the Belgian Order of *Les Dames de St André*, a teaching community in Bruges.

Charles Ilsley senior, father of Charles and Edward, died in November 1879 – a month before Edward's consecration as Auxiliary

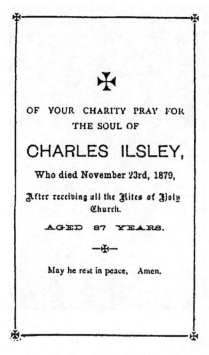

Figure 4.5 *Memorial card, Charles Ilsley. Private collection.*

Bishop. It was therefore a time when a lot was happening in their lives, and they were events and changes which were taking the two brothers still further in very different directions. There are no personal family letters to be found at this time relating to Charles leaving the Rosminians, nor is there any record of his ordination, so presumably he had remained a brother in the Congregation. His brother's behaviour at this time must have come as a great shock and sorrow to Edward, and it must have always weighed heavily on his mind that one so close to him would have acted in this way.

The year 1879 produced one of the highlights in the history of the seminary when, at the age of 78, Dr Newman became Cardinal. Canon Villiers tells how the Rector invited both staff and students to try their hand at drawing up a suitable address from the house, to congratulate the Cardinal – 'on being raised to the purple' was the phrase he used to describe the occasion. 'On looking over the results of their combined efforts, he considered that nothing had been produced that in any way approached what he considered appropriate, so he set himself the task of composing a fitting text, and placed the result in the hands of an artist who would complete the illumination.' A student noted in

Figure 4.6 *Cardinal John Henry Newman. Taken from a photograph in the Birmingham Oratory Archives.*

his diary: 'The address, illuminated and framed was brought by the artist Mr Perry and gave universal satisfaction.'[22] The Revd William Neville gives an account of how two of the seminarians, Edward Hymers and Frederick Crewe, took the framed address to Cardinal Newman at the Oratory on Holy Saturday morning, 12 April 1879, in deep snow. They had not actually expected to see him and only supposed they would hand it in to Father Pope and then leave. Instead, they were shown into the waiting room and were surprised and delighted when the Cardinal himself came in to greet them. They presented the address to him at once, and there was next some difficulty in getting the string undone, so the Cardinal hurried out of the room and returned with a knife to cut it. It was finally unwrapped and he set it upon the mantelpiece to show it to good advantage, and he then leant on the marble and silently read it. Then turning to the students he said, typically, that he felt it was far more than he deserved, but they in their turn protested every word was meant. 'I am sure of that,' he said, 'those things are measured not by words but from the heart.' They told how he then sat and talked with them for about twenty minutes, speaking 'in a sort of meditative way, in somewhat broken phrases ... with an evident feeling that made one warm up with devotion to him'.[23]

## Visit by Cardinal Newman

He returned their visit the following year on the feast day of the seminary, and there is a description given by one of the students of how they prepared for the occasion: 'The students worked hard to give the Seminary a festive appearance. Besides the usual decorations for the feast day, the large corridor was decked with festoons and in each window large spreading ferns were placed in pots.' The pictures of the Cardinal and Dr Ullathorne were decorated with flowers, and over the furthest arch was placed a slogan which read, *Salve Sancte Bernarde*, and over the middle one, *Cor ad Cor loquitur*. (This was the Cardinal's motto meaning 'Heart speaketh unto heart'.[24]) The occasion was also reported in *The Tablet*: 'He was among the first arrivals. On alighting from his carriage, he was received by the Seminarists in cassocks and surplice and as he entered the corridor, after kneeling to receive his blessing, they rose and sang the *'Ecce Sacerdos'*. He stood while the piece was sung, and showed by his approving smile the pleasure the reception gave him ... High Mass was at eleven.' He spoke during Mass as follows: 'My dear children, – I wish I were quite the person to speak upon the subject on which I am drawn to say a few words ... I have not the experience of Seminaries which alone could enable one to do so properly and perfectly.'[25] The sermon he gave lacked nothing on this account. Concisely setting out the advantages of seminary life it contained a great deal of wisdom, being almost a handbook for seminary students and standing the test of time. He finished with these words: 'May we all enter more into the responsibilities put upon us. How much more can we do for God and how much he will enable us to do if we put our simple trust in him.'[26] The final message fitted Ilsley's situation exactly, as he had recently taken on far heavier responsibilities due to Bishop Ullathorne's failing health, having six months previously been designated as his auxiliary.

There must have been some consternation caused on this occasion because Bishop Ullathorne missed his train, and consequently missed Mass. He was in time for the luncheon, however, but Dr Ilsley had to jog his memory during dessert, telling him he was expected to propose the Cardinal's health at the end of the meal. 'The Right Rev. Bishop and Rector of this college has just been whispering in my ears and reminding me that it is our duty to give expression to the great honour that has been conferred upon St. Bernard's Seminary by the presence and discourse of His Eminence who sits at my right hand,' he announced. Handling a difficult situation in his own inimitable way, he began the address in his usual honest manner: 'Unhappily I missed my train, or someone missed it for me ... therefore I am sorry to say I missed both Mass and the discourse,' he told them.[27]

The demands of Edward Ilsley's new position as Auxiliary inevitably drew him away from much of his previous work as Rector and as the condition of the old Bishop gradually worsened, the strain imposed on Ilsley by continuing his work in both positions must have become very heavy indeed. The previous six years spent as 'Father Rector' had been a comparatively quiet plateau in his life, with time to build up reserves – a situation where he became established among his colleagues and the clergy with whom he would be working and directing later on in the Birmingham diocese. These early years at the seminary represented a half-way house where he left behind his earlier missionary work, and prepared to take up the increasingly strenuous loads the future years in higher office were to set upon his shoulders.

## Influence of Newman and Ullathorne

It is significant that during this time Ilsley should have been directly exposed to the influence of two of the most celebrated Catholics of his time, namely, John Henry Newman and William Ullathorne. Newman endorsed his approval of St Bernard's and its Rector through his association with them over the years. His appearances among them, and the special sermons he gave them, testify to this. When the time came, he had no hesitation in pressing his direct influence as Cardinal in favour of Ilsley's nomination as Bishop of Birmingham, openly demonstrating the confidence he had in him by publicly backing the nomination.[28] In a letter to Ilsley thanking the community of St Bernard's for their prayers on the occasion of his eightieth birthday, Newman felt sufficiently close to him to add a descriptive paragraph confiding his feelings on having attained that great age: 'A long life is like a long ladder, which sways and jumps dangerously under the feet of the man who mounts it the higher he goes, and if there is anyone who needs prayers for perseverance it is the man of 80. I rejoice to believe that your and the Seminary's prayers for me include this intention on my behalf.'[29]

One of the great minds of his time, Newman put forward ideas which went far beyond any particular theological school of thought. Unlike Manning, his interest was not along the paths of social reform but in the attitude of men's minds and their spiritual welfare; so whereas Manning outstripped him in practical achievement, 'so Newman outstripped him as a Catholic thinker'.[30] In his 34 years in the Catholic Church, while much of Newman's work had been deeply appreciated, some of it had been viewed with distrust in some quarters as being too independent in outlook, and this caused him to be to some extent isolated as a Catholic. But living at the Oratory in Birmingham as part of the contemporary scene there, he was sustained by the no-nonsense attitude and support of his bishop, William Ullathorne, and by such friends as J. S. Northcote and Canon Estcourt.[31] Ilsley's proximity to these men must have provided him with insight into the mind of the converts coming into the Church at this time, who saw the reality of Roman Catholicism in place of what they had discarded.[32]

Although Ullathorne and Manning respected one another they tended to differ in outlook, often not trusting the other's motives, and it has been said that 'Ullathorne was as natural a representative of one side at Rome, as Manning was of the other.'[33] Ilsley's opinion of Manning may have been coloured by Ullathorne's attitude. But Manning was a man of undeniably great stature, and the work done by him in the social sphere for the working man could hardly fail to make an impression on Ilsley, especially when he witnessed the love and respect paid by the masses at Manning's funeral, at which he offi-ciated. Even so as Bishop of Birmingham, Ilsley by no means adhered to Manning's policies.

Ullathorne's outlook was naturally sympathetic toward the old Church, even though he was instrumental in contributing so much to the formation of the new, and it was on his deathbed he had said, 'The last of the old Vicars-Apostolic is passing.' Working closely with Thomas Grant, who was then Rector of the English College in Rome, he acted as agent of the vicars apostolic for the hierarchy negotiations from 1848 to 1850, and had long since outlived all the others.[34] Mgr Philip Hughes said of him that to his ability as a negotiator he pre-sented a combination of 'native shrewdness, great patience, a liking for hard work, a good business head, practical knowledge of the ways of the Roman officials and a sound knowledge of the law'. To this description of Ullathorne, Hughes added something about his way of living that Ilsley seemed also to have adhered to over the years: 'He was a model of domestic poverty and simplicity to the end of an episcopate of forty years and more.'[35]

On his part Ilsley gained immeasurably from having found favour with such an outstanding man as William Ullathorne, who became the guiding influence in his life from his earliest years. He was in a position not only to gain valuable experience from the old Bishop regarding the practical organization of the diocese and the correct procedures connected with it,[36] but as Ullathorne was the acknowledged 'second in the hierarchy under Manning', the opportunity was there for Ilsley to become knowledgeable concerning development of the Church through him, during all their years of close association.

After Ilsley's consecration in December 1879, Bishop Ullathorne, speaking of the work done by him as Rector of the seminary, summarized it as testimony in favour of his choice of his future coadjutor: 'during the six years Dr Ilsley has occupied that position, everything has been carried out as completely as if I myself had presided over the institution and given all the directions, so fully has Dr Ilsley divined my intention'.[37] Edward Ilsley had in many ways become the instrument whereby Bishop Ullathorne carried through his ideas and ideals. The younger man appeared tirelessly ready to serve, while Ullathorne's role was to direct and instruct, as though consciously fitting Ilsley to be the man who would follow in his footsteps, to preserve and consolidate whatever had been instituted.

On the same occasion Bishop Ullathorne took the opportunity to make it known what he had in mind for the future – clearly indicating that it was his wish Ilsley should follow him as Bishop of Birmingham. He said what a relief and what a source of contentment it had been for him to place his hands, with the other two bishops, on Ilsley's head during the consecration ceremony, because they felt, and he deeply felt, that God had given them one not only who would be able to take a large portion of the burden of the administration out of his hands, but also 'who would be ready to catch the crozier when it fell from his grasp'.

## Notes

1   O.C.A., Parkinson Correspondence, 17 February 1875.
2   *Ibid.*, 7 June 1875.
3   *Ibid.*, 18 October 1875.
4   *Ibid.*, 26 May 1877.
5   *Ibid.*, 27 December 1874.
6   Letter, 2 July 1875.
7   Parkinson, ch. 6. This was in February 1878. The catafalque was first

used for Earl John, the 16th Earl of Shrewsbury, in November 1852. It was subsequently given to the Cathedral.

8  This day may have been chosen because St Aloysius was declared 'Patron of Catholic Students' in 1726, when he was canonized.

9  'The Provost, Canon G. Jeffries and Canons Northcote, Tandy, Ivers, Longman and Revvs. Abbott, Mills, Caswell, Dowling, Fenn and Greany attended.'

10  Diary, 21 June 1875.

11  Literally translated meaning 'Of the founder the cup of charity.' The tradition ended with the move to Oscott, and the Grace Cup was put in the college museum. The engraving of the date 1873 denoted the opening of the seminary, not the founding of the tradition.

12  Chadwick, vol. i, p. 283: 'The ensuing movement called Ultramontane was a rippling wave of Italian influence upon Catholic devotion throughout Europe. The Italian pronunciation of Latin with *ch* instead of *c* became fashionable.' Ilsley uses the soft 'ch' here. The word *charitatis* was used when passing the cup.

13  B.A., B5447. James McCave actually resigned his office of rector on this principle, on 27 May 1884, when Dr Acton was given a stall before him, but the resignation did not come into effect. He was appointed Canon Theologian later that year.

14  Parkinson, 'Jottings during the Rectorship of Bishop Ilsley'. Henry Parkinson's *Brief Sketch of the History of St. Bernard's Seminary, Olton* was drawn up by him from contemporary records and journals. It was compiled for a student's exhibition in 1900.

15  F.R., pp. 7, 8.

16  O.C.A.., Letter from Ilsley to Parkinson, 27 November 1875.

17  Barry, pp. 47 and 122, and obituary, *The Tablet*, 20 December 1930.

18  O.C.A., 25 July 1877.

19  *Ibid.*, Ilsley to Ullathorne, 2 July 1879.

20  Frederick Keating, 'Monsignor Parkinson in pre-Oscott days', *Oscotian* 24, 1924, pp. 161–2. Also Barry obituary, *Birmingham Directory*, 1932.

21  Later recounted by his niece, Catherine Brindley. Some of the Brindleys acted as godparents to the Ilsley children.

22  F.R., p. 4, and J., Holy Saturday, 12 April 1879. See also W. P. Neville, *Addresses to Cardinal Newman*: Taken from Ilsley's address to Cardinal Newman: '. . . Our hearts are full of gratitude when we call to mind the noble services you have throughout your life rendered to the cause of truth and religion. You have fought the good fight, you have guided many to their true home . . .' Signed E. Hymers, W. Waugh, E. Delaney, J. Hopwood, F. Keating, W. Bryon, J. Atkins, A. Villiers, H. Whitgreave, T. Fitzpatrick.

23  W. P. Neville, *Addresses to Cardinal Newman*, pp. 54, 55, taken from an account in a student's diary. The diary would be either Edward Hymer's or Frederick Crewe's.

24  An adaptation of a thought of St Francis de Sales: '*On a beau dire, mais le coeur parle au coeur, et le langue ne parle qu'aux oreilles.*' *Oeuvres de Saint Francois de Sales*, Paris, 1834. See *Letters and Diaries of J. H. Newman*, vol. xxix, p. 108. Barry claims this comes from a Persian proverb in *Memories and Opinions*, p. 36.

25  *The Tablet*, Saturday 3 July 1880, p. 125. Also J., 21 June 1880.

26  W. P. Neville, *Addresses to Cardinal Newman*, pp. 290–9.

27  *The Tablet*, Saturday 3 July 1880.

28  D.B., p. 11. This was at the Catholic Re-Union Meeting in Birmingham in January 1888.

29  *Letters and Diaries of John Henry Newman*, vol. xxix, p. 340.

30  Gray, p. 283.

31  Meriol Trevor, *Light in Winter*, pp. 550–63. Ullathorne assisted in securing Newman's election to the Sacred College in spite of certain misunderstandings that had arisen through Manning's attitude.

32  Chadwick, vol. i, p. 281. Newman, Estcourt and Northcote were numbered among those distinguished converts who had embraced 'the Lure of Rome'. Northcote brought to light the unbroken traditions handed down from the early Christians. He wrote scholarly accounts of the catacombs and lectured widely on the subject.

33  Gray, p. 185. See also Butler, vol. ii, ch. 16.

34  Butler, vol. ii, p. 295. These were among some of his last recorded words. He was appointed Vicar Apostolic of the Western District at the age of 40 in 1846 and was transferred to the Central District in 1848, becoming Bishop of Birmingham on the restoration of the hierarchy in 1850. Vol. I, pp. 137, 150, 165.

35  Beck, pp. 74–5.

36  Ullathorne's aim was for correct protocol and the laying down of canon law. He defended moderate 'English' Catholicism against extreme 'Roman' influences. Norman, p. 305.

37  *The Birmingham Daily Post*, 5 December 1979. Speech by Bishop Ullathorne at the luncheon following the consecration of Edward Ilsley, on 4 December 1879.

## CHAPTER FIVE

# *Auxiliary Bishop*

As his health declined Bishop Ullathorne felt unable to continue his administration further, so he sent a petition to Rome early in 1879 seeking permission to retire from office. Nearly ten years before, in 1870, he had the beginning of an illness 'which continued from time to time to return at intervals, causing him severe physical suffering'.[1] But in spite of this, and although he was now 73, his petition was refused on the grounds that 'your counsel may be of great use in the meetings of the bishops and may bring great light'. However, he wrote in July 1879, 'His Holiness desires me to be relieved of part of my office through an auxiliary but wishes me to continue in the See. Further, which is quite unusual, I am to send one name for approval.'[2] Dom Cuthbert Butler later observed when writing Ullathorne's biography: 'Manning being in Rome when the petition was put in, and doubtless consulted on it, may surely be the inspirer of the reason assigned for his continuance in office.'

In his reply Ullathorne nevertheless submitted three names to be considered. This may have been because of his strict adherence to protocol, making sure the correct canonical form was observed. He was also probably anticipating Ilsley might follow him, as usually when three names are sent in it is a question of nominating a bishop with 'right of succession'. Earlier in the year in March, he considered choosing Edmund Knight from among his chapter, and John Hedley had also been mentioned, but he emphatically decided against both, suggesting to Canon Estcourt that the former was 'stiff minded', and that the latter 'has everything except backbone, but that he wants deplorably. It is a pity, for otherwise he is just the man.' His opinion of these two men was not shared generally – within four months Edmund Knight became auxiliary bishop to Bishop Brown of Shrewsbury, and Hedley became Bishop of Newport and Menevia two years later.

Regarding Manning's interest in the matter, Ullathorne seemed to be distrusting his motives when he wrote to Estcourt, 'I think the question ought not to be delayed because the Diocese will get unhinged. If Manning can get in a man of his own he will ... if he dare, except he is afraid of meddling with me.'[3] Ullathorne may have been afraid that his health would give way before he could get the man of his own choice safely in place, in which case Manning would have had his way. After visiting Oscott that summer, Ilsley remarked in a letter to Canon Estcourt that 'there was much talk about Caswell as auxiliary bishop'.[4] John Caswell, eight years younger than Edward Ilsley, was prefect of studies at Oscott at this time and he was a man well-liked among the clergy.

In a letter to Rome dispatched a month later, on 18 August, Ullathorne wrote, 'I have pondered about it for a considerable lapse of time. I also asked the opinion of the chapter and solicited the prayers of the faithful for that purpose.'[5] He was indicating that he not only valued the opinion of his chapter, but wished to draw his people into his decision concerning what he described as 'this matter of great relevance'. He continued: 'Having taken into consideration more than one person, may I recommend the following ones to the Holy Father.' He submitted the name of Edward Ilsley in the first place and two other members of his chapter, John Hawksford, in second place and Thomas Longman, third. Hawksford, then aged 46, had been the president of Oscott for the past two years. Ullathorne described him as 'well balanced and very pious', but there is a hint in the letter that 'his presence in the college is quite necessary' and that he would be difficult to replace. Longman was nearly 61 and had recently been appointed Vicar General. His previous experience was as administrator at the cathedral. Ullathorne closed his letter about Longman by suggesting in his blunt manner that, being rather elderly and in poor health, he could not see him as an auxiliary bishop.

## Ullathorne's Recommendation of Ilsley

Ullathorne's recommendation regarding Ilsley, then aged 42, is of particular interest because it is written by one who knew him well and summarizes his attitude towards him. There is no overt suggestion of Ullathorne putting him forward as a successor to himself as the future bishop of the diocese, but he is portrayed rather as one who would fit readily into the mould as his assistant, conforming exactly to the Bishop's wishes and commands. The list of Edward's qualifications submitted to the Sacred Congregation tends therefore to discount many of his special merits in favour of portraying a man who would simply obey and follow, rather than presume to act on his own initiative.

At first glance he appears to be positively under-estimating Ilsley, and as the text is in Latin, his individual style of writing is missing. Having first described the extent of Ilsley's work at Longton and his organization of the seminary, in which he emphasized his spiritual qualities, he continues with the following description of him: 'He does not shine either in the breadth or brilliance of his learning since his mind is less swift than firm in judgement; he has an unassuming manner and a capacity for hard work.' His point about Ilsley's capacity for hard work was absolutely right, and for the rest, Ullathorne's testimony gave a reasonably true picture of him. So on closer scrutiny one realizes that this was the manner in which Ullathorne could be reasonably expected to present Ilsley as a candidate for this position.

Aware that the influences of Ilsley's family background would amply supply the necessary springboard for his spiritual life, rather than encouraging any considerable intellectual stimulus, Ullathorne introduced him in this light. Being a man with not many years' classical education himself, having gone to sea at the age of 12 after a fairly basic education from the age of 8, it would particularly suit the old Bishop to work with someone who would pose no problems for him in this field, not tending in any way to outshine his superior with a swift, challenging mind. It is true Ullathorne later resumed his studies again, going to Downside when he was 16, where he studied for a year before commencing his noviciate,[6] but his complaint there was, 'I was pushed up too rapidly through the school & consequently did not get my fair share of scholarship.' Bernard Ward's conclusion was that he never fully overcame 'the want of his early education';[7] however, Ullathorne could by no means be described as an uneducated man by the time he completed his training for the priesthood, because his natural scholarship took him through. In defence of Edward Ilsley's intellectual ability it must be said that although his father was a tradesman, having one uncle a priest, and another a schoolmaster, meant he was quite possibly as well equipped as many of his peers, so Ullathorne's statement in this case did not appear entirely to do him justice. However, this was the attitude the old Bishop chose to adopt towards him in relation to himself.

The remaining passages begin to compensate for his rather stark introduction: 'For all that,' it runs, 'he does have adequate knowledge, together with a great striving towards wherever his duties should happen to lie.' Here Ullathorne appears to be indicating the thoroughness of Ilsley's approach in matters great or small. The last part of the letter reveals the promise of the future years, and relieves the carefully measured constraint at the beginning. It encapsulates much of all that could be said of Ilsley, who was by nature a man of great simplicity: 'Firm of purpose,' he wrote, 'prudent in his actions, good at organising, humble in spirit, cautious in speech – he is the man to whom I would freely confide episcopal duties.'[8]

Further than this it is difficult to assess any more precise reasons for Ilsley's appointment to the hierarchy, because even after his long term of office, spreading over a period of 42 years, very little emerged of his real personality. Although his work embraced a considerable portion of the recent history of the diocese, much that was said of him after his death tended to be written in the official language of newspaper editorials or in carefully chosen words, in the style of the time, in articles which contributed little to the true picture. Even though he was a prodigious letter-writer for well over half a century, he rarely expressed his innermost feelings or even the incidentals of his everyday life – so in many ways he escaped notice. Monsignor J. D. Crichton, who remembered Ilsley's final years at Oscott College when he himself was a student there, wrote this in April 1984: 'One puzzle is why Ullathorne, a very forthright character, should have chosen Ilsley to be his auxiliary, who he must have known was likely to succeed him. Ilsley was the direct opposite of Ullathorne and never had his drive.' He continued: 'I suspect it was the deep spirituality of Ilsley that prompted the choice – all told he was a quiet man and it is said, deeply spiritual.' Possibly Mgr Crichton felt that sanctity precluded administrative ability – in Ilsley's case this was certainly not so. Ullathorne had his own positive reasons for choosing him and underlined them at the luncheon given after Ilsley's consecration when he said: 'The man who so successfully realised the formation of a college, and who has succeeded in presiding over it, is just the man to govern and understand the clergy.'[9] Or it may simply have been through his shrewd observations of the hard-working young curate at Longton showing his ability to take on the details of the building of St Gregory's while at the same time caring so well for those he aptly named 'my little flock' that Ullathorne chose Edward Ilsley as his successor.

## Ilsley appointed Auxiliary

A month later, the Bishop received confirmation from Rome of the final choice of candidate, and it was with considerable pleasure he was able to inform Ilsley that Pope Leo had appointed him as his auxiliary bishop and coadjutor. The interview between the two is described in a letter to the Bishop's old friend and adviser Canon Estcourt: 'The Holy Father has been pleased to appoint Canon Ilsley as my Auxiliary. I saw him this morning, and after certain humble representations as to his disqualities, which I answered, he submitted to the yoke.'[10] On the same day, 13 September, there is a note in Parkinson's *History of St. Bernard's* which tells how the announcement was received at the seminary: 'After dinner the professors adjourned to Dr Schobel's room where the Rector made it known to the professors his nomination as coadjutor. The vice rector assembled the students in the Common Room and announced to them the good news, at which there was an outburst of rejoicing. The students then went away in a body to congratulate the "Father Rector", the title which had been given to him since the opening of the Seminary.'[11]

In spite of Bishop's Ullathorne's recommendation of Ilsley, some doubt as to whether he should accept the nomination still lingered in the minds of his staff at the seminary. They were at that time Henry Parkinson, Victor Schobel and Dr Verres. According to Arthur Villiers, they went as far as advising him against the appointment because they felt 'he had not the intellectual capacity for the office and was sure to make a mess of things'. It is true he did not have the academic degrees they were looking for (for instance Hawksford was a DD and Longman an MA), but his colleagues seemed to have overlooked some of the strengths and qualities of his nature which were to reveal themselves throughout his long episcopate. Besides, even if he had agreed with them, to Ilsley, who had always considered the demands of his superiors to be the *vox Dei*, the request had to be met with unquestioning obedience.[12]

The consecration was arranged to take place early in December, so the next few weeks were full of preparation. Bishop Ullathorne wrote to Ilsley, addressing him 'My dear Bishop elect', and continued, 'I have written to Canon Estcourt to ask him to put £100 at your disposal for your pontificalia, of course you will want your jewelled mitre for the consecration. So far I think the appointment has been well received in the Diocese.' There were many letters of congratulation, including one from Cardinal Manning, and another from Cardinal Newman.[13] Ilsley's reply to a letter from John Caswell had a candid ring about it: 'I had quite made up my mind that it was to be the other way about, and that I should be paying you homage and offering you my congratulations. As it is, let me say how thankful I feel for your kind words and good wishes.'[14]

## Presentation of a Pectoral Cross

Toward the end of October, the clergy of the diocese made a presentation to the Bishop elect of a very beautiful pectoral cross and chain. The cross was a gold reliquary set with rubies. The occasion was informal, so it took place at the seminary, and as they all gathered round in the common room, Canon Longman addressed him: 'We have come here today to present your Lordship this cross and chain, which we hope you will live to wear for many years,' he said. His ensuing speech was a summary of what had already been accomplished by Ilsley, and it contemplated what was yet to come, listing his qualities that would prove to be so precious to his clergy: 'Born in the Diocese, educated among us and having laboured with us, your whole career is before us, and we know you well. We know you to be a man of prayer, that whatever you undertake for God's glory, you anticipate by prayer and so secure God's blessing upon it. We know you for your steadfastness and perseverance . . . and a third characteristic is this: that

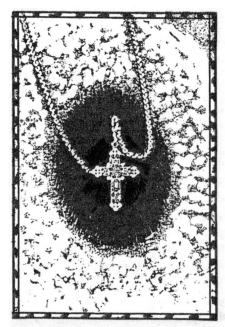

Figure 5.1 *The pectoral cross and chain presented to Edward Ilsley in 1879 by the canons of the cathedral chapter and the clergy of the diocese.*

we shall find in you a father and we shall be able to come to you in our troubles and meet with that sympathy that takes the edge off the sword of authority.'[15]

In his reply Edward began: 'I know that it is a more blessed thing to give than to receive. On this occasion, however, I venture to say that my joy on receiving your token of goodwill, is fully equal to the pleasure with which you offer it.' He then expressed his feelings about his appointment in words that appear gently but firmly to anticipate any further questioning – 'Indeed I needed some token of your sympathy. Not as if I could for a moment doubt the loyalty of the clergy of this diocese, or as if you could fail to welcome anyone whom the Bishop nominated as his auxiliary, and the Holy See appointed. But for myself, conscious as I am that my own resources are so limited, that I am in many ways unequal to the task that is before me – that in point of virtue, and learning, and experience I fall so short of what may fairly be required of me, and accepting the office proposed to me entirely on faith in the judgement of others, I need the moral support that comes of the sympathy of my brethren – the sympathy of hope that I shall be enabled to perform its arduous duties – the sympathy of your prayers too that abundant grace may be given me.'

He then outlined some of his immediate intentions with regard to the importance of his assistance to Bishop Ullathorne: 'But this I now feel my great responsibility – to relieve our much-loved and venerated Bishop of that portion of his labour which is mainly a tax on the bodily frame, so that his valuable life may be preserved for many years in the Diocese and the Church at large.' In fact, the work that Ilsley was about to undertake as auxiliary, by willingly shouldering a large part of the main burden of the work in and around the diocese, enabled William Ullathorne to continue as Bishop of Birmingham for the next nine years, right up to the year before his death. Dom Cuthbert Butler described how Ullathorne used this time: 'They were years of great productiveness, of unremitting reading and writing and redoubled letter writing ... the intellect held out to the end.'[16] It was largely due to Ilsley that the old Bishop gained his reputation of being an 'exception to the common run of non-writing bishops'.[17] Realizing the size of the task ahead of him, Edward continued: 'For this I shall require vaster breadth of mind for my extended sphere of labour, and an immensely enlarged heart to devote myself to work generously as a "good shepherd" and as "the servant of God's servants" ... '

Sadly enough, Ilsley's father, Charles, died on 23 November only ten days before the consecration, and Father Joseph Parker, the old

Bishop's hard-working secretary, whose family also lived in Stafford, recorded in his diary at the time, that his brother George notified him of the death by telegram, so he could take the news across to Dr Ilsley at the seminary.[18] A student wrote in his journal, 'News came during High Mass of the death of Dr Ilsley's father. Announcement to the Students after dinner and the blinds drawn throughout the house.'[19] Joseph Parker's diary gives a brief description of the day of the funeral: 'Thursday 27th. Up at 6.30. Mass at 7.30. *Requiem* sung by Dr. Ilsley at 10.00. I walked with Dr. Ilsley as mourner at funeral in cemetery. Saw Dr. Ilsley off by the 3.45 to St. Bernard's.' *The Catholic Times* reported of Charles Ilsley: 'He was denied the satisfaction of beholding the mitre placed on the head of the Bishop elect. He was vouchsafed, however the consolation of hearing that the Holy See had elected him to the See of Birmingham.'[20]

## Consecration in St Chad's Cathedral 1879

Ilsley was consecrated on Thursday 4 December, in St Chad's Cathedral. The day before, Bishop Ullathorne came there, and 'blessed the elect's crosier, ring and vestments'.[21] The ceremony lasted altogether three hours, and at the commencement over two hundred clergy entered the cathedral in procession and moved up the nave to the sanctuary, the warm light of their candles contrasting with the wintry, snow-clad scene they had left in the streets outside. The bishop elect was brought before the consecrating bishop Dr Ullathorne, who had taken his seat at the altar, and he then took the Pontifical Oath on the book of Gospels. Then, vested in his pontifical vestments, he withdrew with his attendants to an altar in the north chapel where he read the Mass as far as the Gospel. Bishop John Cuthbert Hedley then delivered the discourse, observing that the size of the large congregation testified 'how very interesting and important was the occasion'. Taking for his text the words 'He hath given him the priesthood of the nation',[22] he said, 'The significance of the consecration of a bishop is the significance of the Christian priesthood. There was made that morning a priest of priests – a high priest – one to whom was given the fulness of the priesthood of the Church of God.'

Ilsley was then led a second time before the consecrator, who placed an open book of the Gospels on his shoulders as he knelt before the altar. This signified that though he was to govern others himself, he was subject to the law of the Gospels. Then came the solemn imposition of hands by Bishop Ullathorne and his assistant bishops, Francis

Figure 5.2  *Edward Ilsley, Bishop Auxiliary, Bishop of Fesse (1879–88). From the Oscott College Albums.*

Amherst, the recently retired Bishop of Northampton, and Edmund Knight of Shrewsbury. *The Veni Creator* was intoned as the head of the bishop elect was anointed with holy chrism, and his hands were then anointed to show he had received the power of blessing and consecrating. He was next presented with his pastoral staff as an emblem of his charge as ecclesiastical shepherd and a ring, the symbol of the fidelity he owed to the Church, was put on the fourth finger of his right hand. The book of Gospels was then delivered to him, and the consecrator and his assistant bishops gave him the kiss of peace.

He now presented offerings of bread and wine to the consecrating bishop, and after receiving Holy Communion, the mitre was placed upon his head, and he was solemnly enthroned. The *Te Deum* was sung while the newly consecrated bishop proceeded round the cathedral with his assistants, Revds Henry Parkinson and Victor Schobel, giving his blessing to the congregation, many of whom were his old parishioners from Longton. 'Advancing to the highest step of the altar he gave his benediction, and next kneeling and facing the consecrator, saluted him three times, saying, "Unto many years". The Prologue to the Gospel of St. John having been said and a procession formed, all retired to the sacristy.'

## A Hotel Luncheon

At the luncheon afterwards which was held at the Grand Hotel, Edward Ilsley first spoke of his gratitude towards Bishop Ullathorne, whom he said he could never thank adequately for all he had done for him over the years.[23] He then welcomed the visiting bishops who were with them that day, 'Dr Amherst back again after his labours of well nigh a quarter of a century... They also welcomed their own Bishop Knight who stole away from amongst them, almost before they were aware that he had left them.' Addressing the priests of the diocese, he took the opportunity of thanking them for their goodwill, and especially for presenting him with his pectoral cross a few days before. It would remind him, he said, under all circumstances, to cherish them and keep them, like this cross, very close to his heart. He also thanked the Catholic laity who had travelled long distances to the ceremony, in spite of the difficulties caused by the bitterly cold weather.

Then turning to the venerable figure sitting next to Bishop Ullathorne, he said there was one among them whose presence 'was like beams of sunlight in their midst, one who was the reflection of a more august presence' – who had lived a great part of his life among them, and had become well known to them and much loved in that thirty years. At that point Cardinal Newman rose to say a few words for this kind tribute. He was received with 'loud and prolonged applause', then in his characteristic way, he protested that he could not thank them adequately for their kindness, so would they kindly accept his few words of gratitude for the way in which he had been received. Bishop Amherst, sitting between Dr Hedley (who had delivered the discourse) and Cardinal Newman, said later how well the Cardinal was looking, not appearing to feel the cold, even though it was intense. He also remarked that although the ceremony lasted more than three hours everything went off 'without a hitch'.[24]

On returning from the cathedral, the young seminarians showed their appreciation of the honour that had come upon the seminary by decorating the principal corridor for the reception of 'His Lordship the Rector' when he returned, and by hanging his coat of arms over the door of the refectory. Flowers and lamps were set in the windows, and the festoons they had worked on at different times of the day were hung round the arches. The chapel was prepared for solemn pontifical benediction, and when the Bishop returned at about six o'clock he was met at the door by the students in surplice and the *Ecce Sacerdos* was sung while he vested in the reception room. Finally, at the day's end,

'All the students came into the Bishop's room after supper and remained conversing with the Bishop till 9 pm.'[25] From this time on they always referred to him as 'the Bishop', and the term 'Father Rector' was not used again in their journals or elsewhere.

## The Old Bishop's Move to Oscott

Dom Cuthbert Butler described the situation regarding Bishop Ullathorne at this time: 'But his health was greatly broken and the external administrative work of the Diocese passed more and more into the hands of the auxiliary ... And so having reached 1880, he practically withdrew into retirement.' At this point William Ullathorne moved from Bishop's House, which lay in the rather drab Bath Street opposite St Chad's Cathedral, and went to live at Oscott College, where he devoted most of his time to reading and writing in the seclusion of his rooms.[26] An exceptionally gifted man, he had always appeared to have a need for solitude. In his youth he had chosen the freedom of the sea, and at the age of 56 had petitioned to retire to the Benedictine cloister, but the Pope did not consent to his request.[27] On his first voyage to Australia, at the age of 26, he wrote: 'From my boyhood I had a good deal of the hermit in my composition, preferring to be alone and having no attraction for society beyond the sense of duty. My attraction was for books and my own solitary musings.'[28] He indicated the same feelings on several occasions, writing as early as Easter Sunday 1858, after having been Bishop of Birmingham for only eight years: 'When tempted, as I often am for a moment, to wrench myself out of my position and get free, it is the feeling more than anything else that I may require my position to protect that work that encourages me to go on.'[29]

At this point Ilsley helped the elderly Ullathorne to gain the seclusion he so ardently sought by taking over a considerable portion of the work of the diocese, and when visiting the Bishop to consult him he must have been struck by the excellent facilities the buildings at Oscott offered in comparison with those at Olton. But in contrast to his own experience at St Bernard's, he must also have become increasingly aware that it was not possible for those dealing with the administration at Oscott to develop the training of the future priests of the Church in the way he himself considered it should be done, because of the lay influences that continued to exist there.[30] This must have been one of the main considerations that convinced Ilsley of his case, which later set him on the course he finally chose, back to Oscott.

He continued in the position of Rector at St Bernard's for the next four years. This may have been because Ullathorne saw Ilsley's situation of a bishop living with his students, as fulfilling the Tridentine ideal (even though this applied to the Ordinary at the time of Trent). Or possibly Ilsley had no wish to relinquish his control and pass it to anyone else just then – which would have been very much in keeping with the protective side of his character. But if these were some of the reasons, things did not work out as anticipated, because his increasingly heavy duties as auxiliary caused Ilsley to pass much of the day-to-day working of the seminary over to his Vice Rector, Henry Parkinson, especially as he found it necessary to live most of the time at Bishop's House, returning if possible at weekends to deal with affairs at St Bernard's. His absences from the seminary caused Canon Villiers, writing about Bishop Ullathorne later, to remark: 'We did not easily forgive him when he robbed us of our Father Rector who, elevated to the Episcopate, had other work to do, and for a great part of the year he was for us but a weekender and not always that.'

With Ilsley frequently away, things did not run as smoothly as before at St Bernard's, and Villiers wrote, 'The Vice-Rector did his best but he lacked the *savoir faire* of his superior and somehow or other things went wrong in the absence of Bishop Ilsley.' Some of the students attempted to reorganize their former system of self-government 'and some of us clamoured for written rules'. This caused discontent among them because the older students could see 'the changes were not for the better', and then the Rector took a hand, expressing his strong disapproval. Recalling the firm stand he made on this occasion, Villiers used the descriptive phrase 'the iron had entered his soul'.[31]

## Parkinson's Resignation

It may have been partly through this incident, that in October 1882 Parkinson recorded in his history of the seminary that he found it necessary to take three months' leave of absence 'on account of ill health'.[32] He was away at St Edmund's College until the New Year of 1883 and decided six months after his return he no longer wanted to continue as Vice Rector. This was also the recommendation of Dr Blunt, the local doctor who attended the staff and students at the seminary. So in July 1883 Canon Longman accepted his resignation on Bishop Ullathorne's behalf, and Father C. A. Wheatley, who had been one of the first students to come to St Bernard's in 1873, was appointed in his place.

A letter to Bishop Ullathorne from Parkinson of 8 July 1883, revealed there was some serious difference of opinion between himself and Ilsley at this time, but there is no indication as to the exact nature of the problem: 'On my return this morning Dr Parkinson placed the enclosed in my hands, saying at the same time he had no wish to enter into any explanations,' Ilsley wrote to Ullathorne the following day; 'Thus one difficulty I have been anticipating is obviated.' Parkinson, then aged 30, had been Vice Rector for five years, so he may have disagreed with Ilsley's earlier intervention over his management, and possibly considered he should have been appointed Rector by that time, rather than working on as Vice Rector for Ilsley, who was so often absent.

Whatever his reasons were, Parkinson said to Ullathorne in his letter: 'Things being as they are with the staff of the Seminary I believe it to be extremely desirable that a Professor should be secured to take my place here after this term – for, unless distinctly ordered by my Bishop to do so, I cannot remain any longer where I have experienced that an agreeable understanding with my Rector is impossible. Again I do not think a compromise is feasible. Yet I intensely regret leaving my present work, and cannot say I resign, – while under the present circumstances I feel I cannot stay.'[33] As it happened, Parkinson did not leave St Bernard's at this time. It was Ilsley instead who resigned his rectorship at the end of that term, and subsequently left St Bernard's for Bishop's House. A move that in retrospect would probably have been better all round had it been made two or three years earlier.

Parkinson remained on the staff for another four years until 1887, when he went to the cathedral parish as senior curate and choirmaster under Canon Greaney for two years. Frederick Keating described this period in Parkinson's life as 'a short break in his professional career'. He said 'it was characteristic of him that he "put off" the professor and "put on" the missioner with consummate ease ... he displayed extraordinary activity in every sphere of parochial work, in the pulpit, in the confessional, in the schools, in the organisation of Guilds, and visitation of his districts'.[34] Things appear to have improved between the two men six months after this considerable upset, when in January 1884 Ilsley was able to write to him, 'It is a relief to me to think that we are on better terms than we have been of late. I could not but be pained to observe that those amicable relations which bound us together formerly were passing away; but I have felt all along that the change was owing to causes over which we had little control. I am glad now that the strain is removed & that henceforth there need be no reserve between us.'[35] He suggests neither of them is entirely responsible for what happened and closes with, 'I am thankful to be able to say I have never once been tempted to esteem you less than in the happy days of our early acquaintance.'

The rift in their friendship seemed to have remedied itself at this point, and when in 1889 the seminary transferred to Oscott College, Parkinson agreed to work again as Ilsley's Vice Rector, and their association continued equably from that time onwards. Subsequent events in his life demonstrate that while Edward Ilsley was capable of giving great friendship and support, it was also in his make-up to take a hard line and adopt a dismissive attitude towards some people on certain occasions, should he consider circumstances made it necessary.[36] His own personal loss would have been considerable if he had broken with Parkinson over this troubled patch, so it was fortunate for him that matters righted themselves in time.

## Rules for St Bernard's

As for the written rules for St Bernard's that the students (and possibly Parkinson) were hankering after and which Ilsley had not allowed to be put forward previously, it would seem that both James McCave and Victor Schobel, and Bishop Ullathorne as well, saw the need of having them properly recorded. Particularly as Bishop Ullathorne wrote to Schobel on 28 August 1885, two years after Ilsley had left the seminary, 'I am keenly alive to the necessity of having a body of rules drawn up for St Bernard's, and urged the subject on Dr. McCave only last week. I shall be much obliged to you for any suggestions you may draw up and send me on the subject, the fuller the better.' Victor Schobel duly submitted a draft set before leaving in 1885, and Ullathorne again pressed for 'a written code' for the seminary on his last visitation in July 1886.

Victor Schobel was another member of staff who had become dissatisfied with the situation at St Bernard's, and he wrote quite strongly to Canon Estcourt letting him know how he felt about things early in July 1883, at the same time as Ilsley's upset with Parkinson: 'It is now ten years that I have been at work here, and though others seem quite satisfied with the result, my own experience, I fear, is anything but pleasant. Like my colleague Dr Parkinson I am physically worn out and morally disheartened. It seems to concern me as professor, when in constant effort of flying, my wings are cut off.'[37] It is significant that he coupled himself with Henry Parkinson over the troubles at that time, and he also appeared to be expressing frustrations over personal freedoms. It would appear that it might well have been Ilsley who had clipped Schobel's wings, and there is more than a hint expressed in both cases that Ilsley was not delegating sufficient authority to either of them, especially as this was his tendency throughout his episcopate.

A description of Schobel in *The Oscotian* in December 1915 mentions that 'though robust in build and appearance, his health after a few years of strenuous teaching began to suffer from excessive application', and he was 'troubled by his unrelenting enemy, acute headache'. So the troubles he was expressing at this time could have come about through an accumulation of circumstances.[38] His other complaint to Canon Escourt was that he did not have enough students to work with, and he pointed out that this particular problem stemmed from the fact that accommodation was too cramped at St Bernard's to allow for any substantial increase in the number of students, so their average was fewer than twenty. 'The result is', he wrote, 'that I cannot keep up my system of teaching effectively – of course I have always hoped for an improvement from year to year – but it has always ended in sore dis-appointment.'

The lack of space at St Bernard's had always been a major problem, because although the architect, Edward Hansom, had designed the seminary to have two main wings with a central tower, less than half his plan had been completed at the outset for financial reasons, and so the building had always been too small for diocesan needs. Henry Parkinson wrote in his history of the seminary that on 4 April 1883 'Dr Ullathorne dined here. He sat talking with the Professors ... he expressed a desire to go on with the building of the seminary.'[39] But unfortunately the advancing years had taken their toll of the old Bishop. His motives for not acting to ease the situation earlier are by no means clear, except that it would seem that his fear of overspending had always remained with him. But by this time he was far too ill to undertake any major changes likely to remedy the problem, and the situation was not helped by the fact that the church students at Oscott had always represented a larger rival group to those at St Bernard's. It can only be supposed that the Bishop had no wish to close the theo-logical department at St Mary's mainly through a feeling of kindness toward the president and staff. Or he may have been reluctant to begin to make any such move, bearing in mind that the original foundation of the college was for the clergy, and possibly he cherished a remote belief that this purpose might be one day be restored.[40] But if any of these thoughts were in his mind, he did not publicly express them.

## Ilsley resigns as Rector of the Seminary 1883

With things as they were at St Bernard's, and the precarious state of Bishop Ullathorne's health, it is hardly surprising that by the summer of 1883 Edward Ilsley decided the time had come for him to set aside the role of Rector of the seminary with all its attendant problems, in order to devote his time fully to his duties as auxiliary bishop. He chose to make this known on the feast of St Aloysius that summer when he concluded his after-dinner speech by suggesting he should now hand over to someone else: 'After ten years it might be better if someone else took up the burden,' he said, 'but of course that rests with the Bishop.' This permission was granted, and it was recorded in the history that, 'During the Midsummer Vacation of 1883 his Lordship Bishop Ilsley resigned his office of Rector and took up his residence at Bishop's House.' At this time he handed all his teaching over to Canon McCave, who was subsequently elected Rector in his place, with Dr Schobel taking over as Vice Rector.

## Notes

1 *Letters*, p. 251.
2 Butler, Letter from Bishop Ullathorne. He quotes this within the letter (Latin), 4 July 1879, vol. ii, p. 190.
3 B.A., B6597, Letter from Bishop Ullathorne to Canon Estcourt, 24 March 1879.
4 B.A., B6746, Letter from Edward Ilsley to Canon Estcourt, 17 July 1879. John Caswell became vice president of the college in 1885.
5 B.A., B6762, Bishop Ullathorne to the Sacred Congregation of Propaganda, 18 August 1879.
6 Butler, vol. i, p. 17. Also Norman, pp. 161–2.
7 Bernard Ward, *The Sequel to Catholic Emancipation*, London, Longmans, Green, 1915, vol. ii, p. 16. Also Bellenger, pp. 326–7.
8 B.A., B6762, Petition from Bishop Ullathorne to the Sacred Congregation of Propaganda, for an auxiliary bishop (Latin).
9 *The Birmingham Post*, 15 December 1879. Speech after Ilsley's consecration. Revd Morgan Sweeney, discussing sanctity and administrative ability, points out that 'The false separation of the two seems like asserting that faith will do without good works.' Beck, p. 131.
10 B.A., B6773, Letter from Bishop Ullathorne to Canon Estcourt, 13 September 1879.
11 Parkinson, ch. 6, 1879.
12 F.R., p. 5.

13  B.A., B6774, Letter from Ullathorne to Ilsley, 15 September 1879. These letters from Manning and Newman are not in the archives.

14  O.C.A., Letter from Edward Ilsley to John Caswell, 19 September 1879.

15  *Ibid.*, Olton Seminary scrapbook, newspaper cutting. The pectoral cross was commissioned by Canon Fenn on 21 October of that year and was made by Hardman's at the cost of £40. It was later worn by Archbishop Maurice Couve de Murville in the 1980s but was unfortunately stolen from Bishop's House in 1992. Letter from Fr Giles Goward, Archbishop's Secretary, 6 September 1999.

16  Butler, p. 264.

17  Philip Hughes, 'Bishops of the Century', in Beck, p. 192.

18  B.A., Diary of Joseph Parker, 1879.

19  J., 23 November 1879.

20  O.C.A., Olton Seminary scrapbook, newspaper cutting, *The Catholic Times*, 12 December 1879. Should correctly read as, 'the Holy See had elected him to the See of Fesse, as Auxiliary Bishop of Birmingham'.

21  B.A., Diary of Joseph Parker, 1879. The ring was presented to him by the duchess of Norfolk. His niece Cecilia Ilsley told me this.

22  Dr Hedley's text was taken from Ecclesiasticus 14.5. He was auxiliary bishop to Bishop Thomas Joseph Brown of Cardiff at this time, and later became Bishop of Newport and Menevia in 1881.

23  O.C.A., Olton Seminary scrapbook, press cutting. Over 150 sat down to 2 o'clock luncheon at the Grand Hotel. Also Joseph Parker, Diary, 4 December 1879: 'Including 92 priests and 5 bishops.'

24  Mary Roskell, *Francis Kerril Amherst, D.D.*, pp. 341–2.

25  Parkinson, '*Addendum* to Chapter the Fourth'.

26  Butler, vol. ii, pp. 190–1, 264.

27  *Ibid.*, vol. i, p. 233.

28  *Ibid.*, vol. i, p. 29.

29  Letters, p. 92, and Butler, vol. i, p. 233.

30  The presidents over this period were, Mgr John Hawksford, 1877–80, Mgr Edward Acton, 1880–4 and Mgr Joseph Souter, 1885–9.

31  F.R., p. 6. Ilsley was known among the later Oscott students as 'steel-jaw' when he took a strong line with them. A cousin, Sister Mary Joseph Ilsley, LSA, told me this.

32  Parkinson, ch. 6, 'Jottings of Seminary Life from 1873 to 1883'. Frederick Keating took his place while he went to St Edmund's, Ware.

33  B.A., B8224, Parkinson to Bishop Ullathorne, 8 July 1883, with accompanying letter from Ilsley, dated 9 July 1883.

34  *Oscotian* 24, pp. 161–2.

35  O.C.A., Ilsley to Parkinson, 13 January 1884.

36  This occurred with his treatment of Joseph Souter (Chapter 7), and John Hopwood (Chapter 15).

37  B.A., B8221, Letter from Victor Schobel to Canon Estcourt, 3 July 1883.

38   Schobel, p. 5. He suffered from migraine.
39   Parkinson, ch. 6, p. 50.
40   J.F.C., p. 2.

CHAPTER SIX

# *The Succession*

As the periods of Bishop Ullathorne's illness occurred more frequently, Ilsley's work as auxiliary became increasingly demanding. A letter from him to Bishop Ullathorne's secretary Father Parker, at Oscott College in the autumn of 1884, written at a time of particular concern because Ullathorne was ailing, gives a picture of Ilsley busily travelling out to parishes and convents, while at the same time dealing with urgent matters of the diocese when he returned to Bishop's House late in the day. He wrote, 'Thank God for the improvement that has taken place, thank you for the welcome news.'[1] One characteristic throughout Ilsley's life was his punctuality regarding his departures and arrivals, so that no time would be lost, and he was jokingly described as knowing 'his Bradshaw train time-table as well as his Breviary' in those days.[2]

In spite of his ever-increasing responsibilities, his hands could still accidentally be tied, and when he had to dispatch an urgent message from Bishop's House on one occasion, he had to tell Joseph Parker that he could not lay his hands on certain necessary papers, because 'All the Bishop's drawers are locked and your room also.' Never assuming direct authority in the old Bishop's absence, Ilsley still tried to follow his intentions as faithfully as possible, through close co-operation with Father Parker. This situation became particularly hard on Parker upon whom it fell to co-ordinate things, and he was in effect acting as secretary to both men and moving between the two. Even on Proclamation Day, a tradition introduced by McCave when he became Rector at Olton, when it happened that Bishop Ullathorne was too ill to attend at the end of July 1886, Ilsley still would not put himself forward unduly, and it is recorded that, 'His Lordship Bishop Ilsley said only a few words on his behalf, as the Bishop had not authorised him to occupy his place.'[3]

In September 1885, two years after Ilsley handed over the rectorship to McCave, things seemed to have reached an *impasse* at the seminary. Canon McCave was a man full of drive, and energy and Henry Parkinson said of him that his vocation was to lead and govern. He was an historian, and was described as 'one of the most powerful, learned and eloquent preachers in Birmingham'.[4] He was then aged 47, and from the time of his appointment had worked towards raising the status of St Bernard's to that of a quasi-central seminary, by drawing in students from Clifton and Portsmouth as well as the adjacent Midland dioceses, and expanding the programme of studies. But he was very much aware of the unsuitability of the building due to the inadequacy of the accommodation, particularly as the numbers of his students was increasing to the point where he had to turn down applications. Having reorganized all the available space, he managed to increase the intake from an average of about 20 up to 33.

## James McCave Wants Transfer to Oscott

But in September 1885, two years after his appointment, the tone of a letter that he wrote to Vincent Holcroft, then procurator at Oscott, shows his enthusiasm for a move back there, where his present schemes could come to full fruition. Talking of the numbers of students, he wrote to Holcroft, 'Everybody wonders where I put them. I have fresh applications but I have to decline them through lack of space.' The letter continues in a practical and common-sense vein, with McCave questioning the possibility of 'the laymen' at Oscott College being served with a notice to quit, and with St Bernard's then being used for the purposes of the lay school requirements of the diocese. 'I want Oscott Library, Chapel, Lecture-Rooms etc., to convert them into a Maynooth for the Midlands – I can get the students: and you must help me to their natural training ground, Oscott', he said. This last sentence alone sums up adequate reasons for vacating St Bernard's and returning to Oscott. Although the college library was later considerably enlarged, it already housed a unique collection of books and manuscripts, and the facilities there largely outweighed those afforded at Olton. The chapel was completed in 1837 by Augustus Welby Pugin, who designed a fine reredos above the high altar, and his arched stained-glass windows surrounding the sanctuary flooded it with light. Decorated with the characteristic Pugin colours of blue, red and gold throughout, this chapel must have made the much smaller one at St Bernard's seem very modest in comparison.[5]

Edward Acton, then president of Oscott, obviously had no private part in these discussions, nor apparently did Joseph Souter, who took his place the following January, 1886. So it would seem that the matter was being dealt with in a strictly confidential manner between a small circle of those concerned, particularly Henry Parkinson, who was still on the staff at St Bernard's, and John McIntyre, who was there between 1883 and 1885, and Canon James O'Hanlon, who had been a professor of theology at Oscott from 1872 until 1877 and was a lifelong friend of Ilsley's. Three years later, in the summer of 1889, when Bishop Ilsley announced that the lay school was to be moved out of Oscott, Souter expressed amazement that such things had even been considered, and in a letter to the parents of the lay pupils he announced that during the jubilee celebrations the previous summer 'I had not the faintest suspicion that we were on the eve of so important a change in the destinies of St Mary's.' It may have been partly due to McCave's opinions that Ilsley became thoroughly convinced of the advisability of transferring the seminary back to the far more commodious Oscott.

## Victor Schobel leaves St Bernard's

There appeared to be a continuing lack of fulfilment at St Bernard's during those later years, and Victor Schobel only worked in the position of Vice Rector with McCave for a further two years until the summer of 1885, after which time he was granted leave of absence by Bishop Ullathorne for a much-needed break from teaching which he spent abroad.[6] On returning from Bruges the following year he was invited by the Bishop to work at Oscott. He accepted the offer and 'he entered upon his new field of work with his accustomed spirit and adaptability, and soon endeared himself to his pupils by his thoroughness and sympathy'.[7]

The question of a possible transfer of the seminary at Olton back to Oscott was now obviously continuing to be privately discussed between the two ecclesiastical departments, but although Bishop Ullathorne made a final visitation to Olton in mid-July 1886, and even paid another brief call there in the late August of 1888, just six months before he died, Father Parker said later that he appeared to know nothing about these proposals at any time.[8] The old Bishop was cut off from St Bernard's and the rest of the diocese to a great extent, through his continuing ill-health, and this may well have contributed to the feeling of lack of progress prevailing among the staff there just then. But as he was actually living in Oscott College and had regular visits from Ilsley, it is unlikely that Ullathorne knew nothing of these future plans, particularly as his mind was absolutely clear right up to the end, though at this late stage he probably chose diplomatically to ignore much that was going on.

In August 1886 Cardinal Manning, replying to a letter from Canon McCave, assured him he had no real reason to be anxious over the state of things at Olton. McCave had complained about the considerable amount of financial and administrative work he was involved in and that at the end of term he had no word from the Bishop. This seems unfair towards Ullathorne as he had been unwell at the end of term on Proclamation Day, but had made a visitation only ten days earlier on 4 July. There were also rumours troubling McCave, but dismissing his concern regarding these, Manning suggested many of the present difficulties arose from, 'the silence of the Bishop . . . but he is as you say, not well'. He continued, 'As to the rumours, when and about what, are they not always on the wind? Do not regard them until they come *in concreto*', then you will know how to take hold of them.' He suggested that the patient attitude of Thomas Longman should be adopted at this time, 'My advice to you therefore is to do nothing: and wait for the V. General's by and by' and his final word was 'do not be anxious – it does no good, & only wears one to the bone'.[9] It is interesting to note that the Cardinal's precise and legible script retained its clarity right to the end of his life, and now in his eightieth year, he was still ready to write and give counsel to those who came to him and sought it. It is puzzling though why McCave should have been turning to Henry Manning with his problems at this time instead of approaching Ilsley who would surely have been in a far better position to help him to solve them – particularly in such a sensitive situation.

McCave was obviously a man who was very much concerned about his own rights. He sent his resignation as Rector of the seminary to Bishop Ullathorne on 27 May 1884, only nine months after his appointment to the position, because he objected to Edward Acton being given a stall before him. Ullathorne's proposal that he should be examined by Acton 'with the assistance of one or two others' as a candidate for Canon Theologian (which he judged higher than an ordinary canon) did not please him. It caused him to complain to Joseph Parker that 'coming after my work here the Bishop's speech was intolerable and insulting'. He informed Parker that he considered that as the Bishop seemed to have changed his policy over appointing the Rector of the seminary to a stall to be represented in the chapter, then 'the Rector must also be changed, & hence my resignation'. As it happened things settled down and McCave continued in the position of Rector for a further four years.

## McCave Resigns Rectorship

Then in July 1888, at the age of 50, having worked for five years at the seminary, he resigned his rectorship. The reason given for his resignation was poor health, but he continued to work with the same drive and energy for the following eleven years, dying in harness in 1899. On leaving St Bernard's he first took over the small mission of Abbot's Salford, where he was able to continue with his writing, and then in 1892 agreed to take charge of the Mission of St Augustine's in Solihull. In another two years, as well as continuing his writing, he became secretary to the Birmingham Catholic Schools Voluntary Association. His interest in the early Church in Britain led him to research the subject, and he later brought out a small publication entitled *Continuity or Collapse?*, which covered only a small portion of his copious work.

In his final months as Rector of St Bernard's, in spite of his previous enthusiasm for change, McCave was probably not prepared to deal with the sensitive issues involved in its transfer to Oscott and so thought it best to remove himself from the scene. Any further plans he had in mind at that time were brought to a halt, and the matter placed back into the hands of Edward Ilsley, who had become Bishop of the diocese four months earlier on 22 March.

The pressures of those years are revealed in a letter written by Ilsley to Henry Parkinson on 1 July 1886, explaining why he was not able to return to the seminary for the celebration of the silver jubilee of his priesthood: 'I do not altogether regret that the celebration has been of a quiet character – as you say it secures sincerity and a public affair hardly does. Not that I had any misgivings of that sort about the celebrations at St. Bernard's if it could have been held there – for at the last I shared the disappointment you all felt and expressed.' His dislike of unnecessary fuss and ostentation on public occasions was most marked if it in any way impinged on a church ceremony. Later, when he was Bishop of the diocese, he was asked to take part in the marriage ceremony of 'an ancient and noble house', and when he went to the church to make preparation, he was disconcerted to find twelve special thrones set up for members of the family, but nothing provided for himself. He suggested that either one more throne should be provided, making thirteen in all, or eleven removed, leaving one for himself. The hint was taken: 'one throne was left for the use of the bishop'.[10]

Ilsley's work was lightened at this time with the help of such staunch men as James O'Hanlon, with whom he had been a student at Oscott, and who became his vicar general in 1888.[11] Having been on the staff of Oscott for seven years, it must have worked in well for O'Hanlon to become Rector of St Bernard's for the following two years on McCave's retirement, until the seminary was transferred to Oscott in 1889. He would then have been in the right position to handle many of the immediate details concerning the changeover.

## Ullathorne Suffers a Stroke

In 1886, during the Low Week meeting of the hierarchy at Westminster, Bishop Ullathorne celebrated his eightieth birthday, and he received congratulations from far and wide. He was still deeply absorbed in his writing, but his health was a matter of increasing concern to those around him, and a few months later he was further weakened by a stroke on 30 April 1887, when Joseph Parker noted in his diary, 'First day of Bishop Ullathorne's attack of paralysis'.[12] As soon as he was sufficiently recovered, Ullathorne wrote to Rome that summer, and also to Cardinal Manning, pressing urgently to be released from office, saying that he now needed 'absolute repose free from responsibility'. He requested the Cardinal to second his petition to the Holy See, in order that 'my few remaining days may be relieved from the burden I can no longer carry, that this diocese may be provided with an efficient ruler'.[13] In his reply the following day, on 24 June, although sympathetic, Manning appeared only reluctantly to agree to his request, and even at this late stage, although he knew that Ullathorne was a very sick man, he added this postscript to his letter: 'I cannot forbear to add – why not rest as you are and give the reins to your good auxiliary bishop?'[14]

Manning knew that Ilsley had been guiding the diocese along more or less on his own for the past seven years, and so the postscript was merely echoing a vain hope that things might continue the same for a while longer. He may have made this suggestion with the thought that by attempting to persuade Ullathorne to delay his decision, should he die while still in office, the opportunity would then present itself for Manning to strongly influence the choice of the future bishop. But Ullathorne showed every determination not to be put off making a decision at this stage, and sought instead to settle things regarding his successor without any further delay, while time still allowed. A fortnight later, on 7 July, he wrote to Manning: 'Today I have mustered resolution to write my letter to the Prefect of Propaganda in which I have urged my petition for a speedy deliverance from responsibility.'[15] Manning finally acquiesced, and the following day he replied, 'Your bidding is enough. I will write to Propaganda and the Holy Father.' On 31 July an answer came from Rome saying that the Pope agreed to accept Bishop Ullathorne's resignation, with the proviso that 'you continue your administration till a successor be appointed'.[16]

Events then began to move swiftly to a decided conclusion for Edward Ilsley. Ullathorne first consulted his chapter over the choice of their future bishop. Among its members were James O'Hanlon, Joseph Souter, James McCave and J. Spencer Northcote, who was Provost. They then held a meeting to discuss the three candidates, at the Dominican convent, Stoke-on-Trent, in August 1887 under the presidency of Bishop Clifford.[17] The meeting probably took place there for the convenience of J. S. Northcote, who lived next door to the convent and whose health was failing. The distance chosen from Birmingham was also a diplomatic move, as the chapter were not only choosing a successor to Bishop Ullathorne, but his present auxiliary, Edward Ilsley was among the three names that were submitted for the bishopric. The other two were James Richmond, a Rosminian aged 45, also from the Birmingham diocese, who was working at Ratcliffe College of the Immaculate Conception, at Syston, Leicester, and Daniel Gilbert, aged 59, from the Diocese of Westminster, a Domestic Prelate to the Holy See. He was working at the mission of St Mary Moorfields in London. A glance through the letters of recommendation soon establishes Ilsley as the only real contender, and the decision at their *terna* was in favour of placing Edward Ilsley's name in first place followed by Daniel Gilbert. Delighted at this preference, Ullathorne announced enthusiastically, 'My Chapter has done a good day's work and I am proud of it.'[18]

## Unanimous Vote for Ilsley at Westminster

A month later Cardinal Manning held a meeting at Archbishop's House, Westminster, to discuss the three candidates, and Edward Ilsley was given a unanimous vote by the bishops. They then expressed a wish to add something to the previous submission regarding him which had been sent to Rome by Ullathorne when he had been put

Figure 6.1 *Cardinal Henry Edward Manning, Archbishop of Westminster (1865–92). Taken from a photograph in a private collection.*

forward as Auxiliary Bishop, and Manning's letter to Cardinal Simeoni gives an interesting profile of Ilsley, as he was assessed by the bishops at that time:[19] they praised the spiritual qualities he had fostered among his students when he was Rector of the seminary, and also acknowledged that he had always been well-accepted as Auxiliary Bishop by the majority of the clergy in the diocese. The letter continues: 'Although he is placid and gentle by nature, he nevertheless displays a determination and firmness of character. He is an excellent administrator and very skilled at this. Accordingly, by the unanimous judgement of my Colleagues, especially of the Bishop of Birmingham and my own, without reserve, he appears worthy to succeed to the vacant See.' Manning's letter was dispatched on 7 September 1887, but the official announcement from Rome concerning Ilsley's elevation was held over for a further six months into the following year, because of the celebrations being held for Pope Leo XIII's jubilee.

Throughout his time as Ullathorne's auxiliary, Ilsley's aim had been to shield the elderly Bishop from a great deal of the more arduous work of the diocese, and because he would have carried this out as unobtrusively as possible, some people probably underrated his capabilities, being quite unaware of the amount he had shouldered while

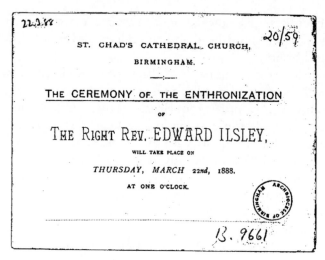

Figure 6.2 *A printed admission card for the enthronement of Bishop Ilsley. Birmingham Archdiocesan Archives.*

still dealing with his own many responsibilities. By his careful effort the extent of Ullathorne's illness was certainly generally not known, so that even as late as the July of 1887 the old Bishop was able to write to Manning: 'I am in fact a wreck and no longer capable of duty. But the fact is kept from the diocese where it is only known that I am ill.'[20]

At this stage of his life Ilsley considered himself in a position of unquestioning service to the older man, and therefore did not presume to act as a personality in his own right. Meanwhile the familiar image of the old Bishop, who appeared among them from time to time, was still preserved in many people's minds. Renowned for his early pioneering days in Australia, he was also still greatly revered for his reputation of assisting in carrying the Church in Britain through to its present position. He had also endeared himself to a great number over the years by his genuine and forthright manner, and was recognized generally as 'one of those rare spirits with a gift for ruling men'.[21]

There was also a considerable physical contrast between Ilsley and Ullathorne. Compared with William Ullathorne's colourful North Country dialect, Edward's cultured delivery may at times have appeared a trifle stilted and prosaic to the Midland ear.[22] But William Barry said his first impression of Ullathorne, seeing him at Sedgley Park, was that of 'a sturdy resolute figure', whereas Ilsley had the advantage of being an unusually tall man whose physically imposing appearance and personal dignity commanded unfailing respect. It was said he could always be picked out at a glance in any gathering or in a procession, as he stood head and shoulders above most of the other priests and bishops.

Some of those not in favour of Ilsley may have been prejudiced by the fact that because he had been born and educated in the diocese he might subsequently prove too closely connected with it, and they suspected this might cause his outlook to be narrow and parochial. On the other hand his familiarity with the diocese and those working in it was to prove to be a distinct advantage to him when he was in the enviable position of knowing his clergy really well, either because he had trained with them, or because they had passed through his hands at the seminary. Those near to him said he always appeared to carry out the responsibilities of his office prayerfully, as though very much aware of his need of divine direction. But Arthur Villiers saw past this very spiritual and unassuming side of Ilsley's nature to the point where he said that although he was 'habitually humble and naturally shy, he still possessed a quiet dignity which forbade familiarity and commanded respect ... Yet in spite of his ascetical demeanour he had the gift of human sympathy and could be all things to all men – though no-one ever dreamed of accusing him of undue partiality.'[23]

## A Message from Cardinal Newman

The Annual Catholic Reunion was held in the Birmingham Town Hall in the middle of January 1888.[24] It was expected that the official announcement of Ilsley's election would have been made from Rome by then, and the members had anticipated that they would be calling on Dr Ilsley as their new bishop to preside over the meeting. But under the existing circumstances he had to be requested to act as president merely as a 'stop-gap' as he later pointed out, while final decisions were being made. He consented to take the chair and for his address spoke eloquently and with feeling on 'The rescue work of homeless children', which had always been his particular concern, and was one of the most urgent and pressing needs of the time. His audience, which on this occasion was largely representative of the most influential Catholic opinion of the day, was obviously moved by his words, and when he finished an unexpected and quite dramatic succession of events took place. Father Thomas Pope of the Oratory stood up to second the vote of thanks to Dr Ilsley for his address, and he then followed this up by making the most unusual announcement, saying 'in clear and incisive tones', that he had brought a special message to that great meeting from his superior, Cardinal Newman: 'His Eminence', he said, 'considered that no more fitting successor could be found to Bishop Ullathorne than the Right Reverend President, Dr Ilsley, and he sincerely hoped that the Holy Father would soon appoint him as Bishop.'[25]

The Cardinal had taken this opportunity to publicly show his support for Ilsley, and the effect on the audience was quite spectacular, as the months of waiting seemed suddenly to fall away. At this point everyone in the hall spontaneously gave wholehearted testimony of the same feeling by 'springing to their feet and cheering with great enthusiasm for several minutes'. Ilsley rose to his feet in an endeavour to reply, but the cheering was renewed, demonstrating that the gathering was in complete agreement with the great man's message and giving proof of the feeling of the majority in favour of Ilsley becoming their next bishop. When at last the hall quietened so that he could speak and be heard, he 'thanked priests and people for their remarkable proof of goodwill, expressing the deepest gratitude to the great Cardinal for his message of confidence and esteem; but for himself, he left the matter entirely in the hands of Divine Providence'. Pope Leo's nomination of Ilsley was made on 17 February, just two weeks after this extraordinary occasion, and when the official announcement came through, Bishop Ullathorne seemed filled with an unbounded feeling of relief. 'The Brief appointing Bishop Ilsley came inside a letter to me on Sunday last,' he wrote. 'So I am a free man and the binding straps have all flown away.'[26]

One of the first to hear about the appointment was Cardinal Newman. There is an interesting letter written to him from Ilsley on 19 March as soon as he received confirmation of the appointment: 'Late last night on my return from Tamworth I found on my table the Brief of the Holy Father appointing me successor to Dr Ullathorne in the See of Birmingham. Knowing the kind interest your Eminence has taken in the matter of this appointment I feel it to be my duty to send you the earliest intimation hereof. Coming as it does on Passion Sunday is rather ominous – yet it would be cowardly to be afraid of what comes with the sign of the cross upon it. I trust however I may count upon your sympathy and prayers.'[27] Cardinal Newman's reply is dated the same day; he addressed Ilsley, 'My dear Bishop of Birmingham,' and continues, 'Your Lordship's letter is as kind as it is welcome to me. I trust to say Mass for you on Thursday. Excuse my bad writing. Your Lordship's faithful and affectte. servant J. H. Card. Newman.'[28]

At this stage no time was wasted, and arrangements were concluded for the enthronement to take place in St Chad's Cathedral on 22 March. Newspaper accounts at last revealed the truth of the whole situation regarding the precarious state of the old Bishop's health and the difficult months leading up to this time. It was reported that Bishop Ullathorne was unable to leave his room in Oscott College to attend the ceremony in that 'trying weather', because he was 'stricken with the infirmities of old age'.[29] The Provost, Dr Northcote, was also unable to be present, so Canon O'Sullivan, who was the senior canon, was appointed to conduct the ceremony.

## Bishop of Birmingham 1888

In chapter 5 of *A History of St Chad's Cathedral*, entitled 'Bishop Ilsley' and written by Father Francis de Capitain, it is recorded that 'The function, shorn of the consecration ceremony, was less brilliant than usual, but the church was crowded to overflowing.'[30] We are also told that 'Today's proceedings were in order that he might receive the acknowledgement and submission of the canons and formally take possession of the diocese.' One hundred and fifty priests of the diocese were present, and most of the chapter also assisted at the impressive ceremonial. Bishop Ilsley was met at the entrance to the cathedral by the canons, and he went in procession under the canopy, arrayed in full episcopal vestments, with cope and mitre, and carrying the crozier, to the Lady Chapel. 'From there he was escorted to the high altar where he formally received the homage of the canons' and he was then finally conducted to the throne.[31] Edward Ilsley might have found no truer message on that day of his enthronement than the one contained in the essay, 'Ornaments of a Bishop', written by his old superior, Bishop Ullathorne: 'It is true that the mitre of glory is lined with thorns and with all the solitude of pastoral care. The crosier is rich with ornaments, but it is given to us at our consecration to remind us of our infirmities and the need of support, whilst we correct and chasten the faults of others.'[32]

Three days before the ceremony Bishop Ullathorne wrote to Ilsley in his old inimitable style, addressing him for the first time, 'My dear Lord,' but hastening to add in his direct Yorkshire manner, 'I never congratulated a man on being raised to episcopal dignity,' and then with a flash of his old humour and kindness, 'but I congratulate myself on having you as my successor and I congratulate the Diocese. I also take the opportunity to thank you for your faithful service as well as founding St. Bernard's Seminary whilst acting as my auxiliary.'[33] This was indeed a gracious message from a man who had acted towards Ilsley not only as a superior but also as a kind and amiable benefactor.

In the months following Ilsley's enthronement William Ullathorne seemed to gather up enough strength to enable him to make a final round of farewell visits to his friends and the much-favoured convents he had always looked after, but by the end of the summer he was back in his rooms at Oscott rarely to emerge again, and here, remarkably enough, he continued to write his letters and revise his autobiography, right up to the month before he died.

Edward's mother Mary Ilsley died that October at the age of eighty-four, so she had the joy of knowing that her son had become Bishop of Birmingham. She had outlived her husband Charles by nine years and left their home in Stafford two years after he died to be cared for by her granddaughter Alice in Wednesfield in Wolverhampton.

## Deaths of Ullathorne, Newman and Manning

Within the following three years, the deaths of three of the most influential Catholic men of their time – namely William Ullathorne, John Henry Newman and Henry Manning – were to bring to a close a period of forty years which was for the Church a time of rapidly accelerating change, and the coming of Archbishop Herbert Vaughan to Westminster marked the beginning of a new epoch.

William Ullathorne died the following spring, on 21 March 1889, just one year after Edward Ilsley had become his successor. In his letter notifying Cardinal Simeoni of his death, Ilsley described Bishop Ullathorne as a man 'strong in vindicating the rights of the Church'.[34] He celebrated the Solemn *Requiem* Mass in St Chad's Cathedral for this remarkable man who had ordained him in the same cathedral, and later consecrated him as his auxiliary bishop there, and who had always given him such kindly guidance over the years.

At the end of the funeral service in St Chad's the cortège travelled some 32 miles to the Dominican priory church at Stone in Staffordshire, where it arrived at about eight in the evening accompanied by a large number of people from the district carrying torches, who had met the hearse about a mile along the road. The coffin was received by Canon Bathurst, and it was taken in procession into the church and laid on a catafalque before the high altar. The Dominican Sisters, having recited the Solemn Office for the Dead, watched and prayed throughout the night. The following day High Mass was sung

Figure 6.3 *Edward Ilsley, Bishop of Birmingham (1888). Taken from a photograph in Oscott College Archives.*

by Mgr Souter assisted by Joseph Parker as Deacon and Canon Bathurst as Subdeacon. He then performed the ordinary funeral service and the body was buried in a vault in the south transept of the church, in a simple bricked grave. Among those present at the ceremony were Bishop Edmund Knight attended by John Caswell, and the Revd Fathers Bernard Ward, John Stringfellow, James Massam, Frederick Crewe and William Sutherland.[35]

Toward the end of the same year, in October, Cardinal Newman was found unconscious in his room, having struck his head heavily in a fall. Father Pope went next day to inform Ilsley what had happened, and Ilsley insisted on returning with him immediately to the Oratory. When he came into the room, 'the old Cardinal sat up in bed and asked the Bishop for his blessing, and when the Bishop made the sign of the cross over him in the usual way he said, "No I don't mean that, begin at the *Adjutorium nostrum*"', and then he bowed down his head while the Bishop gave him the pontifical blessing. It must have been a touching sight and Dr Ilsley was quite overcome.'[36]

He later asked those in the house to keep him closely informed about the Cardinal's condition. There is a letter from Father Pope, written to him the same evening: 'Wednesday night. There is no material change in the Cardinal's state and now we must see what the morning will bring us. I should add that I think you saw him at the worst. He has been much better since.' Another letter was dispatched to him the following morning: 'More grounds for hope, but not out of danger. The only disease is exhaustion ... while it lasts it is a permanent peril of death.'[37]

The Cardinal recovered in the following weeks, and although he appeared more frail than before, he continued quietly on for a further two years into his ninetieth year, but was then suddenly taken ill with pneumonia on Monday 11 August 1890, and Ilsley returned from a holiday to be with him. 'There were no last words. John Henry Newman went out of this world as quickly and quietly as he went in and out of the rooms in it, surprising people who expected formality.'[38] On hearing the news of the Cardinal's death William Barry said it was 'as if my bright particular star had vanished out of the firmament'. The following Sunday Bishop Ilsley preached in St Chad's Cathedral about the Cardinal's life and work. Referring to the lessons to be drawn from Newman's example, he appropriately took for his text, 'The Lord went before them to show them the way, by day in a pillar of cloud, and by night in a pillar of fire, that he might be the guide of their journey at both times.'[39]

The funeral was held on 19 August at the Birmingham Oratory, and Bishop Ilsley sang the Pontifical *Requiem*. The side walls and those around the high altar were sombrely draped in black crepe hung with gold fringes, and many distinguished people from far and wide attended the service. Unlike most cardinals, whose remains are placed in a cathedral tomb, by Newman's expressed command he was to be buried with his friend Ambrose St John, in the same simple grave, with a plain headstone in the form of a cross. This is in the little graveyard on the side of the hill, near the Oratory House at Rednal, on the outskirts of Birmingham. He composed for his epitaph the brief and simple words, *ex umbris et imaginibus in veritatem*, meaning 'From shadows and images to the truth'. They are to be found inscribed on a memorial tablet on the wall of the cloister in the Oratory Church.

It fell to Cardinal Manning to give the address at the memorial Mass in London at Brompton Oratory, a task not easy for him as his route in the Church had in many ways not led in the same direction as that of Newman. However, he was said to have delivered his words with 'equal generosity and skill', saying, 'The history of our land will hereafter recall the name of John Henry Newman among the greatest of our people, as a confessor for the faith, a great teacher of men, a preacher of justice, of piety and compassion.'[40]

## Ilsley Officiates at Manning's Funeral

There was a genuine sense of loss among the ordinary people when Archbishop Manning, 'the people's Cardinal', died seventeen months' later on 14 January 1892. His popularity with the working man reached its zenith when he mediated on behalf of the London dockers and helped to resolve their strike for higher wages and fairer conditions in 1889. The solemn *Requiem*, which took place at Brompton Oratory, was celebrated by Bishop Clifford. Afterwards when the procession made its way through the London streets in a dismal fog for four miles to the cemetery, there had never been such a mass demonstration of the people's feelings shown on the London streets before, and the crowds lining the route were so dense in places that the traffic was brought to a halt, and the police had to struggle to force their way through, for the cortège to proceed on its way.[41]

Bishop Ilsley officiated at the service held at the graveside, and a description of the scene is taken up by the Cardinal's biographer, Edmund Purcell: 'The final Rites of the funeral at the grave were performed by the Bishop of Birmingham ... In the dim twilight of the January day, the tapers making darkness visible, the plaintive chanting of the *"Miserere"* faintly heard amid moans, ejaculations and prayers of the dark masses which filled the Catholic Cemetery at Kensal Green, all that was mortal of Cardinal Manning, "Earth to earth", was reverently lowered into the silent grave.'[42] The following June Ilsley arranged for letters to be sent out to notify all the clergy in the Province of Westminster that it had been decided, as Manning's primary attachment was to the poor, a fitting memorial to him would be in the form of 'a refuge to the destitute, to be placed in the East End of London'.[43]

## Notes

1 B.A., B8561, Edward Ilsley to Joseph Parker, 3 October 1884.
2 D.B., p. 21.
3 Parkinson, ch. 6, 'The Rectorship of the Very Rev Canon James McCave'.
4 Obituary, *The Tablet*, Saturday 14 October 1899. James McCave took his doctorate in theology in 1862. While Rector at Bilston he set up a library in the town, and when he was transferred to Kidderminster between 1871 and 1877, he wrote a history of the town.
5 B.A., B8919, James McCave to Vincent Holcroft, 25 September 1885. Judith Champ gives a description of the chapel in her *Oscott*, p. 9. The room which was originally the chapel at Olton now serves as the present library and conference room. Approximately 46 feet in length by 24 feet wide, it is upstairs, above what was then the seminary refectory. The altar stood in the window recess surrounded by four large Gothic-type windows. Undoubtedly the main feature of the room, which has great dignity, is the beautiful vaulted ceiling finished in dark wood. Taken from a description by Revd T. Sheridan, SCJ, in a letter dated 14 July 1999.
6 Schobel, pp. 5, 6.
7 *Ibid.*, pp. 6, 7. Frederick W. Keating took over as Vice Rector at St Bernard's under James O'Hanlon in 1887, and Edward B. Hymers then continued in the post between 1888 and 1889, at which time the seminary was transferred to Oscott.
8 Butler, vol. ii, p. 187.
9 B.A., B9247, Letter from Cardinal Manning to Canon McCave, 30 August 1886.
10 *The Tablet*, Saturday 11 December 1926.
11 O'Hanlon became Provost in 1905, on Northcote's retirement. He was headmaster of St Chad's Grammar School in 1868 and in 1872 was nominated to the chair of theology at Oscott. Others were: John

McIntyre, later Ilsley's secretary; Henry Parkinson who became Rector of Oscott; and members of the chapter, such as Frederick Keating and Charles Cronin, to name but a few.

12  Thomson, p. 27. Also Father Joseph Parker's diary, 30 April 1887.

13  Butler, vol. ii, pp. 280–1.

14  *Ibid.*, p. 281, reply from Cardinal Manning, 24 June 1887.

15  *Ibid.*, p. 281, Letter from Bishop Ullathorne to Cardinal Manning, 7 July 1887.

16  *Ibid.*, p. 180, Letter from Cardinal Simeoni, 31 July 1887.

17  Thomson, p. 27. Cardinal Manning, now in his seventy-ninth year, did not travel to such meetings at any great distance from London, and so the senior suffragan, Bishop Clifford, presided.

18  D.B., p. 11. Also, details of the candidates according to *Acta S. Cong. de Prop. Fide*, 1888, vol. 258, f. 37, A. 1888, no. 3.

19  Sent by Cardinal Manning to Cardinal Simeoni, Prefect to the Sacred Congregation of the Propagation of the Faith, 7 September 1887 (Latin). The bishops at that meeting were those of Birmingham, Clifton, Liverpool, Menevia and Newport, Nottingham and Southwark.

20  Butler, vol. ii, p. 281.

21  Beck, pp. 74–5.

22  Toplass, p. 131.

23  F.R., pp. 8, 9.

24  D.B. p. 11. Revd Patrick O'Toole reported this in later years. The meeting was described in *The Birmingham Post*, Tuesday 17 January 1888.

25  D.B., p.11.

26  *Letters*, p. 159. Bishop Ullathorne now became the titular Archbishop of Cabasa.

27  Birmingham Oratory Archives. Letter from Bishop Ilsley to Cardinal Newman, 19 March 1888. Ilsley wrote to Cardinal Simeoni on 21 March 1888 accepting his appointment. Archives of *Propaganda Fide*, *Scritture Riferite nei Congressi*, *Anglia*, vol. 27.

28  John Henry Newman, *The Letters and Diaries of John Henry Newman*, vol. xxxi, p. 247.

29  B.A., press-cutting, scrapbooks.

30  *St Chad's*, p. 62.

31  B.A., press-cutting. 'Afterwards the Bishop entertained the clergy, the Mayor & many of the laity, to luncheon in St. Chad's Schools.'

32  Glancey, *The Ornaments of a Bishop*, p.14.

33  B.A. B9651. From Bishop Ullathorne to Bishop Ilsley, 19 March 1888.

34  Butler, vol. ii, p. 293, 22 March 1889 (Latin), to Cardinal Simeoni, Prefect of the Congregation for the Propagation of the Faith, Rome.

35  *The Tablet*, Saturday 6 April 1889: 'Archbishop Ullathorne, the interment at St. Dominic's Priory, Stone'.

36  Meriol Trevor, *Newman: Light in Winter*, p. 637.
37  B.A., Letters from Father Pope to Bishop Ilsley, dated 31 October and 1 November 1888.
38  Meriol Trevor, *Light in Winter*, p. 645.
39  Barry, p.188. Also *The Catholic News*, Saturday 23 August 1890. The text was from Exodus 13. In 1832 Newman wrote a poem called 'The Pillar and the Cloud' using this text. This was later sung as the hymn: 'Lead kindly light, amid the encircling gloom, Lead thou me on!'
40  Gray, pp. 315–16. Cf. pp. 67–8.
41  Gray, pp. 1–3. The Duke of Clarence's funeral on the same day was eclipsed by this event.
42  Edmund Sheridan Purcell, *The Life of Cardinal Manning Archbishop of Westminster*, 1896, vol. ii, ch. 24, p. 184. The body of Archbishop Manning was later translated to Westminster Cathedral.
43  B.A., B10726, 3 June 1892. Donations were to be sent either to Bishop Ilsley or to the Duke of Norfolk.

## CHAPTER SEVEN

# The Closure of St Bernard's

## First Pastoral Letter

Bishop Ilsley issued his first pastoral letter on Easter Sunday, the week following his enthronement.[1] In his message to his people he expressed a feeling of great responsibility for the care of all those souls now entrusted to him and, taking the opportunity to thank Bishop Ullathorne for the good inheritance he had passed on, he paid tribute to him for the 'immense work' he had accomplished during his administration. In the concluding passages of his letter he gave more than a hint of what was in his mind regarding the future of St Bernard's, of Oscott College and of St Wilfrid's,[2] when he said that the care of such establishments spurred him on to greater diligence, 'lest the happy fruits of so much industry and sacrifice should begin to fail'. By this statement he was indicating that the questions regarding the seminary, the college and the school now needed his immediate attention.

The problems facing him were certainly not straightforward, the main difficulties weighing largely on the side of Olton Seminary. The building in its present form was proving too small for its purpose because the second stage in the design had not been carried out as planned, so it had never come to function on the scale originally envisaged by Bishop Ullathorne and his architect. Meanwhile, Oscott College continued to maintain its clerical department, and the two establishments were interdependent in many ways, sharing ordination ceremonies, retreats and lectures, and there was also an exchange of staff from time to time, or an occasional transfer of students between the two. This situation was unsatisfactory because it imposed a heavy drain on diocesan resources, and the original idea of separate education for the ecclesiastical students could not altogether be achieved in the diocese while Oscott still functioned with mixed lay students and divines so closely mingling.[3]

When he established St Bernard's, Bishop Ullathorne probably intended leaving things arranged this way only as a temporary measure, having no wish to disturb the ecclesiastical department in the college, which was working satisfactorily at that time. He may have delayed partly from a feeling of sensitivity towards the department at St Mary's, and financial considerations were also involved at the beginning. He nevertheless said at his golden jubilee in 1874, a year after his seminary was founded, that it was his fervent hope that it would become 'a centre of light to the whole diocese'.[4] But eight years later the situation remained the same, and in his speech made on the feast of St Aloysius in 1882 he even went so far as saying that 'he rejoiced that Oscott had a large class of divines, even larger than that of the Seminary'. He then followed up this statement by saying that 'The Seminary was to ultimately absorb all the ecclesiastical teaching of the diocese,' presumably meaning that the department at Oscott College would finally be closed. Henry Parkinson also recorded in his history of St Bernard's, that on the annual feast day in 1883 the old Bishop said he 'would consequently have to act in order to carry out his intention. He seriously contemplated the extension of the building.' Such statements constantly posed St Bernard's as a distant threat to the department at Oscott, where the divines were used as a necessary supplement to the teaching staff in order to keep the fees at a low rate. This arrangement alone may have presented an appreciable reason in Ullathorne's mind for not hurrying things along, and as time went by he appeared to be finding no will to shift the divines from the ecclesiastical department.

There is no doubt that a far more suitable building could have been completed had the will been there, but as the years moved on no move was made in this direction. The question remains as to why Ullathorne did not complete his plan for the seminary when the opportunity was there, and the need for the building to be enlarged was so obvious, particularly as he would have been able to pass all the details over to Ilsley at that time. It would seem that either he had grave doubts about finally moving the ecclesiastical department out of Oscott, or he may simply have always assumed that Ilsley would carry the work forward for him in future years. But by 1883, after ten years at St Bernard's, Ilsley was about to give up the rectorship, and James McCave who took his place favoured a return to Oscott. So the great end wall of the seminary building still has the keystones in place, waiting for the extension that was to remain only a vague vision in the old Bishop's mind as some future undertaking, instead of ever becoming a reality for him.

## Chosen Course back to Oscott

Some might argue that a wrong turn was taken by Bishop Ilsley in 1889, by not putting into motion the idea of completing the seminary, by doubling its size according to the original plan. In this way he could have left Oscott College intact as a public school. But as far as he was concerned there was no doubt in his mind as to which course to take, and it was fortunate that an ecclesiastical department still remained in Oscott College, because this meant the door was conveniently left open, and the way paved for him to make the return to St Mary's. This was the move he chose to make – a move which might not have been so easily achieved had the ecclesiastical department not still been functioning there.

Bishop Ullathorne's death, occurring a year after Ilsley became Bishop of Birmingham, seemed to bring with it the closing of a chapter, during which time the Catholic Church had emerged from the uncertain times of the emancipation, and moved forward through the restoration of its hierarchy, to become the rapidly growing Roman Church of the day. It was against this developing background that Ilsley grasped the nettle firmly and brought about the necessary changes which had been lingering as such a vexed question over the past years. By taking certain positive and decisive measures, he was to be responsible for taking Oscott College a stage further in its development.

His close association with both establishments meant he was at the heart of the matter, and as soon as he was appointed Bishop, discussions took place to decide what steps should be taken toward some satisfactory solution to the problems involved. The final outcome was that in April 1889, just one month after Bishop Ullathorne died, 'the project of the transference of Olton Seminary to St Mary's College, Oscott was first made known at a meeting held at Olton'.[5] Although the new Bishop had felt compelled to start putting things in motion even before the old Bishop died, Dom Cuthbert Butler, who was by no means in sympathy with Bishop Ilsley's policy in this matter, did however write significantly with this assurance regarding Bishop Ullathorne, 'The one who knew him most intimately at the end of his life, his devoted secretary Rev Joseph Parker, assures me that he had no knowledge of the closing of his seminary.'[6] Certainly, right up to the end of his life, Bishop Ullathorne appeared to consider St Bernard's as the future establishment for ecclesiastical training in the diocese, but his lack of decision over the completion of the project might well be taken as an indication that he was by no means entirely convinced as to how to bring this about, especially if it meant altering the status of Oscott in any way.

## Ilsley's Views Differ from Manning's

Cardinal Manning was Archbishop of Westminster when Ilsley became Bishop of the diocese. Through his interpretation of what had been laid down by the Council of Trent, he was notably in favour of small localized diocesan seminaries such as St Bernard's.[7] But Bishop Ilsley took a different view. His own practical experience made him aware of the drawbacks inherent in the present system, which was costly to maintain, and made uniform standards of ecclesiastical education between the dioceses difficult to achieve. He knew he had within his reach the potential of the large 'central' seminary inherent in Oscott, in which he could bring together a staff of the necessary calibre, and introduce a system of working suited to the training of a well-educated clergy, throughout the Midlands and beyond.

When speaking about the merits of separate education Bishop Ullathorne acknowledged that a lot had been achieved by the earlier priests 'with but a few advantages of training, while the present generation has special advantages – separation from the lay element and professors whose sole duty was the intellectual and spiritual training of the students'.[8] There was obviously in Ilsley's mind a determination that, added to these advantages, sooner or later 'Oscott would function as a seminary for all the dioceses of the Midlands,' because, apart from all the other benefits that would accrue, he said, 'it would thus be financially viable'.[9]

In his proposed reorganization of administration within the diocese, Ilsley was subscribing to a broader concept currently shared among a number of other bishops. They believed that their ideas transcended Manning's, whose outlook, they considered, unavoidably reflected the views of the Anglican converts, and that he therefore had no innate understanding where English Catholicism was concerned.[10] They believed it was still within the provisions of the Council of Trent to consider a small country such as Britain as one whole district which could then be served by one central seminary on the same principles that had held good for the great college of Douai for three hundred years.[11] They proposed that under this system their students would attend one large centre, and some would then complete their training in Rome. The moves Ilsley was now making pointed to the fact that he

Figure 7.1 Canon James O'Hanlon, the rector of St Bernard's with a group of students in 1888. Drawing made from a photograph in Oscott College Archives.

was looking ahead in the direction towards this type of centralization. His originality of thought and forward-planning at this time earned him the reputation, in retrospect, as being 'one of the best organisers and administrators among the Roman Catholic Bishops in England'.[12]

The transfer of Olton Seminary to St Mary's College was primarily dealt with by Ilsley and his chapter with the sanction of the Holy See, and the whole business was completed in a few short weeks during the summer of 1889, four months after Bishop Ullathorne's death which occurred at the end of March. Ilsley had in fact taken hold of his first opportunity to make this move with the least disturbance to both establishments, by carrying it out at the end of the academic year when the students were away for the holiday.

## Positive Action over Transfer

Having been Bishop of the diocese for just over a year, he was now making his actions seen in a very positive manner over the transfer of St Bernard's to Oscott. He could of course have delayed this move and engaged in lengthy consultations. But by taking such a decisive step so early in his episcopate he was able to come forward out of the shadow of his predecessor William Ullathorne, where he had been for the last ten years, and clearly reveal himself as a man prepared to make far-reaching decisions in his own right.

By closing down St Bernard's he was also making a first decided move against Manning's policy regarding seminaries. The significance of his action may not have been fully appreciated at the time, but by moving back to Oscott he must have felt he was now in command of his own seminary, instead of retaining St Bernard's, which had always been of particular interest to the Cardinal as one of the first important examples of his idea for small separate establishments.

There was of course another issue of paramount importance which needed to be resolved at the same time, namely the position of the lay school at present housed within the college. From the layman's point of view, 'the policy of converting Oscott into an exclusively clerical college seemed to offer, to many, room for legitimate difference of opinion. St. Mary's College had attained a unique position among the Catholic colleges.' They claimed that 'the great men that governed the college had given it distinct status. Oscott was the centre of religious life and culture not for one diocese alone, but for the whole kingdom. It touched the Oxford Movement, the Mediaeval Movement, and the development of the Irish Church. Lacordaire who visited it in 1852, said it was more like a palace than a college. Weedall, Wiseman and Northcote by their high principles, culture and scholarship had impressed their own strongly marked individuality on it, and crowning all, Newman's sermon "The Second Spring'', preached in the College Chapel at the First Synod, had shed an imperishable lustre upon Oscott.'[13]

These arguments were in some ways true. R. H. Kiernan, writing the history of the college sixty years later, when reflecting on all that had taken place within its walls, said of Oscott: 'but what is more important is that this College became a dynamo driving Catholic energy through the Midlands and beyond'.[14] But for Ilsley the time had come to act, and what is more he seemed in no mind to negotiate the future of the lay school. The only conference the school authority appears to have been drawn into on the subject was when an invitation was issued to Monsignor Joseph Henry Souter, the president of the college, to attend a meeting of the cathedral chapter to be held at Bishop's House on 18 June, just one month before the end of term. By the time this was arranged, all the main decisions had already been arrived at, and he was presented with a *fait accompli*, the principal subject for discussion on this occasion being 'The closing of Oscott College as a lay college'.[15] At this meeting it was made clear that the dual system of education must come to an end, and it was decided to close the lay school in favour of making Oscott the diocesan seminary, whole and entire.

## Joseph Souter

The manner in which these important decisions were taken regarding the fate of the lay school, with no prior warning to Joseph Souter, seems particularly unfair to him. He had served the diocese well over the years, having always been placed in responsible positions in charge of schools and colleges, and he surely merited better consideration.[16] The reason for this seeming lack of courtesy and consideration toward such a senior priest by Ilsley as his Ordinary might have been because, knowing that Souter was against the thought of any change, Ilsley felt that unless he acted quickly and decisively in the matter, once the facts became known, the weight of opinion marshalled against him could possibly have delayed or even prevented him from carrying out what he had in mind, particularly as far as such an influential man as Monsignor Souter was concerned. Another reason could have been that Ilsley considered that in his position of Bishop of the diocese he needed only to notify Souter of his intentions and not engage in any further discussion concerning the merits of the case. Either *modus operandi* would have fitted in with Ilsley's disposition and his determination to see things through over this matter.

Dr Schobel wrote a letter to Ilsley from Oscott College on 18 June, the day that Joseph Souter attended the chapter meeting.[17] Written in his rather colourful style, his opinion was that more time should be given both in thought and prayer before any action was taken concerning moving St Bernard's back to Oscott, 'in order that light may be given to you', and he advised Ilsley that he should take at least a year to prepare his move: 'Two points come very vividly before me,' he wrote, 'I mean two great obstacles against the plan of making Oscott the Seminary at present. The first is that closing the lay school just now with still 60 students and no debts and the President unwilling and a large section of sympathisers, might raise a quite unnecessary storm against your Lordship, and it would not be improved by the fact that also Olton is suddenly closed as a Seminary. Secondly the Seminary at Olton is just now weak and a sudden amalgamation with 18 Oscotian Divines (with strong anti-seminaritical animosities) would be a little risky.'

Having worked with Joseph Souter for the past two years Schobel's letter was probably written as much in sympathy with him as for any other reason, and it is unlikely that Ilsley would have welcomed Schobel's cautioning attitude at this crucial time. But there was certainly much truth in what he had to say, for the Bishop and his staff were to meet with just such challenges as he predicted, particularly Henry Parkinson in his position of the new Vice Rector. Victor Schobel was at the hub of the situation at this time, in charge of the divines at Oscott and working closely with Joseph Souter. He would therefore be sensing all the pressures that had arisen in that highly charged situation and for this reason he was moved to write in this vein. He warned Ilsley of what might well occur if the students from St Bernard's linked up with the existing ones at the college, and Canon Edward Godwin later described what actually did happen: 'The lay boys had gone, but the advanced church students remained. Therein lay the peculiar difficulty, to be met chiefly by the Vice-Rector. He had to strive to blend into one, two widely differing spirits; that of the divines at Oscott, under the old regime, and that of the seminarists from Olton. The former had enjoyed a much greater measure of liberty than the latter, and in the process of curtailing those liberties and bringing the Oscott divines into line with the stricter seminary discipline, the Vice-Rector had to suffer many unpleasant experiences.'[18]

Godwin would not reveal the exact nature of the difficulties that Parkinson encountered, but apparently by the time the Westminster students were transferred to Oscott in 1893, he began to feel himself to be in a position of being disliked generally, particularly as they bore the added resentment of being wrested from their own diocese. But he was wrong. Apparently although many of them grumbled about his strict discipline, there was a great deal about him that they liked and respected, and they soon came to appreciate their new situation. As for Victor Schobel, in spite of his apparent holding back at the very moment when everything he had previously found so unsatisfactory was about to be changed, he was later to prove himself in the years ahead to be passionately determined that the Central Seminary should be brought into being, and had a great deal to do with its successful formation.

## A Well-Thought-Out Document

Two days after the chapter meeting had taken place, Joseph Souter received a letter from Bishop Ilsley underlining his reasons for taking these decisions.[19] The letter is outstanding as a well-thought-out document, and it shows the Bishop knew very clearly what he had in mind at the time for the future development of the college, and at the same time it gives his clear, indisputable reasons for the actions he was about to take. In the first rough draft of this letter it can be seen that among the carefully chosen words others have been thoughtfully substituted here and there, or a fresh phrase added. It was as though he was carefully weighing the meaning of every passage, being fully aware both of its immediate importance and of its historic significance. It is explicit and uncompromising, but at the same time it does contain certain elements of sympathy and understanding. It begins: 'During the last few months various circumstances have combined to direct my attention to the subject of our aspirants to the priesthood. As the matter affects the College over which you preside it is my duty to make known to you the conclusion at which I have arrived'. He then went on to quite rightly point out the difficulties involved which had always existed in the maintenance and upkeep of the two schools of theology, one at Olton and the other at Oscott: 'Of late the anomaly of maintaining a double staff and two bodies of students has been only more apparent and the conviction has been forced upon me that, sooner or later, the unification of the two schools was inevitable. When therefore it became necessary to choose between the two, the advantage was manifestly on the side of Oscott, and Oscott has been selected as the permanent home of the diocesan Seminary.'

Certainly St Bernard's did not bear any comparison with the palatial Oscott, so wonderfully described by Newman in his sermon 'The Second Spring' as, 'a large edifice, or rather a pile of edifices ... with many fronts and courts, and long cloisters and corridors, and story upon story'. No further additions to the small seminary at Olton, such as had been considered earlier by Bishop Ullathorne, would have remedied the matter so satisfactorily, because Oscott College was unique in its advantages; hence the choice had been made.[20] It would also seem that Bishop Ilsley had more than a diocesan seminary in mind when he added: 'It was founded, as you know, primarily for the purpose of educating priests for the Central District.' He was, in this instance, actually taking his argument back to the historical past, and the origins of St Mary's College when it was housed in the building known as 'Oscott House', which had been rebuilt in 1753; and although his claim regarding these times, chronicled in the early annals of Oscott, may not have exactly matched his present circumstances, it was nevertheless correct in essence.[21]

## The Lay College Must Go

His letter went on to say that, although it was true the college also served for the education of the laymen, the double purpose had only been approved by the Holy See temporarily, until such a time as separate establishments for the laity and the clergy had been created. The time had now come for this to be put in motion. The Bishop continued: 'The mind of the Church is clear. She will have aspirants to the priesthood provided with such an education and training in a congenial atmosphere and such surroundings as afford a reasonable hope that they will come forth, not merely possessing the requisite technical knowledge, but thoroughly imbued with the priestly spirit and fully equipped for their work.' He was pointing out that the Church now demanded the best possible opportunity to be provided for the training of her future priests, 'hence she will not tolerate the existence of a lay college within the walls of a seminary'. Here the tables had been sharply turned by the Bishop – the seminary did not happen to be housed within the walls of the lay college but vice versa – therefore the lay college must go.

He was willing to go no further in this case, and obviously saw no good reason to rehouse the lay college, or to embark on the foundation of another public school at this time. His final word was dismissive on that score – the lay students could easily find accommodation elsewhere – 'especially in a country like this where colleges abound'. His attitude could not be judged unreasonable, as educational opportunities for Catholics had increased in recent years, and the choice was there, without any special help needed from him. Now was not the time for the distraction of transferring and setting up a public school elsewhere, involving added expense and the attendant difficulties with staffing. James McCave had envisaged the rehousing of 'the laymen' at St Bernard's at one time, but no further mention was made of this, and the idea had obviously been set aside.[22] The selling-off of St Bernard's had probably been dictated by the need to cover the costs of the move to Oscott anyway, in order to set the college on a sound financial footing for the future. Besides all these considerations, Ilsley may well have had in mind his care of Cotton College and its future development, in order to accommodate the growing needs of the diocese.

Rarely, if ever again, did he speak of his personal feelings in quite the same way as on this occasion when he stated that, 'my duty to the diocese, and loyal obedience to the dictates of the Church in the discharge of that duty, must outweigh every other consideration. And it is this sense of duty alone that has nerved me for this painful task of closing to the laity the doors of my own *Alma Mater* and erasing from the roll of Catholic colleges one which can boast such a glorious record of useful service, and one whose history, extending over well nigh a century, is bound up with such distinguished and honoured names in every profession and sphere of life.' The letter concluded on a note of regret that 'this decision will, I fear cause you serious disappointment, and give pain to your excellent body of clergy and students.' But at the same time such a decision had not been brought about 'without mature deliberation and consultation with the Cathedral Chapter and other friends of the college'.

Every aspect of the move was handled with a calm sense of resolution and conviction on Ilsley's part. It must not be forgotten that he had been a student at the college for eight years, from the age of 15 to 23, and so had first-hand experience of the drawbacks of the present system of mixed lay and church students, and he therefore had a clear vision of the benefits this changeover would bring with it.

## The Cathedral Chapter

The cathedral chapter at that time consisted of J. Spencer Northcote, who was Provost, John Hawksford and Edward Acton, all three having been former presidents of Oscott, also the Vicar General, James O'Hanlon, who was later described as having served the Bishop 'as his right hand'.[23] The other canons, Thomas Longman, James McCave, Michael O'Sullivan, Henry Davies, Stuart Bathurst and Thomas Ducket, were all old members of the college as church students – Canons O'Hanlon and McCave having both been rectors of St Bernard's at one time as well. All these men may not have been in absolute wholehearted agreement with the Bishop's scheme because they shared among them some poignant memories of the lay college. But at the same time they were familiar with the present difficulties involved and must have recognized this was the opportunity to solve them, particularly McCave and O'Hanlon, who must have readily welcomed the transfer. As members of his chapter the majority of them would have given him their ready support, and their endorsement of his decisions would in turn lay a strong seal on his actions. The friends of the college he mentioned would have been former students, or members of the Oscotian Society, or leading Catholics, such as Edwin de Lisle, the MP for Mid-Leicestershire, who, when speaking publicly at the college jubilee celebrations, hinted at his interest in the college becoming the diocesan seminary again in future years. His speech was described at the time as being 'cordial, but a little hard to Mgr. Souter'.[24]

As President of the college Monsignor Souter, then a considerably experienced man of 61, was justifiably very bitter about what was happening so suddenly and unexpectedly to the lay school, and he was not prepared to comply gracefully with the Bishop's new plans. On receiving Ilsley's letter on 21 June, he first read it to the clergy in the *Receptorium* at 9am, and then to the whole college in the Northcote Hall. He finally read out a letter that he was proposing to send to the parents and friends of the college, and there is no attempt in it to defend what was about to happen. On the contrary, they were all about to bear the brunt of the drastic changes that were soon going to take place, so he felt it his duty to lay the whole matter clearly before the parents and students, and it is written very much from his own standpoint. He said that the following term the college would be open only to the ecclesiastical students, and that naturally nothing else remained for him to do under the circumstances but to tender his resignation immediately. He also hastened to explain that the college had never been on a sounder footing financially, or academically, and that no internal condition contributed to the change 'which so many deplore'.[25]

The letter from Monsignor Souter, with copies of Bishop Ilsley's letter enclosed, were both sent out the following day. The college diary for the remainder of that day speaks for itself: 'No work done for the rest of the day – the saddest day in the college record.'[26] According to a rather favourable account written fifty years later by Canon Toplass, the students behaved admirably over the closure. He says: 'There seems however, to have been a complete absence of rancour and on the whole they duly submitted to the will of God as manifested by the mouth of the Bishop. The manly and uncomplaining spirit of resignation was highly recommended by the Bishop in a letter to the President before their final departure.'[27] This letter makes sad reading. It begins, 'I cannot let you disperse without saying a parting word. It would be unfeeling as well as ungracious on such an occasion ... I cannot say "farewell" to the boys without expressing my admiration of the way they have borne themselves under the very trying circumstances of the last four weeks ...' In the final passage he attempted to offer some small compensation for what had taken place. Though kindly enough meant, his words seemed to convey a lack of feeling towards the lay boys who had been forced to leave the college under what must have been for many of them, rather sad circumstances. He said 'Let me assure them that if at any time they desire to visit the college, and so recall the memories and revive the impression of their college days they will be heartily welcome.'[28]

The blow was in no way softened for Joseph Souter by this final message either,[29] and although it would seem, as far as diocesan provision was concerned, that the most obvious destination for any of these boys needing to complete their education should have been Cotton College, where he was previously President, there is no evidence either in the school registers, or in the annals, of any of them going there from Oscott. Arrangements were made instead for fifteen of them to go *en masse* to St Augustine's College, at Ramsgate, which was in the Southwark diocese. This may have been as a result of Souter's disapproval of what was happening at the time, or possibly simply through a lack of accommodation at Cotton.[30]

## William Barry's 'Fall of Oscott'

Monsignor Souter next sent an open letter to *The Tablet*, together with the letter he had received from Bishop Ilsley, and the two were published on 29 June under the uncompromising title, 'The Fall of Oscott'. William Barry, whose sympathies were with Joseph Souter at this time, wrote an article which was published the following week in *The Tablet*, entitled 'The Record of Oscott'. It was a catalogue of the college's triumphs and traditions over the years, voicing deep regret at its passing. Barry was to confess 36 years later, in 1925, when writing his book, *Memories and Opinions*, that the words 'Fall of Oscott', 'still echoes my feeling'. Giving his argument in favour of the retention of the dual system, he offered his own personal reasons in retrospect: 'I was helped on my path by Oscotian comrades who never thought of becoming priests. The loss of such a meeting-place for English and Irish Catholic youth has proved unspeakably great; I shall mourn it while I live.'[31]

The published letters and Barry's article stimulated considerable correspondence during the following weeks, from those standing either for or against the changeover. These appeared in the principal Catholic journals and newspapers, and the differences of opinion on the matter were to range far and wide. Objections were raised that St Bernard's Seminary, so very much cherished by Bishop Ullathorne, should come to be disestablished immediately after his death, especially when a considerable sum of money amounting to £2,200 had been generously donated by the clergy specifically towards its foundation. Others deeply regretted the changes that St Mary's College was about to undergo. There were of course also many who entirely supported the Bishop, seeing the value of his changes for the years to come, and the editor of *The Tablet*, John Snead-Cox was one of those who took a sympathetic attitude towards the Bishop's action. On presenting Barry's article, he dismissed the general tone of regret by countering: 'There must now be a looking forward as well as a looking back: the closing of one chapter in the story of Oscott means only the beginning of another, and possibly of a wider and truer usefulness.'[32] Herbert Vaughan, then the Bishop of Salford, approved of Ilsley's move. He expressed his opinions through *The Tablet*, which he had owned since 1868. J. Snead-Cox, who was his cousin, was the editor from 1884 until 1920.

Once the President's letters were sent out, the news of what was about to happen to Oscott College soon spread further, and although the course that was about to be taken by Bishop Ilsley seemed right to some, the thought of the fate of the lay school must have been quite shocking and unthinkable to others. However, a letter written to Monsignor Souter by Charles Welman, JP, on 27 June 1889, a week after the news of the changeover broke, only indicates fond memories and regret, and at the same time there is an acceptance of the new policy as a whole. His name is listed among the 'nobility and titled' students in the Oscott jubilee edition. He and his five brothers had attended St Mary's College during the 1850s and 1860s, and he must have expressed the feelings of many others at this time: 'I cannot hear the news about dear old Oscott without writing at once to tell you how sorry I am to learn it. You will have very many to sympathise with you, and I for one, who will feel in addition their regret that the Oscott they knew and loved should be of the past, have very keen sympathy with you personally in the trying position in which you are placed.' In spite of all this sadness there is a ray of light in the letter. It comes just at the end and projects hope for the future, as it concludes: 'May the Oscott of the future, however, long be preserved and give many holy priests to the Church.'[33]

## College Jubilee 1888

The situation was exacerbated by the fact that only a year earlier, in July 1888, the golden jubilee of St Mary's College had been celebrated amidst great rejoicing, with Bishop Ilsley as one of the principal guests of honour, and Bishops Bagshawe, Knight, Clifford and Bryan were also present. 'It had been hoped that Cardinal Manning would be there, but Old Hall were keeping their centenary the same day, and Cardinal Newman excused himself on the grounds of ill-health.' As no mention was made of Bishop Ullathorne it is doubtful whether he made an appearance at the gathering that day. It was on this memorable occasion that the president of the college, Canon Joseph Souter, was created Domestic Prelate by Pope Leo XIII, and he also accepted a gift of £1,000 from the Oscotian Society on behalf of the college, which cleared the college's debt to them. He clearly had no idea at the time what the following year was about to bring.[34]

The Oscotian Society, which was composed of many influential past students, voiced its opinion loudly against the closure of the lay school. Justifiably disconcerted by the unwelcome train of events brought about by Ilsley's policy, they even raised the question among its members as to whether they should now disband and discontinue their support of the college altogether. Members were balloted to this effect, but the Society weathered the storm and continued its existence as a body, although it was now represented by noticeably fewer lay members.[35]

Ilsley must have found himself in a 'cleft stick' at the time of the jubilee celebrations, needing to retain complete secrecy regarding his future plans as far as Souter and most of his staff were concerned, while at the same time being carried along with the momentum of all the celebratory events. He must have known by then what was in his mind regarding the wide-ranging changes he would implement within the year, and would have recognized that those changes were to bring to a sudden end so much that was being rejoiced about at that time. At the luncheon on the third day he was called upon to propose the toast of the president 'remarking that the principles which Mgr. Souter had enunciated that day had the true ring about them', and finding himself forced to conclude by using the unlikely words: 'Long might he live to preside over the destinies of the College'.[36] It is of course possible that Ilsley may have considered that Joseph Souter could be persuaded to agree with his plans the following year, in which case this speech was a diplomatic move to help win him over.

With opposition to his policy very apparent in some quarters, Ilsley must have been gratified to receive unquestioning and positive support from where it mattered most, with the neighbouring bishops of Northampton and Shrewsbury. He had wasted no time in contacting them about his revised schema, and Bishop Arthur Riddell of Northampton replied at the end of August: 'I am very pleased you have decided to make Oscott a thorough seminary ... I write with satisfaction that the ecclesiastical students of the other dioceses may be admitted.' Edmund Knight, the Bishop of Shrewsbury wrote: 'I have been studying your proposed Constitution with the greatest interest and am much impressed with the careful and practical way in which its provisions are made.'[37]

## Seminary Buildings Sold

The college term had now ended, and the pace of things continued to go swiftly ahead toward the time Ilsley aptly termed 'The closing chapter'. The seminary estate and buildings were sold to the Capuchin Fathers, and during the summer vacation some forty van loads of furniture and books from St Bernard's were transported to Oscott. Dr Clayton supervised the packing-up at Olton, and Vincent Holcroft received the goods as best he could at Oscott, while Joseph Parker superintended the general organization by overseeing the arranging of the house and chapel furniture and installing some of the books in the library.[38] In a letter to Joseph Parker, sent by Ilsley from Bishop's House on 9 September, he mentions his staff returning to the college and needing time to settle in to the new situation: 'Dr Schobel will turn up I hope, towards Thursday or Friday & Dr Parkinson too – But the latter will want a day or two to arrange the things in his own room. We must assign the rooms for the students by Friday as well as for the professors.'

For some time the front cloister and St Michael's and St Gabriel's dormitories were piled high, and made almost impassable, with books and furniture of all kinds, most of which were gradually and almost imperceptibly absorbed into the vastness of the rooms and halls of the college. So the first part of Ilsley's vision of the changeover was completed, and history has since proved him justified in the development of Oscott in the years that followed.

By the unusually forthright manner he employed at times during the handling of this issue it would seem that Ilsley consciously sought to use the situation as a way of making his mark on the diocese, wishing at the same time to prove himself to be his own man, particularly *vis-à-vis* Manning, whose policy regarding small seminaries he was clearly discarding. By pursuing this particular course he must have known he would raise a great deal of controversy, but because he saw his vision as right for Oscott he had no hesitation in seeing it through.

## Notes

1  B.A., Bishop Ilsley, Pastoral Letter, 28 March 1888.
2  His old school, Sedgley Park, had moved out to Cotton Hall, Oakamoor, North Staffordshire, in 1873. Although first known as 'New Sedgley Park School', this was dropped in favour of 'St Wilfrid's, Cotton Hall', and the name 'Cotton College' was also frequently used.
3  The Fourth Provincial Council of 1873 had called for church students to be taught philosophy and theology apart from lay pupils.
4  Parkinson, ch. 6, 12 March 1874.
5  *Ibid.*, ch. 7, 'The Rectorship of Canon O'Hanlon, V. G.'.
6  Butler, vol. ii, p. 187. Abbot Butler frequently consulted Joseph Parker when he was writing his biography of Bishop Ullathorne.
7  Beck, p. 36.
8  Parkinson, ch. 6, 'Jottings from Seminary Life from 1873 to 1883'.
9  J.F.C., p. 18. Also, Canon McCave had already started to draw in

students from the four adjacent dioceses when he was Rector of St Bernard's.

10  Beck, *Diocesan Organisation and Administration*, pp. 128–9. Wiseman had supported Manning's election in the anticipation that he would be the most suitable man to lead in the expected influx of Anglican converts. This ultimately did not materialize.

11  McCormack, p. 266, and Snead-Cox, vol. ii, pp. 41–2. Herbert Vaughan, the Bishop of Salford, was strongly of this opinion.

12  Obituary, Archbishop Ilsley, *The Times*, 2 December 1926.

13  Jean-Baptiste Lacordaire, a French Dominican, was described by Canon T. B. Scannell, in the *Catholic Encyclopaedia*, as the greatest pulpit orator of the nineteenth century. He visited Oscott when he was 50. See also D.B., p.13.

14  Kiernan, pt I, p. 22.

15  Thomson, p. 30.

16  *The Oscotian*, 12, (Christmas 1911). He was the first headmaster of St Chad's Grammar School, which he founded in 1858. When appointed President to Sedgley Park, he straightway transferred it to Cotton in 1873. He remained there till 1885, when he was appointed President of Oscott. He was appointed Domestic Prelate by Pope Leo XIII in recognition of his service to the college in its jubilee year of 1888.

17  B.A., B10068, Letter from Victor Schobel to Bishop Ilsley, 18 June 1889.

18  *Oscotian* 24, Canon Edward Godwin, 'Monsignor Parkinson, Vice-Rector of Oscott', pp. 163–4.

19  O.C.A., Letter from Bishop Ilsley to J. H. Souter, 20 June 1889.

20  J.F.C., p. 14. Many major improvements had been undertaken at Oscott during the presidency of James Spencer Northcote in the 1860s in the way of a lecture theatre, swimming pool and gymnasium. In his sermon 'The Second Spring', John Henry Newman describes Oscott as being 'story upon story'. Present-day British spelling is 'storey'.

21  *Ibid.*, p. 2. The elements of its earliest history were possibly unknown to most by this time. The whole of Oscott House Estate was left in 1702 in perpetuity to the Vicar Apostolic for the purpose of supplying priests to help the poor. The original benefactor, Andrew Bromwich, used the words 'for the maintenance of a secular priest', with Oscott House 'as the chief place of his residence'. What he may have envisaged as to any future development in this respect remains a moot point. See Bernard Kelly, *Historical Notes on English Catholic Missions*, p. 806. Also *Birmingham Faces and Places*, 'St Mary's Seminary, Oscott', 1 January 1890.

22  B.A., B8919, Letter from James McCave to Vincent Holcroft, 25 September 1885.

23  B.A., Myerscough, p. 163.

24  Thomson, p. 28. Attention should be drawn here to one noticeable incident that occurred that may also have raised some enquiring

eyebrows at the time: When toasts were given at the Oscotian Society dinner which was held on 28 July 1888 as part of the jubilee celebration of St Mary's College, Mr Edwin de Lisle MP proposed Monsignor Souter's health with some extraordinarily prophetic words, expressing the hope that, 'one day the College would resume its high place among the Seminaries of England which it held under the presidency of Dr Northcote'. This could of course have been a mere *lapsus linguae*, but it rather prompts the question: Did this indicate that future policies were being fairly widely discussed behind closed doors even at this stage?

Also: Thomson, pp. 30, 31, and the account in *The Birmingham Daily Post*, 29 July 1888.

25 Thompson, p. 30.

26 O.C.A., College Diary, 21 June 1889.

27 Toplass, p. 132. An article brought out for the centenary of the college in 1938.

28 *The Tablet*, Saturday 27 July 1889.

29 *The Oscotian* (Christmas 1911). In his obituary it was said of him that 'the very suddenness of the blow prevented him from seeing that, however glorious had been the past, the future would and must be more glorious'. Also, 'In spite of the sorrow he always felt at this unexpected move, he was always absolutely loyal to his Bishop.' He was first stationed at Kenilworth and then Leamington, where he later died in 1909 at the age of 82.

30 Abbot Parry, *Scholastic Century*: This unusual transfer may have been partly due to the influence of Father Jerome Vaughan (brother of Cardinal Vaughan), who was contemplating joining the Ramsgate community at that time, and had achieved 'a surge of success' in St Augustine's College. Some of the boys may have gone to the Oratory school near Birmingham, as the immediate intake increased there.

31 Barry, p. 197.

32 *The Tablet*, Saturday 6 July 1889.

33 O.C.A., Letter from Charles Welman, JP, to Monsignor J. H. Souter.

34 Thomson, p. 29. Revd John Henry Thomson recorded all these events in his *History of Oscott College*, which was inserted in serial form in *The Oscotian*.

35 O.C.A., Uncatalogued letters of July 1889.

36 *The Birmingham Daily Post*, 28 July 1888.

37 B.A., B10111, B10112.

38 Parkinson, ch. 7: 'amongst other things, the best furniture in the students' rooms is from St. Bernard's, some of the most beautiful vestments, and about six thousand volumes, the greater part of which are now in the library of the Common Room'. Also Annals, 1889.

CHAPTER EIGHT

# A Return to Oscott

There is a letter from Bishop's House written by Edward Ilsley to Joseph Parker on 30 August 1889, just after the changeover had been made. He does not mention the upheaval that has just taken place, but his mood is rather that everything is calm again, and ready to go steadily ahead: 'I will go over to Oscott tomorrow, please God, by the 3.5 train which reaches Erdington at 3.20 – I want to be quiet for a day or two – and I can say Mass for the household on Sunday and Monday morning. Probably you can find a boy in the neighbourhood who knows how to serve Mass.'[1] He goes on to say that they will then make an opportunity to discuss Father Parker's new appointment, as his work of acting as Bishop Ullathorne's secretary had now finally come to an end.[2]

Events in the months that followed are again outlined by Canon Edward Godwin, who was a student of Oscott College under the new regime from 1890 to 1897. He described what happened after Monsignor Souter and his vice president, John Caswell, resigned: 'The Bishop of the Diocese undertook the responsible task of Rector and brought with him from the Cathedral Parish Dr Parkinson as his Vice-Rector.'[3]

## College Staff – Holcroft, Schobel, Hopwood and Ward

Ilsley selected three members of the previous college staff to work with him: Vincent Holcroft, who had always staunchly supported the idea of the changeover and was previously procurator, Victor Schobel, and John Hopwood. He also brought in Bernard Ward, who was the son of William George Ward. Dr Schobel, who had filled the post of professor of theology for the past two years, now became prefect of studies, taking dogmatic theology and Hebrew. John Hopwood had worked there for two years as professor of theology and he now took church history, sacred eloquence and music, and Dr Bernard Ward, physical science and liturgy. Ward came to the college in 1880 and was ordained there in 1882. A man of considerable acumen, he began a new mission at Willesden in North London in 1886 and then went to teach at Oscott in 1889 when he was 32. He only remained a year with Ilsley, when he was appointed Vice President of St Edmund's in 1890, becoming the fifteenth president there in 1893. In 1917 he was consecrated Bishop of the newly formed diocese of Brentford. Ilsley also appointed James O'Leary onto his staff at this time to take moral theology and canon law, and John McIntyre took over as bishop's secretary and also worked on the staff teaching sacred Scripture, but was non-resident, as he was working much of the time at Bishop's House.

Canon Godwin gives an account of how things progressed initially: 'A new era was beginning for the famous college, and critical eyes watched the early stages of the innovation. A heavy and anxious responsibility rested upon the shoulders of the two chief rulers of Oscott.' He went on to describe the difficulties of merging the seminarians from St Bernard's with the divines at Oscott. Many of the divines had not taken kindly to the change, having always had far more liberal treatment in the past than the students at St Bernard's. This was largely due to the fact that they were used as teachers in the dual system and so were on a social footing with the staff, taking their meals with them and sharing certain duties.[4] They were also used to mingling freely with the lay boys, taking part in their recreational activities. The students from St Bernard's were of course far more acquiescent. Godwin continues: 'All honour to Dr Parkinson that he was able, out of those two divergent spirits, to create a new one which we all came to recognise as the spirit of the seminary of Oscott.'

During his inaugural address to the students at the beginning of term in September, Ilsley stressed the importance of the spirit of seminary life – 'the object for which they had all been brought together'. In his customary manner of appearing unwilling to receive any acclaim for what he had achieved, he made the point 'that the change in the place had not been brought about by any one man, but by the overwhelming force of circumstances which pointed to its necessity'.[5] It is doubtful whether he managed successfully to cloak the fact that he had just played the principal role in what had occurred as it must still have been a major topic of conversation among the students at the time.

The final chapter in Henry Parkinson's *History of St. Bernard's* gives

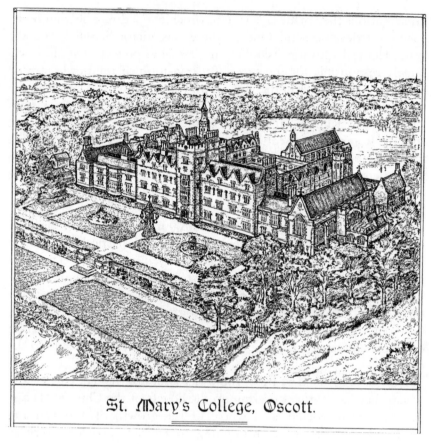

St. Mary's College, Oscott.

Figure 8.1 *A view of Oscott College, c. 1880, taken from an engraving by Hall and English. Oscott College Archives.*

no hint whatsoever of any regret or doubt about what had taken place over the departure from Olton. On the contrary in the final passages he conveys a message for future loyalty to Bishop Ilsley and his chapter. His exhortation is as follows: 'Students should ever remember that the ample provision of every kind which they find at Oscott is due to the advice of the Venerable Chapter of Birmingham and to the courage and foresight of the present Bishop of Birmingham. *Floreat Oscotia! Floreant Oscotiani!*'

## Victor Schobel and Henry Parkinson – Their Contribution

Many have played a prominent part in making the history of Oscott College, but two men should be particularly remembered for the contributions they made at this time which had a direct bearing on its successful development. One of these was Victor Schobel, and the other Henry Parkinson. Schobel, in his role as prefect of studies, was largely responsible for the successful transition of the newly formed seminary. He later led the way in the formation of Oscott as the Central Seminary, which enhanced its position and influence within the Catholic Church in Britain, while at the same time looking towards Rome as its essential guide. His influence was reflected in the general improvement in the standard of ecclesiastical education which embodied the most forward-looking advances of the Church taking place in Britain and on the Continent.

This partly came about because as a student he had the good fortune to attend the lectures of Bernard Jungmann, a very brilliant professor of philosophy and theology at the ecclesiastical seminary in Bruges at that time. 'To him it was mainly due that the custom of regular scholastic disputations and *casus morales* became one of the traditions of the seminary' – a practice which was maintained for over forty years. He introduced a wider programme of studies extending over a period of six years, and 'in his own lectures he gave a generation of Oscotians some of the best theological formation available in the country'.

He was very much aware of the wider issues of the day, particularly where they had a direct bearing on the beliefs of the Church. He saw the dangers to society as a whole of the growth of Marxism and Modernism, which were threatening to envelop people's everyday lives. In his opinion there was a need for the Church to make a stand against them, particularly through a clear interpretation of the Scriptures 'while distancing itself from any of its presuppositions that were dangerous to the Faith'.[6]

His talent also lay in music. When he was President of the Cecilian Society he was responsible for the introduction of harmonized singing into church music. It is largely through his use of polyphony in his musical arrangements for the college choir that the development of that aspect of the liturgy can be traced in those days.[7]

Henry Parkinson was another who left his mark on Oscott for all time. From the time of the re-establishment of the college the success of the new undertaking began to be apparent, and this was due to a great extent to his influence. He devoted his next 35 years to every side of college life, until he died at the age of 72 in 1924. He had been constantly associated with the seminary since his earliest days, arriving as a student at St Bernard's in 1873, and leaving for only a brief spell to

Figure 8.2 *Mgr Henry Parkinson, Vice Rector of Oscott College (1889–97), Rector (1897–1924). Oscott College albums.*

serve in the cathedral parish from 1887 to 1889, at which time Ilsley appointed him as his vice rector at Oscott. Under his personal guidance 'by the beginning of the present century Oscott was well established as a centre of Catholic learning'.[8] It was his concept of priestly training and self-discipline, coupled with 'his enormous capacity for hard work', that built the foundations of the modern Oscott.[9] He was noted for his meticulous care over the liturgy and his great devotion to the development of church music, and his dedication to Latin as the ever-living language of the Church was another of his commitments throughout his life. Monsignor Francis Ross, writing about him later in some reminiscences of his student days at Oscott, said, 'I often noted a small trait which filled me with awe ... the Rector never said his grace without previously doing that which we associate with the Last Supper: *"Elevatis oculis in Caelum"*. That and many other instances of the same kind made one realise the two dominant features of his piety: a profound reverence for the presence of God, with the accompanying sense that every moment of the day had its duty to be fulfilled.'[10]

It was in spite of his devotion to the college that 'to many it seemed a marvel that in the midst of his duties carefully or even punctiliously performed in connection with Oscott, he found time for other interests involving much writing and speaking'.[11] Social science filled what was probably the most interesting part of his life, particularly in his capacity as the first president of the Catholic Social Guild, which came into being via the Catholic Truth Society, through the work of his close friend Charles Plater, the Oxford Jesuit. Henry Parkinson was a principal founder of the Guild in 1909 and was a very active member. He regularly attended executive committee meetings in many parts of the country till the summer of 1919, by which time his health was failing.

In this sphere of his activities much that he was engaged in was not directly connected with his life immediately within the Church. He stepped outside this when his work came more broadly within the realms of purely socialist concepts such as those of the Fabian Society, 'and it is from members of the society that we get accounts of Mgr Parkinson's kindliness and human concern'. The people who encountered him in those days admired him as much as his priestly colleagues and for the same reasons – his hard work, his devotion to duty, his attention to detail and his ability to cope with a great deal of material clearly and concisely.[12] J. M. Cleary in his history of the Social Guild observed, 'Two forces lay behind his interest in social studies: compassion for the workers arising from his years as curate in the Birmingham slums, and his strict Roman sense of obedience to Papal directives.'[13]

In 1912 Parkinson wrote an informative introduction to the Catholic Truth Society publication *The Pope and the People*. This was a book of select letters and addresses on social questions by Popes Leo XIII, Pius X, Benedict XV and Pius XI, which was originally published in 1902. A year later, in 1913, he brought out *A Primer of Social Science*, a booklet explaining the general principles underlying social reform, in which he explained 'the precise object of the science and its abiding interest is the material, intellectual and religious well-being of each and all as members of society'. Throughout this aspect of his work, Pope Leo's social encyclicals were his inspiration and his guide. As professor of philosophy, he watched over both the spiritual and academic sides of seminary life, keeping pace with modern developments, and through extensive reading, he gained first-hand knowledge of the work of Darwin, Huxley, Tyndal and others. He also studied biology and physiology at Mason's College, from which the University of Birmingham sprang.[14]

## Ilsley's First Diocesan Synod

The academic year had already begun at St Mary's when Bishop Ilsley chose his first diocesan synod, held on 16 October 1889, to outline the new policy he had effected. It had probably originally been thought by many sitting at that meeting that the new bishop, having worked so closely with his predecessor for the last ten years, would now be steering a steady course, keeping in line with whatever had gone before, and appropriately enough, he opened his address by stating that he was completely in accordance with what had been established by Bishop Ullathorne regarding church law. He said 'his venerated predecessor had formed a body of law so complete that little was left for further legislation, and it was his duty to enforce those decrees as necessity arose.'[15] Then taking his theme from Pope Leo's recent encyclical, *Exeunte jam Anno*, in which the Holy Father had given a warning concerning the decline of Christianity in the world, Bishop Ilsley conveyed his concern for this subject of 'vast and vital importance'. Charity, he said, was growing cold, and hope declining to a point where the light of faith was being extinguished. He announced his wish for the revival of 'the good old practice' of publicly reciting the acts of faith, hope and charity at the principal Mass on Sundays, to help counteract these evils.

He then came to his final announcement which concerned the diocesan seminary, and he said that the transfer of Olton Seminary to Oscott College was now complete, and accordingly asked for the warm support of all towards the newly constituted seminary. He paid tribute to the clergy who had served the College of St Mary's for the past fifty years, who 'by their prudent management had secured it as the exclusive property of the diocese'. He also drew attention to the fact that the clergy had contributed the largest portion of the funds out of which Olton Seminary had been founded.

As the reorganization had occurred three months previously, the gathering was already well-acquainted with the facts, and opinions among them were varied. Many who objected to the changeover were undoubtedly still dismayed by the speed with which it had been carried out, and the lack of consultation on Bishop Ilsley's part. They argued against what had been done because they considered 'the education of the clergy and laity side by side was on many grounds a distinct advantage to both' and they cited Ushaw and St Edmund's Old Hall as examples. Others held the view that St Mary's held a unique position in the country, with a history that was full of tradition, and they considered this new procedure caused a break with the past and all its associations.[16] But if his audience was prepared for Bishop Ilsley's announcement, he was equally ready with his arguments to counter any objections raised, and was able to strongly back his reasons for bringing about the changes.

## Holy See Approves Ilsley's Action

Although Edward Ilsley had been described at times as being gentle by character and in many ways reserved, he was also portrayed as one who 'never swerved from a prefixed course of action, no matter how difficult of completion, were he but once convinced of its Divine sanction'.[17] The moves he had made in the previous weeks had been backed by his absolute conviction that he had embarked on the right course, and it was this certainty of mind that now carried him through. He firmly began to reiterate the main points he had previously included in his letter to Joseph Souter. First he underlined his authority in making this unprecedented move so early in his period of office, giving his reasons why 'he decided to unite and concentrate his forces upon Oscott which had a decided advantage over Olton, hence Oscott was selected as the permanent home of the Diocesan Seminary'. Then he stated that the most important aspect of his message to them on this occasion was that he was 'on the side of the Church'. He said he had in view the mind of the Church as regards the training of priests, and it was his duty to the diocese, and his loyal obedience to the dictates of the Church, that 'must outweigh every other consideration', and also that 'this great changeover was brought about after consultation with the Holy See which approved of his line of action'. It was of course Pope Leo's great hope that through a professionally trained clergy would come the conversion of England. Knowing little of the English scene he may have been influenced by Wiseman's over-optimism in his earlier years.

When talking of the 'mind of the Church', Ilsley was also referring to the fact that the idea of separate education for church students had been put forward and approved at the First Provincial Synod by Bishop Grant of Southwark as long ago as 1852. Nothing was done at the time, and although these resolutions had been renewed at subsequent synods to the point where Cardinal Manning urged the bishops at the Fourth Provincial Council in 1873 that they 'should leave no stone unturned' on this account, no steps had ever been taken to remove the lay boys from any existing colleges (probably through financial considerations as much as for any other reason). He took his argument back to Bishop Walsh in the 1830s, whose original plans for the old college of Oscott and the new had been for the setting-up of a 'purely ecclesiastical seminary',[18] but Walsh's hopes remained unfulfilled. The restoration of ecclesiastical seminaries had also been one of William Ullathorne's chief priorities. Ilsley was now coming into line with all those in the past who had advocated these moves, with the vision of bringing in the next phase of Catholic revival.[19]

## College Now Properly Established

He concluded by announcing to the synod that he had finally made it possible for the original purpose of the college to be properly established. His very positive action over Oscott had brought to a decided conclusion the debate about mixed lay and ecclesiastical education which had been argued with considerable intensity some forty years earlier regarding the shortcomings of the system.[20] The concern of the Anglican converts had been that the lay students suffered by being tutored by young ecclesiastics, who in their turn were inadequately educated. They claimed this resulted in a Catholic laity unqualified to take their place in the professional world. Although it had initially been Northcote's policy to discontinue the use of clerical students as tutors to the lay boys in the college, the practice continued among those remaining there after the setting-up of St Bernard's. Ilsley now closed the matter by approaching it from the opposite standpoint and making it clear that the Church wished to 'have aspirants to the priesthood provided with such surroundings as will afford a reasonable hope that they will come forth possessing the requisite technical knowledge, but thoroughly imbued with the priestly spirit, and fully equipped to do their work'.[21]

Although he was uprooting some of Ullathorne's work by transferring St Bernard's to Oscott, the move had been made in order to afford a continuation of just the same undertaking, but it was now placed in the ideal location for its future development, and one that Ullathorne would have no doubt chosen for himself had it been possible for him to do so. Dom Cuthbert Butler, when writing Ullathorne's biography in later years, described the closing of St Bernard's by 'the man of his choice' to be 'a tragic irony of fate'. Nevertheless, he had to admit that Olton Seminary was 'not capacious enough', and also that the running of the two ecclesiastical departments was a costly anomaly. What is more, he went on to say, 'it is true that Oscott had, after the retirement of Dr. Northcote from the Presidency, fallen on evil days, for the Presidents appointed after him by Ullathorne had proved incompetent'.[22]

From the nature of the protests against the dismantling of the lay school one is easily led to imagine that it was considered to be on a par with the other Catholic colleges that were gathering such prestige at this time, but this was not the case. The college had reached its zenith under Northcote, who had retired in 1877, and since that time standards had rapidly fallen, until in 1880 it was described in Thomson's history as being in 'low water', so it was certainly not as financially viable and generally successful as Mgr Souter claimed. A cutting pasted in the college diary in the January of 1885 indicates that confidence had not been fully restored by that time. It was a letter sent by a former student, Walter Austin, whose brother Alfred was later to become poet laureate. The letter he published in The Tablet on 17 January was complaining about the frequent changes in the presidency, and he remarked that Dr Acton, who had been 'called to the rescue' four years earlier when 'the very existence of Oscott was imperilled', was now suddenly to retire. He feared the results of this. 'It is not improbable that the College will soon miss from its muster roll the few representative names that it still possesses, and may even disappear altogether from the list of public schools,' he wrote. Judith Champ observed in her history of the college, 'It is probably true that by 1889 the heyday of Oscott School for the sons of gentlemen was long past,'[23] and it would certainly seem from the persistently low numbers on roll by the time Ilsley made this move, that the school was losing its lay boys to other Catholic colleges.

It should be noted here that although the Oratory School was near Oscott, it did not represent such a rival institution as may be supposed, in spite of Newman's reputation among the old Catholic aristocracy. This was simply because he had set a policy of curtailing the intake to no more than 70, and the numbers available should have sustained both establishments. Founded by him to suit the requirements of the sons of the affluent converts and the old Catholic gentry, the school was an alternative to the 'dual' system afforded at Oscott. Before establishing it, Newman diplomatically approached the rector of Oscott, Dr Weedall, concerning any possible encroachment, and had his assurances that there was no reason why the two schools should not grow together, which they did for the next thirty years. But Newman's prime purpose in keeping his numbers down was to keep a small select establishment, rather than to consider the effect on Oscott in any way. Joseph Souter used the term 'the friendly rival school' to describe it at the time of the jubilee in 1888.[24]

It is true that some old Catholic families who sent their boys to the Oratory School might well have otherwise sent them to Oscott, but the sons of converts were now an additional source of supply, so stability should have been well maintained. An examination of the intake at the Oratory School over the years shows an increase only after Oscott closed its lay school. This suggests that some of the former Oscott boys may then have transferred there.

*The Oscotian* recorded that in December 1887 there were only 21 boys on roll at Oscott, 'the lowest number on record'. It continued, 'the circumstance does not appear to have caused much anxiety, the College speaks of nothing but the preparations for the jubilee'. The numbers picked up to 65 by April, and although the matter caused no immediate concern (the issue being clouded by the preparations for the jubilee celebrations), nevertheless there was need for some action to be taken sooner or later over this question. At the prize distribution at the time of the jubilee, Mgr Souter explained away the criticisms that had been levelled against him because the college had not in recent years been represented at the London University examinations, by claiming 'that the greater part of the Oscott men entered professions such as the Army and the Bar, to which the London University examinations were not the channels of entry'.

## Divided Opinions

The question as to whether Ilsley was acting for the best in making this change is more easily answered once these facts are known. Had he allowed the lay school to stay in existence, how it might have developed in the future can only remain a matter of conjecture. But when speaking publicly to the diocesan synod he did not reveal any of these shortcomings but instead praised the college's glorious past, and so loyally preserved its image. Views were to remain sharply divided at the time, and it was only eight years later when it became the Central Seminary, that opinion turned generally in his favour over Oscott.

He also began to turn his attention to Cotton College at this time. Canon Hawksford had been President there since 1885, and the Annals record changes made in their 'course of studies' with an introduction of 'the system of Commercial classes as well as Classical'. There is a note that the Bishop 'wished his boys in the 1st class to go up to the London Matriculation' with the senior church students remaining at

Cotton instead of completing their course at St Edmund's. The Annals also mention that these moves were not approved of by the other bishops, but it would seem that Ilsley was aiming for the school to provide as good an education as that given by the other Catholic colleges at the time, and 'in 1893 Cotton had more successes in London Matriculation than any other Catholic school'.[25]

There were other circumstances then existing in the Church that had a significant bearing on why these changes that Ilsley carried out were particularly well-timed. For the past two decades, since 1865, when Manning became Archbishop of Westminster, Catholics had been admonished by him not to attend university for fear of coming under adverse influences likely to jeopardize their faith. Exceptions were made only in rare cases, and church leaders were aware of the limitations such restrictions were imposing on clergy and laity alike. Through their affiliation with London University since 1835, Ushaw and Oscott and other leading Catholic colleges had been able to pre-pare and present their students for degrees, and although this alle-viated the situation in some ways, it was generally recognized that the 'university experience' was missing.

Nicholas Wiseman, during his presidency of Oscott in the 1840s, had entertained an ambition that the college might one day evolve into a Catholic university.[26] He wrote in 1847: 'I walked in front of the College and casting my eyes towards it, exclaimed to myself, "No, it was not to educate a few boys this was erected, but to be the rallying point of the yet silent but vast movement towards the Catholic Church." I felt assured of this as if a word of prophesy had spoken it.'[27] The idea that Oscott should act largely as a vehicle for the edu-cation of the young sons of wealthy Catholic families was therefore not entirely acceptable to him, but he later came to acknowledge that the time was not yet right for any great changes of this kind, so his self-styled prophecy had to wait for some other time to be fulfilled.

## The Facilities of University Life

Ilsley was inevitably linked with the 'University Question' because Oxford University was in his own diocese. By widely opening the doors of the college to students coming from beyond the diocese, as soon as the transfer from St Bernard's was accomplished, he began to build up the concept of a central seminary not only for the Midland area but beyond. By doing this he was able to compensate largely for the lack of opportunity previously suffered by clerical students by now

offering them something corresponding more nearly to the atmosphere and facilities of university life. The Revd George H. Bishop
from the Westminster diocese, a student who entered the college in
1898, described that 'there was developed something of the university
atmosphere, so that the students of widely variant antecedents mingling together in their new common life soon lost their youthful
prejudices and learnt to look to the good they could gather from each
other'.[28]

Canon Toplass, writing in *The Oscotian* in 1938, half a century after all
this took place, was to comment, 'It is only fair to the memory of the
innovator to point to the flourishing state of the seminary to justify
his decision . . . indeed Bishop Ilsley is one of our greatest benefactors.
He is our greatest friend.'[29]

## Notes

1  B.A., B10113, dated 30 August 1889.
2  *The Birmingham Directory 1936*: 'For the first 18 years of his priestly life he
was secretary to Bishop Ullathorne. After the Bishop's death, Father
Parker was appointed to Woodlane where he laboured for 46 years until
his death.'
3  *Oscotian* 24, p. 163.
4  In January 1885 it is recorded in the Oscott College Diary: 'During the
holidays the floor at the top end of the Refectory was boarded to make
a suitable dining-place for Priests, Professors and Divines.'
5  O.C.A., *Records of St Mary's College 1830–1900*.
6  Schobel, pp. 3, 4. Also Mervyn Tower, 'A Missing Link: Oscott's
Bavarian Connection, Victor Schobel (1848–1915)', in Essays, p. 142.
7  Parkinson, ch. 6, 2 May 1882, 'The little Hymn book, *Laudes Marianae in
usum clericorum*, the work of Dr. Schobel and the Cecilians, was used
tonight at the May devotions for the first time.'
8  Kiernan, p. 22.
9  J.F.C., p. 21, and *Oscotian* 24, p. 194.
10  *Oscotian* 24, p. 196.
11  *The Tablet*, Saturday 28 June 1924, p. 890.
12  David Evans, 'Henry Parkinson: Philosopher-Rector', in *Essays*, p.167.
13  J. M. Cleary, *Catholic Social Action in Britain 1909–1959*, p. 28.
14  *The Oscotian*, 22/3 (Autumn 1922), pp. 165, 180, 191. Also David Evans,
'Henry Parkinson: Philosopher-Rector', in *Essays*, pp. 166–7.
15  D.B., p. 12. These decrees came into fruition in the reign of Pope
Benedict XV when in 1918 canon law applied fully in England, and the
ordinary parishes came into existence in consequence.
16  D.B., p. 13.

17  Toplass, p. 134.

18  Peter Dennison, 'Thomas Walsh's Vision of Oscott: Hopes and Realities', in *Essays*, p. 43.

19  Norman, p. 159. Also, Judith Champ, 'The Crown of the Diocesan Structure', in *Essays*, p. 96.

20  V. A. McClelland, 'Tractarian Intellectualism and the Silent Heritage', in *Essays*, pp. 89–90.

21  J. Champ, in *Essays*, pp. 95–6: 'Ullathorne's anxiety to remove clerical education from lay colleges reflected the increasing influence of Ultramontane thinking in the Church in the second half of the nineteenth century.'

22  Butler, vol. ii, p. 186.

23  J.F.C., p. 18.

24  Thomson, p. 26.

25  Roberts, p. 138.

26  V. A. McClelland, *English Roman Catholics and Higher Education 1830–1903*, p. 65.

27  Wilfred Ward, *Life and Times of Cardinal Wiseman*, vol. i, p. 349.

28  *Oscotian* 24, 'Monsignor Parkinson, Rector of the Central Seminary', p. 172.

29  Toplass, p. 132. An article in *The Oscotian* brought out in 1938 to celebrate the golden jubilee of Oscott College.

## CHAPTER NINE

# *The Central Seminary*

When Cardinal Manning died in January 1892, Herbert Vaughan, then 59, who was Bishop of Salford, was appointed to succeed him. After forty years' friendship with him, Vaughan was considered in many ways to be a disciple of Manning. But there were inevitably certain differences in outlook between them, and Herbert Vaughan had never been in agreement with Manning's policy concerning diocesan seminaries.

One of Vaughan's earliest appointments was that of Vice President of St Edmund's Seminary at Ware, a position offered him by Archbishop Nicholas Wiseman shortly after he was ordained in 1854, when he was 22. He had received a special dispensation from the Vatican, petitioned for him by Mgr George Talbot, which enabled him to receive holy orders eighteen months earlier than was laid down in church law. Before taking up the position of Vice President, he visited some of the principal seminaries on the Continent to study their methods, and in this way he developed his ideas and discovered some of his preferences regarding ecclesiastical education.[1]

## Mixed Seminaries – Vaughan's Opinion

St Edmund's was a mixed seminary, and from the outset Vaughan held strong opinions about the mixing of lay and church students because he considered the presence of lay students reduced the 'ecclesiastical spirit', but he nevertheless did not favour the excessive isolation and severe discipline he met with in some of the Continental seminaries. While he acknowledged that the practice of mixing church and lay students might produce good priests, he considered it did not foster the best,[2] so his views on the running of a seminary coincided closely with those of Edward Ilsley in that respect.

As Bishop of Salford he set up a small 'Pastoral Seminary' in 1874 which was attached to the cathedral. Its purpose was to give his students

Figure 9.1 *Cardinal Herbert Vaughan, Bishop of Salford (1872–92), Archbishop of Westminster (1892–1903). Drawing made from a photograph in the archives of St Joseph's College, Mill Hill.*

the benefit of a year's practical experience of parish work while still continuing their theological studies. But after five years it was forced to close down through the costs involved and the continuous shortage of priests, and although it was not a diocesan seminary as such, 'as time went by he came to wonder whether, after all, the whole policy of separate diocesan seminaries was not a futile waste of men and money, made possible by a disastrous interpretation of the decrees of Trent'. Long before he left Salford he had arrived at the conclusion 'that no diocese in England came within the rules which made it an obligation to establish a separate seminary'.[3]

Vaughan's visits to Archbishop's House at Westminster during Cardinal Manning's final years convinced him of the drawbacks in the present diocesan system, involving disproportionate expense and often resulting in small, weak seminaries. As early as 1882 he had written: 'Proficiency will not come about by multiplying theological seminaries, but rather by increasing their number of students, raising their standard of studies and prolonging their years of culture and training.'[4]

On his arrival in London as Archbishop of Westminster in 1892, Vaughan was therefore in no mind to embark upon the enterprise of a separate diocesan seminary, and his plan for the future was instead to seek an amalgamation with a suitable existing establishment with a view to planning for its future growth as a central seminary. To pave the way for this, an article by J. D. Snead-Cox was first published in *The Tablet* determining the merits of the case.[5] He often acted as Vaughan's mouthpiece in this way, editing his speeches for publication or writing articles on his behalf.

Characteristically Vaughan wasted no time in putting his ideas into action, and within the year, on 29 December 1892, he sold off his seminary of St Thomas at Hammersmith because he felt its position was too near a busy built-up area in London to be of any use for his plans for expansion. Although St Edmund's College in his own dio-cese at Ware in Hertfordshire appeared suitable for his purpose, he had no wish to be seen to be entirely reversing Manning's policy by taking his students back from whence they had originally come in 1869. It was that year that Manning had transferred his theological students to Hammersmith leaving St Edmund's as a college for lay boys only.

Vaughan felt that although he had considered reorganizing St Edmund's in the past, the prospects regarding his health were now too uncertain to undertake the entire reorganization and building-up of such an establishment, so he decided to look for a more immediate solution elsewhere.[6] 'His thoughts turned for a moment to Wonersh' in the neighbouring diocese of Southwark, but he was soon to discover Bishop Butt would entertain no such proposal, wishing his seminary to continue in what he considered to be the manner laid down by the Council of Trent.[7] Chief among the opponents to Vaughan's policy was Father Francis Bourne, the recently appointed rector in August 1891 of the newly built seminary at Wonersh. Unswerving in his dedication to diocesan seminaries, he was quite open in giving his views both to Vaughan and to Ilsley. In the summer of 1893 he wrote a letter to Ilsley presenting his ideas: 'I feel more and more that our strength will lie in independent Diocesan Seminaries that are willing to take students also from those Dioceses which cannot maintain a seminary: and that a joint Seminary under dual, triple or multiple control is hardly likely to succeed even for a time and cannot be permanent.'[8] Bourne did not favour sending his students to Rome like those trained at Oscott, because he felt that as they were being prepared for the mission, a wider training was unnecessary for many of them. He also warned Archbishop Vaughan that the individual bishop soon lost the educational control of his students in a central seminary system, and there was to be a ring of truth in this statement which the Cardinal came to realize in later years.

## Oscott Chosen for Vaughan's New Scheme

Herbert Vaughan heard he was to be created Cardinal within a year of his appointment to Westminster. By then he had decided on a far bolder scheme with the idea that Oscott College would be the most suitable choice for an officially established central seminary for the greater part of southern England and further afield. As he was proposing quite sweeping changes in the field of ecclesiastical education, it was a considerable help for him to be able to put forward the proposal of using St Mary's College with all its ample facilities when carrying out his present plan, instead of having to face the difficulties and costs of acquiring and equipping a new building.[9] This proposition also disposed of any arguments given in an article by Father John Morris SJ in *The Month*, which was presented shortly after Manning's death, when he wrote in favour of the continuation of diocesan seminaries because of the considerable cost involved in the setting-up of a central seminary. Vaughan was also aware that St Mary's had already been running on the lines of a central seminary under the guidance of the Bishop of Birmingham for the past three years, since its transfer from Olton, and it was already attracting an ever-increasing number of students from the Midlands and the South.

He journeyed to Rome in January 1893 to be created Cardinal, and seeing this would be a good time to draw the attention of the Holy Father to the idea of establishing Oscott College as the recognized Central Seminary of Britain, he took the opportunity to present him with a memorandum setting out his full plans before returning to London. Pope Leo shared the Cardinal's interest in an improved and economical system for England as he happened to be engaged in the same task in Italy at the time, and the answer came swiftly back from Rome within the month on 1 February, endorsing the proposal with these words: 'We entertain good hope that we shall be able one day as joyfully to congratulate you on the prosperous and happy result of work well done, as we now warmly encourage you to begin it.'[10] On 18 March, four days after the final lecture was given at St Thomas's, Vaughan transferred his Hammersmith students to Oscott as their new permanent home.

In an article in *The Tablet* shortly after making this move, Vaughan argued that according to the decrees of Trent young divines should have the advantages of a thoroughly equipped and endowed institution such as Oscott. He even suggested that the inefficiency of smaller establishments was in violation of the spirit of the decrees and that they 'by no means represent the seminaries for which the Council was legislating'. After this time, the diocesan seminaries that had been so expensively founded at Manning's behest were closed one by one over the years until Liverpool and Southwark alone survived.[11] Vaughan rightly considered all these to be too parochial in outlook and generally having a narrowing effect on the training of his clergy compared with the expansive education afforded in a much larger college such as Oscott. At the annual meeting of the bishops at Westminster in April 1893, he set things in motion by reading out the Holy Father's letter approving of the idea of a 'Central Seminary of Philosophy and Theology for the Southern Dioceses of England'.[12]

## The Amalgamation of a Group of Dioceses

The plan he set before them was to amalgamate the resources of a group of dioceses in support of a central seminary. So the months following his succession to the See of Westminster proved to be the most stirring ones for Oscott, which was now seen to be developing its full potential. In addition to the students from its own diocese, the seminary was taking them from the dioceses of Northampton, Nottingham and Shrewsbury in the Midlands, and Portsmouth in the South. It was also affording temporary accommodation to some of those from Southwark while the buildings at Wonersh were being completed, and it had recently absorbed those students from the Diocese of Westminster as well.

From the speed with which Herbert Vaughan acted at the outset over this plan by selling off his own seminary at Westminster, the impression was given that he expected to bring the whole business of establishing the central seminary to a conclusion within a few months, and he may initially have had this idea in mind. He was aware of his own impatience and habit of hurrying over his undertakings and of his 'liking to get things done'. But the completion of the scheme finally proved to be a fairly long drawn-out business, and the official status of the central seminary and the final arrangements for its recognition were not to be completed for another five long years. It was said that during this time the prestige of Oscott continued to soar, 'above the narrow boundaries of diocesanism',[13] but it should be noted that as well as opening the doors of St Mary's so wide, it was also Edward Ilsley who took the protective measure of arranging for secure railings to be erected all round the grounds as well,[14] and this could almost be considered as a symbolic gesture on his part, because to the end of his days, the welfare of the college was to be his constant care and protective concern.

Vaughan and Ilsley approached matters in very different ways. Writing in his diary as a young man, Herbert Vaughan gave an intimate portrayal of his own personality, confessing some of his faults that were to be a source of anxiety to himself throughout his adult life: 'My line is to arrive,' he said. 'I cannot walk but I must run ... Everything savours of impatience, of hurry, of the love of the object to be attained and of recklessness as to the means. I am imprudent because I have not time and patience to consult people's feelings and ways of thought.' Even at the personal risk of being trampled on, he would push a horse's head aside in order to cross in front of a moving carriage, in his haste to cross a busy street.[15]

Ilsley's ways were very different. As bishop of the diocese owning the college, he adopted a careful, watchful attitude concerning every detail that was being laid down regarding its foundation as the future central seminary. Diligently sifting through every rule and regulation, he made sure that whatever the later years might ultimately bring, the interests of St Mary's would remain secure for Birmingham.

He made good use of his time in this respect when he was in Rome in the summer of 1893. He wrote about it on 23 July to Canon McCave, saying, 'On hearing that the Card. Prefect of Propaganda was also interested in the project, I interviewed him and explained the precise position of Oscott and the work of the Central Sem$^y$ that was being carried on there.' He told McCave he was now being pressed by Cardinal Vaughan as to the basis on which he would consent to negotiate terms with him and the Southern bishops on the matter of placing Oscott under their joint control – 'I named certain conditions the chief of which were that 6 bishops should each endow a chair at Oscott and found five burses & that the Constitution as fixed should not be altered until the experience of 3 years had shown the expediency thereof.' He said he had reported all these matters to his chapter and to Cardinal Vaughan on his return from Rome, and ended his letter with the somewhat cryptic observation, 'I added that I did not anticipate that 6 bishops would be found to undertake such a responsibility.'[16]

## Ilsley Protects Diocese and College

The position Herbert Vaughan found himself in over these negotiations was never to be an easy one. Not only was Oscott College outside his own diocese, but Edward Ilsley was in the unprecedented position of being both bishop of the diocese concerned, and at the same time holding the position of rector of the establishment in question, and as such he was naturally anxious to protect both the interests of the college and his own diocese. Added to this, since its reconstitution in 1889, the changed ethos of the seminary merited the approval of the bishops of the neighbouring dioceses, who already sent their students there, and so Ilsley could count on their automatic support. So whereas Herbert Vaughan was anxious to conclude negotiations as soon as possible, Ilsley was content to let things develop at their own pace. One matter that concerned Bishop Riddell of Northampton when the agreements were being made, was that the City of Birmingham might increase so much in size that it would surround Oscott in time, and so render the site unsuitable for a seminary![17]

In May 1894 the Cardinal wrote to Ilsley complaining, 'The terms your Lordship now proposes seem to be far more onerous than those proposed in Rome, and of course they are such as the smaller dioceses could not possibly carry out.' He suggested that more reasonable terms could be worked out 'if due economy is practised'. He then hinted that he himself would put forward more generally satisfactory terms were he to decide on Old Hall in his own diocese for the site of the central seminary instead of Oscott: 'I should have thought you would have been willing to accept such an arrangement as I should myself consider satisfactory were Old Hall instead of Oscott chosen as the site for the Central Seminary,' he said.[18] He may well by then have been considering it a mistake not to have used St Edmund's for his purpose, but must have decided to set the thought aside as he did not mention it again to Ilsley.

Negotiations continued to pass back and forth between the two men, and the months began to lengthen into years. Vaughan made a stand against any permanent thought of 'the one-man management system' which was operating at Oscott during this interim period with Ilsley at the helm, but Ilsley was by no means ready to give up his personal control at this stage. One of his chief mentors at this challenging time was his vicar general, James O'Hanlon, who warned him: 'The plain English, I suppose of the Cardinal's letter is, that the interested Bishops are willing to take their full share of the advantages but not of the liability of Oscott',[19] and he insisted 'that until the partnership should see its way to undertake all its financial liabilities, the seminary as heretofore should remain under the control of the Bishop of Birmingham, and the other bishops to have a consultative, and not a decisive voice in its management'. Unwilling to accept any financial compromise, Ilsley brought up the added argument that he could foresee his certain need in the future to set up a new bishop's house to match his requirements. He wrote to Vaughan: 'and I shall be met with the taunt, "Why did you give up Oscott as a residence?", when I appeal to my people'.[20] As it happened, Ilsley never gave up Oscott as his place of residence, and it was to be another 21 years before he purchased a large house in Norfolk Road at Edgbaston for a new archbishop's house. By this time the requirements of the archdiocese had far outgrown the original house in Bath Street, in the overcrowded area surrounding St Chad's Cathedral.

## The Pope Urges 'Completion'

Two years later, in January 1895, Herbert Vaughan made a note in his diary, while he was in Rome: 'Central Seminary – the Pope asked me how this was progressing; he urged me most strongly to use all my influence to promote it, getting good studies and a learned clergy, &c, as the best means of converting England. He pressed this matter with great urgency.' A few months later, in April, there is another entry: 'The Holy Father urged me again to make the Central Seminary my great work – a university of ecclesiastical studies.' At 63 his frame of mind was that of a man aware of the urgency of the amount he must get done before his death, and among his commitments at this time he was about to begin another of his 'grand visions' – the prospect of building Westminster Cathedral. Owing to his precarious state of health, particularly in these later years, he constantly felt that death was not far away, and lived with the prospect very much before him. He had to slow down and adjust at times to what he termed 'a lowered scale of vitality', but while in the process of slowing down he was at the same time in a constant state of anxiety to hurriedly get on and embark on still further undertakings. It has since been analysed that the constant need to be active on behalf of various 'great schemes' was a weakness in his leadership, because although he familiarized himself initially with the necessary details and made careful preparation each time he embarked on some new undertaking, his temperament and his wanderlust made it difficult for him to apply himself to any one task for long enough to see it satisfactorily through to the end.[21] This apparently had always been the case since his first appointment at St Edmund's. At the time of Vaughan's death in 1903, Bernard Ward described how his restless energy 'could not find sufficient scope within the walls of the college, and he frequently undertook work outside which interfered with the continuous residence so essential for college life'.[22]

Ilsley, on the other hand, was always in favour of steadily 'making haste slowly', and in the knowledge that his seminary was already well established, he wished to deliberate with care and consideration over the formulation of all the finer details. Naturally calm and unhurried, the description given of him by Canon Toplass that he was 'dogged' in his approach seems very apt, but credit is due to him for his concentration on the job in hand, and his skills at steering things through. He showed early in the negotiations that he could not be rushed into any decisions that he considered unfair to the diocese through what he termed 'my innocence in diplomacy',[23] and the notes he made at this time reflect a very different attitude from that of Vaughan. When considering the changeover of Oscott from a diocesan seminary under his control to management by a board of bishops, he appeared to view the whole situation with a degree of caution, and there is no indication that he was in any hurry to conclude matters until he was sure everything was in place.

## The Arrangement Lacks Stability

In February 1895 Ilsley pointed out to Vaughan that in his view the present scheme needed modifying – 'Your Eminence regards the Scheme with satisfaction as it was drafted and as it was accepted by your Chapter. To my mind it lacks the element of stability which it surely ought to possess. It is a temporary arrangement whereby the control of Oscott is relinquished by me and handed over to a Board of Bishops; but it commits no-one to any permanent acceptance of the scheme. The bishops are free to join and free to withdraw; they may send their subjects to Oscott or they may place them elsewhere for economic or other grounds, the only penalty for withdrawal the forfeiture of any building they may have erected. But who would care to build with such a prospect before them?' The point that he raised was to have crucial significance later on. He went on to say that he was anxious to co-operate, 'in the important work which the Holy Father has commissioned your Eminence to undertake', and he said he was willing to make any personal sacrifice that was demanded of him, 'But for the sake of an arrangement that is of an ephemeral and experimental nature, I think we ought not to sacrifice the living, organic, working institution we have got, which is the steady growth of the last 22 years and enjoys the confidence of many of our Brethren.'

The task Ilsley now appeared to set himself was that of convincing the Cardinal of the soundness of the present organization of the seminary, which therefore needed to be left intact. He seemed, in fact, to be taking the role of adviser to his superior, suggesting to him how best to proceed in order to open up the way for final decisions to take place: 'I have given my candid opinion of the scheme in the spirit of friendly criticism. Let me now as frankly make a suggestion. The Holy Father having laid upon you the task of establishing the Central Seminary, or University of Ecclesiastical Studies, you will have first to determine in your mind the form and shape of the work to be created – the ideal which you hope will be realised some day. This you will have to set before us and we shall discuss it with you; and if we can agree about this there will be little difficulty about the stages whereby we mean to attain it – they will resolve themselves into the question of ways and means for the most part!'[24]

## Schobel's Views Published in *The Tablet*

Two years previously Victor Schobel argued the case for the Central

Figure 9.2  *Victor J. Schobel, St Bernard's Seminary (1873–85) and Oscott (1885–97).*
*Drawing made from a photograph in Oscott College Archives.*

Seminary in *The Tablet.* He had been mainly responsible for outlining
the seminary's schemes of work since his earliest association with the
Birmingham diocese at St Bernard's in 1873. Now over twenty years
later in 1895 he published his views in a pamphlet entitled *De Seminaro
Centrali*,[25] arguing further that Oscott was in the forefront by reason of
its specially selected staff, and the courses it pursued. One of the
strongest points he made was that, due to the passage of time, the
intellectual requirements of the priesthood were now far greater than
at the time of the Council of Trent. His fear, he said, was that many of
the existing diocesan seminaries might not be adequately resourced,
and insisted that the central system was the only means of attaining the
necessary requirements to secure a well-educated clergy in England.
The pattern was to be found in Rome, he said, 'If we cannot reach it,
we have to try to come as near as possible.'[26]

Vaughan asked Ilsley to have the pamphlet distributed among the
bishops, and Dr Schobel's far-reaching experience in the traditions of
the seminary, and the clarity of his arguments, meant his work was
well-received and generally applauded by them. For Schobel, 'there
was no doubt that Oscott was the only Southern Seminary that could
meet such requirements'.[27] The following weeks appear to mark a

turning-point in Herbert Vaughan's approach towards the negotia-tions. From that time on he seemed content to let Ilsley go ahead and take the lead, giving assent to most of his suggestions with little fur-ther questioning. It was as though he appeared to realize that the necessary spadework for the 'great work' that he had expected to make his own had already been done by others, and all that was needed now to bring things to a satisfactory conclusion was, as Ilsley suggested, through 'ways and means'.

Expressing a liking for Schobel's learned paper, Vaughan wrote enthusiastically, 'There will be no difference between us on the point of stability. I am quite ready to cut my cables and become wholly committed to Oscott.' During this time the restless speed with which Vaughan wrote letters to Ilsley was indicated by his habit of joining two or three words together in a string, dashed off, and sometimes linked together right across the page, with words occasionally crossed out, and others inserted. This could be an indication that his interest in the project was on the wane.[28] On the other hand Ilsley's commu-nications to him, often written from a well-thought-out first draft, were always eminently clear and legible – this was his system of approach throughout his life. By this time the Cardinal's health was in decline, and he was far from well. The condition of his heart was beginning to affect him to such an extent that he often had to adjust the pace of his life and was forced at times to break away from his work and take complete rest in an attempt to regain his strength. In spite of his constant illness, throughout the years the picture of him that still remained stamped in people's minds was of a man of great presence, and they considered he fitted magnificently into the position of Cardinal-Archbishop.[29] He may have begun to feel the sands of time were gently running out for him, and the fragmentary notes he kept in his diary show that the Pope was constantly urging him on to complete his work of founding the Central Seminary, trusting that in its wake it would help bring about his great hope for the conversion of England.

By the spring of 1896 a letter was circulated by Bishop Ilsley on behalf of Cardinal Vaughan, to the bishops concerned, stating 'I have pleasure to inform you that the founding of a Central Seminary at Oscott has been favourably received.' The letter continues, 'The Cardinal hopes that without further delay a Deed of Foundation may be agreed upon by the cointerested Bishops to be subsequently sub-mitted, together with regulations respecting studies and discipline, for approval by the Holy See.' However, even at these closing stages, several hurdles still needed to be cleared before final agreement could be reached. An important point for Birmingham was brought forward by Canon Fenn, who drew attention to the fact that the freehold of the college should on no account be made over to the board because this would take control out of the Bishop's hands: 'It is a mistake to give power away,' he remonstrated.[30] The freehold at that time was held in perpetuity by the Bishop, and he said it should remain so. It would have been unlike Edward Ilsley to let any advantage of this kind go out of his hands, so this difficulty was overcome by him 'granting use of the college', and so the freehold remained intact. Another point the Canon raised was concerning the Bishop's three trustees who were at present subject to him in canon law. He feared if these were replaced by others from outside the diocese, the Bishop's case would again be weakened. Cardinal Vaughan eased the situation by allowing the three to remain, and bringing in three others, thus creating a fair balance.

## Vaughan's Failure to Insert Protective Clause

Another decision was taken by the board concerning a situation only remotely being envisaged at the time: 'It was agreed that the funds and property should revert to their original owners only in the case of Oscott being dissolved as a Central Seminary.'[31] This condition, recorded and signed by Cardinal Vaughan, was to prove to be the weak link in a chain of events leading from the establishment of the Central Seminary to its untimely demise only six short years later. If he had sought to cement the foundation of the Central Seminary permanently in a manner officially approved of in Rome, by inserting a protective clause, rather than going in the opposite direction by providing for the possibility of its dissolution, then Francis Bourne's unfortunate reversal of his policy, begun in 1905, could not have come about, and any question of its discontinuation would have been averted. Ilsley's words written to Vaughan a year earlier, that 'the scheme lacked stability because no-one was committed to any permanent acceptance', showed astute perception on his part, but sadly enough at the time it seemed not to have registered with the Cardinal as a vital consideration to be acted upon, and so a serious loophole in the foundation was overlooked. The conclusion arrived at concerning such failures on Vaughan's part is summed up by Robert O'Neil, who detected his lack of application right back to his years as a student: 'Any weaknesses in Vaughan's work can often be traced to his temperament and health problems and a consequent inability to take on the everyday tasks of his office as a seminarian, Church leader or founder.'[32]

But it is apparent throughout all these negotiations that the Cardinal continued to treat the Birmingham diocese with special consideration. As his biographer J. G. Snead-Cox was to observe in later years: 'The Cardinal never forgot that Oscott belonged to Birmingham and that the Bishop in surrendering his control with six other interested bishops was giving up a great deal. To make that sacrifice as little difficult as possible, and to make sure of the harmonious co-operation of all in the future, was throughout Cardinal Vaughan's great, and indeed only aim.'[33] It was his own diocese of Westminster that provided the largest proportion of money, amounting to £7,000, toward the new endowment, but Ilsley countered any suggestion that this was in any way excessive by pointing out that 'Birmingham is prepared to contribute as its share in the enterprise the Oscott furnished building and grounds, value say £50,000. Is it too much,' he wrote, 'to expect that a like sum should be raised by all the other dioceses concerned.'[34] It was to Ilsley's credit that he always kept a clear-sighted and businesslike view of how finances should be fairly proportioned among the bishops concerned in the scheme at this time.

## All Birmingham Staff Re-engaged

When at last the final stages were being worked out, Cardinal Vaughan seemed ready to accommodate Bishop Ilsley yet again on another key issue. In order 'to encourage harmonious co-operation' the Cardinal agreed that all the old staff – all Birmingham clergy – should be re-engaged.[35] Victor Schobel had advised Ilsley fairly and precisely on this matter two years earlier in June 1895: 'After mature consideration of the subject of our conversation last night, I am of the opinion that the most promising procedure would be the following. First settle the broad issue of the financial part of the Central Seminary. Next proceed to the appointment of the Superior i.e. Rector & Vice-R., Prefect & Procurator . . . It would seem right if one of the two heads (Rector & Vice-Rector) were from different Dioceses. In other words B'ham should have the post of either Rector or Vice R. but not both.'[36] This advice would appear sound and it was given by the man who was considered to have the expert knowledge that shaped the pattern they were all to follow. It would undoubtedly have provided the essential balance that was later found to be lacking as far as the other dioceses were concerned. But to Bishop Ilsley it would seem that theory was one thing and practice another as far as Schobel's advice was concerned, and to suit his own interests at that time he decided not to follow it.

The arrangement he chose of using his own staff at that time was a happy one for him, but in all probability it may have been one factor, in the long run, that helped to shorten the life of the Central Seminary. In the first stages of the reorganization his attitude of wishing to protect those who had served the college throughout the years can be understood, because he reasoned that they already had the experience needed for the task ahead. In fairness to him, he may have considered that at this time of change and development within the seminary it was sound policy to keep his own experienced staff in charge at the initial stages rather than weaken the forward thrust by bringing others in from other dioceses who were unfamiliar with the system. If this was the case, Ilsley was quite right to do so.

But Ilsley's mistake lay in the fact that, for one reason or another, the practice of employing his own staff was to persist unchanged. Schobel asked him in June 1895: 'Will it be a principle with the Cardinal and your Lordship that both St Edmund's and Oscott might draw professors from any interested Diocese without ceasing to belong to their own Diocese?' But his suggestion was not acted upon, and the first appointment from the Birmingham Diocese was that of Edward Henry Godwin, then aged 28, who took his place on the staff a year later in 1898 and remained until 1902, to return again in 1906 as Vice Rector. He came as a student to Oscott in 1890 and was ordained in 1897. Whatever his ability, it would seem that someone with more experience, coming in from another diocese on the recommendation of his own bishop, would have inevitably been a more suitable choice for the position on the staff in 1898. But when considering the financial side of things in October 1896, Ilsley expressed an opinion in his notes which suggested he assumed the Birmingham staff were remaining in place, when he wrote: 'One thing is certain that whereas the staff is now provided by the Diocese of Birm & are willing to give their services at a lower rate of remuneration for the benefit of the diocese, they will require better pay if they are placed under the Management of a Board of Bishops in the interest of many dioceses.'[37]

John Snead-Cox gives a clear picture of the situation that Edward Ilsley created by insisting on the reappointment of the entire Birmingham staff who were then under Henry Parkinson as Rector and Francis Lloyd as Vice Rector. They were John McIntyre, Frederick

Sandy, James O'Leary and John Hopwood. He mentions the Cardinal's desire to keep things running smoothly, and goes on to say: 'It was for this reason that the whole of the old staff was re-engaged. All belonged to the diocese of Birmingham, knowing the needs of Birmingham but little acquainted with those of Westminster; and if at any time as the years wore on, the Cardinal felt that his plan had not worked out to a perfect success, or that the students from other dioceses were slow to think of Oscott as their *Alma Mater*, probably the explanation may be found in this decision to retain the services of a staff recruited solely from a single diocese.'[38]

## A Lost Advantage

But even if the Birmingham diocese was satisfied with the arrangement over staffing, the situation must have caused quite considerable dissatisfaction among the other bishops. Moreover, this arrangement must have robbed of all its force one of the arguments on which the Cardinal relied in urging the advantages of a central seminary. It was contended that such a seminary, commanding the resources of many dioceses, would be able to secure the services of a teaching staff such as no single diocese could hope for.[39] But as it worked out, the staff of the Central Seminary was neither better nor worse than it had been previously – it was just the same. For the following six years, throughout the remaining part of Cardinal Vaughan's lifetime, any new appointments or changes of staff took place solely from within the Birmingham diocese. After that time names from other dioceses began to appear on the staff list, but by then the struggle for survival had begun.

There was more than one reason why this unsatisfactory situation came about. Vaughan was struggling with poor health and was losing interest in the undertaking. There was also a noticeable contrast between the attitude of the two men towards their clergy. The Cardinal's constant ill-health contributed towards the impression that he held himself aloof from them, particularly in his later years when, as Archbishop of Westminster, a great deal of his time was taken up with administration. He was in fact by no means an unfriendly man, and Snead-Cox noted that 'he cared nothing whether peer or peasant or anyone else were invited to meet him',[40] but he saw very little of his clergy at this time as he invariably referred them to his vicar general, Canon Michael Barry. This meant he was never to come to know them individually, and the situation of always being at a distance from his clergy caused him to have difficulty in remembering their names, particularly as he always had a problem in remembering faces. These combined circumstances could furnish the reason why he so freely handed the staffing of the Central Seminary over to Ilsley without realizing the possible future outcome of his action, and when things did not work out entirely satisfactorily with the Oscott staff it was too late for him to alter his decision in any way.

In his circular letter distributed to the bishops of the governing board on 3 April 1896, Ilsley included a copy of eight basic Articles of Agreement that he had drafted at the request of Cardinal Vaughan for discussion by them 'at Archbishop's House in Low Week after the usual business of the Hierarchy has been concluded'. The Bishops were invited to make any further observations at that time, and the final draft was to be subsequently submitted for the approval to the Holy See. But even as late as 21 October 1896 Ilsley seemed to be entertaining certain reservations regarding the bishops' scheme for Oscott and was quite open in his views about it in a letter to Cardinal Vaughan: 'Personally I regard the proposal as an experiment which may prove advantageous on the whole, or on the contrary a cause for trouble and regret.' But having given his considered opinion in the matter, he continued in a more conciliatory manner: 'However the Holy Father has notified his desire for the establishment of a Comm. Sem$^y$ in founding & maintaining which the Bishops of several dioceses are to join their forces & this inspires the hope that we shall reap results in proportion to the prudence with which we have taken the work in hand.' His letter concludes: 'If it commends itself to the General Committee I shall be glad to give it my formal approval.'[41] Ilsley has been described as worldly-wise,[42] and the fact that he did not come to accept the developments concerning Oscott at this time without questioning the possible outcome, and even with a certain degree of scepticism, certainly shows the mind of a man with penetratingly wise vision.

In the following May 1897, it was Bishop Ilsley who, accompanied by Henry Parkinson as his secretary, travelled to Rome to hand over the Constitutions of the Seminary to Pope Leo, telling him that it had now finally been adopted, and that it was awaiting the approbation of the Holy See. He wrote a letter from the English College to James O'Hanlon at that time, addressing him as 'My dear Vicar-General', and telling him all about his audience in the Vatican. 'I have just returned from my audience with the Holy Father – needless to say he received me in his accustomed paternal manner – and began straightway to talk about what was nearest his heart – the conversion of England.' This he hoped would be brought about through the improved training which was now about to be provided for the clergy and which would in turn reflect upon the people.[43]

When Ilsley handed him the *constitutio*, the Holy Father asked who had drawn it up – 'I told him it represented what was now actually in operation at Oscott,' he continued, 'and had been gradually developing for the last 24 years in the Diocese of Birmingham. He glanced through its pages.' By this reply Ilsley intimated that the idea of a central seminary had been developing in his own mind ever since he had been appointed Rector of St Bernard's twenty-four years ago in 1873. Parkinson was then called to join him at the papal audience, and Ilsley described to O'Hanlon, 'Parkinson was thrilled with emotion as the H. F. spoke with that beaming face and bright eyes fixed on him – and we both retired from the august presence filled with consolation. We were very favoured, indeed almost beyond expectation, for it had been said that "as so many bishops are about we should have to go in batches".'

## The Central Seminary, July 1897

Two months later, on 15 July 1897, St Mary's College, Oscott, became *de jure* as well as *de facto* the common seminary for Westminster, Birmingham, Clifton, Newport, Portsmouth, Nottingham, North-ampton and what was then the Vicariate of Wales. So it covered the Midlands, the South and the West of England, while Ushaw covered the North. The previous evening the bishops assembled at the college, and on the following day they held their first meeting as the govern-ing body of the seminary, and signed the legal documents by which the endowments of the chairs were secured. Cardinal Vaughan was to act as President of the Board, which was to meet annually in October 'and as frequently at other times as found desirable'.[44]

All this took place four years after Herbert Vaughan began to develop his idea of establishing Oscott College as the Central Seminary. A note in the college diary says that at lunch Cardinal Vaughan announced that Dr Parkinson had accepted the rectorship of the college and that Father Hopwood was to be secretary to the board of bishops. We are told in the Oscott diary that on that day, 'Dr Parkinson took his place as rector at the head of the table during lunch.' An article in *The Tablet* entitled 'Important Ecclesiastical Change' mentioned that Francis Lloyd was Vice Rector, and John McIntyre prefect of studies and that 'we understand also that the Rev. Dr Butler of St Charles' College will act as spiritual Father, and will visit St Mary's during each month'. Ilsley had now been Rector of Oscott for eight years, since 1889, as well as being Bishop of the diocese, and yet it was not until this point that it suited his purpose to hand over the reins entirely to Henry Parkinson.

Ilsley's inability to delegate final authority has been called in question. His method was invariably to oversee any key situation until he came to a point when he felt it appropriate to remove himself from the scene. He worked closely in this way with Father George Hudson, whom he appointed to take charge of the mission and children's homes at Coleshill in 1898, and in 1917 when he was 80, he still found the time and energy to take an active interest in Father Thomas Newsome's work with the mentally disabled children at Besford Court. He was very thorough in his approach to things: 'Nothing missed his keen eye,' was one accurate summary.[45] It was probably for this reason he was slow to hand over entirely to others, preferring to concentrate on certain main issues in the administration of a scheme and to work closely with whoever he had selected finally to take over in the future until he felt the time had come to let go.

In the case of Oscott, Henry Parkinson would of course in many ways have already been fully acting as rector while Ilsley only nominally held the office. But there were special circumstances prevailing that gave sufficient reason for Ilsley holding on to the position while negotiations were in progress that required him and not Parkinson to be 'in command'. The fact that so many of the institutions he established by working in this way continued successfully over the years must speak for itself, because they give testimony to the fact that his system worked.[46] But even so, valid criticisms of some of his judgements and procedures still remain.

## Notes

1   O'Neil , p. 63. George Talbot, having previously taken Anglican orders, was received into the Catholic Church by Wiseman and ordained in 1846. In 1851 he was sent to Rome by Wiseman as his personal representative. He immediately became a papal chamberlain and from that time forward had considerable influence there. A severe illness had prompted Vaughan's wish for an early ordination Also p. 82. Wiseman suggested to him the same itinerary as he himself had used in 1835 and gave him letters of introduction. He travelled to Italy, Austria, Germany and France, and his first interview was in Munich in 1855.

2  McCormack, p. 39.

3  Snead-Cox, vol. ii, pp. 41–2.

4  These words are taken from Herbert Vaughan's preface to *St John the Baptist de Rossi*, a book translated from the Italian by Lady Herbert and published by Burns & Oates. In this introduction he dealt largely with matters to do with ecclesiastical training.

5  Snead-Cox, vol. ii, pp. 41–3.

6  O'Neil, p. 110

7  McCormack, p. 266.

8  B.A., B1100, Letter from Bourne to Ilsley, Guildford, 12 July 1893. Bourne wrote two anonymous letters to *The Tablet* on 11 and 18 March 1893, and in May, backed by Bishop Butt, produced a pamphlet under the name of Francis A. Bourne, entitled *Diocesan Seminaries and the Education of Ecclesiastical Students*.

9  Snead-Cox, vol. ii, p. 40.

10  St Joseph's College, Mill Hill, Scrapbooks, PCW 3 35.

11  Beck, p. 36, 'The Coming Century'. The seminaries in question were Westminster, which closed in 1893, Birmingham (Olton) 1889, Salford 1879, Nottingham 1902, Northampton 1908, and Clifton 1893. Leeds, which was established in 1878, was the only one which had more lasting qualities. It continued for 61 years, until 1939.

12  B.A., B10947, Annual Meeting of the Bishops, April 1893.

13  The Revd George Bishop, *Oscotian* 24, 'Monsignor Parkinson, Rector of the Central Seminary', pp. 171–2.

14  Toplass, p. 133. Some of the original ones have now been replaced.

15  Snead-Cox, vol. i, pp. 49–50.

16  B.A., B11066, Letter from Ilsley to Canon McCave, 23 July 1893.

17  *Ibid.*, B11752, Letter from Bishop Riddell to Vincent Holcroft, 17 December 1896.

18  *Ibid.*, B11262, Letter from Archbishop Vaughan to Bishop Ilsley, 28 May 1894, referring to St Edmund's, Old Hall. Also O'Neil, p. 48: 'He also had a strong opinion about the mixing of church students as was done at St Edmund's.' Also Snead-Cox , vol. i, p. 76.

19  B.A., B11261, Letter from James O'Hanlon to Bishop Ilsley, 25 May 1894.

20  Westminster, Bo 5/24, Letters from Ilsley to Vaughan, 12 July and 20 September 1895. The new Archbishop's House, 'Lawnside', was not finally set up until 1915. Also, Southwark, Letter from Ilsley to Bishop Amigo, 26 November 1915.

21  O'Neil, p. 496. See also David Parry, *Scholastic Century*. Herbert Vaughan's brother Jerome was described as having a roving career consisting of unfinished enterprises, so it would seem the two brothers shared the same characteristics in this respect.

22  'Cardinal Vaughan', *The Edmundian*, 5/3 (July 1903).

23  Westminster, Bo 5/24. Letter from Ilsley to Vaughan, 20 September 1895.

24 *Ibid.*, Bo 5/24. Letter from Bishop Ilsley to Cardinal Vaughan, 28 February 1895.

25 *The Oscotian*, 3rd Series, 16/1 (December 1915), p. 10.

26 *The Tablet*, 4 March 1893, p. 442.

27 M. Tower, 'A Missing Link: Oscott's Bavarian Connection, Victor Schobel 1848–1915', in *Essays*, p. 151.

28 B.A., B11422, Letter from Cardinal Vaughan to Bishop Ilsley, 3 March 1895.

29 *The Weekly Register*, 1892, 'Piccadilly Portraits'. When he became Archbishop of Westminster an article in *The Weekly Register* began: 'The Vaughans of Courtfield belong to the untitled nobility of England. They can trace back their descent further than many of those whose names are written in the peerage.'

30 B.A., B11762, Notes in Canon Fenn's hand.

31 *Ibid.*, B11227, 16 April 1876, Recorded in notes by Cardinal Vaughan during a meeting of the bishops.

32 O'Neil, p. 497 and pp. 56–7: '. . . life was not going well for Vaughan in Rome. From Snead-Cox, and his sources, another Herbert Vaughan emerges, one who was not accustomed to the studies and self-discipline required of students at the Academy and the Roman College.'

33 Snead-Cox, vol. ii, p. 64.

34 Westminster, Bo 5/24, Letter from Bishop Ilsley to Cardinal Vaughan, 16 September 1895.

35 McCormack, p. 269.

36 B.A., B11480, Letter from Victor Schobel to Bishop Ilsley written from Oscott College, 23 June 1895.

37 *Ibid.*, B11570, Notes written by Bishop Ilsley, 21 October 1896.

38 Snead-Cox, vol. ii, p. 64.

39 *Ibid.* Also this point was argued strongly in Victor Schobel's pamphlet *De Seminario Centrali*.

40 Norman, p. 346 and also Snead-Cox, vol. ii, 388. Robert O'Neil described how the Cardinal would sometimes engage man-to-man enthusiastically in conversation with any workman, discussing details of building work in progress on one of his projects. A paper given to the Catholic Record Society, on 'Cardinal Herbert Vaughan', at Plater College, Oxford, 3 August 1995.

41 B.A., B11570. Notes made by Bishop Ilsley, 21 October 1896.

42 V. A. McClelland, The Catholic Record Society, 1996, 'Bourne, Norfolk and the Irish Parliamentarians: Roman Catholics and the Education Bill of 1906', p. 251.

43 B.A., B11900, Letter from Edward Ilsley to James O'Hanlon, from the English College, Rome, 22 May 1897.

44 *The Tablet*, July 1897, pp. 14, 15. This was the year of Queen Victoria's diamond jubilee. Her jubilee thanksgiving, kept throughout the

Empire, was held a month earlier on 23 June.

45 An observation made by Rosie Martin as a child in *My Lord and the Angel*, p. 52.

46 Notably, Oscott College itself, and the Homes at Coleshill, which have now developed into a Social Care Agency for the Archdiocese. Besford Court School continued until the economic climate, which brought about cuts in local services, caused it to close on 31 August 1996. St Gerard's Hospital was forced to close in 1998 for the same reason, and the following press statement was issued on 2 March: 'It is with regret that Father Hudson's Society has today announced that Warwickshire Orthopaedic Hospital (St Gerard's) will close on 30 April 1998. Strenuous efforts to expand the NHS Orthopaedic Business and develop new initiatives have proved unsuccessful despite a vigorous public campaign supported by the Staff, the local community, the Hospital League of Friends and local Politicians.'

## CHAPTER TEN

# The New Order of Things

## Ilsley continues to Reside at Oscott

Although he was now no longer Rector, Bishop Ilsley continued to reside at the college. His time there added to that spent at St Bernard's had lengthened into 24 years, and the habit of being among his staff and students suited him well. His abiding interest was in the training of priests, and for that reason his ties with his students were never to be broken. This fact is summed up in an appreciation written in *The Oscotian* in 1927 by Father Patrick O'Toole: 'He kept in contact with every student and by kindly advice and encouragement and interest in them became a personal friend to each.'[1]

But at this point certain questions need to be asked about Bishop Ilsley's decision to remain at Oscott College, now that it had become the Central Seminary under the jurisdiction of a board of bishops. Two years earlier, in September 1895, he had mentioned to Vaughan, 'The change will further involve Birmingham in the expense of a new Bishop's residence,' so it would seem he was proposing to move out of Oscott. In retrospect the fact that Ilsley continued to live in the seminary could be considered an error of judgement on his part. If the retention of the entire Birmingham staff was not looked on generally with favour by some of the other dioceses involved in the scheme, the Bishop's presence in the seminary would seem like going one step further in the wrong direction, causing repercussions at a later stage brought on largely because it was considered that too much influence rested with the Diocese of Birmingham.

Vaughan had mentioned in the initial stages of the negotiations, as early as May 1894, that he had no wish 'to subject the college to the uncertainty of sudden changes according to the views of succeeding Ordinaries' and gave his reasons: 'This would be to perpetuate the one-man-management system, to reduce our strength and follow the example of Italy which the Pope is doing all he can to change.'[2] But the question as to whether any attempt was made by him to persuade Ilsley to live away from the college has to remain unanswered, as there appears to be no further reference to the subject in any correspondence between them. Invariably when Ilsley was referred to in the future in commentaries or written articles to do with his own diocese, it was as someone who was considered as a permanent and inseparable part of the seminary community within which he had chosen to remain.

In the wake of recent events, the Oscotian Society adjusted the view they had previously taken against the changeover of Oscott College to the diocesan seminary, taking the opportunity at their first general meeting 'to express their thorough appreciation of the high and important position that Oscott has assumed through the new order of things'. They conveyed this change of attitude in a joint letter to the board in October 1898, and the message continued, 'any regrets therefore, at the change are softened and in a great measure removed by the knowledge of the greatness of the work Oscott is now called upon to perform'.[3]

The long article in *The Tablet* by Snead-Cox, written with Vaughan's approval and entitled 'Important Ecclesiastical Change', naturally had nothing but praise for the new arrangement. It began: 'Large as has been the part which Oscott has played in the story of latter-day Catholicism in England, it seems destined for a wider role in the future.' He emphasized that Ushaw was the principal seminary for the North, while Oscott was to serve the South; both establishments having stability brought about by the administration of a board of bishops.[4] There were no letters of dissent on this occasion. The mood seemed generally to have changed over the years to one which, in acknowledging the development of Ilsley's earlier work in transforming Oscott into a *Grand Séminaire*, now appreciated its final evolution into a Central Seminary.[5]

Describing this phase in the history of the college as 'a fresh start', George Bishop, who came to Oscott from the Westminster diocese in 1898, later wrote in *The Oscotian*, 'This time it was Dr Parkinson to whom as Rector was given the responsibility of carrying to success the ideals that were in the Bishops' minds.' His article described the feelings of some of the students on going outside their own dioceses to the Central Seminary: 'There is no need to conceal the fact that to many of us the idea of going to Oscott was extremely distasteful ... rumour had been busy and given us a distorted idea of the life there

Figure 10.1 *Bishop Ilsley with a group of servants in the courtyard outside Oscott College.*

... but in the shortest time all prejudice was swept away, for the reality showed beyond a doubt that we had entered a life of happiness and brotherly companionship.'[6]

## Disappointment for Victor Schobel

Victor Schobel was not included among the Oscott staff at this time. Two years earlier in a letter to Ilsley written on 23 June 1895 he said: 'While perfectly ready to help your Lordship in every way I can, to promote this great scheme of clerical education, my own personal desire would be to retire to make room for younger enthusiasts. A quiet mission would suit me well for a year or two until I regain my strength for harder work in a more populous mission.' Two months later on 11 August, Ilsley reported to Vaughan, 'Dr Schobel is in need of 12 months' rest, but I have made arrangements for a course of lectures during his absence.'[7] A temporary appointment begun by Schobel that September as Chaplain at Oulton Abbey, was destined in his case to become a permanent one, so 'at the time that the Central

Seminary, for which he had hoped so long and laboured so hard, became a reality, his health continued to give anxiety, and when the staff was reconstituted in September 1897, the veteran professor had been superseded'. Mervyn Tower in his commemorative essay on Schobel suggests that 'it was a bitter blow for him not to be appointed to the Staff of the institution that he had nurtured', and according to his obituary in *The Oscotian*, 'This was a severe disappointment to him, perhaps the keenest and most enduring in his life.'[8]

Schobel was 49 at this time, and although from the very first he had always made such valuable contributions to the life of the seminary in his teaching, writings and schemes of work, Mervyn Tower also observed of him that, 'It is one thing to promote the highest possible standards; but it is quite another to be unadaptable and unrealistic.' This is a reference to the exacting demands he made on his students. 'Herein might have been Schobel's greatest weakness and this could have been a contributory factor to his poor health, leading to what appears to have been a breakdown in 1895.'

From this time on, as well as periodic depression and times of exhaustion, his general health continued to decline. It is possible he may briefly have considered a return to Oscott again, and finally facing the reality must have caused him understandable disappointment. But to a certain extent his mission was completed and under the circumstances Ilsley could do no more than accept his continued retirement, and duly acknowledge his work over the years: 'It was no coincidence that it was at the opening of the term of the new Central Seminary that the Bishop wrote to Rome for a prelacy for Schobel. It was certainly a recognition for all he had done for Oscott and Schobel well deserved this recompense for all his labours.'[9]

## Vaughan's Plan Not Working Out in Practice

According to Snead-Cox, Herbert Vaughan did not feel wholly satisfied by his efforts on behalf of Oscott, and in spite of all the years of careful preparation for the Central Seminary he always looked back on his work connected with it 'with perhaps a shade of disappointment, that was certainly not due to any misgivings as to the soundness of the principle to which he had tried to give effect', but because 'success in its completeness eluded him'. The Cardinal approved of the agreed plan, but not the way in which it 'had worked in practice', and there were some among his own chapter 'who from the outset thought the arrangement whereby students were sent to study outside the diocese derogatory to the dignity of the Metropolitan See'. This was because they seemed unable to come to terms with the idea of their students receiving their training in a provincial setting rather than within the Archdiocese of Westminster.[10] It is also possible that they may have considered the outlook of some of those on the staff of the Central Seminary rather too socialistic. Vaughan nevertheless subscribed handsomely toward the endowment, and provided the greatest number of students. When the college opened with 74 students, 29 came from Westminster and 26 from Birmingham.

But in a short time he must have felt he had forfeited too much in order to protect Ilsley's interests, particularly by sanctioning the reappointing of all the original Oscott staff. Vaughan experienced problems in this respect only a year after the new system had been set up, and this happened because it reached his ears 'that the Oscott Professors drank spirits regularly once a week and that they placed them on the table whenever there were visitors'. Confiding the matter to Bishop Riddell of Northampton in a letter written on 27 October after the meeting of the board in 1898, he said that when he had visited the college a year earlier he expressed an earnest hope to the Rector, 'that the practice might be given up on account of the great influence which the example of Oscott must exercise upon the clergy in the South of England'. He mentioned he was 'agreeably surprised' when the Rector seemed to immediately concur with his wishes, 'telling me at supper on the same day that they were going to begin that night the disuse of spirits while the Bishops were present'.

But when Vaughan returned to Oscott a year later in September 1898 he was dismayed to find nothing had changed, and because he had then pursued the matter further he now found the professors had sent out a circular letter to the board on 26 October commenting strongly on his request to them. He told Riddell 'I have been surprised by a Circular from the Professors at Oscott, received this morning, which is based on a misapprehension.' He continued, 'Now I did say to the Rector I should be very glad if they would give up the use of ardent spirits and limit themselves to wine because of the importance of doing all we can to discourage the use of spirits among the younger clergy. I pointed out that my efforts would be of little avail when the example of the staff of Professors at the Central Seminary could be quoted against me.' He said that he had also suggested to Henry Parkinson it would be best if the professors carried out his wishes through a 'spontaneous act of cooperation' to prevent the matter having to come before the bishops. He regretted that his proposal had later been presented to the professors accompanied with the threat of his intention of bringing it before the board. They now appeared be resenting his manner toward them as much as his request over the use of spirits. 'I propose to write them a kind letter at some length,' he told Riddell, 'I hope to show them that I have no distrust of them but I am seeking cooperation in a grave matter.' [11]

Writing a week later on 4 November to the Vice Rector Francis Lloyd, Vaughan conveyed his feelings on the matter in the effusively apologetic manner that he sometimes characterstcally used, saying 'the last thing on my mind would be to treat the Professors, in whom I have placed my highest hopes for the future of our ecclesiastical life and spirit, with reserve and distrust. I would ask you to let me speak with openness & offer such explanations as I hope may remove mis-apprehension.'

He then embarked on several lengthy passages in order to make his point: 'My experience as Bishop in the North and South of England', he began, 'has convinced me that one of the most insidious evils besetting the people & clergy in this country is the drink evil'. After giving a number of examples to back up his argument he continued: 'If the Bishop is striving to meet the evil in one way & the priests who have in their hands the formation of his clergy, condemn his method by setting it aside every week, doing the very thing he is striving to induce his clergy not to do, there must ensue a serious clashing of counsel & authority, where all should be working together.'

## Difficulties with Birmingham Staff

It was for this reason, he explained, that a year earlier he had expressed 'an earnest hope' that the practice should be given up. He continued: 'Now what has occurred? On my visit to the College last month I was grieved to learn that no change had been made. I knew that the practice had become a matter of comment not only among strangers, but among some of my own students & priests.' [12] At this point he did not explain how he had come to know that the business had become a matter of general debate, but it would seem most likely that he was one of those who had led the way by discussing it among the other bishops.

It was possible that the staff had not taken the Archbishop's comments seriously the previous year and so the matter had been set aside. But now with Vaughan basing his action on his precise powers as Chairman of the Board, they had seen beyond the immediate question in hand, and looked on the whole concern as a serious threat to the agreed constitution by which they now lived. They considered that Vaughan was exercising more power over their personal lives than they had previously envisaged, and that is why they had sent out their circular letter to the bishops on 26 October, making it clear that they believed the 'threatened enactments' at which Vaughan hinted, 'against our harmless weekly symposium', would reach 'down to the most innocent details of our daily life'. Their words were strong – 'If we are liable at any moment to be fettered by enactments like that now threatening us, we fear that all our confidence would be broken, and that we should be continually harassed by painful expectancy as to what might next come upon us.' The letter was signed by Francis Lloyd, John McIntyre, F. J. Sandy, J. O'Leary, John Hopwood and E. H. Godwin, all being Birmingham men constituting the whole Oscott staff.[13]

Figure 10.2 *John McIntyre on the steps of the entrance to Oscott College. Oscott College albums.*

In his reply to Francis Lloyd, Vaughan answered them in conciliatory terms saying, 'I much regret that I did not take pains to lay before you the reasons which had been working my mind. These, I feel sure would have rendered a misunderstanding impossible.'[14] Even acknowledging the authority of Vaughan, which as Cardinal-Archbishop he had over his clergy, at this point his letter makes it difficult to realize he was speaking to a group of intelligent and highly educated men, as he continued, 'You speak of "our harmless weekly symposium". No doubt "harmless" so far as you are personally & directly concerned – of this there can be no question or suspicion. But this pagan or classical word is used, not only in the purely literary sense of the Nineteenth Century, but in its Etymological & dictionary sense, of a Drinking Feast. Now Oscott stands on a great eminence. The eyes of the clergy will naturally turn more & more to Oscott. Would it not be sad if the clergy were by degrees to feel encouraged to Establish Drinking Feasts every week or oftener in imitation of the Professors of Oscott?'

## Rules and Regulations

It was perhaps not surprising that Francis Lloyd made no immediate reply to this extraordinary letter, and eleven days later on 15 November Vaughan wrote again and reminded him 'At the beginning of the month I sent a letter & hope it reached you, though I have not heard that it has.' By this time he must have begun to realize the disadvantage he was up against by having the 'united opposition' of the whole Oscott staff to deal with. He therefore attempted to counter the situation by submitting to them this further letter which came in the form almost of an ultimatum, laying out the rules and regulations under three main headings, by which the lives of superiors and professors were governed while living under the authority of the Board of Bishops in a central seminary.

He reminded Francis Lloyd that in the same way as a diocesan seminary came 'under the absolute direction and control of the Ordinary who has the right and the duty to make from time to time such regulations for the instruction and training of his clergy as he may think most suitable to the needs of the Diocese and the Church,' so the exercise of this right was transferred to the Board of Bishops in the case of a central seminary. He pointed out that the advantage of this was that 'a Board has a collective wisdom & prudence' and so they in turn had 'a greater security for permanence, continuity and for freedom from ill-judged arbitrary interference & changes than if they lived under a succession of Ordinaries'.

Under his next main heading he passed on 'from the question of principle to practice'. He first listed the duties of the bishops concerned under this permanent and unchanging constitution, and then in the last part described that it was 'our duty to look carefully into the material, financial, educational and religious conditions of the College & to act accordingly'. He commented that he supposed 'you would raise no objection to this, nor does your circular convey to me an impression that you do'.

Under the third and last main heading he said, 'It comes, I think to this – whether you have confidence or not in the judgement & prudence of the Board of Bishops.' Talking of this confidence he continued, 'it may be shaken & destroyed by a series of obviously imprudent or mischievous acts, or by a radical difference on main principles'.

He said their circular was 'sufficiently explicit' and hoped that his previous letter would have dispelled the apprehension they expressed. By this time he may have realized the deep water he was in, particularly when he said he hoped 'that you will not draw a general conclusion from a particular case'. But on returning to a more conciliatory tone (but still with some reservations), 'I may say at once that nothing could be further from my wish than to interfere with "the most innocent details of your daily life" or with any details whatsoever, unless they happen to exert an injurious influence on the younger clergy. I am confident that all apprehension on the part of the Professors is quite groundless; & here I can speak for my colleagues. It is not our custom to harass with useless regulations those who are filled with the ecclesiastical spirit and are sharing with us the Apostolic heat and burden of the day.'

His final observation was: 'During the first stages of its existence the Board would naturally be likely to make more regulations concerning details than later on when it will have impressed its mind on the College. But the Board would be placed in a painful position were its action resented or a desire expressed that it should curtail its freedom or discretion.' Is it possible that at any time Vaughan came to realize that it was not the regulations imposed by the board that the professors were objecting to, but his own personal intervention? He concluded 'I will be obliged if you will read these letters to your Colleagues.'[15]

## Possible Resignation

The professors dispatched a joint reply to Vaughan just over a fortnight later on 2 December, pointing out that their reply had been delayed 'In our desire of avoiding anything like a hasty or ill-considered reply to your Eminence's carefully written letters.' Unfortunately the mischief had already been done, and the tone of the professors' reply to him, if not entirely lacking in respect, was about to turn all the arguments that he had so elaborately given to them, right round in their own favour.

They made a veiled suggestion of the possibility of their resignations, slipped in among the text of their letter, by saying that should the service they unquestioningly agreed to carry out 'prove distasteful to us, there will always be to us an easy and honourable way out of it'. The letter was also concise and to the point. Regarding his original direction in October a year earlier for the custom to be changed, they began: 'When, and to whom such a wish was expressed we have no means of knowing; but what we do know is, that no hint of it ever reached our ears.' The implication being that his original complaint had not been considered of any significance, and so had not been reported to them. It is of interest to note here that the Rector, Henry Parkinson, appears to have distanced himself from any direct involvement in the matter by neither sending out nor signing any of the letters to do with it. This leaves the question open as to whether or not he ever attempted to carry out the Cardinal's wishes. On further consideration he may have decided to ignore Vaughan's request or, not wishing to deal with it personally, subsequently chose instead to leave the matter in the hands of his vice rector, Francis Lloyd.

Deeply criticizing the way in which Vaughan had handled the affair they explained 'that we should not have felt it to be in the slightest degree unfriendly or inconsiderate if the matter had been referred to the Board; but we certainly did feel it most keenly when the matter was informally set before us as if to be settled by ourselves by our own choice, and yet at the same time being given to understand that we should not be allowed to vote on it'.

They were even more critical of the Cardinal's announcement that their practice 'had become a matter of comment'. They declared 'We can hardly express the shame and pain that those words caused us. A sense of ignominy of our position certainly comes strongly upon us, when we think that mere idle tittle-tattle enters into serious consideration, & actually finds a place among motives which seem to call for legislation against us. – When we think how, on hearing of the enactment, those irresponsible gossips will rejoice to see the success of their whispering. – But most of all, when we think how students will be elevated in mind above us, when they come to understand that our lives are liable to be ruled and governed in accordance with their comments.'

Herbert Vaughan must surely by then have seen the folly of attempting to make the drinking of spirits a major issue of either discipline or legislation among the enactments of the Central Seminary, and this must have been particularly so when he read the final somewhat facetious paragraph of the professors' letter, saying: 'In conclusion, it will be only just to ourselves to say, that as soon as a Crusade of the Clergy against Spirits is publicly organised or announced, we will be ready at once to give our names publicly.'

Bishop Riddell wrote a brief reply to Francis Lloyd a fortnight later which could be construed to have more than one meaning. It ran, 'Your letter signed by yourself and six other Professors is to hand. From a few words of H. E., whispered to me after supper on 18th, I gathered that the Professors had taken the initiative in the matter you refer to: we certainly did not!' Vaughan kept Riddell informed on the matter by sending him a copy of the professors' letter the following January. 'On receipt of it I contented myself with sending merely a formal acknowledgement,' he wrote, 'but the tone which the professors have adopted is such that I shall be obliged to bring matters before the Board at our next meeting.'[16]

## Vaughan's Remoteness toward his Clergy

The fact that Herbert Vaughan was by no means a teetotaller and drank moderately himself makes his attitude toward the Oscott staff hard to understand, particularly as it was so desirable that above all he should have good relations with them. But his treatment of them follows the usual pattern of his apparent remoteness towards his clergy on the whole. Now in these, his declining years, with his strength failing, he was no doubt to be sharply reminded that Francis Bourne had been right in one respect, and that he had in reality surrendered control not only over his own students, but over his staff also, certainly as far as this ludicrous issue was concerned, and with hindsight he must now have realized the power weighed far too heavily on the side of the Birmingham diocese.

The immediate problem he had involved himself in must have been considered by most of those concerned as trivial. Snead-Cox observed: 'The question at issue was one upon which opinions might legitimately differ, but it was one on which he felt strongly.' Certainly if this episode was typical of Vaughan's way of handling things at Oscott it is not surprising he looked back on his work there 'with a shade of disappointment'.

But Edward Ilsley's attitude of initially continuing to keep a firm hand on the things that mattered can also be well understood, particularly if Archbishop Vaughan was allowing himself to be side-tracked by such issues. There is a final reference to be found among the minutes of the Bishops' Meeting a year after this, on 17 October 1899, that it had been agreed unanimously at the morning session: 'That the Rector be told that the Bishops will be gratified if serving spirits be discontinued at the Professors' meetings' – they were, in so many words, suggesting that the whole episode should be forgotten!

## An Advantage for Edward Ilsley

The choice that had been made of Oscott for the Central Seminary, and the personal attitude of the two men mainly responsible for its foundation, were bound to bring about certain repercussions that are worth examining here. If Herbert Vaughan had been able to use Wonersh, or had used the site of St Edmund's College, which was in his own diocese – a vague thought he momentarily conceived and as quickly laid aside – the whole project of the Central Seminary would have been more his own. As it turned out, because he had chosen Oscott College for the Central Seminary, the control he sought tended to elude him from the outset. This seems almost inevitable partly because he lived away from the seminary, in London, while Ilsley had the advantage of living right within its walls. As Edward Ilsley was so closely concerned with the seminary, it was in the natural order of things that he would see himself in many ways as needing to continue as the leading figure in the proceedings, particularly as it was his natural tendency to show the way. He also had the tremendous advantage of knowing all his staff very well, whereas Herbert Vaughan had the added difficulty of not remembering names and faces. Arthur McCormack, in his biography of Vaughan, summed up the situation for him at this time, as 'a difficulty to be overcome', and he portrays him as 'having recourse to prayer and to Rome. Patience would do the trick, not hustling.' [17]

Towards the end of the negotiations, Vaughan not only appeared patiently willing to take account of what Edward Ilsley had to say, but in most cases would attempt to carry out his wishes as far as possible. He possibly took this attitude in respect of Ilsley's experience and knowledge of the internal workings of the seminary, feeling that Ilsley could manage things better than himself, or he may have come to recognize the Bishop's unbending tenacity, and so ultimately decided that this would be the easier way to arrive at a solution and so bring things to a conclusion, sooner rather than later. The worsening condition of his health could have forced him to lean on Ilsley finally in this way, or perhaps it was simply the fact that some of his greatness lay in his ability to be flexible and to give way if he thought it for the best.

However it was that the Central Seminary ultimately came into being, the final outcome resulted in the creation of a unique institution. There were bound to be problems occurring at the beginning of its foundation, but it can be seen that they were by no means insurmountable, and they would have automatically been solved by the carefully defined regulations gradually coming into satisfactory working operation over the years. The opinion of Mgr Philip Hughes in his essay 'The Coming Century', was that the Central Seminary was 'a remarkable success, and it gave every promise of becoming the long desiderated centre of Catholic thought'.[18]

## Notes

1  D.B., p. 15.
2  B.A., B11262, Letter from Vaughan to Ilsley, 28 May 1894.
3  St Joseph's College, Mill Hill, Scrapbooks 1898, p. 27. Letter from the Oscotian Society to the Board of Bishops, October 1898.
4  Snead-Cox, vol. i, p. 181: 'Among the results of Father Vaughan's first visit to America ... must be counted a new appreciation of the power of the press. On his return to England he determined at once to have a paper of his own. In the summer of 1868 he was in negotiation for two of the existing Catholic papers and decided to buy *The Tablet*.'
5  B.A., B11955, Letter from Bishop O'Neil to Bishop Ilsley, from Port Louis, Mauritius, 27 August 1897.
6  O.C.A., *Oscotian* 24, Revd G. H. Bishop, 'Rector of the Central Seminary', pp. 171–2.
7  Westminster, Bo 5/24, Letter from Ilsley to Vaughan from Cortina, 11 August 1895. B.A., B11480, Letter from Schobel to Ilsley.
8  Schobel, pp. 8, 9.
9  M. Tower, 'A Missing Link: Oscott's Bavarian Connection 1848–1915',

in *Essays*, pp. 151–2. He went to the parish of St Augustine's, Solihull, in 1908, but returned to Oulton a year later on account of ill-health. Diabetes became his chief ailment, and he died in 1915 at the age of 66.

10   Snead-Cox, vol. ii, p. 63.
11   Northampton, Letter from Cardinal Vaughan to Bishop Arthur Riddell of Northampton, 27 October 1898.
12   *Ibid.*, Letter from Cardinal Vaughan to Francis Lloyd, 4 November 1898.
13   *Ibid.*, Circular letter of the Oscott professors, to the Board, October 1898.
14   *Ibid.*, Letter from Cardinal Vaughan to Francis Lloyd, 4 November 1898.
15   *Ibid.*, Letter from Cardinal Vaughan to Francis Lloyd, 15 November 1898.
16   *Ibid.*, Letter from Cardinal Vaughan to Bishop Riddell, 25 January 1899.
17   McCormack, p. 268.
18   Philip Hughes, 'The Coming Century', in Beck, p. 36.

## CHAPTER ELEVEN

# Policies Reversed

## Deaths of Pope Leo and Herbert Vaughan 1903

Within six years of St Mary's becoming the Central Seminary, Cardinal Vaughan died, in June 1903, and the death of Pope Leo occurred one month later. This sad coincidence meant that the two main supporters of the ideals of the Central Seminary were now gone, and mainly because of this, the burgeoning stages of its early development were unfortunately to be cut short. The new Pope, Pius X, translated Bishop Bourne of Southwark, who was then 42, to the See of Westminster as successor to Cardinal Vaughan, and Mgr Hughes in a few well-chosen words describes the course of events and its outcome: 'When in his place, the founder of the Southwark Diocesan Seminary was named archbishop, the older policy was restored, and the Central Seminary, deprived of its main support, ceased to be: after forty years one can safely say a major tragedy.'[1]

After attending Ushaw, Francis Bourne's training took place at St Edmund's when he was 16. He continued his studies at St Sulpice and Louvain University and was ordained at the age of 23 in 1884. He was 28 when he started the foundation of the Southwark Diocesan Seminary at Henfield in Sussex, and was appointed Rector when it was moved to Wonersh a year later in 1890. Cardinal Vaughan's plan to found a central seminary threatened Wonersh in 1893 when it was hardly more than a *petit séminaire*. But this was averted through the joint efforts of Bishop Butt and Father Francis Bourne, so the seminary remained outside Vaughan's scheme with the approval of the Holy See, and has continued on its way as a diocesan seminary ever since.[2] Three years later, in 1896, Bourne was consecrated coadjutor to Bishop Butt, and the following year, in 1897, he became Bishop of Southwark – the same year the Central Seminary was officially founded at Oscott.

Knowing that his own views did not in any way coincide with those

Figure 11.1 *Cardinal Francis Bourne, Bishop of Southwark (1897–1903), Archbishop of Westminster (1903–35). Drawing made from a photograph in the Westminster Archdiocesan Archives.*

of Francis Bourne, Edward Ilsley must have been well prepared for the policy the new Archbishop of Westminster would predictably pursue, and surely enough, as Chairman of the Board of Bishops, Bourne gave some indication of what was in his mind at their annual meeting held at Oscott in early October 1903, just six weeks after his translation. The enthronement of the new Archbishop took place that year in Westminster Cathedral on 29 December. A month earlier he had travelled to Rome to receive the *pallium*, which distinguished the Metropolitan from the suffragan bishops. He read his first Westminster Pastoral from the steps of the sanctuary in the cathedral on the morning of his enthronement, and having praised Archbishop Vaughan for the legacy he had left behind him, he then intimated that he was about to reverse his predecessor's policy of the Central Seminary by restoring St Edmund's to his diocesan seminary. His words must have left little doubt in the minds of his hearers as to what his future policy would bring. Some must have feared that the days of the Central Seminary were numbered, while others were ready to rally to his support.

Because the Westminster chapter had never been entirely in favour of the arrangement whereby their students attended the Central Seminary, and as 'in the meantime at St Edmund's Mgr Ward had made numerous additions to the School buildings and had restored the College to something of its former prestige and position',[3] Bourne was able to go straight ahead without encountering any untoward difficulties, with the preparation of his plans to bring back into line his ideals for the system of localized diocesan seminaries. Within four months of his appointment he ordered considerable work to begin on the enlargement of St Edmund's for this specific purpose, and the foundation stone for the new building was laid by the President, Mgr Bernard Ward, on 20 February 1904 with due ceremony.[4] The work was pushed forward by employing a huge team of over 80 workmen on the new buildings, and a massive block later to be known as 'Allen Hall', the new wing for the divines, was soon nearing completion. By 22 September 1904 St Edmund's was once more opened as the diocesan seminary and 'the return of the exiles' was warmly greeted by Mgr Ward and Dr Burton, the vice-president, who cordially welcomed this rehabilitation of 'Douay in England'.[5]

## Bourne's Change of Policy

The previous 25 December 1903, even before his enthronement had

189

taken place, Bourne wrote to Monsignor Parkinson telling him about his intentions: 'I propose in future to have a school of Theology in the diocese of Westminster. This means that I shall not be able to send any more Divines to Oscott. The students who are already with you will remain, if you will kindly allow them ... as I do not wish to interrupt their course. The reasons for this change of policy are to my mind absolutely convincing,' he wrote. In his reply to this most unwelcome letter, Henry Parkinson made his feelings quite clear: 'The Bishop of Birmingham gave me your message on his return from the meeting of the Bishops at Archbishop's House; and while I cannot but deplore the decision at which your Grace has arrived, I am grateful for the courtesy and delicacy with which you have followed up your verbal message by a letter ... forestalling the public announcement of Tuesday next.'[6] Apart from his obvious leanings towards Trent, Francis Bourne was endorsing the general attitude of his chapter by withdrawing his students from the Central Seminary and setting them up again in his own establishment. This they considered altogether more fitting for the Archdiocese of Westminster. Unfortunately, Bourne's concept of things generally was ultra-conservative and narrow, in contrast to Ilsley, who was more percipient and practical pastorally.

In 1904 a meeting of the Board of Bishops was held at Oscott on 26 January, in order that they might put forward their opinions on the present situation regarding the Central Seminary, and in addition to Bourne, five out of the seven of them were there – Bishop Cahill of Portsmouth, who was now also secretary, Bishop Burton of Clifton, Bishop Mostyn of Menevia, Bishop Brindle of Nottingham and Bishop Ilsley. They first appointed Archbishop Bourne trustee in succession to Cardinal Vaughan. Bishop Riddell of Northampton was in Rome at the time and Bishop Hedley of Newport was also unable to attend. On Bishop Riddell's return at the end of February, Bishop Ilsley wrote to him to let him know what had taken place, and in his letter he gave an indication of his concern about the turn of events that had come about since Francis Bourne had become Archbishop of Westminster. Ilsley mentioned: 'Unfortunately the Bishop of Newport was detained by urgent matters at home that day so only 5 of us met ... and we began to talk about the future of the Central Seminary. The Archbp. told us why he felt constrained to carry out the measures contemplated – and it seemed to me that the Bishops of Portsmouth and Clifton were in sympathy with the Archbishop. Whatever was urged by the Bp. of Menevia and myself was addressed to unwilling ears – so it seemed to me – and we proposed no resolution for the simple reason that it had no chance of passing. So things have remained as they were.'

The 'measures contemplated' outlined by Bourne of withdrawing his students from Oscott and restoring St Edmund's as his own seminary would be disastrous ones as far as Ilsley was concerned, and he was obviously sensing that things were on a very uncertain footing with some of the bishops on the board as well, so he decided that it would be wiser to appeal directly to the Holy See rather than spending precious time at this stage trying to bring them round to his way of thinking. He now explained his reasons for this to Bishop Riddell: 'So convinced, however am I that the existence of the Central Seminary has not been brought to the notice of the New Authorities in Rome, & so strongly do I feel that they ought to know of the solemn compact we entered into in compliance with the repeated wish & desire of the Holy See, & that the Holy See as well as ourselves is fully committed to the Central Seminary Scheme ... therefore such a step as that in contemplation – the withholding of nearly one half the number of our students & setting up of a rival seminary in the South – ought not to be taken without full knowledge & approval of the Holy See.' Ilsley told Riddell that the Bishops of Newport and Menevia were both prepared to write independently 'in the same sense'. He then went on to ask him if he 'might not see your way to throw your weight into the scale for maintaining the Central Seminary and saving it from the disaster with which it is threatened ... This would mean the wrecking of what Cardl. Vaughan regarded the greatest work of his life after the Foreign Missions.'[7]

## Bishop Riddell of Northampton

From the way Ilsley wrote to Riddell it would seem that he must have imagined that as a member of the Board who had worked with Cardinal Vaughan for some years, Riddell would owe his allegiance to the Central Seminary, and it would be on these grounds that he trusted him to do so, especially as Herbert Vaughan had tended to confide in Riddell over some of his difficulties. But he was to discover that this was by no means the case. As it happened, Riddell had already communicated with Bishop Cahill on 5 January, the day before the Oscott meeting, telling him that he would be unable to attend and putting forward the views that he wished to have represented: 'As in my opinion Bp. Butt was right to start Wonersh so the Archp. is right to restore Old Hall as the Westminster Seminary,' he wrote. 'I do not see this as the annihilation of Oscott. His Grace might push Old Hall without detriment to Oscott, & might lessen only slightly his students at the latter.' He was already thinking of the financial benefits that might accrue – 'If any part of the Professorial fund be withdrawn I shall certainly go in for repayment of the Northampton £2000.'

Although Riddell, who had become Bishop of Northampton in 1880, had been co-operative in the past when Oscott was the diocesan seminary, he probably did not like Ilsley's continuing control once it had become the Central Seminary. He may also have resented Ilsley's association with Vaughan, who was his own metropolitan in the Province of Westminster, and so he was now ready to make a stand with Archbishop Bourne against Ilsley. Cahill's somewhat sanguine reply to his letter shows that Riddell was fully conversant with the situation – suggesting that there must have already been considerable discussion about it behind closed doors. 'I am sorry we are not to have the advantage of your attendance,' Cahill wrote, 'I suppose that we can hardly come to any final conclusion yet. The Archbishop has notified Oscott that he will not remove any who are there belonging to him, but he will send no more. As to the Professors' Fund, I understand the Bishop of Birmingham contends that it always remains for Birmingham. The statutes do not provide for the return of the money; but the Archbishop thinks that the trust deed does so provide. He must inspect it.' There is no mention of the value of the system itself as a training ground for future priests, but the financial side of things had obviously already been carefully weighed up in his mind. 'I should be glad to have back my £2000 as it makes my one student cost me practically £150. I would rather be in a position of an outsider paying £70, and surrendering my £80 worth of control – a dear commodity.'

It must have come as a shock for Ilsley to discover that Bishop Riddell already had a natural leaning toward Archbishop Bourne's views, and this became apparent when he replied to Ilsley's letter on 4 March, clearly defining his outlook on the whole matter: 'As the Council of Trent, and the present Holy Father, advocate a diocesan seminary where possible, I hold that Abp. Bourne is right in restoring Old Hall as the Westminster Seminary: for years I have held that it was a mistake for Card. Manning to transfer his students to Hammersmith and another mistake for Card. Vaughan not to take them back to Old Hall when he sold Hammersmith. Archbp. Bourne is repairing these two mistakes & I could not oppose him.'[8]

## Riddell Supports Bourne

Bishop Riddell's reply revealed that he held absolutely opposite views to Ilsley's way of thinking, and this apparently had always been so, to the point where he must have acted on the first possible opportunity that presented itself in a deliberate move to bring in the present opposing system. It was his suggestion that the name of Francis Bourne was included in the *terna* at the bishops' meeting he presided over (as senior bishop of the province) to consider the successor to Cardinal Vaughan, which ultimately led to his selection as Archbishop of Westminster. So in this way Riddell had very largely contrived this present change of policy. Francis Bourne's appointment was a grave disappointment to those who favoured the other two candidates, Dr Hedley, Bishop of Newport, and Dom Aidan Gasquet – both were Benedictines and they were 'desired on account of their scholarship, their industry and their learning'. Had either of them been appointed this present unfortunate circumstance would not have come about.

With regard to his attitude towards Bourne, Riddell wrote in the same letter: 'Another reason for not opposing him is that when the Holy See sanctioned the scheme of Card. Vaughan to make Oscott into the Central Seminary, it at the very same time sanctioned the Bp. of Southwark having his own seminary at Wonersh & standing aloof.' Certainly when Ilsley was in Rome in August 1896 he had written a memorandum to himself regarding Oscott, which bears this out. When he looked into the matter he ascertained that 'Propaganda confirms: no bishop is obliged to send his students there, and has a right to establish his own seminary.'[9] This was to be the considerable loophole Bourne was to use in order to establish the authenticity of his present policy.

Riddell made another fairly devastating point to Ilsley that he was later to convey to Archbishop Bourne, saying that he could well remember the time when 'Oscott as the Birmingham Seminary flourished and the Bishop and Chapter of Birmingham did not desire a change: in fact they opposed the scheme of Cardinal Vaughan'. All the points that Riddell made to Ilsley at this time he repeated in a letter to Bourne ten months later in January 1905 'in the hope that it may help towards a settlement of the question now before the Sacred Congregation'. As one of the bishops connected with the Central Seminary he said he now supported Bourne's policy, and continued, 'As a Bishop in the Midlands I did not like the scheme of Cardinal Vaughan & very unwillingly joined in the project & paid £2000 towards the Professorial Fund.'[10]

Riddell gave no comfort to Ilsley at this time, especially when he wrote, 'I should be satisfied if the Holy See sanctioned Oscott ceasing to be a Central Seminary and becoming again the Birmingham Diocesan Seminary.' Ilsley seemed grateful that Bishop Riddell had at least given him all the facts concerning what was in his mind, because at least he now knew where he stood. He replied the following day, 'I thank you for the frank expression of your sentiments re the Central Seminary. It is a matter of regret that we cannot count upon your Lordship to support my appeal to Propaganda.' Ilsley then pointed out to him that whereas his own argument to Propaganda was that the Central Seminary was a wise move on the part of Cardinal Vaughan, Bishop Riddell regarded it 'as a mistake. So the whole argument falls to the ground in your view.' Already seeing clearly what the future might bring, particularly without Riddell's support, Ilsley did not hide his feelings, and at this point became scathing in his tone: 'If the authorities in Rome take your view of it, the Central Seminary is doomed. You are not serious when you suggest that Shrewsbury & Salford, whose interest is in Ushaw, and Nottingham which has scarcely any funds, can compensate for the withdrawal of the Westr. contingent – which has been on an average nearly half the College.'[11]

## Ilsley's Appeal to Propaganda

At his request, Ilsley dispatched to Riddell a copy of his appeal to Propaganda, in which he gave the full history of how the formation of the Central Seminary had come about. Riddell may have been right in remembering that at one stage Bishop Ilsley and his chapter, concerned with the possible loss of control of Oscott, had not particularly wished it to become the official Central Seminary. The fact that Ilsley had been in no hurry to commit himself when negotiations were in progress is further evidence of this. But circumstances were now very different, and Ilsley now had a much clearer vision of the value of the system that he himself was largely responsible for setting up, particularly as it had begun to show the benefits that such an organization brought with it. Now it was a reality, whereas in those early days it had only been a developing theory. Now he could see all that was so good and so generally beneficial about to be torn down.

His appeal to Propaganda touches on the truth of the matter, at one and the same time conveying the sheer waste of past effort, and the futility of the present situation. It also expresses some of the anguish Edward Ilsley must have been feeling over the devastating turn of events: 'Seven years have not passed and the Central Seminary is threatened with ruin. And to what end? What reason shall we give to our flock why the advice of the Holy See after being carried out with great labour has suddenly come to nought? The same state of things endures as before, yet we are compelled to make a complete change of front. What confidence will the faithful have in us when they see us moved now in this direction, now in that? What do we make ourselves when we build up again what we have destroyed?'

Realizing that he would not get the support he needed from the board now that a number of the Bishops were already siding with Archbishop Bourne, he became convinced that the answer to the problem lay with Propaganda, especially if the facts were put clearly to them. But here he was not to be right either, as testified by a letter written by Mgr Bernard Ward two months later, on 8 May 1904, when he was in Rome. Ward's letter indicates that there was certainly no automatic support there for the Central Seminary, as it would seem that as Birmingham now no longer had the support of Westminster it followed that, for right or wrong, it no longer had the support of Rome. He described to his Vice President, the Revd Edwin Burton, that Bishop Hedley's fight against Bourne in connection with the Central Seminary seemed to be getting him nowhere: 'My dear Vice,' he wrote, 'Have seen Bishop Cahill. Dr. Hedley fighting hard for Oscott & Propaganda evidently cornered and don't know what to answer. Practically we can't see what they can do – And it seems they don't see – but Bp. Hedley carries great weight, and they don't know what to say to him.' A footnote mentioned 'Bourne in first rate frame of mind.'[12]

## An Audience with Pope Pius

In December 1904 Bishop Ilsley went with John McIntyre to have an audience with Pope Pius X in the hope of putting across to him the urgent need to preserve the Central Seminary. McIntyre was familiar with the workings of Propaganda, and the tone of Ilsley's letter to Henry Parkinson seems to convey that this was their last hope: 'I am hoping for a private audience on Tuesday – We shall have done all that is possible to save the situation at Oscott,' he wrote from Rome on 18 December.[13] Enclosed was a letter written to Parkinson by McIntyre, an amended copy of which Ilsley was handing in to Propaganda that day, 'It is brief, but very forcible,' Ilsley told Parkinson. In his letter to Parkinson McIntyre said that Cardinal Satelli was very much in sympathy with them and was particularly angry at the dismantling of a good and promising work. Concerning Bourne he pointed out that 'the Archbishop's strict right cannot be denied, or its exercise forbidden', and he clarified further, pointing out Vaughan's previous shortcomings in the matter: 'The late Cardinal, although warned, rushed the matter through: he failed to set a seal in a *congresso generale* of Propaganda, which would have made Oscott as secure as Maynooth.'[14] He said that in his letter to Propaganda he had demanded that since Archbishop Bourne's right was only in creating a diocesan seminary, he should be restricted to that right and not be allowed to admit students from the Central Seminary to St Edmund's 'to the destruction of Oscott'. He also said that he had hinted that 'to prevent trickery we shall have recourse in the last resort to the Holy Father himself'. McIntyre's conviction was that Bourne had a wish to make St Edmund's the future Central Seminary. He said that although there could be no absolute evidence of this at this stage, he was nevertheless demanding a 'precautionary prohibition' against him doing so. Whether his suspicions were valid over this point or not, the realization had obviously come into his mind by then that Bourne's objection to the Central Seminary had come about through rivalry as much as anything else, and that once it had been closed down at Oscott there was the possibility of St Edmund's taking over as the new Central Seminary in its place.

In spite of the strong representations Bishop Ilsley made in Rome at this time, there was no real examination of the matter by Propaganda, so his words had no positive effect by way of saving the Central Seminary, and Archbishop Bourne was allowed to continue to freely pursue his own aims. The irony of the situation was that the Board of Bishops, set up by Vaughan in the belief that they gave permanence to the scheme, were instead to become the agent of its destruction. Ilsley and McIntyre were also faced with the discovery of Cardinal Vaughan's ultimate failure to guarantee the security of such an important structure that had the outward appearance of being settled for all time. This had come about through what Vaughan recognized as a matter for concern about himself – his habit of rushing things through too rapidly to swift conclusions – so the critical detail of the absolute securing of the Central Seminary was bypassed at the crucial stages.[15] Throughout all their negotiations, in his wisdom, Ilsley's main concern had been to keep Oscott intact for Birmingham at all costs, but Cardinal Vaughan, it would appear, had failed to 'set the seal' on the Central Seminary in its own right. This had occurred even though Ilsley had advised him that the scheme 'lacked stability', and also despite the warning given to Vaughan by Propaganda for the need of a permanent and binding agreement with them at that time. Even so it is questionable as to whether anything would have been effective at this time, as the attitude in Rome appeared to be no longer favourable towards the Central Seminary, since the death of Pope Leo.

## Dissolution of the Central Seminary 1905

Events began to draw to their inevitable conclusion when, in April 1905, the Bishop of Portsmouth, John Cahill, sent out a letter to the bishops concerned saying that he had been directed by the Archbishop of Westminster to call a meeting of the Oscott Board, to be held at Archbishop's House on Thursday 4 May at 3pm.[16] At the meeting the Bishop of Portsmouth moved the following resolution: 'That the *"Conventio Seminario Communi"* be dissolved, and the Capital contributed by the six Bishops be returned to them or their successor.' According to the notes made by Bishop Riddell on that occasion the resolution was 'proposed by the Bp. of Portsmouth and seconded by the Bp. of Northampton', and it was 'carried 4 to 3'.[17] Those in favour of the dissolution were Cardinal Bourne, Bishop Cahill of Portsmouth, Bishop Riddell of Northampton and Bishop Burton of Clifton.

John Baptist Cahill was described by Ernest Oldmeadow as 'Francis Bourne's loyal follower and admiring friend'.[18] Also it would be natural for Arthur Riddell, who recommended Bourne as successor to Cardinal Vaughan, to support him on this issue, especially as he had always stated his preferences for diocesan seminaries. As George Ambrose Burton had been consecrated in the pro-cathedral at Clifton in 1902 by Bishop Riddell it was predictable that he would vote the same way as well. Ilsley had the support of Francis Mostyn, the Bishop of Menevia who had trained at Oscott, and John Hedley, the Bishop of Newport, a Benedictine who had been associated with Ilsley since Ullathorne's time and had preached at Ilsley's consecration. Bourne's was the casting vote, and so the resolution was passed.

So yet again the hierarchy showed themselves to be over-preoccupied with authority and control, rather than preserving the development and progress they had attained in the cause of priestly training. During the course of the second half of the nineteenth century and beyond, a continuing pattern, in which what one generation built up so the next was set on demolishing, seemed to persist. This was set to continue long after Bourne's time.

Three weeks later, at the opening of the new buildings at St Edmund's College, Archbishop Bourne took the opportunity to make his views clear on the dismantling of the Central Seminary which his predecessor had so ardently built up. Knowing the power now lay in his hands he was easily able to steer the arguments at will in his own direction, saying that as Manning's policies had been relinquished by his successor, so he in the same way did not look upon Cardinal Vaughan's policies as continuous or binding. Describing the development of the Central Seminary, he continued, 'when it had assumed a more definitive shape, it did not even then realise the intentions of Cardinal Vaughan with whom it originated ... I do not say that my revered predecessor would have adopted the policy to which we are now committed, but I am certain if God had spared him to us, he would have found himself face to face with the grave contingencies which confronted me, and would have been obliged to reconsider the whole question.'[19]

His arguments were of course not logical as it was far too soon to decide whether the scheme was working satisfactorily or not. His real reasons for pursuing this course were that he opposed it from the start and he had now taken the opportunity to restore full authority to Westminster in the matter of training his own priests. He was also making claims as far as Herbert Vaughan was concerned that had no real bearing on the case. Vaughan's main problem was that because the seminary he chose was not within his own diocese he never felt that the project was quite his own. He nevertheless approved of the scheme wholeheartedly in principle and would never have entertained any thought of giving it up. His disappointment stemmed from purely personal feelings that had nothing to do with the working of the system, so Bourne's suppositions here were entirely without substance.

## Judgement Against Bourne

Some judgement must surely be laid against Francis Bourne for doing far more than simply reversing the policy of his predecessor – he was reneging on whatever had been established by all those churchmen, going right back through the years, who advocated the removal of the lay-element from ecclesiastical education, and at one stroke reintroduced all the inward-looking policies perpetuated by the small diocesan seminaries that had been superseded for the past two decades. One of his principal biographers, Ernest Oldmeadow, explained why

Francis Bourne reasoned in favour of a system wherein his church students could once more join up with the lay pupils. Although it had been decreed otherwise by the Fourth Provincial Synod under Manning in 1873, Bourne formed the opinion for himself that everything was 'intended to be understood reasonably. It did not preclude arrangements such as afterwards were made at St Edmund's, where Church students could study secular subjects with pupils not intended for the priesthood. The essence of the decree of the Fourth Council of Westminster was that the teaching of philosophy and theology must be for Church students alone and that such students must grow up in a purely ecclesiastical atmosphere.'[20] In other words Bourne was prepared to bend the rules to suit himself. Oldmeadow acknowledged 'some people were astonished at this', but went on to explain: 'Merely formal consistency did not interest Francis Bourne'; he considered that to have sent the lay boys away 'would have been unjust to the boys and also to the traditions of the school'. So he assigned to the divinity students their own refectory and other rooms to give them a life apart. Whatever his true opinions were regarding separate versus mixed seminaries, he had decided not to alter things as they stood at St Edmund's, even though he knew that the mood of the Church for over half a century had been to turn away from the dual system.

During 1909 official decisions were finally made by the governing board that the Central Seminary should discontinue, and so Oscott was once more taken over by Edward Ilsley as his diocesan seminary. In his address to the students at the opening of the new term in September, he characteristically displayed a positive and optimistic view when he told them the news that they were about to make a fresh beginning which in spirit and aspiration would be like a return to the days of fervour and enthusiasm which ensued on the foundation of St Bernard's in 1873. Summing up the position they were now in, he said they had far greater advantages than in those early days, with more students, a full staff of able professors, a splendidly equipped establishment and the experiences and traditions of nearly forty years.[21] It was certainly true that the college had considerably advanced since the days of St Bernard's, and Ilsley would have had no wish to present a negative attitude to them by dwelling on any recent loss of prestige, even though there were obvious difficulties to be faced when the numbers declined as students from the other dioceses completed their courses and moved on.

Ilsley, now aged 71, found himself in the position of having to negotiate the future of his seminary once more, but this time he needed to attempt to restore the situation as far as he could, and it was not an easy task. 'I send you notes of our interview this morning,' he wrote to Archbishop Bourne in June 1909; 'I stated that as it was the wish of your Grace and all the other Bishops of the Oscott Board that the Board should be dissolved I should not oppose any measures that you and the Board might be disposed to take for that object.' But as Ilsley had been forced to accept the dissolution, he seemed determined once more to set his own terms as far as possible, and he spoke out clearly to Bourne, pointing out all the disadvantages that were accumulating due to the changes and the effect they were having on the college. Characteristically he stated first that he did not wish anything to be concluded hastily; then he continued, 'I should further stipulate that a reasonable compensation should be made to the Diocese of Birmingham for the altered condition of the College compared with that in which it was handed over to the Board. It was then in a flourishing condition in point of numbers and prestige – it is now declining in numbers and reputation.'[22]

## Dispute over the Minute Book

A final matter of dispute between the two men regarding Oscott College property came about in 1911 over the minute book kept of all the Central Seminary proceedings. Cardinal Bourne wished to have it in his possession, claiming that it contained business affecting all the dioceses of the province. In a letter to Bishop Amigo in February 1911, Ilsley described how he handled the matter: 'I have replied that that might hold good if the business were of a provincial character affecting all the dioceses of the province – But these concern the history of Oscott far more vitally than any of the 6 other dioceses of the province which for a time had an interest in the College but now have ceased to have. I claim the Minute Book therefore for the College as a record of its history.'[23] Monsignor Crichton said, 'There was a considerable tension between Ilsley and Bourne. I heard they were not on speaking terms for years. Ilsley disliked Bourne's assumption of the leadership of the English Church.'[24] This situation does not shed a favourable light on either of them, but from the experiences Ilsley had of Bourne, both at this time and in the years to come, his attitude was understandable.

During Archbishop Bourne's time in office, for the next 25 years, he continued to spend a great deal on every kind of improvement at St Edmund's. In July 1914 an extensive fire broke out at Allen Hall and destroyed about one third of the new wing, but undeterred he set about rebuilding it on an even grander scale. The Revd Gordon Wheeler, writing nearly forty years later about Bourne's policy in Beck's *The English Catholics*, gave this judgement of him: 'It is thought by many today that he made a mistake in departing from Cardinal Vaughan's idea of a central seminary, and by pouring all his resources into St Edmund's he narrowed the outlook and potentialities of many students who might otherwise have been sent to Oscott or Rome.'[25]

When he died in 1935, at Bourne's own wish his remains were interred in the Galilee of the college chapel.[26] He believed that he had established the seminary question for generations to come, but this was not to be the case. There is a sad comment in *The Edmundian* for 1973 which observes that he was 'destined to lie amid a silence bereft of the comings and goings, the prayers and chants of the candidates for the priesthood, in whose cause he devoted so much of himself and his resources'.[27] In spite of all that had been done for the college over the years, an awareness grew of the need for it to be nearer London with the greater opportunity the capital provided for the students, both for their studies and for pastoral work. So after nearly seventy years the Westminster diocese reverted to the Manning policy of over a century ago and prepared to move their students back there in 1973, to Allen Hall in Beaufort Street, while St Edmund's became solely a lay school once more.

## Recovery of Oscott

Although Oscott had been stripped of her official status of being the Central Seminary, once the initial disappointment was sustained, she began to recover from the blow which had been dealt. Two years later, when Birmingham became an archdiocese, William Barry wrote, 'Its record is too honourable and its spirit is too large and gracious to break with the past. May we not now cherish the anticipation that as the intellectual centre of the new Province, capable of holding in touch with Oxford on the one hand, with Birmingham University on the other, St Mary's College will rise to its manifest destiny and do great things for the Midlands, for Wales and the West under the Archbishop's Standard.'[28]

There were repercussions though, and 'It was the Rector, perhaps, even more than the Bishop of Birmingham, upon whom the blow fell most heavily.'[29] Although during the first years the drop in numbers was gradual so that the change made little outward difference, in time as the Westminster students began to leave, 'the lack of numerical strength began to tell'. Then the war years took their toll, and 'when conscription came Oscott shrank to a skeleton of her former self'. However, Henry Parkinson brought the college through these difficult years and 'with his keen common-sense and cheerful energy carried on', and 'even before the end of hostilities the numbers of students began to rise, and Oscott was full again to overcrowding'. This was partly due to the influx of refugees from the Continent who had a number of Belgian seminarians with them. Because of the sound traditions which had been built up over many years, and its special architectural qualities and natural geographical position, and not forgetting the careful legal footing on which Ilsley had insisted it should stand during the negotiations for the Central Seminary and his care over the way in which things were handled during the time of its subsequent withdrawal – all these factors helped to overcome any setbacks suffered by St Mary's College in past years.

When preaching at Archbishop Ilsley's funeral on 6 December 1926, Frederick Keating, the Archbishop of Liverpool, bore testimony of how firmly things stood once more as a result of the earlier moves made by Edward Ilsley to turn Oscott into an exclusively clerical college: 'the change undoubtedly raised the standard of studies for the clergy. It must have been a great joy to him in his declining years to see Oscott with close upon eighty students, with additional buildings and improvements on modern lines and with a highly efficient and devoted staff.' He went on to say that as an old teacher of the Gregorian Chant, it must have gladdened his heart to listen to the chant 'rendered by the students in the college chapel with such exquisite skill and precision'.[30]

St Mary's was never to lose the characteristic of being the Central Seminary, which she retains to the present day. The four English seminaries have now broadened their outlook into the wider secular world of today. Oscott and Allen Hall run degree courses linked with the Catholic University of Louvain; Ushaw with Durham University, and Wonersh with Southampton. Academic courses have been adapted to meet the needs of the sudden influx of former Anglican clergymen, and resource centres set up to accommodate requirements of lay students. Oscott's academic programme for Years 1–3 is now validated by the University of Birmingham for a BA in Applied Theological Studies, in addition to the STB degree from Louvain.

Well over a century has passed since Edward Ilsley made his decisive changes to Oscott, and much of the organization that was put together then still stands. Archbishop Patrick Kelly of Liverpool, when he was Rector of the college from 1979 to 1984, described Oscott as 'The Gentle Octopus', drawing many and many towards herself over the years. This apt phrase suggests firmness and strength and at the same time flexibility. A fair description that will be approved of by most.

# Notes

1 Philip Hughes, 'The Coming Century', in Beck, p. 36.
2 Oldmeadow, vol. i, pp. 140–1.
3 'The Migration of the Westminster Seminary', *The Edmundian* 28 no. 194 (Winter 1973), p. 473. Bernard Ward was installed as a member of the chapter in 1905.
4 *The Hertford Mercury*, 20 February 1904. Bernard Ward's strong allegiance lay with St Edmund's, particularly as his father, William George Ward, was professor of dogmatic theology there between 1852 and 1858.
5 'The Migration of the Westminster Seminary', *The Edmundian* 28 no. 194 (Winter 1973), p. 473.
6 Westminster, Bo 4/2/3–1, Letter from Francis Bourne to Henry Parkinson, 25 December 1903. Parkinson replied 27 December, Bo 4/2/3.
7 Northampton, Letter from Ilsley to Bishop Arthur Riddell, 1 March 1904.
8 8 Northampton, Letter from Bishop Riddell to Ilsley, 4 March 1904.
9 B11686, Memorandum in Bishop Ilsley's hand, Rome, 24 August 1896.
10 Northampton, Letter from Bishop Riddell to Bishop Ilsley, 4 March 1904. Bishop Riddell conveyed this point to Archbishop Bourne later on 19 January 1905.
11 *Ibid.*, Letter from Bishop Ilsley to Bishop Riddell, 5 March 1904. Ilsley's use of 'Westr.' here, is short for 'Westminster.'
12 Westminster, Ward Papers, 26, Letter from Bernard Ward to Edwin Burton from the Hotel d'Angleterre, Rome, 8 May 1904.
13 O.C.A., Letter from Bishop Ilsley to Monsignor Parkinson from 45 Via Castlefiderato, Rome, 18 December 1904. McIntyre's letter was enclosed.
14 The centenary celebrations held at Maynooth in June 1895 must have left an abiding record of stability. Maynooth had no ecclesiastical foundation document, but by a series of Acts of Parliament (Irish 1795, 1800; UK 1808, 1869) the college authority became a 'body corporate with seventeen trustees, all since 1869 being Catholic bishops'. Revd P. Coish, letter, 20 August 1992, St Patrick's College, Maynooth.
15 O'Neil, pp. 61–2. In an address to his clergy in June 1893, Vaughan said 'The great success and popularity of St Cuthbert's College, Ushaw, are attributable in great measure to this stability, which has been secured to

it through the fact that it is under the general government of six co-interested Bishops.' Snead-Cox, vol. ii, p. 59.

16  Northampton. Circular to the Oscott Board of Bishops, 17 April 1905.

17  *Ibid.*, Bishop Riddell often made additional notes in pencil of the main points at any meeting, and Bishop Cahill and Bishop Riddell corresponded frequently and were in agreement over most major policies.

18  Oldmeadow, vol. i, p. 398.

19  *Ibid.*, p. 249.

20  *Ibid.*, p. 142.

21  *The Oscotian*, 3rd series, 10 no. 1 (Christmas 1909), p. 42.

22  Northampton, Copy of a letter from Ilsley to Bourne, 21 June 1909.

23  Southwark, Letter from Archbishop Ilsley to Bishop Amigo, 11 February 1911. There are two minute books in the archives at Oscott College. Both are listed as 1897–1902. One is 'Minutes of the Bishops' Conferences' and the other is 'Minutes of the Board of Bishops'.

24  Right Revd Mgr J. D. Crichton, observation given in a letter, 2 April 1984.

25  G. Wheeler, 'The Archdiocese of Westminster', in Beck, p. 174.

26  Oldmeadow, vol. ii, p. 342, 'In obedience to a deathbed wish of the Cardinal's his heart was placed in the chapel at Wonersh, the seminary he once ruled and always loved.'

27  'Migrations of the Westminster Seminary', *The Edmundian*, 28 (Winter 1973). Allen Hall was moved to Beaufort Street, where the students enjoy the advantages of studying at Heythrop College, the Catholic Central Library, the Westminster Archives, etc.

28  B.A., Scrapbooks, Press cutting.

29  Revd B. V. Miller, 'Rector of the Birmingham Diocesan Seminary', *Oscotian* 24, p. 178.

30  D.B., p. 14.

Figure 11.2  *The Archbishop's arms carved on the panelling in the centre of the oak stalls mounted on the west wall of the Chapel of St Edward at St Chad's Cathedral, Birmingham. The Motto: Justus et tenax propositi, meaning 'Just and Firm of Purpose'.*

Figure 12.1 *Edward Ilsley, Bishop of Birmingham (1888). Taken from a photograph in Oscott College Archives.*

## CHAPTER TWELVE

# Rescue, Emigration and Welfare

Edward Ilsley was 49 when he became Bishop of the Birmingham diocese. An official portrait taken at Colliers in New Street at this time shows him to be comparatively youthful-looking for his years, with a pleasant, open expression (see Figure 6.3). The words he used for his motto, *Justus et Tenax Propositi*, meaning 'Just and Firm of Purpose', were taken from Bishop Ullathorne's letter to the Holy See when Ilsley became his auxiliary. He described Ilsley as firm of purpose, and his words appear to be well-chosen, as the photographer seems to have captured a feeling of strength and decisiveness in his manner.

In his first pastoral letter, given on 28 March, a week after his enthronement, he told his people that he 'accepted the weighty charge laid upon us ... we have signified our willingness to undertake the administration of this important diocese ... And now although we are addressing you for the first time as your Bishop we venture to speak out to you out of the fulness of our heart ... the more freely because of that personal knowledge of each other which has been acquired during the eight years we have been called upon to share the pastoral labours of our predecessor.' He added the ever-abiding phrase which invariably prefaced any undertaking he was about to embark on, 'yet with no little confidence in the Divine assistance'.

## Visitations

In this message to his people Bishop Ilsley spoke of his 'overpowering sense of responsibility which is bound up with the Pastoral charge entrusted to us', and it forecast his approach to his people: 'Behold I will seek my sheep and I will visit them',[1] was the passage he chose on this occasion. It was to prove appropriate, as he always followed this principle, liking to familiarize himself with every corner of his diocese by regular visitations. Father Patrick O''Toole, who had been one of his students at St Bernard's in 1882 and therefore knew him well, fills in some of the details of Ilsley's administration in an essay he wrote for *The Oscotian* in 1927, entitled 'Diocesan Bishop'. The keynote of his visitations was his 'downright earnestness in going into every matter connected with the parish', he said. He knew the principal people in all of them by name and expected his priests in their turn to visit those in their care. 'A house-going priest is a church-going people,' was his constant watchword. 'He listened patiently to the representations of the people', and although he would praise the work of the parish community on these occasions, 'he rarely praised the priest in public'.

O'Toole said that 'the Bishop took such a high view of the priest's work that although he knew quite well that praise acts as a seasonable tonic, and helps people at times to put forth their best efforts, yet he would not descend to the human side: a priest's work spoke for itself and he must go to his Divine Master for his reward, and not look to the Bishop for any praise or advantage on this account.'[2] But the Bishop well knew that the pastoral ministry is not entirely spiritual and so would certainly have found the right time for passing a word of encouragement to them, having received the same himself from his superiors on many occasions.

The energy and interest he gave to his work is also described by O'Toole in a memoir published in *The Tablet* in 1926: 'Physically the Archbishop was a Saul among his brethren: endowed with a fine constitution, he had an insatiable appetite for work and was capable of great endurance. After singing a pontifical Mass in St Chad's Cathedral on Whit Sunday, he gave an address in the afternoon and confirmed 1200 candidates. The same evening he proceeded to a large town in the Midlands, gave another address and confirmed upward of a thousand, returning home without showing any trace of fatigue.'[3] In a letter to Father Boniface Mackinlay of Douai Abbey in 1891, he proposed a visit to Coughton in the morning to administer confirmation, and Alcester at night, with a procession in the afternoon. He added a footnote to his letter, 'But possibly you would think we were crowding too much into one day, and you are the best judge of your people's power of endurance.'[4] Evidently the thought of whether it might prove to be too tiring for himself had not occurred to him!

## The Birmingham Archdiocese

The Birmingham archdiocese covers a very considerable area. From Staffordshire in the north it stretches down through Warwickshire and

Worcestershire, southward on through Oxfordshire, finally bordering on the banks of the Thames. Ilsley was described as one who attended to the concerns of his growing diocese 'without haste and without rest',[5] and although he had been born into an age of mainly horse-drawn transport, he discovered the rapidly developing railway system to his liking and made a thorough use of its timetables: 'He would be most punctual in his appointments,' and often when making an arrangement for a priest to meet him for the regular conferences he had with them at Bishop's House, 'would advise him as to the time of his train, etc.'[6]

In addition to much travelling at home, he frequently visited places abroad as well. William Barry observed, 'His visits to Rome, and his presence at the great Catholic gatherings — such as the Maynooth Centenary, the consecration of the Armagh Cathedral, and the Eucharistic Congress in Montreal — have made him a traveller.'[7] When addressing two thousand members of the Union of Catholic Mothers who came from all over the diocese to assemble for an outdoor service and procession at Oscott during the war, Ilsley said to them he had not seen such a great gathering of Catholic women, except when he attended the Eucharistic Congress in Montreal.

## 21st International Congress

The 21st International Congress, which took place in Canada in 1910, was evidently a remarkable one conceived on a grandiose scale: 'The gardens of half the continent had been ransacked of flowers to strew before the Blessed Sacrament,' wrote one eyewitness. The procession, passing through the crowds to the altar on the open mountainside, started in the broad sunshine of high noon, only reaching its destination when darkness fell five hours later. 'The Benediction, lighted by countless electric lamps, was a moment never to be forgotten.' Ilsley's signature is to be found in the *Livre d'Or* of visitors to the congress, which was held from Wednesday 7 to Sunday 11 September. He took the opportunity of making the train journey from Montreal to visit St George's Home in Ottawa with the Archbishop of Westminster the day before the congress began. St George's was the reception centre for the children who had been brought out from England through the Catholic Emigration Association, and the work being carried on there had always been one of Ilsley's great interests, especially as it was largely under his auspices and through the advice of Father Hudson that the administration had been set up there in 1907 under the care of the Sisters of Charity of St Paul from Birmingham.[8]

An appreciation written by Monsignor William Barry, in the official booklet printed at the time of Ilsley's investiture in 1911, throws a light on his readiness to accept whatever was required of him in the ministry. Barry aptly borrows phrases from the concept of 'the Church militant'[9] to express his meaning: 'It has often been said as regards these various promotions that they came not only unsolicited but unthought of by the recipient. They were accepted as a duty in the spirit of discipline which makes it all one for a priest, whether he marches as a private or an officer in the ranks of the Church. Edward Ilsley would have lived and died as a curate in the Potteries had his superiors so disposed of him in that fashion.' This feeling of service is evident in Ilsley's reply to a woman who protested that she ought to have been overlooked by him when he spoke to her in passing, during one of his visitations. She said, 'My Lord, I don't think you know who I am; I am only a servant.' But he replied, 'Well I am only a servant too, so we are both on the same level of equality in that respect, each having a different duty, but called upon by God to fulfil it faithfully according to our opportunities.'[10]

## Ilsley's Concern for Destitute Children

His early missionary work in the Potteries taught Edward Ilsley a great deal about the living conditions of the poor, and he always involved himself with the most genuine concern in the rescue work for the thousands of homeless and destitute children in his diocese who were a product of that industrial age. Father O'Toole wrote of him: 'Whatever the task the Bishop undertook, he put his whole strength and energy into it,' and describing his dedication, he continued, 'he took up this work vigorously in 1889, and true to his motto pursued it with unswerving tenacity to the end.'

Throughout his episcopate a great proportion of the work of the Church was directly concerned with care of the poor and destitute arising from the rapid increase in the size of the working population at that time. The problem was immense, and its urgency meant that policies had to be clearly formulated and quickly pursued, and Ilsley tirelessly appealed for the active co-operation of both clergy and laity.[11] As for Birmingham itself on the eve of the restoration of the Hierarchy, the population of two-hundred-and-twenty thousand contained some ten thousand Catholics. When Ilsley became Bishop of Birmingham in 1888 the Catholic population in the city numbered nearly 24,000, so it had more than doubled in size in the span of less than forty years since 1850, and it now represented nearly one third of all the Catholics in the entire diocese.[12]

Birmingham was centred in an area where industrialization had turned the district for several miles around into one vast, sprawling workshop, and a steadily increasing working population had crowded in from the surrounding rural areas and beyond, to find employment. There were more working people in Britain living in towns at this time than any other country on the Continent, and many of them, unused to urban living, soon found themselves living in slum areas, in extreme poverty. At best they were able to eke out a mere existence, struggling to avoid starvation, and were often forced, out of sheer necessity, to abandon their children to the streets at a tender age, to fend for themselves through begging, stealing or child-prostitution.[13] Many of these children were known to be Catholics, and Ilsley's particular concern was that provision should be made to rescue them from the dreadful circumstances they were in and preserve their faith by providing shelter for them before they could be swept away into prison or local authority workhouses, or orphanages run by other denominations.

In a letter to his clergy in October 1890, he alerted them, as a matter of pressing importance, to the drinking habits of the workers which caused so much misery in their lives, even though it might provide a temporary escape from the harsh reality of the world about them. From a practical point of view he pointed out the difficulties of grappling with 'a disorder so deep-rooted and so widespread'. He realized that remedies had been tried and failed, but nevertheless during his administration he wished a well-directed effort to continue throughout the diocese in an effort 'to check the torrent of so much evil'. He advocated an organized crusade on the same lines as the earlier temperance crusades, with the priests now enlisting the help of lay helpers to assist them. His past experience in the training of young people is evident in a further requirement that as an added precaution, all children of twelve years were to be instructed and trained in the practices of the crusade, as 'the policy of prevention will act as a protection for them'. He suggested the statistics they were dealing with should be tabulated and asked for reports on the measures they were adopting to be sent regularly to the administrator at the cathedral outlining the results they were achieving. This was so he could be kept informed as to the progress of the movement throughout the diocese.

## Early Stages of Rescue Work

In the early stages of rescue work in Birmingham, when shelters for children were being built in different areas, each Home operated independently with little contact between them. In 1880 some Catholic children who had been removed from workhouses in the borough were living in the newly built cottage homes in Marston Green at Coleshill, a small straggling village in a rural area on the outskirts of Birmingham. These homes were run by the Birmingham Guardians of the Poor, and when they were opened in the district, Father Charles Wheatley, who was in charge of the local mission, was appointed to give religious instruction to them. He had been among the first students to come to St Bernard's when it opened in 1873 and was ordained there in 1877. There was no church at the mission at the time, and he said Mass in a stable off the main street there until he built St John's out on the Coventry Road in 1882. But by April 1884 Bishop Ullathorne decided the time had come to establish his own home in Coleshill for poor and destitute children. With this in mind, Edward Ilsley, who was then auxiliary bishop, had called a meeting at Bishop's House a month earlier on 3 March, on behalf of Bishop Ullathorne, and formed a committee of interested gentlemen, 'for the purpose of providing and carrying on Homes for the Catholic poor'.[14] It was Bishop Ullathorne's wish that both Bishop Ilsley and the vicar general, Canon Longman, should become *ex officio* members of this committee (which was called 'the Birmingham Certified Poor Law Schools Committee') – so they could then report back to him on the progress that was being made. Bishop Ullathorne was living in semi-retirement at Oscott College at the time, so they would consult with him there.

The outcome of this first meeting was that an arrangement was made by Ullathorne with the Guardians of the Poor, for any Catholic child coming under their care to be transferred to his own poor law schools. It also led directly to the planning of St Paul's Home for Boys, which was opened seven months later in the village of Coleshill, in November 1884, and was run by the Sisters of Charity of St Paul. The same year the Sisters of Mercy opened a House of Mercy for older girls at Handsworth, and the setting-up of the poor law committee encouraged them to begin St Mary's Home and Orphanage at Maryvale in 1888.[15] St Paul's Home was housed in quite an imposing three-storey building standing on the main street. It had once been a tannery and was large enough to accommodate 68 boys, and the

Guardians of the Poor allowed five shillings a week for the support of each child.[16] When the Home was enlarged in 1889, a newspaper cutting from the scrapbooks at Oscott College, dated 19 July, commented favourably on the design of the new building. It also described the healthy, happy condition of the boys they found there: 'The playground lying between the old and the new buildings was formerly a tanyard. Part of it was under cover, so that in all weathers the boys have a spot where they can work their own sweet will ... some dozen were engaged at ninepins while others were constructing parachutes out of newspaper and string and proudly informed the sister from the adjoining convent – the nuns who have the home under their care – that they had made an invention.' The newspaper account went on to say that as well as their basic learning, the boys were taught 'to make themselves useful' by making their beds neatly and sharing in the tidying up and cleaning of the Home. They also washed up dishes, cleaned the windows and, by way of a trade, were trained in shoemaking and tailoring, and to this some even added the skills of knitting. Ilsley continued to work with the poor law committee right up to the time he became Bishop of Birmingham in 1888. After this he kept in touch with them through the chairman and attended their annual meetings.

## George Vincent Hudson

Bishop Ilsley was said to have an acumen for 'selecting the best men for his purpose and infusing into them his indomitable courage and energy'.[17] With his choice of Father George Vincent Hudson this certainly seemed to be the case. Hudson's appointment to Coleshill to take charge of the mission and act as chaplain to St Paul's Home was made a week after he was ordained on 1 November 1898, when he was a young man of 25, and it was later said of him that 'Father Hudson seemed to have been raised up providentially to help the Bishop in all his plans for the fulfilment of this grand scheme.'[18] A month after he came there he wrote to Bishop Ilsley suggesting that it would be better if St John's Church, which was at some distance away, should be moved to a site next door to St Paul's Home. His reasons for wanting this move clearly demonstrate that he was already immersed in his work and that his sympathies were particularly with the children in need who had come into his care. His letter gives a summary of the ideas and ideals for them which he adhered to from the very outset: 'Perhaps the most important part of my work here is to gain the confidence and love of the boys. This can only be done by daily and personal contact with them. Now, My Lord, I feel that as I am at present placed it is impossible for me to do this in the way I should like. I am a mile from the Home; every visit there means at least an hour, and consequently is only taken for a very definite purpose, and for some formal object. And this feeling of formality is, I am sure, shared by the boys – they cannot but feel that I am in some sense a stranger. Of course I share in their games, such as football, once or so a week, but this is not enough. I feel that I ought to live amongst them, be able to mix with them at all hours, make their interests my interests, teach them to feel that they can always come to me in their difficulties. In this way I should gain a much stronger influence over them, an influence which I could turn to good account during those three or four critical years after they leave the home.'[19]

His ideas of dealing with each child as an individual by encouraging their freedom of expression in order to develop their abilities, rather than imposing a regime of strict discipline upon them, were unusually enlightened for their time. He said he felt that he owed it to each child coming into his care that they should have a better education than the ordinary child because without their own families they had to rely entirely on themselves, so they needed any extra advantage he could provide to help them later on in life. Kind and gentle in his manner, his dedication was said to be an inspiration to his fellow workers, and he possessed the imagination and courage necessary to widen out this work with a clear-sighted view of what was needed for the task in hand. It was shown in his realization that an alternative to the large children's homes could be made in some cases by using suitable Catholic families to foster some of the children, and also in his extension of the work outside the homes, by helping boys after they had left the security of Coleshill to make their way in the world.

## Dedication of the New Century

At the turn of the century it was Pope Leo's wish for Catholic bishops world-wide to undertake some special work of charity by way of dedicating the new century to Christ. Bishop Ilsley gave his response to the Holy Father's request in his Advent Pastoral in 1899, when he outlined his intention for the diocese to extend the work of rescue and protection of homeless children.[20] He did not follow up George Hudson's suggestion of moving St John's Church next to St Paul's Home, because at this time he began to develop the idea of bringing

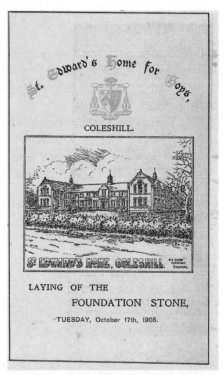

Figure 12.2 *From the archives of the Father Hudson's Homes, Coleshill Birmingham.*

Figure 12.3 *Father George Hudson in 1898, aged 25. From the archives of the Father Hudson's Homes. Coleshill, Birmingham.*

together onto one site as much as possible of the rescue work being undertaken in the diocese. His vision was to concentrate any future building in that connection in an area of open land outside Coleshill and so have several children's homes working in close co-operation with one another. In 1904 he authorized Father Hudson to purchase a suitable site out beyond the village, opposite the church which had been built out there by Father Wheatley. A start was made when the foundation stone of St Edward's Home was laid a year later in 1905, and as the scheme expanded so more land was acquired.

To consolidate the work in hand, in 1902 he had appointed Father Hudson as honorary secretary to the newly formed Birmingham Diocesan Rescue Society, with himself as chairman of the project and Canon Frederick Keating as vice chairman. Among the ten priests serving on the first advisory committee of the Society as *ex officio* members were Michael Glancey and Arthur Chattaway, and Bishop Ilsley's *Ad Clerum CXXVI*, dated 5 April 1902, stated that 'the laity of the diocese are invited and exhorted to render assistance by supplying information and contributing to the fund. The Lenten Alms, and the collection on the second Sunday in October are the two main sources on which we have to depend to carry on the work.'

Two years later at the end of September 1904, George Hudson read a paper at the Catholic Truth Society Conference on 'Rescue Work in the Birmingham Diocese'.[21] Dealing with the problem of leakage he stressed the point that 'the rescue of the children is essential to the well-being and growth of the Church in England. Its importance is well-illustrated', he said, 'by the fact that it formed one of the chief works of the two great English cardinals, Manning and Vaughan.' The development of rescue work in Birmingham coincided with the time when the many difficulties previously arising from Catholic children in Dr Barnardo's Homes being lost to the Catholic faith had now finally been resolved. This was because in the autumn of 1899, Cardinal Vaughan had come to an agreement with Dr Thomas John Barnardo that John Snead-Cox described as 'friendly', although this was hardly so. Barnardo, who had begun to have more children than he could now handle, undertook to notify the Catholic authorities of any destitute Catholic child coming into the receiving wards of his homes, and although he would not hand back any Catholic children already in his homes, this arrangement began to clear the way for Catholics to reclaim many more of their own.

George Hudson soon saw that since the boys left St Paul's Home at Coleshill at the age of 14, it was becoming increasingly evident that more adequate provision was needed for them at that stage. In Birmingham some help was given to them by individual members of the St Vincent de Paul Society, but far more was needed to be done. In 1900 this was sadly made clear in a quotation from an account written on the subject of 'Working Boy's Homes' by the Revd E. Bans, the administrator of the Homes for Destitute Children of the Archdiocese of Westminster, on page 11 of the seventeenth annual report of St Paul's Home. The following year George Hudson sent out a letter to the clergy to draw their attention to it: 'Anyone who has any experience of boy-life in a great city, must often feel his heart ache at the thought of so many young lives, once full of promise, hastening, helplessly perhaps, to wreck and ruin,' he wrote. 'It is a problem that has filled my thoughts, as one by one our boys have left the Home to fight their own way in life. Many succeed, but far too many sink lower and lower, never perhaps to rise again.'

## St Vincent's and St Edward's Homes

To help solve the problem Bishop Ilsley agreed to urgently steer funds in this direction, and with his support a working boys' hostel was opened in the centre of Birmingham in 1901 where there was accommodation for twenty boys from 14 to 18 years of age. The following year a move was made to larger premises in Moseley Road acquired at the cost of £1,112. 10s, which would accommodate about 45 boys, and this came under Father Hudson's overall management.[22] The cost of each boy worked out at about eight shillings a week at that time, but the aim for the hostel with its daily supervision was that it should be largely supported through their own earnings, while at the same time providing them with the necessary care and shelter to see them through. As these boys were mostly working in good trades with wages amounting to about six shillings a week, they were able to contribute to about 75 per cent of their keep, while retaining a small sum for pocket money. The rest was made up by government grants or weekly payments from the Board of Guardians. The hostel was later named 'St Vincent's Home' after it had been extended in 1907, at which time it was transferred to the management of Father Hubert Sandy, who had come to Coleshill as assistant administrator in 1906.

St Edward's Home for Boys, built at a cost of £9,000, was opened in 1906 and was designed to hold 120 boys between the ages of 5 and 14. It was arranged in the form of a square, one side being open and the centre forming the playground. The decision in this case was for a further boys' home to be provided because several girls' homes had already been established in the diocese. The severe social problems of the day are defined in a letter written by Bishop Ilsley to mark the occasion of the laying of the foundation stone a year earlier: 'In nearly every considerable centre of population, especially in such a large city as Birmingham, numbers of such unfortunate children are to be met with who, either through being orphans, or through the degraded or dissolute habits of their parents, are practically set adrift at far too early an age to earn an honest living, but old enough in most cases to learn the ways of sin, and knowingly to live on its wages. The present aim', he continued, 'is to rescue such as these from the fearful fate before them – to supply them with the parental care and affection they never knew or lost – to feed, clothe and educate them in the way of salvation and fit them in the way of becoming good and useful members of society by training them in the knowledge of the love of Our Lord and in obedience to his Divine commands.'[23]

One of the most important aspects of the work of the Rescue Society was the taking into their care of any Catholic children coming before the Birmingham Children's Court. In October 1909 a description of this work was given on a page of informative notes added to the invitations to the society's annual meeting which were sent out by George Hudson on behalf of Bishop Ilsley to subscribers and friends: 'Nearly ninety children are brought before the Court each year charged with various offences. All these are handed over to our care. We do not give up supervision of them until they have been reclaimed to the practice of their religion and given a good start in life.'[24] Many of the children they received were crippled with rickets through malnutrition, or suffering from tuberculosis, which meant they had to be treated in hospital before coming into the homes. To solve the problem, funds were moved in that direction, and St Gerard's Hospital was built on the site in 1912, which consisted of a central administration block and two ward blocks, providing overall accommodation for 38 patients. George Hudson's work marked him out as one of its ablest pioneers in this field, and he made St Gerard's into a training school and took over the orthopaedic clinics for the county of Warwickshire. With continued building in progress, Coleshill took on the look 'of a Collegiate town', and the work continued to grow.

The progress of Catholic schooling was seen in the building of St Edward's Elementary School adjacent to St Edward's Home in 1914. Well-built to accommodate 120 of the younger boys from the homes, it consisted of four classrooms opening on to a central hall according to the latest prescribed design of the day. As St Edward's Primary School it flourished over the years, being finally moved from the site in 1997 when a decentralization plan was brought into operation and the school building was converted to a day centre. As the century progressed and the number of children coming into care steadily reduced in numbers, so the pattern of help given by the Society adjusted itself accordingly in order to accommodate the varying needs of society.[25]

## The Catholic Emigration Association

In 1904 Father Hudson became the treasurer of the Catholic Emigration Association, and the following February 1905 he became its secretary. The Catholic Emigration Association, which was an amalgamation of several emigration agencies, had become a central organization with Coleshill as its headquarters, mainly under the joint control of the Dioceses of Westminster, Southwark, Liverpool and Birmingham, dealing with child emigration to Canada. Catholic emigration work had begun in connection with Canada under Father James Nugent as early as 1870, but things became more organized in 1880 when the Liverpool Catholic Children's Protection Society set up a hostel in Liverpool as a gathering point for child emigrants, and another in Montreal called 'St Vincent's Home', as a centre for their distribution.

In Canada the work of the Catholic Emigration Association originated through the Southwark Catholic Emigration Society when they rented a house in Ottawa, and which originally called 'New Orpington Lodge', and it was opened as a receiving centre for emigrant children in October 1895. Ten years later, in April 1905, after the building had been enlarged and refitted, it was renamed 'St George's', and on 1 May it officially became the headquarters for the Catholic Emigration Association in Canada.[26]

Those in charge of children's homes like Barnardo's and the Methodist Children's Home, were evangelical in outlook, but all of them, the Church of England and Catholic ones included, saw child emigration as the answer to many of the considerable social and moral problems confronting them in those days. In this way child emigration naturally became a major extension to their work of assisting orphans and abandoned children in Britain to a better life. The same attitude prevailed among the group of separate individuals involved independently in helping children, such as John Middlemore, who opened his own emigration home in Birmingham in 1872. It is a sad fact that in those days, before any official regulations had been laid down or children's rights considered, he was able to take children out to Canada entirely on his own motivation, and left them there with no established receiving home or organization they could turn to for their protection after his return to England.

By the mid–1870s standards of procedure among many emigration societies began to improve, but the uncertain nature of many of the schemes and the vulnerability of the young children in question, meant that the situation as a whole was open to some very valid criticism throughout all the years it was in operation. In the 1880s and 1890s some people in Great Britain voiced their concern for the welfare of the children, 'separated from family and inadequately supervised in Canada, where they were subject to exploitation and abuse from their employer'. On the other hand objections to the schemes were also expressed on the other side of the Atlantic by many Canadians, because they felt that owing to their unfortunate background these children were not the kind of emigrants their country was looking for, and there were also critics among them who argued that the child workers took employment away from their own people and contributed to a drift to the cities.[27]

## Canada

One of the chief motivations behind the development of child emigration schemes was the concern of the people engaged in rescue work that some of their children were in danger of reverting to a life of poverty and crime should they return to their former backgrounds on leaving the care of the Home. Taking them abroad prevented this. Another incentive was the relief brought to the rescue societies, whose financial resources were strained to the limit by the ever-increasing number of cases they were handling as the population steadily swelled in size, and as legislation brought more children into the courts over the years. It cost them less to equip children and pay their passage overseas than to keep them in charitable institutions in Britain. Seeing the possibilities in Canada for opening up entirely new lives for young people through the constant demand in that country for labour on the land or in domestic service, Father Hudson assisted in taking groups of children from crowded urban areas by working through the emigration organizations, and he accompanied his first party, which numbered eleven, out to Canada in 1903. After this time, between twenty and fifty boys and girls were sent out each year in the care of priests or reliable laypeople and placed with Catholic families either to work for them, or in some cases to be adopted as their own children. After coming to Coleshill in 1906, Father Sandy also took parties of children out there.

In April 1907 Archbishop Bourne wrote to Archbishop Duhamel of Ottawa saying that the Catholic Emigration Association was considering putting St George's under the care of four nuns instead of having it under the management of the Emigration Office, as they considered it would be more beneficial for the children and more economical if it were run in this way. Archbishop Duhamel's approval was requested by him with the promise that 'the number of Sisters should never, without your Grace's sanction, exceed four, and that no other work than managing the Home would be undertaken by them'.

It was hoped that the Sisters of Charity of St Paul from Selly Park, Birmingham, would be in charge, so Bishop Ilsley wrote an accompanying letter to Archbishop Duhamel. As Father Hudson was to personally deliver this letter to the Archbishop for him, it commenced 'Allow me to introduce the Rev. G. V. Hudson, the Bearer of this letter', and having recommended him 'to the favour of your Lordship' he explained that Hudson 'greatly desires to see St George's Home in your Lordship's Diocese placed under the care of a small community of the Sisters of Charity of St Paul whose Mother House is in this diocese, and who take charge of the Homes for Boys at Coleshill near Birmingham to the satisfaction of us all'. He continued: 'The Mother General and council of the Congregation are quite willing to take up the work at St George's Home if your Lordship approves of their doing so.' He concluded, 'All detailed information on this matter he will be glad to lay before your Lordship.'

Archbishop Duhamel had no objection to such an arrangement, and although his approval was required for the entry of the nuns into his diocese, they were never actually under his diocesan jurisdiction, nor did the home receive any financial help from the Diocese of Ottawa, so it would seem their work was done more on a reciprocal basis. They were mainly funded by the Catholic Emigration Society with the addition of the two dollars for each child which was paid over by the Canadian Government to all emigration societies.

## Mother Evangelist O'Keeffe

There was a last minute delay to do with the final arrangements, brought about by a misunderstanding on the part of the Cardinal

Prefect of Propaganda at the Vatican. He wanted the home to be put in charge of men because he thought that only boys were being sent out from Britain. Bishop Ilsley wrote to Archbishop Duhamel explaining that he was taking on the task of writing to the Vatican to correct this mistaken opinion: 'I am writing to remove that impression by explaining that we emigrate girls as well as boys, many of whom are of tender age and require a woman's care,' he wrote. He also said that it might be desirable at some future date to set up a receiving house for boys under the care of men – 'But the Society cannot bear the expense of two houses at the moment.'

With the Vatican finally reassured by Ilsley's letter, the sisters arrived in October 1907 with their superior, Mother Evangelist O'Keeffe, who was appointed Agent for the English Catholic Emigration Association. George Hudson had remained in Ottawa to welcome them, and on 11 October he informed the Archbishop that they had arrived and that they would esteem it a great honour if he would grant them an interview. 'If you will let me know what time would be most suitable to you I will arrange to call with them,' he wrote.[28] By December more help was required with the work in the office, so permission was requested by Father Hudson to send out a fifth sister. Two years later Mother O'Keeffe noted that her total staff, including herself, then amounted to ten – five sisters, two gentlemen visitors and a further two clerks. Testimony to Ilsley's caution concerning the setting-up of a home for boys at that time was borne out by the fact that St George's remained the sole reception centre over all the years.

The Birmingham Diocesan Rescue Society claimed in 1909 that the home in Ottawa kept 'an oversight over the children until they were eighteen',[29] and apparently the system worked out well on the whole as the Catholic Emigration Association gained a good reputation for the care they extended over the children they were dealing with. Good reasons for selecting Ottawa as the chosen destination for their emigrant children were given in the first edition of the Southwark Catholic Emigration Society's quarterly magazine, *Boys and Girls*, published in 1895. The home it said was situated in 'the centre of a splendid country in Ontario, where we can place a large number of children with prosperous Catholic and Irish Canadian farmers; it is essential that the children should be with men fairly prosperous, otherwise they will be made to do labour for which their age unfits them, the unprosperous men being too poor to hire help, or at any rate glad to escape the necessity...' Families who took in the children signed an agreement to treat them in all respects as their own, and the Sisters of Charity undertook a certain amount of inspection by travelling about visiting the places where the young people were working. Even so, as growing numbers were placed on farms and homesteads scattered over an immensely wide area where there were often no proper roads, such an undertaking would seem a difficult assignment to carry out. Also the agreements signed by the families who took them into their homes were of course not binding in any way, so the histories of some of these young people tell of suffering and hardship. But others of course found fulfilment and happiness in their adopted country.

Altogether, 8,228 British children were registered as passing through St George's during its years as the primary receiving home for Catholic children in Canada. Although three hundred of them were taken out by the Emigration Association in the first decade of the twentieth century, there was a sharp decline in numbers brought about by the First World War, and because of the risks involved in sea travel, all emigration was stopped by 1917. Both Mother O'Keeffe and Father Hudson made applications at that time for grants from the Canadian Government to ease their financial situation. This was on the assumption that they were still working with the children they had brought over to Canada previously. But their requests were turned down.

## British Government Schemes

After the 1914–18 war, the Canadian Government was ready to resume its pre-war undertaking once more and began to replace the original payment per child with a system of generous grants. By that time the nature of the system had undergone a change because the British Government, in an effort to deal with the overwhelming numbers of unemployed, began to take an active hand in encouraging the emigration to the Dominions of its surplus people, many of whom had returned from war service. They promoted schemes of land distribution with financial assistance through the Overseas Settlement Committee, and child emigration played an important part in their schemes.[30] The numbers of children placed by St George's were soon rising above four hundred annually, and imposing new buildings were added to accommodate them.

But by the beginning of the 1930s things went into decline once more with the start of the Depression which took its toll on both sides of the Atlantic, and by 1934 the home was closed. Mother Evangelist had remained in charge until 1926, when she was succeeded by Mother Francis. George Hudson made 30 journeys to Canada before retiring in 1934 when he was 61. He was appointed a Domestic Prelate in 1920 when he was 47, but to the children he always remained 'Father Hudson' rather than 'Monsignor'. One of his main considerations was that 'Canada offered most advantages because of its strong Catholic population where the children's faith would be assured' and the Rescue Society reported that 'This work has the active support of the Archbishops and Bishops of Canada, and of Mgr Sbarretti, the Apostolic Delegate of Ottawa.'[31]

In later years the whole system of child emigration was called into question for continuing to function too long after it was considered to be either desirable or necessary (and certainly no longer beneficial) for children to be removed from their home backgrounds and sent off to fend for themselves in a very different environment. Gillian Wagner, in her book *Children of the Empire*, wrote that, 'From these well-intentioned beginnings, this work, in other hands, later became linked with the building of an Empire rather than making the good of the children the prime objective.' The debate still continues.[32]

## Barry Speaks Out on Social Problems

As President of the Catholic Truth Society, Edward Ilsley was present in the lecture theatre of the Midland Institute in 1890 when Dr William Barry read a paper questioning why Christianity had ceased to influence the lives of the masses living in our large towns, and asking what methods could be used to combat the problem.[33] Barry called it 'a stormy conference' and later said 'I startled some of those Midland magnates by my doctrine of a fuller share due to Labour ... but my resounding stroke was delivered from the platform where I read my paper, in the presence of Bishop Vaughan of Salford, somewhat to their consternation.' Barry took both a sympathetic and a practical view of the cause of their present-day heathenism, which was to be found not so much among the lapsed masses, he pointed out, but the abandoned masses. He pointed out that this was prevalent because many had to work for such long hours on six days in the week, that they considered the seventh as a day of rest. The enormous majority of them seldom entered a church, he said, and he could not blame them. The number of churches existing would be insufficient if everyone attended, but where were the crowded churches and chapels?

Canon Ducket followed by saying that the Church must take an interest in the social problems of the day. It was the only channel through which they could speak to these people – they must take a special interest in strikes, settlements of wages and any disputes which arose. There was a feeling among the poor, he said, that the Church was on the side of the rich and against the poor. The responsibility for this could originally be laid at the door of the Established Church, which would always listen to the squire rather than the worker. There had been a religious revival, but it had not been enough to Christianize the masses of the people.

He asked what had given rise to the Salvation Army and said they needed to distinguish the elements of good from those of evil in this movement. He also asked 'in what way can the Church meet the need or the craving which the Salvation Army points to?' He said they could not point a finger to anything about it that was directly against morality or religious feeling and the sole plan of attack could only be against the spiritual legality and its mode of action – 'it now seemed to reach where no voice had yet been heard in the cause of God and Salvation. That it had elements for good was obvious; that it had elements for evil they could not but suspect most strongly.'

He said that anyone could be carried away in the whirlwind of their street parades and the excitement of their public meetings. But how was it the Church had not led a way in these matters? 'Surely it is not through a lack of zeal of her pastors. Might it not be due to the slowness on their part to rise to the occasion and to a lack of knowledge of the necessities of the times?' There was a realization at this meeting that ignorance about the masses was 'dense and widespread'. The solution lay in more active and ubiquitous work of the clergy – to reach them some priests approved of taking religion out into the streets, but not with drum and bell, they said.[34]

They touched closely at this conference on what was later to be termed 'a secularisation of social consciousness'[35] among the working classes. This occurred among that fastest-growing sector of Victorian society in the big industrial cities where the realities of city life revealed the truth of social relationships to the working people. They had understandably become disillusioned by their own exploitation, and consequently lost their religious belief and practice as a result. Barry, then aged 40, identified and realistically faced up to the reasons for this decline, and he startled his audience by proclaiming that before attempting to rescue the soul of the proletariat, 'you must first attend to the body that housed it', and he enforced his argument with statistics, maintaining that 'to make the people Christian they must be restored to their homes and their homes to them'. He said if they were shown how to live a human life in this world – 'then perhaps they will believe you about the next'. He concluded, 'When I had finished amid the applause and wonder, Bishop Vaughan shook hands with me.' The Bishop congratulated him for his 'fearless and outspoken views' and did this enthusiastically right in front of the audience, which Barry said was 'uncommonly brave of him'. 'The tempest followed in the hall,' he said, 'then in the newspapers.'[36]

## Pope Leo's Great Encyclicals

Throughout his reign, between 1878 and 1903, Pope Leo wrote a series of great encyclicals on 'the welfare and happiness of his people in a rapidly changing world'.[37] Bishop Ilsley strongly endorsed the social teaching given in *Rerum Novarum*, which dealt with the aspirations and conditions of the working classes. Speaking at the evening service on the opening of Hanley Church in October 1891, he devoted his remarks to the labour question, which he said would never find a practical solution in civil legislation. The answer was bound up, as the Pope had said, in the precept of perfect justice, which demanded the rate of wages should correspond to the labour done.[38]

He said the Pope had 'stepped in between capitalist and workman, the statesman and legislature' and he pressed the point that the Church recognized the dignity of labour, making a strong plea against long working hours: 'There were men, women and children now serving for miserable pittances which were nothing like just payment for the labour done, and they worked for 13 or 14 hours a day without getting sufficient hours for rest and the duties of life. Such masters as did that were absorbing what they had no right to, and were living at the expense of the poor man's life, and doing injury to society.' Observing that no solution had yet been found and no conclusion arrived at, he said the answer stood 'in the domain of human conscience'. But although Ilsley always showed great sympathy for the cause of the working man and abhorred the exploitation of child labour, he nevertheless cautioned those who, in the name of socialism, might go too far by working along non-Christian lines in striving to overthrow the social order, to the detriment of all.[39]

## Notes

1   The pastoral office in the Christian church, described in Ezekiel 34.

2   D.B., pp. 20–1.

3   P. O'Toole, 'Archbishop Ilsley, A Memoir', *The Tablet*, 11 December 1926, p. 11.

4   Douai Abbey Archives, Letter to Father Boniface, 13 May 1891.

5   B.A., Scrapbooks, Canon Barry, newspaper article, 'The Archbishop of the Midlands'.

6   D.B., p. 21.

7   B.A., William Barry in an official booklet printed for the investiture, 8 December 1911.

8   Oldmeadow, vol. ii, pp. 64, 65, and Thomas M. Schertwerner, *The International Eucharistic Congresses*.

9   A term used in the Catechism from the time of Vatican 1. The militant aspect here comes from the ninth article of the Creed in which it was explained that the Church was divided into the Church triumphant, the Church suffering and the Church militant.

10  D.B., p. 26.

11  *Ibid.*

12  Kiernan, pp. 38, 42.

13  Gillian Wagner, *Children of the Empire*, Introduction, p. xi. They would often steal for their parents.

14  Marston Green Cottage Homes, Report no. 1, 1881, Birmingham Library. Also Archives, Father Hudson's Home, Coleshill.

15  Records left at Maryvale by the Sisters of Mercy.

16  The Birmingham Diocesan Rescue Archives, Annual Reports. Bishop Ullathorne acknowledged the 'Resolution of the Guardians of the Poor' in a letter to Mr Bowen, clerk of the Guardians, 8 April 1884.

17  D. B., p. 27.

18  *Ibid.*, p. 26, and Obituary, *The Tablet*, October 1936. George Hudson's appointment was initially a temporary one, but he was to remain for 36 years! There was a special Mass on 31 October 1998, to celebrate the centenary of his arrival at Coleshill. Father Wheatley left Coleshill in 1885 and was followed by Fr James Giblin. In 1887 Fr Clement Gottwaltz took over and remained until 1898.

19  B.A., B12312, Letter from Revd George Hudson to Bishop Ilsley, 14 December 1898.

20  The Seventeenth Annual Report of 1900 of the Roman Catholic Certified Poor Law Schools, concerning St Paul's Home for Boys, Coleshill, states: 'the year 1900 has been remarkable for the great increase in the number of boys in the Home. Commencing the year with 139, the number rose steadily to 176 on December 31st, giving an average for the year of 158.'

21  *Birmingham Daily Post*, 29 September 1904. The full title of the Society was 'The Birmingham Rescue Society for the Protection of Homeless and Friendless Catholic Children'. The Catholic Truth Society Con-

ference was held on 27 and 28 September 1904 in Birmingham at the Temperance Hall, Temple Street.

22  The hostel was first in Whittall Street. The following year in 1902 it moved to a larger and more suitable house in 102 Moseley Road, and the formal opening of this new Home took place on 12 December at the first annual meeting.

23  Tuesday 17 October 1905. Bishop Ilsley's words were later to be written into 'The Objects of the Birmingham Diocesan Rescue Society':
1. To rescue the friendless and homeless boys from vice, misery and crime of the streets.
2. To shelter and provide for them.
3. To save their faith.
4. To give them a Catholic education.
5. To train them to earn their living and give them a good start in life.

24  The work of the Children's Court is described in detail by Sylvia Pinches in her book *Father Hudson and His Society: A History 1898–1998*, p. 23.

25  D. B., p. 24. Also Mgr Hudson founded the Catholic Child Welfare Council in 1929, which is today one of the leading organizations in the country, assisting with negotiations with local authorities and central government. As well as caring for children in need and their mothers, the society today supports family situations and looks after the elderly. Special care is also given to the mentally handicapped.

26  This work in Canada in the hands of James Nugent from Liverpool in the 1870s was followed by that of Father Thomas Seddon, one of Manning's secretaries, from 1874 until he died in 1878. The emigration work of the Southwark Catholic Emigration Society was carried forward by Canon Edward St John, and in 1903 Arthur Chilton Thomas of Liverpool and Father Emmanuel Bans of Westminster formed yet another society called 'The Catholic Emigrating Association'. Detailed in Frederick J. McEvoy's paper, 'These Treasures of the Church of God: Catholic Child Immigration to Canada', pp. 6–10, and Beck, pp. 575–6.

27  *Ibid.*, p. 16.

28  The Archives of the Archdiocese of Ottawa, file 'Immigration d'enfants 1880–82', Archbishop of Westminster to Archbishop of Ottawa, 6 April 1907 and Bishop of Birmingham to Archbishop of Ottawa, 4 April and 31 July 1907 and Revd G. Hudson to Archbishop of Ottawa, 11 October, 7 November and 11 December 1907. Archbishop Duhamel died on 6 June 1909 and his successor was not announced until 22 September 1910. Archbishop Charles Hughes Gauthier was installed 18 February 1911.

29  O.C.A., Notes attached to invitation to the annual meeting in 1909 of the Birmingham Diocesan Rescue Society. Much of the work done by the Sisters of Charity in Ottawa is described by Sylvia Pinches, in *Father Hudson and his Society*, pp. 26–9.

30  The Empire Settlement Act of 1922 formed the basis of this state-aided empire settlement. The history of the development of the work at St George's Home at this time is described at length by Frederick J. McEvoy in 'These Treasures of the Church of God: Catholic Child Immigration to Canada', pp. 14–18.

31  Rescue Society notes 1909 and Beck, p. 575. Mother Evangelist O'Keeffe died on 19 September 1926 and was buried in Ottawa. George Hudson died in 1936 at the age of sixty-three.. He was assisted by Father James O'Connor from 1914 until his retirement in 1934.

32  Gillian Wagner, *Children of the Empire*, pp. xiv, xv. Children were still being taken out to Australia in the 1950s. Frederick McEvoy presents a picture of the opposition to child emigration on both sides of the Atlantic in 'These Treasures of the Church of God: Catholic Child Immigration to Canada', pp. 16–17.

33  The Midland Institute, Tuesday 1 July 1890. Also Barry, p. 185.

34  *Birmingham Post*, 2 July 1890. A reference to the Salvation Army.

35  Friedrich Engels, *The Condition of the Working Classes in England*. The opposite view was put forward by Robert Vaughan in *The Age of Great Cities*. He argued that the Christian religion would find its fullest expression in city life, thus making the Protestant religion triumphant. Time of course proved this to be incorrect.

36  Barry, pp. 185–7, and *Birmingham Directory*, 1932.

37  *Rerum Novarum* and *Providentissimus Deus*. The last 'seemed to open the counter attack by authority against the Modernists'. Norman, p. 334. See Manning's influence, Beck, pp. 27, 163, 582.

38  'The Bishop of Birmingham on Labour', *The Tablet*, Saturday 3 October 1891.

39  These were the tenets of the Catholic Social Guild, and this was the age of Catholic Action. The Church encouraged her members to get elected to public boards. It was considered of great value for priests and people to protect their own by knowing the regulations regarding the guardianship of children, housing of the poor, offences of breaches of the Factory Acts and employer's liabilities ... through setting-up information bureaux and the provision of Catholic Libraries. M. Costello, Birmingham Town Hall, 30 June 1890.

CHAPTER THIRTEEN

# The Struggle for Catholic Education

At the beginning of the nineteenth century the Church of England saw itself as having charge of the nation's Christian faith, and because their aim was to have an Anglican school conducted on church principles in every parish, some among their churchmen regarded the country's education as coming solely within their province. These schools usually owed their creation to the parson or the squire, and because they were connected with the 'National Society' which had been formed in 1811 to promote 'Education of the Poor in the Principles of the Established Church',[1] they were generally termed as 'National' or Church schools and were seen as the usual mode of popular education.

Following their segregation in penal times, the majority of the Catholic population in Britain were educationally isolated at the beginning of the nineteenth century, knowing little or nothing of public schools or universities. The wealthier classes had largely overcome their problems throughout the troubled years by educating their sons abroad in the Continental colleges such as Douai – two exceptions to this were Sedgley Park and Standon Lordship.[2] But after the passing of the Act of Emancipation in 1829 the Church began to strive to make up for their lack of schools, particularly at the level of elementary education. Although on the surface the immediate problem for the Catholics appeared to be largely a financial one, the underlying principles of political and religious freedom also played a major part throughout their educational campaign on behalf of their schools.

## First Catholic Day Schools

However, even before the turn of the nineteenth century and on towards the time of Catholic Emancipation, there had already been a decided awakening among the Catholics to the general needs of their people, and many Catholic day schools had their beginnings in Sunday schools similar to those of the Anglicans.[3] Typical of the small day schools of the time was the one built in 1818 that was attached to St Austin's Church in Stafford, where the Ilsley family probably received their early education. Sir George Jerringham, the future Lord Stafford, contributed largely to the building of this school. Another such school was the one provided at Harvington Hall by Sir George Throckmorton for the village children, and this was where Edward Ilsley's uncle Joseph was headmaster. It was set up in the old Georgian chapel in the grounds of the hall, as the building was no longer being used for services after the opening of the church there in 1825. Sir George died in 1826, and although the Throckmorton family no longer lived in the hall, they continued to support the school. Described by Father Brownlow in accordance with the usage of the time as 'a Poor School', it was still in existence 88 years later, in 1913.

Although in the early years of the nineteenth century government policy tended toward non-intervention in education, an awareness began to grow among some politicians of the general need of more educational provision among the poor. Poor people were not to be educated above their station, but the basic instruction they would receive would come with a training in attitude, supposedly to enable them to work more efficiently and to make them more aware of their duties towards their superiors. So in 1833 the first grant aid consisting of £20,000 was voted in 'for the erection of school houses for the Children of the Poorer Classes in Great Britain'.[4] But no parliamentary grants were allocated to Catholic schools at this time, and there were comparatively few men of importance in the Catholic community in either industry, trade or politics who could make themselves heard on this account, so any applications for such grants were ignored.

By 1843 a Catholic population of under a million represented 5 per cent of the population of England and Wales when a Catholic Institute report registered 236 day schools and 60 Sunday schools, providing for nearly forty thousand children.[5] Although this number of schools represented a tremendous amount of self-help in education on the part of the lay people, it still left a shortfall of well over a hundred thousand children in the Church without schooling. The Vicars Apostolic of England and Wales recommended in 1846 that every mission should have a parish school. In order to organize their own fundraising for the support of their schools by co-ordinating the correct procedures with the government in the educational field, they appointed the Catholic Poor Schools Committee in 1847, which was also to disseminate educational information through its members throughout the country. This was a prestigious body which had among its ranks the Earl of Arundel and Lord Shrewsbury, and their policy was to secure a fair share in the Central Exchequer grants for Catholics. Had such support been given to the Catholic schools from the initiation of the government's grant aid scheme, they would have benefited by what would have presumably amounted to £110,000 by 1846. So wasting no further time, the Poor Law Committee negotiated the following year with the Committee of the Privy Council on Education for financial aid for apparatus and equipment for Catholic poor schools, and for the awarding of building grants toward new schools. The outcome of this was that grants finally began to be awarded to the Catholics towards fulfilling their educational requirements.[6] So although Catholics were in some ways reluctant to accept money directly from state schemes for fear of giving away their independence,

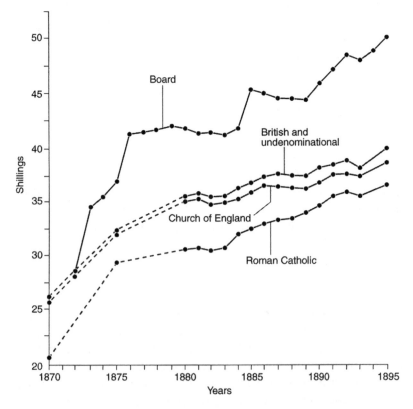

Figure 13.1 *Growth of expenditure on maintenance. From Dr Gillian Strickland,* Policy-Making in Elementary Education 1870–1895.

these grants were accepted by them through their own poor school committees working in line with the government, and these schools were then open to inspection.

## The Unschooled Catholic Poor

The bishops of the restored hierarchy inherited problems in the field of education related to the rapidly increasing numbers of unschooled Catholic poor. This was partly caused by the sudden influx of Irish immigrants coming into Britain due to the potato famines which struck the Irish crop with such ferocity between 1845 and 1851. Added to these were numbers of workers moving in from the countryside and looking for employment in the towns. This was brought about by the forced enclosures of the land, which had taken their living from them. However, the bishops were to discover that the foundations of popular education had been laid down by 1850, because Catholic schools with daily attendance were already existing by this time in some of the towns and villages. But it was only to be through a hard and determined struggle on their part well into the first decade of the next century that their schools finally became established with acceptable fairness of treatment.

A lack of education was common at this time among all the nation's poor of whatever denomination, and during the century a series of Factory Acts were designed to alleviate the appalling conditions of child workers caught up in the industrial scene who were made to work long hours in factories and mills. As these unfortunate children, often taken from workhouses, could be 'apprenticed to a master', through no choice of their own, for up to seven years, these acts attempted to enforce a minimum of education for them by shortening the hours of their working day and forbidding night work. The provisions of the 1870 Education Act now referred to all children in the land including those who had previously been covered by the Factory Acts.

Among the denominations that were steadily growing with the development of the population in the large industrial cities, that of the Catholics was expanding proportionately at the most rapid rate throughout the Victorian period. Census returns showed large congregations at their services, and the reason for this was not hard to find. It was the ever-increasing numbers of Catholics of Irish origin who provided the largest proportion of all church attendances in the areas where they had settled. But this growth in numbers was also due to conversions. An assessment of these made in the Birmingham diocese for the three years between 1881 and 1884 numbered the best part of two thousand souls. It was also noticeable that whenever a new mission was founded, people from the surrounding districts would come in their numbers, seeming somehow to have instinctively retained the knowledge that they were Catholics even though they never had the opportunity of instruction and practice.[7] But in spite of the rapid increase in numbers, a constant preoccupation among the hierarchy was the possibility of leakage slowing down any real progress and even leading to recession. The word 'leakage' was first used by Herbert Vaughan in 1885 when he was Bishop of Salford to suggest that the losses to the Church were like water trickling away from a leaking pipe. This was when he realized that thousands of Catholic children were being lost to the faith through active proselytization and that this was a further challenge that had to be faced.[8]

## Manning, Vaughan and Bourne

The struggle to provide Catholic schools, in which the three successive Archbishops of Westminster – Cardinals Manning, Vaughan and Bourne – were prominently involved with the governments of the day, was at its fiercest throughout Ilsley's years as Bishop of Birmingham. These men concentrated a great deal of their time and interest on 'the schools question' – so the ensuing struggle to maintain their rights and principles, when providing primary schools for the masses, became a considerable part of the story of the bishops of that century and the decades to follow.[9]

As regards secondary education, the Church initially relied largely on the work of the religious orders, though there were some small grammar schools for boys established which were run by the local secular clergy, such as St Chad's in Birmingham which was begun in 1858 by the Revd Joseph Henry Souter, and Salford Catholic Grammar School ten years later, which was begun by Bishop William Turner in his own house.[10] In the case of private schools and colleges it was not considered necessary for a course of professional training to be provided for those who taught in them.

To counter the difficulties facing them and to prevent the revival falling back, the bishops of the restored hierarchy directed their efforts towards the provision of the new churches, schools and children's homes that were urgently needed, particularly in the large centres of population. Bishop Ilsley followed these priorities, and 'within the thirty-three years of his episcopacy he established some forty churches and Mass centres throughout the diocese',[11] and 'almost all the 123 Elementary Schools existing in the diocese in 1926 had been opened during the years of his Religious Life'.[12]

Over these years the numbers of Catholics grew principally because of Irish immigration, and because of their subsequent movement into the larger urban areas like Birmingham, Manchester and Liverpool, and parts of London, these became the main centres of a growing Catholic population throughout the rest of Queen Victoria's reign and beyond. The Catholic population in England, which numbered 700,000 in 1840, had grown to 1.3 million by the end of the century, and by that time 'the general framework of the Catholic community was already formed. Within the last twenty-five years of the century the number of Catholic churches and chapels in England and Wales had grown steadily from one thousand to one thousand five hundred, and the priests, secular and religious, from two thousand to three thousand.'[13]

Cardinal Wiseman, on discovering the dreadful conditions to be found in the slums of London in mid-century in the Westminster area, wrote, 'there lie concealed labyrinths of lanes and courts and alleys and slums, nests of ignorance, vice, depravity, and crime, as well as of squalor, wretchedness and disease; whose atmosphere is typhus, whose ventilation is cholera; in which swarms a huge and almost countless population, in great measure, nominally at least, Catholic'. His concern for these neglected masses led him to instigate far-reaching social and educational work there among the destitute.[14] A training college for men was founded in his time in 1850 at Brook Green in Hammersmith at the expense of the hierarchy, and another was founded in Liverpool in 1856 by the Sisters of Notre Dame de Namur.

## Training Colleges

Cardinal Manning, who proved himself to be perhaps the greatest advocate among the hierarchy for the care of the poor, is quoted by Robert Gray as being so firm in his absolute conviction concerning the obligation to provide for destitute children, that he pronounced, 'the care of children is the first duty after, and even with, the salvation of our own soul'.[15] One of his main undertakings was the provision of Catholic elementary education for the masses. His Educational Pastoral of 1866, given on the first anniversary of his consecration as Archbishop, outlined many of the problems of the day, one of his chief concerns being the losses to the Church caused through the lack of schools and the serious shortage of teachers. Because the newly established churches were so acutely short of money, he at once established a Diocesan Education Fund to help combat financial difficulties. In 1874 a training college for women was opened at Roehampton by the Sacred Heart nuns; and as tremendous costs were involved in these undertakings, such provision made by religious was a great relief.[16] Herbert Vaughan considered the sponsoring of the training colleges that had been established in Hammersmith, Liverpool and Roehampton of vital importance, and directed money towards their support through the Catholic School Committee in 1892.[17]

As in recent years standards of English education had been falling behind in relation to many of her European neighbours, mainly through the lack of schools throughout the country, the 1870 Education Act was concerned primarily with the supply of schools. Through the Act the government sought to fill in the gaps existing in the voluntary schools system by introducing publicly controlled 'board schools', and in order to raise standards further throughout, the level of government grants to all schools, voluntary and board, was increased. The new board schools which were governed by their own School Boards, were maintained by these grants and were also paid for out of local rates. The Catholic schools, on the other hand, received less by way of grants and had to manage on voluntary subscriptions and the parents' fees. Initially the new structure, such as it was, was formed through the system of voluntary schools being augmented by board schools, and over the years the movement of population to towns and cities increased the part played by these board schools.

When the 1870 Education Bill was being debated, the bishops were involved with the Vatican Council which opened on 8 December 1869 and continued until 20 October 1870, so they set up a committee of lay people to defend their interests during those months while such a great deal of their time was being occupied in Rome. Though few in number compared with the Anglicans, the Catholics presented a more coherent policy at this time, because their bishops worked together with a common sense of purpose, and this continued on throughout the years as they struggled for equal rights for their schools. When the Education Act was in the committee stage, Gladstone acknowledged that it was within their small minority that the Catholics made themselves responsible for 'a tenth, an eighth or even a sixth of the educational destitution', which he said was out of all proportion to their numbers and therefore weighted the scales of 'exceptional poverty' heavily against their schools. As time went by the Catholic claims crystallized into an effort to gain an equitable share in the rates in comparison with the government board schools, to help maintain their everyday requirements.[18] This was strongly pursued, particularly when it became apparent that although the voluntary schools were giving equal service to the state alongside the board schools, there was nothing like equal reward given them for equal service. Snead-Cox pointed out that 'the 17s per child paid at that time to the Board schools annually out of the rates had a poor equivalent in the case of the Denominational schools in the average of 6s 10d supplied by voluntary subscriptions'.

## The 1870 Education Act

Because the Act brought in a national system of education, although requirements for attendance were not yet compulsory, the fear of Catholics was that many of their children might be lost to the Faith by eventually being compelled to attend other schools, unless Catholic schools could be provided for them. Aware of the added gravity this brought to the situation, Bishop Ullathorne, who was opposed to the Act, set up a diocesan committee in Birmingham in the October of that year to deal with what he termed 'the education crisis'. The 1870 Act forbade any religious teaching 'distinctive to any particular denomination' in their own schools, and this in practice led to the use of a type of 'uncontentious biblical study', the kind that Cardinal Manning said he regarded as 'No religion at all'. William Gladstone, then Prime Minister, whose sympathies were with the Catholics, was not in favour of 'undenominational instruction' either. He critically remarked that the attitude of some members of the House tended to be that voluntary schools were 'admirable passing expedients, fit to be tolerated for a time ... but wholly unsatisfactory as to their main purpose and therefore to be supplanted by something they think better'.[19] He was probably aware that these men, entrenched in their opinions, saw no future for the voluntary schools, which they thought would eventually be forced from the system altogether and swept away out of existence.

Edward Ilsley was working as Father Massam's curate in Longton and also serving as manager of the church school at St Gregory's at the time when the Government created the school boards and some boroughs began to enforce the school attendance of children between the ages of 5 and 13 years. Probably on Ullathorne's recommendation

Ilsley was put forward and voted onto the first school board in the area in 1871, coming third in the voting poll out of the nine candidates standing at the time. In this way he would have gained first-hand experience in local administration over the next three years. As Bishop of Birmingham he later showed himself to be vigilant about developments in education, and his interpretation of the Government's legislation affecting the voluntary schools is evident throughout his pastoral letters, particularly 'An Education Peril' given in 1904, and 'The Education Crisis' in 1906.[20]

Although there was an improved level of grant for the Catholics when the 1870 Education Act went through, Herbert Vaughan, on becoming Bishop of Salford in 1872, sought to modify it further by procuring a more equitable allocation of funds for the Catholic schools from the local education rate. Seeing that Manning in spite of his immense work for Catholic education 'had no hand fitted to make a direct appeal to the constituencies', he started the Voluntary Schools Association in 1884, as a militant interdenominational body, believing in specific religious instruction in schools. In this way he was able both to support the causes of the other religions and also to gain the widest backing for his own programme.[21] Although divisions in outlook among them meant the denominationalists never became 'a united Christian front', they were able to put across many of their grievances with one voice through this association. After Manning's death in the January of 1892, Vaughan continued the fight for the schools as one of his priorities when he was appointed Archbishop of Westminster. But Robert O'Neil saw that Herbert Vaughan at this time, 'though active and influential, was representing the Catholic Church, a minority school-proprietor in England and Wales. He was one participant, although an important one, in an effort waged by the Church of England and others on behalf of denominational education.'

## Cost of New Buildings

As time moved on pressures grew steadily on the voluntary schools, one of the main considerations being the matter of staff salaries, and this was because they could not hope to match the improved conditions for staff working in board schools. The Catholics still had to provide a proportion of the running costs for their own schools from fees and donations, and the full cost of new buildings was still supported by them. But although these circumstances compelled many schools among the other denominations to give up and allow themselves to be taken over by the board school system, there was no fear in Archbishop Vaughan's mind that the Catholics would ever give up theirs, because he saw that they had all held firm and none had given way. In 1887 they adopted the phrase 'Catholic Schools for Catholic Children' as their motto, to show their determination to win through. In 1900 Sir William Throckmorton wrote to Bishop Ilsley to tell him that in spite of the fact that the numbers of children were at times very low he intended keeping the school at Harvington open. He said he considered that the Government had insulted the voluntary schools by their treatment of them and continued, 'I have a patent objection to helping the rates in any way as far as education goes ... but I know that there is no more important time as far as regards religion & religious instruction than the time when children are at school.'[22]

In a letter to *The Times*, in September 1895, Archbishop Vaughan proposed a practical solution to the problem, through 'the adoption of a comprehensive policy which shall place the whole of the elementary education in this country upon a common basis which shall as far as possible end or minimise all grievances'. Commenting on his letter, *The Times* replied, 'We welcome Cardinal Vaughan's letter as the first important sign that action will be taken on a matter of grave concern.' The Education Act of 1897 freed voluntary school buildings from rates and increased their grant, but as things stood this was seen by the Catholics as only a temporary measure, and the work to achieve permanent rights still had to go on. They had in mind the fact that many of their teachers were still existing on meagre salaries made up through the ignominy of fundraising, and by this time it was clear that some form of large-scale assistance was going to be needed if they were to make any real progress.

## General Reform Needed

In 1899 the Board of Education Act provided a unified central administration, and before long a progressive partnership between the central and local administration was established. But by the turn of the century responsible opinion held that wider consideration needed to be given to a general reform throughout the educational system if the country was to hold her own against her rivals in world power such as the United States and Germany. Anticipating the problem, Manning had written in a report to the Diocesan Education Fund as early as May 1890: 'Though our great productive supremacy has in time past been attained without systematic technical instruction, we can hardly hope to retain it in the competition with foreign countries which are now systematically instructing their youth in the principles and practices of arts and manufactures. It is of absolute necessity that we should keep pace with them in this also.'[23] Four years later a Royal Commission was appointed to inquire into these matters, and they advocated the setting-up of an overall central authority, headed by an education minister, for public education in England.

At the beginning of the twentieth century it was evident that there was an urgent need for improvement in elementary education and the voluntary schools. Marjorie Cruickshank observed that these schools were educating more than half of the nation's children and that the poor voluntary schools must indeed pull down the general level of education. Nationally the overall daily attendance in the 14,360 voluntary schools at the time, was 2.5 million children. The Anglican children made up 76 per cent of this number, owning nearly 12,000 schools, while the Catholic children constituted a mere 10 per cent of the whole and owned only 1,045 schools.[24] On the basis of these numbers this meant that the Catholic schools were very overcrowded in comparison with the Anglican ones, even though they represented a comparatively small community in number. So there was a considerable shortfall to be caught up with by the Catholics to relieve a serious problem. There was also a shortage of teachers, and to help combat this, Archbishop Vaughan directed the efforts of the Catholic Poor School Committee towards the sponsoring of the Catholic training colleges, in order to support this desperate need.

It was obvious that some far-reaching adjustments needed to be made by the state, but no further major changes came about until the passing of the Education Act of 1902, by which the school boards were replaced, and all schools, elementary and secondary, came under a new system of control which was introduced by local education authorities. The Act emphasized 'the welding of secular education into an organised whole', but at the same time the Conservative Prime Minister, Arthur Balfour, stated that the voluntary schools had their place, and must not only remain as part of the system, but 'must be invigorated', and he increased the grants to help balance the situation for them.

## Cardinal Vaughan in 1902

The 1902 Act was passed on 18 December just six months before Cardinal Vaughan died, and although he could see that some safeguards still needed to be put in place, he wrote, 'In principle we have made a large and important advance.' The Government acknowledged the ownership by Catholics of their own buildings, and stipulated that the costs of the everyday workings of their schools were to be paid out of public funds by bringing them into the system of rate aid. The Nonconformists, especially those in Wales, made their protest against the Act, refusing to pay their rates 'for denominational schools', singling out the Catholics with the rallying cry of 'Rome on the Rates'. The idea that they were 'on the rates' any more than any other religion was of course absurd, particularly as the Church of England through weight of numbers had most to gain from the Bill. The Government was compelled to take strong measures in order to cause the protesting local education authorities to comply with the Act, by bringing in the Default Act of 1904.[25]

On the death of Cardinal Vaughan in 1903, it came into the hands of Cardinal Bourne to carry things forward and make a stand against further encroachments, and it was soon found by the Catholics that although relieved of some of their financial burdens, further obstacles began to present themselves. In his first pastoral letter, Archbishop Bourne pointed out that the new laws fell short of what they had hoped for because 'with the abolition of the old school boards the use of the cumulative vote in elections of public representatives who would have oversight of educational matters, had also disappeared, thus no longer ensuring Catholic representation on the new local authorities'. It was also apparent that Catholics appeared to have less control over the employment of unsatisfactory teachers than previously, and there were difficulties restricting the opening of new schools, and the threat of others being closed should their numbers fall below 30.[26]

## Ilsley's 'Education Peril'

It was concerning these problems that Bishop Ilsley pointed out some of the drawbacks in his pastoral letter in 1904, which he so aptly named 'An Education Peril'.[27] 'There are certain aspects of this recent legislation which concern us so vitally, as constituting a grave peril, that even at the risk of wearying you with a worn-out theme we feel in duty bound to set them before you,' he said. He pointed out the difficulties imposed by the apportioning of the rates. This system dictated that their schools needed to be of a sufficiently economical size to be acceptable to the authorities, and if there were not enough children attending, the school could be closed down by the local authority. 'Now a small school is proportionately more costly to maintain than a large one. Suppose then we desire to build a small elementary school for our own children in the district of a new mission, we may expect to meet with local opposition on the ground of "economy of the rates" ... In the event of our efforts proving unavailing there is the Board of Education to appeal to ... Meanwhile, arrangements must be made for these children of ours who are compelled to frequent non-Catholic schools, so that they may receive instruction in the Christian doctrine and be prepared for the sacraments. The responsibility for these arrangements being carried out rests with the priests and the parents.'

'The most serious aspect', he continued, was 'the provision for recruiting the ranks of our Teachers.' A scheme had been started as early as 1846 whereby selected boys and girls were indentured as pupil-teachers for a five-year apprenticeship. They were formally apprenticed to the headmaster for five years, and if they passed the scholarship examination they moved on to a training college for two or three years and became qualified, while others continued to work as uncertificated teachers. But the Act of 1902 brought in fresh regulations for their training which put further pressures on the provision of teachers in Catholic schools. Ilsley explained that their children previously 'could be transferred from the highest class in an elementary school to the status of Pupil teacher ... After a satisfactory term of pupil-teachership he could take a post of assistant teacher, or pass on to the training college and in a course of two years apply for a certificate. All this is now changed. No-one under 16 is eligible for a pupil-teachership in a town school, no-one under 15 in a rural school, and no-one is eligible who has not spent two years under tuition in a higher school than the elementary.'

The old systems were changing, and after the Education Act of 1902 the pupil-teacher system was losing ground because it was now more common for boys and girls wanting to become teachers to attend secondary schools until they were 17 or 18 and then go straight to training college. The Catholics, in striving to create their own system, were up against formidable odds in those days, and the requirements of the local authorities cut across the stringently economical practices they were forced to employ through lack of funds and inadequate training facilities.[28] But this was the path they needed to tread at the time, and fearing that a resulting fall in the number of Catholic teachers at elementary level might mean the placing of non-Catholic teachers in their schools, the Bishop still urged his people to face up to their difficulties, continuing: 'Here however is the peril, let us realise it, and then we shall try to see how we shall meet it.'

A year later, in September 1905, constantly aware of the problem of leakage, Bishop Ilsley instructed his clergy concerning a joint Declaration of the Bishops of the Province of Westminster on the frequentation by Catholics of non-Catholic schools. Reminding them that by the Code of Canon Law there were censures on parents who sent their children to non-Catholic secondary schools without special permission, he said, 'the matter is too important, to be dismissed with a mere reading of a document,' and admonished them to preach 'on an early day' on the Church's teaching and tradition on the subject, 'so that the force and meaning of the official warning may be brought home to their mind and conscience'.[29]

## Joseph Chamberlain

The bishops were described as standing shoulder to shoulder 'in a solid phalanx at this time with a policy of no surrender', and meetings were held all over the country to denounce some of the government proposals in the 1902 Act. Bishop Ilsley took the opportunity at the opening of a school in the Midlands to speak out against the government policies. He maintained that although Joseph Chamberlain had attempted in the past to threaten their schools with 'painless extinction' through the Birmingham Educational League, he had not succeeded. In the 1870s Chamberlain had campaigned for free education, and there was a certain irony in the fact that at first the Catholics, in spite of their poverty, were against the idea, seeing in it the loss of control of their schools. Bishop Ullathorne was against the acceptance of increased grants at that time, fearing that as the Catholics drew more financially from the state, so their hand in their own management would be relatively reduced, and he was strongly opposed to Joseph Chamberlain's principle of separating secular and religious education. But when the 1891 Act made all elementary education free, such fears were eventually forgotten. Ilsley, who was obviously influenced by Ullathorne in many ways, was always ready to denounce 'the other side', particularly as Chamberlain had been the local MP for Birmingham from 1876 to 1903, having been a member of Gladstone's cabinet in 1880.[30]

After the return of the Liberal Party to power in 1906, the Birrell Bill threatened the essential character of voluntary schools, though its

Clause 4 offered reliefs thought to be more applicable to Catholic schools than Anglican ones. The Duke of Norfolk presented the case in Parliament for the Catholic Education Council. But their members were divided in their opinion. Some followed the Duke, who considered that there should be an outright rejection of the bill, whereas others considered that the position of the Catholic schools could be improved if acceptable amendments were introduced. Cardinal Bourne, representing the bishops, was not in agreement with Norfolk's handling of the proceedings and he was assisted throughout by Mgr William Brown, the future Auxiliary Bishop of Southwark who was expert on handling matters to do with education. After the Conservatives defeated the bill in 1906 with the help of the Irish Parliamentarians, Bourne formed the opinion that the Catholics would have gained financially through the concessions offered, while retaining their educational requirements had the bill been passed. So it would seem a considerable advantage had been lost on this occasion.[31]

Looking into the future, Bourne considered that the Catholics needed 'to remain above political fray' if they were going to make satisfactory gains for their schools and their teachers, and he thought the Catholic cause would fare better if it were not linked with the style of opposition as represented by the Duke of Norfolk. By the new year of 1907, the rift between the two men had widened, and when Norfolk wrote to each bishop individually on 1 January suggesting future procedure, Bourne straightway notified them on the 4th that he himself would reply to the Duke on their behalf. However, from the tone of a letter Ilsley sent to Bourne on 4 January, having first received Norfolk's letter, his very genuine concern was that the bishops must above all keep their unity and be seen to do so. Writing in his characteristically straightforward style, he did not hesitate to play the part of instructing the Archbishop as to the manner in which he considered he should proceed: 'I don't know whether Your Grace intends to call us together to discuss the situation as described in the Duke of Norfolk's letter of the 2nd inst.,' he began, 'I sincerely hope you will, & that you will intimate this to us as early as possible. Otherwise our Colleagues will be replying directly to the Duke & conveying each his own impression on a matter of great moment to the Catholic Body, upon which there ought not to be divided councils.'[32]

It might well appear that Norfolk was attempting to divide opinions among the bishops for his own purposes at this time,[33] but it would also seem that Ilsley was astutely observing that Archbishop

Bourne's attitude was endangering their single-minded stand in order to pursue his own policies. Ilsley's main concern was that if an early ecclesiastical meeting was not called, the bishops would not have the opportunity to come to agreement among themselves on matters of the first importance 'to the Catholic Body'.[34] But at this time Bourne's concern did not lie with the involvement of the bishops but with his own wish to avoid any compromise with Norfolk and his political party as far as Catholic education was concerned.

## Lack of Trust

At a meeting held at St Chad's Girls' School in the summer of 1907 Bishop Ilsley conveyed his lack of trust in the Government and the fear of how they might act without any prior warning. He told his audience that as new buildings were to be constructed on the site belonging to the Sisters of St Paul, it was proposed to help them privately by giving them financial assistance. The new buildings were then to be made over to the Sisters 'as their own property ... the same as had been done elsewhere'. The money could never then be said to be raised through public subscriptions, he said, 'lest some day a Government might unscrupulously seize the property as belonging to the public'.[35] Speaking at the opening of a school in Cobridge, his message was clear as he outlined the guiding principles of: 'Catholic Schools with Catholic teachers for our Catholic children', which he said the parishioners there had adopted, and they had 'by their erection of these splendid schools at the cost of so much sacrifice, conclusively shown that they will never haul down the flag of Catholic Education'.[36]

After 1906, several government initiatives affecting voluntary schools were unsuccessful. Then after 1910 the Liberal Party did not have a majority without the support of the Irish party, who were in favour of assisting the Catholic schools, and thus ended any serious threat to the voluntary schools under the Liberal Government. But another forty years were to pass before the Catholics were eventually to gain many of the real advantages they sought by right to have incorporated by the state into the running of their schools. This was ultimately due to a more open and expansive exchange of ideas brought about through the immediate effects of the Second World War. During this time an attitude for general improvement was adopted towards education as the main hope for the future, in line with the determination to make facilities more adequate and easily accessible to all.

# Notes

1    There was another society known since 1814 as the 'British and Foreign School Society', which attracted some (Low Church) Anglican support, as well as Nonconformist support. Nonconformists played little part in the educational system until after 1870, when they became champions of the school boards.

2    Sedgley Park School in Wolverhampton and Standon Lordship in Hertfordshire. See Chapter 1 at note 17. The boys would go there at the ages of 8 to 9 and leave at 13 or 14 to go abroad, or as in Edward Ilsley's case, to continue training at Oscott.

3    'In Manchester in 1784 Catholics had participated in establishing the Manchester Sunday School Movement, opening a Sunday School in Blackfriars under Robert and Mary Turner.' Sr Dominic Savio Hamer, CP, 'A Phase of Struggle for Catholic Education: Manchester and Salford in the Mid-Nineteenth Century', Catholic Record Society, May 1996, p. 110.

4    *Commons Journal*, 88, pp. 692–3.

5    These figures were only an estimate. Sunday schools were an important source of education in the 1830s–40s.

6    Westminster, Catholic Poor School Committee Reports, 1848, pp. 13, 14. The Honourable Charles Langdale was its first chairman and Scott Nasmyth Stokes its first secretary. Thomas William Marshall, although not a member of the committee, was Her Majesty's Inspector for Catholic Schools. This body finally developed into the Catholic Educational Council in 1905, later to provide a religious syllabus and inspectors for their schools. Sr Dominic Savio Hamer C.P. discusses these points in her Catholic Record Society paper: 'A Phase of Struggle for Catholic Education: Manchester and Salford in the Mid-Nineteenth Century', May 1996, pp. 110–23.

7    Chadwick, vol. ii, p. 401 and Kiernan, p. 43: 'This suggests the teaching of mothers, keeping at least a spark of the Faith somewhere in the background of their children's minds.'

8    O'Neil, p. 271. 'It was towards the end of 1884 that Vaughan became aware of a serious problem affecting children of the working class in his diocese ... his information indicated that there were many church members being lost. The term popularized at the time was "leakage". Especially alarming to him was that poor children were being lost to the Catholic Church due to the charitable works of other Christian bodies who were helping orphans and the homeless.'

9    One of the most prominent men in government at this time was William Gladstone, who became Prime Minister for the first time in 1868. He was a Liberal.

10   Kiernan, p. 44. St Chad's Grammar School was begun in Spring Hill

under Revd Joseph Henry Souter in 1858 and it was later moved to Bath Street. Bishop Turner established Salford Catholic Grammar School in 1868.

11    T. E. Bird, 'An Archbishop in Retirement', *The Clergy Review* (May 1955), p. 280.

12    *The Archbishop Ilsley School Magazine.*

13    Denis Gwynn, 'The Growth of the Catholic Community', in Beck, p. 422.

14    Nicholas Wiseman, *An Appeal to the Reason and Good Feeling of the English People on the Subject of the English Hierarchy* (London, 1850), p. 30. Also Norman. There are graphic descriptions of Wiseman's work for the poor on pp. 155–6.

15    Gray, p. 296.

16    Beck, pp. 347–9. They moved to Wandsworth that year, returning to Roehampton in 1946 and taking the title of 'Digby Stuart'. *Brief History of Digby Stuart College*, Roehampton Institute.

17    O'Neil, p. 443.

18    Richard Cunningham, 'Public Control in Education', an article in *Law and Justice: the Christian Law Review* (1995): 'The first expenditure on elementary education took the form of the Parliamentary Grants which began modestly in 1833 and increased thereafter. These represented one of three forms of income for voluntary schools, (as all assisted schools were until 1870), the other two being subscriptions from supporters and fees from parents. When board schools joined voluntary schools after 1870, they too had three forms of income, but in their case rates took the place of subscriptions.'

19    Gladstone's last word on the Third Reading, July 1870. His sister Mary was a convert and he also had certain sympathies in this direction. See also Beck, p. 276.

20    B.A., CLI, 'An Education Peril', 16 November 1904; CLIX, 14 September 1905; and CLXVIII on 'The Education Crisis', 1 May 1906. Bishop Ullathorne was suspicious of the influence of the local boards, so it was part of his policy to have Catholics sitting on them to protect their own interests.

21    Snead-Cox, vol. ii, ch. 4, 'The Fight for the Schools', p. 91: 'To end this chapter of uncertainties, and to replace hesitations and doubts by a definite programme which should have all the Catholic forces of the kingdom at its back, was the first object which Herbert Vaughan now led into view.' Also O'Neil, pp. 289, 444.

22    H. R. Hodkinson, 'Further Notes on Harvington Hall', a paper given in 1944: 'The school was still in existence in 1913. In that year it appears for the last time in diocesan records and is described as a mixed school of 64 pupils. It was closed presumably about this time by the local authority who were unable to furnish the actual date of closure.'

23  Gray, p. 294.

24  O'Neil, pp. 444–5. See also Marjorie Cruickshank, *Church and State in English Education*, London, Macmillan, 1963, p. 62.

25  McClelland, p. 232. This campaign was led by a Baptist, John Clifford, with the backing of Lloyd George. Archbishop Bourne thought its success was due to lack of Catholic representation on the new local authorities. Lloyd George's slogan at this time was 'Clericism is the Enemy.'

26  *Ibid.*, pp. 232–3.

27  B.A., Pastoral Letter, CLI, 'An Education Peril', The last Sunday after Pentecost, 1904.

28  By 1854 there were 137 pupil-teachers in Catholic boys' schools and 243 in Catholic girls' schools. This system continued generally, but it was largely phased out between 1910 and 1914, mainly because of incentives offered by the Liberal Government. At the same time Catholic teacher training was expanding. See Beck, ch. 12.

29  B.A., '*Ad Clerum*', CLIX, 14 September 1905.

30  D.B., pp. 17–18.

31  McClelland, pp. 236–54. 'Bourne's quarrel with Norfolk centred upon the realisation that the Tory aristocracy was in danger of actions of a militant opposition. It was to be almost forty years before an educational measure was to become operative that would presage a like measure of advantage.'

32  Westminster, Bishop Ilsley to Cardinal Bourne.

33  *Ibid.*, This situation is discussed on pp. 250–4.

34  Westminster, BO 1/178 item 5, Bishop Ilsley to Archbishop Bourne, 4 January 1907. The bishops at this time were: Edward Ilsley of Birmingham, William Gordon of Leeds, John Cuthbert Hedley of Newport, Arthur Riddell of Northampton, Robert Brindle of Nottingham, Charles Graham of Plymouth, Thomas Wilkinson of Hexham and Newcastle, John Baptist Cahill of Portsmouth, Samuel Allen of Shrewsbury, Francis Mostyn of Menevia, Peter Amigo of Southwark, and Louis Charles Casartelli of Salford.

35  'Birmingham and Catholic Education', newspaper report, 29 June 1907.

36  'New Catholic Schools', newspaper report, Cobridge, 22 October 1906.

## CHAPTER FOURTEEN

# *Diocesan Bishop*

## John McIntyre as Secretary

When Oscott became the diocesan seminary in 1889, Edward Ilsley took up residence there as both Bishop and Rector, and he chose Father John McIntyre to act as his secretary. The choice was bound to prove successful as McIntyre had been with Ilsley since his early days as a student at St Bernard's and he shared with him the same great attachment to Oscott. Speaking of his brief times away from there, McIntyre used to say, 'he always left the College with regret, and returned to it with joy and thankfulness'. McIntyre remained in this position of secretary, 'which he held in addition to his academic duties at Oscott',[1] for the following 25 years, continuing after he became auxiliary to Archbishop Ilsley in 1912. He was sympathetic towards the Bishop's views, and 'in this capacity was the right hand of his venerated chief'.[2]

Apart from his normal round of duties, McIntyre proved to be particularly resourceful over the revision and final composition of the Bishop's pastoral letters, and he also acted as a useful channel of communication, keeping Ilsley closely in touch with his clergy. The Bishop achieved this end by having regular meetings with his priests at Bishop's House. He considered his discussions with them to be of the first importance, and always looked forward to them because they gave him the opportunity 'to enter all their works and difficulties'. It was in his nature to readily give his time to people, and he was particularly delighted to have his priests at his table. So in spite of his elevated position as their bishop and, later, archbishop, it could never be said he was in any way remote from the clergy in his diocese.[3] The story goes that on one occasion while visiting a parish, he discovered the organ to be out of repair, and some time later the Bishop was found up in the organ loft with his coat off working away at the instrument. There he remained until he had restored it to his satis-faction, expressing his obvious pleasure at being able to help out in this way.[4]

In spite of his busy life, Edward Ilsley always found time for all those in his care, and when he died this was one of the many qualities he was particularly remembered by. Talking of his accessibility, one writer said of him not only that he was approachable but also that it was easy to talk to him.[5] Archbishop Maurice Couve de Murville of Birmingham told a story in his Advent Pastoral of 1984, which showed Archbishop Ilsley's readiness to give of his time whenever it was needed. 'In one of the Birmingham parishes I visited I met an old lady who had been a little girl in Rushall, near Walsall, in the time of King Edward VII. Her mother was a Catholic and her father was not. One day her mother had a stroke and although she recovered slightly, she felt she was dying. She was very worried about her little girls and what would happen to their religious upbringing once she was gone. At the time the great Archbishop Ilsley was on a visitation in the parish, so the mother sent a message to him, asking as a special favour that her two girls could be confirmed, although they were only little. Archbishop Ilsley not only agreed to their request but when he found out that the mother was too ill to come to the Church, he insisted on coming to the house so that the two little girls were confirmed in the front room with their mother looking on.' The old lady went on to say that life became hard for them after their mother died. Her father remarried and her stepmother tried to prevent them from going to Mass by punishing them when they came home. But they persevered, and they kept their faith, and never forgot that very special day of their confirmation.

## Edward Elgar at St George's

On 9 October 1888 Edward made his first visit as Bishop to St George's Church in Worcester on the occasion of the inauguration of the Apostleship of Prayer and the League of the Sacred Heart.[6] Edward Elgar, then aged 31, who had been appointed organist there in November 1885, was asked at short notice to compose some pieces for the visit. He managed to turn them out in less than two days, and in the end time was so short that the organist and the choir had to manage with hastily written manuscript copies. Writing to a friend a few days later, Elgar described what had happened: 'Our Bishop has been down – last Sunday, and for the special service some special things had to be sung for which we had no music, thus I had to set to work and copy out the parts. Had to get it in anyway and nearly broke my neck doing it. Anyway the leading paper says the new composition was "exquisite" so I suppose twas good enough.'[7] One result of his efforts was a beautiful rendering of the traditional introit, *Ecce Sacerdos Magnus* – 'Behold the Great High Priest', for the entrance of the Bishop. This piece has since been used on countless ceremonial occasions, and Ilsley, being a musician himself, must have very much appreciated and enjoyed Elgar's compositions.

There is a very fine letter written by Bishop Ilsley to Edward Elgar on 10 October 1900, to congratulate him on the performance of *The Dream of Gerontius* which had taken place on 3 October at the Birmingham Triennial Festival. The letter is very frank:

> During the past week I fear you have been overwhelmed with correspondence following upon the production of your *Dream of Gerontius* at the Birmingham Festival. But now you have had a breathing space I hope you will allow me, as your diocesan, to offer you my very sincere and hearty congratulations on the success you have achieved.
>
> It was a bold undertaking to set to music that sublime poem of the illustrious Cardinal. I confess that I went to the festival with a certain misgiving as to the possibility of any musical setting doing justice to the poem. As it proceeded my fears vanished; for it was evident you had entered with all your soul into the treating of the subject, and were employing the ample resources at your command to give it worthy expression. In this age of materialism it is no small matter to have called the attention of thousands to a poem which described the death bed scene of a Christian & the journey into the other world so truthfully and graphically. More than this, you have added to it a new charm which will enhance it in the eyes of the musical world, to so many to whom the poem was a sealed book. In this respect your work is a triumph of faith, on which I once more sincerely congratulate you.[8]

As it happened Ilsley's opinion was not held by the majority at this time. The magnificent oratorio setting had not been well received in Birmingham and was even considered to be a failure – a deeply disillusioning experience for Elgar. This came about because the production had suffered from difficulties from the start, involving lack of time for preparation and rehearsal, and Hans Richter, the conductor, had first seen the score only ten days before the actual performance.

But Ilsley saw past these temporary drawbacks and in his letter to the composer gave his work the appreciation it deserved. His analysis of the dramatic power of the composition, which had taken its own creative approach to bring home positive Christian beliefs in a materialistic world, showed sensitive perception on Ilsley's part. He obviously recognized the important position Elgar's oratorio was destined to hold in English church music and particularly the Catholic Church. Subsequent performances over the years were received with increasing enthusiasm and *Gerontius* soon came to be recognized as a work of enormous originality, taking up a high position in the choral repertoire for all time.

It was in his later years when he was Archbishop of Birmingham that Edward Ilsley, then aged 78, ordained three candidates to the priesthood in St George's on Sunday 30 July 1916 during the time of the Great War. They were Joseph Parsons, SJ, a native of Worcester, Leo Twiney of the diocese, later to become a canon of St Chad's, and Brother Gregory Raupart, a Dominican. There were fifteen priests present in the sanctuary, among them the provincial of the Jesuit Order, the Very Reverend John Wright, who presented the candidates to the Archbishop, also Monsignor Cronin, who was Diocesan Chancellor at the time, acting as master of ceremonies, and Father Percy Styche, who was crossbearer. This was the first ordination held in the church which had been opened 87 years earlier in 1829 in Bishop Walsh's time, and it may well have been the first Catholic ordination that had taken place in Worcester since the time of the Reformation.

The high altar was banked with flowers that day, and a photographer up in the choir gallery during Mass took a picture at the moment during the rite of ordination when the Archbishop and priests, each with their right arm outstretched, prayed over the candidates kneeling before them. This was after the Archbishop, now facing the congregation, laid his hands on the head of each ordinand in turn, followed by all the priests present. The view captured from the gallery was taken at the most significant part of the ceremony with the camera focused midway between the tall pillars of the chancel arch into the sanctuary below.

## Letters

It was one of Ilsley's assets that he liked to maintain contact with people through his own private letter-writing. His personal style was always essentially honest, and not lacking in a touch of humour from time to time. These letters are a particularly valuable source of information because they reveal exactly what was in his mind, and are also a key to his exchange of ideas with others. We are told that in spite of the many demands on his time, 'as regards his correspondence, most of his letters he answered with his own hand, and he was known to sit up to the early hours of the morning with his letters'.[9] His replies would often start with such words of encouragement as – 'Your letter gave me great satisfaction in more ways than one.'

Some of the draft copies have been preserved in which he would use the style of a writer carefully sifting through, and rephrasing certain passages, or adding a further considered thought or word here and there, before committing himself to the finished copy. His correspondence might range widely from the first rough note he made for a letter to Alfred Austin, written in January 1896 to congratulate him on being appointed Poet Laureate: 'As rector of this college I hope I may be allowed to say what lively satisfaction the announcement of your appointment to the Laureateship has afforded me and our College Staff and Students – This feeling will, I know be shared by very many past Alumni who are to be found all over the world. They will rejoice that a son of Oscott has been singled out by our Gracious Sovereign as worthy of so eminent a distinction; and they will feel with us that your elevation reflects glory on our Alma Mater, though of course in a less degree than upon Stonyhurst. You will scarcely remember me, except, perhaps as one of 8 students who arrived in January 1853. But I remember distinctly the active part you took in a movement for promoting the cultivation of literature – You were the leading spirit in the "Academia" of the day and thus gave promise of the brilliant career which has been so worthily and happily crowned.'[10]

Or he might be dealing with the acceptance of an invitation to dine with the Lord Mayor at the Mansion House in the company of Archbishop Vaughan and the other bishops.[11] Or giving the expression of his astonishment to Father Parker, who had to delay his move to Woodlane because Father Morris, who was about to leave, had been farming the land at the mission with cattle and pigs, and was now trying to sell off his stock and equipment before his move: 'I hope you won't think of taking to farming,' he quipped, 'the sheep the flock of Christ would be the sufferers.'[12]

We are told that Ilsley's aim in his pastoral letters was 'to indoctrinate priests and people alike with his own principles',[13] and that they were 'the result of much thought and labour'. He would tend to work out the general idea, and then spend some time turning it over in his mind before getting down to writing it out. His concise interpretations of the Papal encyclicals over the years caused him to touch on a wide range of subjects. In 1891, referring to Pope Leo's moving encyclical on slavery, he deprecated 'the deplorable conditions of the natives of Central Africa, and the iniquitous traffic in human beings that, even in these days of enlightenment, is being carried on'.[14] In 1897 he spoke graphically of the plight of those suffering in the Indian famine, 'scattered over an area more than that of Great Britain and Ireland in extent, there are some 37 millions on the verge of starvation'. He urged his people to make extraordinary efforts in their offerings to help relieve the suffering in this calamity.

One of the most notable of his pastorals was entitled, 'On Devotion to the Pope'.[15] Early in his episcopacy, in March 1892, a controversial address had been given to the Annual Catholic Reunion in the Birmingham Town Hall, on 'The Temporal Power of the Pope'. This was a major issue in the Church at the time. The speaker, a Mr W. S. Lilly, who was a well-known London writer in current journals, and also secretary of the Catholic Union, put forward suggestions in his address which not only would curtail Pope Leo's freedom by placing him in the position of being dependent on the Great Powers, but also ran directly contrary to his declaration affirming his rights of sovereignty over the City of Rome. Lilly's ideas shocked and alarmed his audience who listened throughout in chilly silence, and a great deal of correspondence in the press followed, notably in *The Times* and *The Tablet*, which subsequently took up the cause of the Holy See. Realizing his diocese had been put in an invidious position by this man, and particularly as his speech had been made in Birmingham, Bishop Ilsley published this pastoral defending the Holy Father and demanding support for his liberty. He said, 'in these days of levelling down and of revolution, it behoves us to pay heed to that reverence for the sacredness of his person. He is the highest representative of Christ on earth.'

## Pope Leo's Jubilee

His pastoral in 1893, given at the time of the celebration of Pope Leo's episcopal jubilee, is most interesting in the way it describes the sights and sounds of the English pilgrimage to Rome: 'From various European Nations bands of pilgrims have been travelling Romeward, and for months to come, the stream will be flowing from America,

Figure 14.1 *Pope Leo XIII. A portrait in the albums at Oscott College.*

Australia and the remotest parts of Christendom.' His ability to cap-
ture a scene and share the experience with others is at its best on this
occasion as he describes the appearance of the 83-year-old Pope being
borne aloft on his throne into the basilica above the heads of the
crowd of pilgrims: 'That Jubilee Mass was a spectacle to witness. But
no tongue can describe that slender figure of the Pontiff, arrayed in
white, like a vision from heaven, as he appeared at the extremity of the
basilica; and as he was borne slowly along, giving his blessing on the
right hand and on the left, the *evivas* of the dense crowd rose like a
mighty wave, and died away, and rose again with ever increasing
volume, and their enthusiasm reached its climax when, as he arrived
beneath the great dome, within view of both transepts, the united
voices of all 60,000 who thronged the vast nave, transepts and choir,
broke into one soul-stirring chorus of acclamation.'[16]

The specific objects to be promoted by the pilgrimage were set out
in the official programme. The second of these read: 'To obtain the
return of England to her ancient faith, and to the fold of Blessed Peter,
her ancient patron, and much-loved shepherd and teacher.'
Commenting on the prayers offered for the conversion of England by

the pilgrims, Bishop Ilsley observed, 'What the precise effect of these prayers may be in promoting the other objects of the pilgrimage we cannot tell. God accomplishes His works in His own time, and in His own way. We may not live to see the return of England to the faith; and the restoration of temporal power seems as far off as ever.' He softened his words with the assurance that the prayers offered 'will some day bear fruit in the conversion of our country'. He may have been moved by Pope Leo's hope for 'the conversion of England', but chose this point in his pastoral letter to indicate that in his own opinion this had now become only a distant realization.

There was an awareness towards the end of the century that, despite the growing number of churches being built, and an increase in the numbers of Catholics, there was occurring at the same time among them a considerable assimilation into the rest of the community through mixed marriages. This, and a general movement in the world away from religion, was causing the problem of substantial loss of numbers within the Church, 'which was given justification when Bishop Vaughan of Salford issued an enquiry in 1885 into the state of Roman Catholics in Manchester and found leakage'.[17] So the hope for the conversion of England had now moved into the realms of a very distant possibility, rather than the immediate prospect it had once presented in some minds forty years before. In his experience over the years of what was happening in the realms of religion in his own country, Bishop Ilsley had apparently discerned that the tide had turned, and was already flowing in the opposite direction.

## Winters Spent Abroad

Although he was always considered to have such a strong constitution, several newspaper accounts mention the fact that the Bishop was advised to 'winter abroad' in the years of 1899 and 1900 because he was experiencing periods of ill-health.[18] A postcard written to Henry Parkinson from Menton in the January of 1900 mentions that 'the cold weather of the last two days is very trying to me'. He also wrote from Rome to Dame Laurentia Ward, then the Prioress of Oulton Abbey, on 18 March 1900, regretting his absence at such a critical time as the death of the Abbess, Agnes Beech. He explained 'but the cold winds and wet weather have hindered my recovery. They say however that after St Patrick's Day the genial weather returns to last in Rome.'

It would seem that he was suffering from recurrent attacks of bronchitis at this time, but this did not prevent him from continuing to work with his usual energy as soon as he was recovered. There is another letter written to Dame Laurentia Ward on 31 May 1900, a few weeks after his return. She was now the newly appointed Abbess of Oulton, and from that time on he addresses her as 'Dear Lady Abbess'. The letter shows his habit of dealing with the practical everyday details to do with the Abbey as well as the spiritual matters. Having settled who should conduct a general retreat for the sisters, he then moves on to another matter: 'The next time the joiner calls at the Abbey ask him to look at the tribune gate, & put the hinges right – he will see how a socket can be fixed in the wall to receive a small bolt which can be fastened on the gate & drawn whenever the sacristan is engaged in the sanctuary.' It is certain the Bishop would check the workmanship during the weeks to come.

Writing again in the July he sympathized with her when she confided to him some of the difficulties encountered in dealing with the Community. At the same time he made light of anything he had to deal with himself: 'No amount of work of other kinds is half so exhausting – Blessing bells, and Abbesses & consecrating altars and churches, are only a recreation in comparison with the other – the putting of square people into square holes.' There is no sarcasm in this letter, that was not his way, but there is that light touch of humour he put across so well.

This correspondence continued for over twenty years, with the Bishop showing the same detailed concern covering every aspect of their lives. In an address he delivered on a visitation to Oulton Abbey on 3 December in 1901, he 'congratulated the Community on the contented and cheerful spirit of the lay-sisters; this he desired to be fostered and maintained. He also exhorted the Community to cultivate a spirit of recollection such as befits contemplatives living under the rule of St Benedict.'

In 1900, in spite of the fact that he was some considerable distance away from them in Rome, his pastoral letter written to his people on Quinquagesima Sunday has a particularly personal quality about it, as though he nevertheless felt close to them in spirit. Regretting his absence, he immediately drew them into his own experience, describing his recent private audience with Pope Leo in quite a realistic manner: 'To the detailed account we gave him of the spiritual condition of the diocese and of special works of religion and charity that are in progress, he listened with an interest as keen as if Birmingham were a favourite or an only child.' His letter concluded with a typically kindly observation about the Pope: 'It was a great joy to see His Holiness looking even stronger than he did three years ago – He several times mounted and descended the eight steps between his throne and the *prie-dieu* with a firm tread marvellous in a man who is about to enter his 91st year.'[19] Ilsley showed this same kindly interest toward his people in his Lenten Pastoral in 1908 when he suggested that far from regarding Lent solely as a season of self-denial, they should look upon it 'much as does the mariner the friendly harbour, where he can carefully examine and repair the damages that the wind and the waves have inflicted upon his barque, and put her in fit condition to face the dangers that the rest of the voyage may have in store for him'.

## Modernism

Throughout his 65 years as priest and bishop, Edward Ilsley could be measured as a man who expressed himself as much through his actions as with his words. He appeared to take the great issues of his day in his stride, and would be seen to support or condemn them as they affected the Church, or the lives of those in his pastoral care. Modernism was at its height at the end of the nineteenth century, and there were further important developments in the first decade of the next. Among the leading figures in the movement were Professor St George Mivart, whom Darwin styled 'the distinguished biologist', a convert who had been received into the Church in 1844 by the Revd John Moore who later became the president of Oscott. Another was Father George Tyrell SJ. The Modernists sought their own personal freedom of thought, which tended to move away from ecclesiastical authority, and they were liable to ignore the dogmatic principles of religion when expounding their theories. The movement did not deter the Bishop's endorsement of university education. His own students benefited from the broad training they received at Oscott College, described by R. H. Kiernan in his history of the archdiocese as being 'well-established as a centre of Catholic learning'. So they were familiar with the various developments and movements of the time, being well armed against them where necessary. Schobel wrote to the Abbess of Oulton, 'The Encyclical on Modernists will give the Dames of Oulton an idea of how necessary it is to have a really well-educated clergy and Episcopate, to see thoroughly the dangers when they crop up.'[20]

It is noticeable that Ilsley made no public comment through his own pastoral letters on *Lamentabili Sane* and *Pascendi Dominici Gregis*, the papal documents given in 1907 by Pope Pius X which touched on Modernism.[21] Nor did he appear to enter into any discussion regarding the difficulties presented by the movements in question in any of his private correspondence, in spite of the fact that this was considered a major crisis in his time.[22] As both priest and teacher Ilsley made constant use of the Bible, so it is unlikely that he would have wanted to give his time to the Modernist theories, not wishing to involve himself with something so contrary to his own beliefs. He may have felt that the joint pastoral of the bishops dealing with liberal Catholicism, issued in 1900 by Cardinal Vaughan, covered whatever was required for him in that region.

In contrast to Ilsley, his close friend and mentor of many years, Bishop Amigo of Southwark, was confronted with a series of far-reaching problems in this connection, particularly in relation to Father George Tyrell SJ when he was resident in the diocese, at Storrington. As far as Ilsley was concerned, he may have considered that the far-reaching questions dealt with in Pope Pius's encyclicals on Modernism applied particularly to his clergy rather than the laity, having no wish to draw his people's minds into these complex issues. The problem probably lay behind many of their subjects for discussion at their monthly meetings.[23] Living within the walls of the college would have made Ilsley aware that his rector, Henry Parkinson, was always taking a lead in following up and interpreting all these developments, while his own role would be mainly to approve and sanction whatever might be put forward by him.

Birmingham was also well-represented in the fight against Modernism by William Barry, who described it as a 'mighty tempest bearing down on Catholic established beliefs'. He realized that by attempting to do away with the foundations of all religious faith, it would threaten to destroy the possibility of all religion, and he argued intelligently against it in his writings. He was well qualified to speak out, as he had personal acquaintance with two priests principally concerned, namely, the French professor Alfred Loisy and the Irish Jesuit George Tyrell. Loisy rejected the Bible as a collection of documents having no historical value when related to supernatural or miraculous events. Barry said Loisy had 'reduced the gospels to a tissue of legends ... He has done nothing but destroy.' In 1926 he wrote in his memoirs: 'In my considered judgement all these modernist Catholics mistook a phantom for reality, and their triumph would ensure the disappearance in one generation of the Christian religion ... Modernism and the Catholic Faith cannot be reconciled. The

Roman Church cast it out in good time; and its defeat is a signal victory over agnostic devices.'[24]

A great deal of controversy surrounded the final publications of St George Jackson Mivart, who died in April 1900. There was a division of opinion among churchmen as to whether he wrote so vehemently on Modernist lines simply because he was ill, or whether he had defected from the Catholic faith. Barry had been on friendly terms with him for the last fourteen years before he died, and he described how he remembered talking with him in 'his good old Catholic days', but in that time he had seen him change from a man who strongly defended the Church to one who sought to undermine its beliefs. 'But after a severe illness he became an utterly changed man,' he said, 'and when we last talked together his intellect had altogether given way.' Cardinal Vaughan refused Mivart the rites of a Christian burial, but four years later, after making further enquiries, Cardinal Bourne granted permission to Mivart's widow to have her husband reburied in consecrated ground.

## Professional Standards of the Priesthood

One of Ilsley's main aims in life was to raise the professional standards of the priesthood. This he made clear at his first synod when giving his reasons for setting up Oscott College as the diocesan seminary. In a letter written jointly to Henry Parkinson and John McIntyre to congratulate them on their ordinations and the completion of their studies at the English College in Rome, he confided to them what he felt to be his own inadequacies: 'I am now turning back to your letter to see what the questions were to which you are expecting a reply – but what is now in my mind to say is, as for preaching don't be anxious – have been trying myself at St Catherine's the last three Sundays – I could do very well if I had my theology at my fingers' ends & could give a tolerable exposition of the Catholic Doctrine on any point I speak about – I mean I can't carry it in my head & produce it as required – but you will have had a proper course and need not fear on that score.'[25] He was being typically self-effacing here, and it was as though he felt that there were a number of things he was ready to hand over to them, knowing that they were better equipped academically to deal with them than he was. But in this case he was not doing himself justice, because it was said of him in a later appreciation 'His exposition of the dogmas of Faith, however difficult, revealed the sure touch of the theologian; his use of passages from the scriptures was the fruit of habitual reading and re-reading.'[26] His experience in preaching is revealed in the word of advice he ends with: 'Then as to selecting what to say – as soon as you come into contact with people you will find out what they know & don't know, & you will see almost at once where to start from, and what to say.'

Because of his own particular way of putting things across to them when he was Rector at St Bernard's Seminary, his students thought of him as belonging to the 'old-fashioned school of religion', placing before them the Holy Spirit and devotion to the Sacred Heart and advocating a close study of the Gospels. He must have witnessed the religious and social ferment surrounding the publication of Charles Darwin's evolutionary theories in 1859 while he was still training for the priesthood. But the deeply spiritual side of his temperament meant he was unlikely to involve himself in such matters, and through his early upbringing his sympathies would naturally remain partly with 'the older Catholics', so it could be supposed that because of this he was not prepared to adjust his views to any great extent to suit a rapidly changing world.

## The Middle Path

Arthur Villiers, in a memoir of Ilsley as the Father Rector, summed him up as being of 'the old school of Gother, Challoner and Ullathorne'. So it would seem that he stood on the middle ground, holding on to the values of the old Catholics while at the same time adhering to the Roman outlook and that of the new converts.[27] He also trod this middle path in his attitude toward the personal training of his students; and while promoting the beauty of the 'Romanized' liturgy, he still handled things in moderation. Villiers observed that although 'contrary to the general practice of even exemplary priests' the Rector said Mass every day, he was in no hurry for them to adopt some of the new Continental ways which were being brought in just then, such as the familiarity of taking daily communion.[28] On the other hand it must be recognized that it was through the policies he laid down as Bishop of Birmingham, for clerical education in his diocese, that Oscott College took an important lead in the country in the training of priests in a system that moved away from the old styles and into the attitudes of the new. So in this way Edward Ilsley greatly assisted in taking the Church in Britain forward into the twentieth century.

In England, throughout the nineteenth century and beyond, the

Roman Catholics as a body continued to be unpopular. They were still generally regarded as an isolated community, and the feeling of 'no-popery' among the ordinary non-Catholics remained strong, particularly as they were unable to accept such things as the miracles at Lourdes, or devotions to the Sacred Heart or Our Lady.[29] Through his Anglican background, Cardinal Manning deeply felt the 'social ostracism' which held Catholic men back in public life, and he wrote in 1867 that the prevailing hostility was only 'a more civilised hostility than previously'.[30]

The Queen's religion, tinged with Presbyterianism (an influence brought about through her connections with Scotland), initially meant her relation towards Catholics was only one of toleration, and on their part there was still the feeling among Catholics, including their bishops, of 'heretic' Protestants, an attitude which did little to encourage any real reconciliation. The Royal Declaration made by the sovereign at the coronation was another barrier. Cardinal Vaughan found it unacceptable and 'he felt deeply and strongly about it' throughout his life – and so the prejudices lived on.[31] In May 1887, a more assuring move was made when an envoy from the Pope was present at the Queen's jubilee. But difficulties were raised when the Catholic hierarchy proposed to present an address of congratulation to her on this occasion, only to discover that as her 'loyal Catholic subjects' they were not on the privileged list, so a deputation would not have been received in person anyway.[32]

In spite of all this, by the turn of the century such newspapers as *The Times* and *The Spectator* treated Roman Catholics with respect.[33] But a letter to Dame Laurentia Ward, from Bishop Ilsley in October 1900, gives an idea of how, just below the surface, the relations of the Catholics toward royalty had not progressed to any great extent. Queen Victoria was dying: 'Poor Queen,' he wrote, 'She was as good as she knew how to be – and I trust that God will show her mercy. I offered my Mass for her this morning – we can't do this publicly.'[34] It would have given scandal for a priest (and more so a bishop) to make an announcement at this time that he was offering his Mass for any Protestant and above all for the Queen. Percy Fitzgerald in his book, aptly titled in this case *Fifty Years of Catholic Life and Social Progress*, gives a clear picture as to how things stood when she died: 'During her illness the prayers of the congregation had been invited, but after her death certain reserves were made. The Cardinal pointed out that Masses could not be offered for her soul, which seems not unreasonable: as most Protestants renounce the Mass as superstitious, it could not be an acceptable proceeding. But there was nothing against anyone heartily praying for her soul, and much praying there was, I have not the least doubt.'

## The University Question

When Herbert Vaughan became Archbishop of Westminster in 1892, Edward Ilsley was 53, and he had been Bishop of Birmingham for four years. With Cardinal Manning gone, the question of finally lifting the prohibition of Roman Catholics from attending English universities was brought to the fore by both the clergy and leading members of the Catholic laity at that time. Among them were the Duke of Norfolk and Wilfrid Ward, both long-standing friends of the new Archbishop, and Bishop Hedley and Bishop Ullathorne were among the bishops who, in the last ten years, had attempted to bring about a change.

The question had been a matter of serious concern for the past forty years, and it had been commented that 'in this long and serious question it should be noted how careful were the authorities in every step they took not to wholly close the door, as it were: they seemed almost to imply that under proper safeguards, education at such places might be acceptable'.[35] But Cardinal Manning had always rigidly opposed lifting the prohibition, and Herbert Vaughan, on his appointment as Archbishop, was now seen to adapt Manning's policy to his own. Not having been to university himself, he appeared to have even less understanding of the problem than his predecessor. He saw universities as centres of worldliness and of liberalism of the Continental variety that had recently alarmed Rome, and this ruled out any appreciation on his part of the advantages to be gained from them either in intellectual training or for the urgent need to fit Catholic men for public life.[36]

Meanwhile, it was acknowledged at this time that some parents were ignoring the ban and allowing their sons to go to Oxford and Cambridge, while others did so with special permission from the bishop of their diocese. The provincial universities were also playing a role in the emergence of the Catholic professional classes, for it was becoming the tendency for increasing numbers of the middle classes to attend them. So for the hierarchy to continue to make a stand against all these developments was simply to go against the tide. Vaughan considered that the solution to the problem lay in the setting-up of a Catholic university, and he thought of renewing Manning's plan for a university at Kensington. In preparation for this he even considered asking Rome 'for a more stringent decree in favour of the exclusion of Catholics from Oxford and Cambridge'.[37]

But the mood among both clergy and laity was for the ban now to be lifted altogether, and there was no enthusiasm for Vaughan's plan. It was felt generally that there would be insufficient support for a Catholic university in Britain, and besides this the lack of success of Manning's venture twenty years earlier gave them no encouragement.

## An Oxford Summer School

The question was suddenly brought out in the open in May 1894, when the Cardinal's fears and prejudices against universities went so far as to cause him to forbid a summer school for Catholic elementary teachers to be held in Oxford.[38] As Oxford was in Bishop Ilsley's own diocese, and as he had already given the summer school his full approval, he was justifiably annoyed at this intervention. Vaughan's insistence over the cancellation must have seemed hardly rational to him – because Ilsley took a far more judicious and practical view of the situation, being sympathetically concerned for the wasted effort on the part of the staff appointed to give the tuition, and of the teachers who were going to attend it. He also showed his open-mindedness on the university question by describing those assisting at the summer school as 'our young Catholic friends among the Undergraduates' and at the same time showed his appreciation of those he described as 'our laborious teachers who are anticipating with much interest the plea-sure the proposed holiday would undoubtedly afford them',[39] being mindful, no doubt, of the particularly hard conditions they were working under.

Ilsley first communicated with Cardinal Vaughan over his objection and ascertained that his grounds for his prohibition were because the summer school had been arranged to take place in an Oxford college – albeit that it was to take place during the long vacation. This appeared to suggest his doubts had little foundation, but the Cardinal nevertheless said he considered it would indirectly encourage 'mixed education and the frequentation of non-Catholic Universities by Catholic youth'.[40] On 5 June Ilsley wrote to Sidney Parry, the secretary of Newman House in Kennington Park Road who was involved in organizing the summer school, to convey to him Vaughan's virtual ban on it: 'So strongly does he feel on the matter that he has resolved to refer it to the consideration of the Hierarchy, and, if necessary, to invoke the guidance of the Holy See.' He continued: 'Under these

circumstances I am constrained to appeal to your loyalty and obedience to withdraw the scheme for this year.'[41]

The letter sent out two days later by the two secretaries of Newman
House, the Hon. Everard Fielding and Sidney Parry, to announce the
cancellation, shows veiled sarcasm: 'Since we learned by the Bishop's
letter that his Eminence places his direct veto on the plan, we have
only frankly to withdraw, content to believe that those in high places
have more extended vision than those who are in the plain.' The
annoyance over the cancellation had further repercussions as it caused
the Duke of Norfolk to take a step that had been contemplated by him
some months before. Within the month he called a meeting of interested laity with a view to drawing up a petition to the hierarchy in
favour of allowing Catholics to attend universities, 'under adequate
safeguards'.

The two secretaries were asked by him to assist in drawing up a first
draft of the petition, and in his pencilled notes made in preparation
for this, Parry assumed that 'The Bishop of Birmingham's letter
implies that the whole question of Univ. Education is likely to come
before the Hierarchy.'[42] This was Parry's interpretation of the situation, not Vaughan's and not altogether Ilsley's. Vaughan's idea was to
enforce the prohibition more forcibly if anything, and Ilsley's letter to
Parry was meant to warn him of just this happening. But Parry's
assumption that the business was to be brought before the hierarchy as
a matter for discussion (an interpretation he may well have contrived
for his own purpose) simply ignited the whole university question
further, as the impression was given by him of the likelihood of a
broader approach being made to Rome.

## Intervention of the Duke of Norfolk

No further time was now wasted as the matter as it stood had incited a
keen interest among the clergy as well as the laity who were anxious to
go ahead in the direction of getting the prohibition lifted. The delay
Vaughan was causing at this time seemed to denote a characteristic
lack of sympathy and understanding on his part with the voice of
those people he should have been most closely concerned with, and by
July 1894 the Duke of Norfolk, who always had close and friendly
relations with him, thought it best to tell Vaughan about the petition
drawn up by the laity, which by then had 448 signatures on it. Even so
Vaughan again brought up the suggestion that he considered it would
be preferable if some attempt was made to set up a Catholic university

instead. But this was turned down once more on the grounds that although the idea of a Catholic university might perhaps seem to be ideal, the time for it was now past and the support in the country would be altogether inadequate to sustain it. The Duke of Norfolk earnestly conveyed to him that 'the present state of affairs was unsatisfactory' suggesting there were serious reasons militating against further delay, not least that the middle classes were already attending Manchester, Durham and London Universities, and there were some fifty Catholic undergraduates at Oxford and Cambridge at this time.[43]

Referring to Wilfrid Ward's assessment of Herbert Vaughan's character, Robert O'Neil observes in his biography, *Cardinal Herbert Vaughan*, 'If there were certain qualities in Vaughan that created problems, there was one which Ward admired which made change possible.'[44] It was at this point Vaughan agreed that some change was needed, saying 'that if the Holy See thought well to change its policy he would be willing to concur'. The laity forthwith sent the petition to Rome in December 1894 and three months later on 26 March 1895 the General Congregation of Propaganda decided in favour of the petition and their decision was approved by Pope Leo on 2 April.

It was in Herbert Vaughan's favour that he showed his ability not only to change his mind over the university question, but to follow it up with his wholehearted support. Because his attitude tended to be narrow and dogmatic he was liable to find himself faced with controversial issues of this kind from time to time. But it was not in his make-up to continue with any policy once he found it was not working out satisfactorily, and he had no concern about losing face by changing his mind and turning in a different direction.

The irony of this situation was that, although the end of the prohibition seemed to be yet another reversal of Manning's policy, subsequent events proved that this was not entirely so. When the petition was sent to Propaganda, Cardinal Vaughan endorsed it by writing to Cardinal Simeoni saying that the new policy did not in fact go against Cardinal Manning's intentions: 'Cardinal Manning, a year or two before his death, said to me that circumstances had changed, but that he was too old to change his attitude towards Universities, but that the change would have to come after his death.'[45]

This poses the question as to why Vaughan took so long and appeared to be so reluctant to effect a change regarding this important question that was seen by both clergy and laity to be urgently pressing, knowing as he did that Manning had more or less given him this directive on the matter 'a year or two before his death'. Was he hoping to embark on yet another of his great schemes, this time in Kensington? Or did he lack the intellectual foresight of Henry Edward Manning that would have led him to act more promptly instead of being more or less forced into a decision that was not entirely his own?

Once the policy had been formulated the final decision was announced to the English Catholics in August 1896, and time proved the new permission to be successful; but, as is often the case in times of change, there was some opposition at the initial stages. 'A good majority' of the bishops agreed to sign the petition, but the Bishops of Northampton, Leeds, Middlesborough and Salford objected on the grounds that the Archbishop had been subjected to too much pressure from the laity, and they were quite shocked by his change of attitude.[46] John Snead-Cox was to note that eight years later 'some five months before his death', Cardinal Vaughan in a memorandum to Propaganda wrote enthusiastically alluding first to Catholic laymen, and then to ecclesiastics attending Oxford and Cambridge: 'I must report most favourably of the effect of these two permissions. Catholics have done themselves great credit in both universities.'

## Silver Jubilee 1905

In January 1905, when he was 66, Edward Ilsley celebrated the silver jubilee of his consecration, and as St Chad's Cathedral was to become the centre of attention at this time, it was decided by the cathedral clergy that it would be particularly appropriate to mark the occasion by producing an illustrated history of the chief events relating to the cathedral over the years. Produced in a convenient half-foolscap size, the book deals with the years from the opening of St Chad's in 1841, to the year 1904. It was compiled by Francis de Capitain, John Gibbons and Frederick Keating from among the cathedral clergy, and William Barry who was a member of the chapter, and it was dedicated by them to Bishop Ilsley.

In Chapter 5 in this *History of St Chad's Cathedral Birmingham*, which was written by Francis de Capitain, he described the many events which had crowded into Edward Ilsley's life in the past 25 years, since he became auxiliary bishop. It was during this time that the liturgy had begun to flourish. Writing in *The Dublin Review* of 1884, St George Mivart listed St Chad's as one of the principal churches in the land 'where the liturgy was confessed to be beautiful'.[47] Some idea of the remarkable ceremonial presentation at that time is given in this history

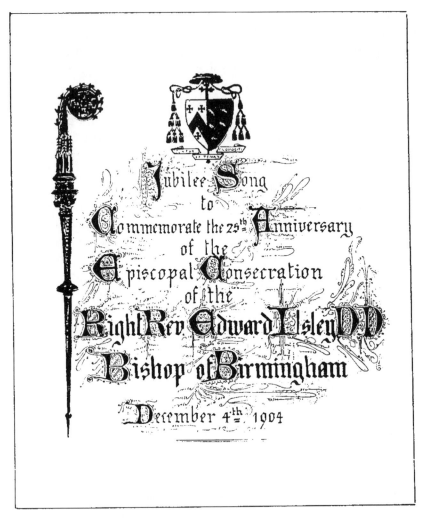

Figure 14.2 *Title page of a Jubilee Song from Oscott College.*

in a description of the special service given on the Sunday preceding the Feast of SS Peter and Paul, in 1889: 'The Bishop of Birmingham sang High Mass and the choir, which should have a classical reputation among English Catholics, sang the Gregorian chant in a manner which I should think is probably equalled and not surpassed (save in rare moments) by the Gregorian chant of Fort Augustus.'[48] Undoubtedly it was due in no small way to Bishop Ilsley's influence that this lofty reputation was maintained.

To prepare for the celebration of his silver jubilee, £2,000 was spent on repairs and decoration to the cathedral, which had collected a coating of industrial grime over the years. It was restored to Pugin's former glory, and colour glowed in every corner. Electric lighting was installed and the organ was rebuilt.[49] The celebrations for the jubilee should have been held on 4 December in 1904, but Bishop Ilsley was in Rome at that time, so the occasion had to be held over until the new year, when it was linked with the golden jubilee celebrations of the Catholic Reunion, on 24 January. The reason for Bishop Ilsley's absence was his pressing need to attempt to restore the uncertain position of Oscott College as the Central Seminary, and urgently put his appeal on its behalf to Propaganda. He obviously decided his own celebration could wait. Oscott was his priority.

## Tributes to Bishop Ilsley

Tributes to the Bishop were recorded in both local and national newspapers. An article entitled *Familiar Figures* published on 4 May 1905 in *The Birmingham Evening Dispatch* claimed: 'In Midland Catholicism there is no more beloved figure than the Rt. Rev. Dr. Ilsley'. *The Catholic News* in the January of the same year, in a 'testimony of regard and esteem', pronounced him to be 'a born leader', and the emphasis was on the Bishop's many achievements throughout his busy career. The celebrations for the jubilee took place at the Birmingham Town Hall, and the Earl of Denbigh, the President of the Catholic Reunion, spoke in recognition of Edward Ilsley's 25 years' work in the diocese, and presented him with a purse of gold and an illuminated address as an expression of 'the warmest affection' from all his people on the occasion. He said that from the day of his appointment to the See of Birmingham 'you have possessed our hearts. Your life has been a record of journeyings many times over to every spot in these four counties where a centre of Catholic life is to be found.' He spoke of the Bishop's unflagging interest in his clergy, of his appreciative words and never-failing kindness and encouragement towards them. 'You are our Bishop – you are our Father. Kindness to us has governed your thoughts and actions. The homely frankness of your manner has won us; your sense of Christ has strengthened us. Your palpable faith has guided us.' The message the Bishop gave back to his people was one of grateful thanks for their congratulations to him, and of appreciation for the harmony and understanding that prevailed between his priests and the laity throughout the diocese.

Figure 14.3 *'In Midland Catholicism there is no more beloved figure than the Right Reverend Dr. Ilsley, Bishop of Birmingham.' 'Familiar Figures' 637, from the* Evening Dispatch, *May 1905.*

Looking back over the 25 years since his consecration as auxiliary bishop, his people became very aware how much the diocese had grown and developed in their Bishop's care, and in the Earl of Denbigh's words how 'under the benign rule of your episcopate the faith has been greatly extended'. Since he had become Bishop of Birmingham, not only had the lay population of the diocese increased by nearly 11,000 to the 85,000 souls represented at that gathering, but whereas in 1888 there had been 197 secular and religious priests in the diocese, now only sixteen years later, there were 276 in number.

## Assistant at the Pontifical Throne 1906

The following year, in 1906, Bishop Ilsley was summoned to Rome by Pope Pius X, to confer on him the honour of becoming Assistant at the Pontifical Throne. This meant he would now belong to the Papal Chapel (*Capella Pontificia*) and would hold towards the Pope much the same relationship as cathedral canons do to their bishop. He was presented on this occasion with a Mandate in the form of a slim volume beautifully scripted on fine vellum, and signed by the Pope. A small plain postcard is also preserved from this time which he sent to his elder sister Ellen on Tuesday 25 July, just over three weeks before the ceremony was due to take place on 17 August. It conveys much of the euphoria the forthcoming event was to bring. It ran: 'Reached Rome last night. Said Mass this morning over the body of St Peter and saw the Holy Father for the first but not the last time. Particulars will reach you in a few days'. He continues, 'So much to do and see I haven't time to write letters. I am trying your patience I know but I can't help it.'[50]

Three months later, in November, a 'Pulpit Sketch' in the local press described his visit to St Thomas's Church, Erdington. We are presented with a quiet picture of Bishop Ilsley, now 69, still enjoying that special relationship he had with the children at Longton in his early years as a young curate: 'In the afternoon, before he confirmed the candidates, he drew from them by way of question and answer the meaning of that particular rite and of the other sacraments of the Church. Again, one heard only a pleasant high-bred voice talking so naturally to the boys and girls, with little ejaculations and interruptions and skilful attempts to draw out the desired answer. He was winningly human to the ear. It must surely have been a red-letter day

Figure 14.4  *Postcard from Edward Ilsley to his sister Ellen Brindley, sent from Rome in 1906. Private collection.*

for every candidate. And while the stately figure and his gorgeous vestments no doubt had their due value in their eyes, there seemed only respect, not awe or fear in the frequent "Yes my Lord,'' that answered his questions, and sometimes the way in which a reply was received and commented on even raised a smile.'[51]

## Eucharistic Congress 1908

Press photographs show Bishop Ilsley with thirteen other bishops of England and Wales at the 1908 Eucharistic Congress which took place in London from Wednesday 9 September to the 'Blessed Sacrament' Sunday on 13 September.[52] This Congress had a remarkable outcome, culminating in a surge of what could only be described as 'a pinnacle of religious fervour', and it was attended by the hierarchy from countries all round the globe. They came from Spain, Italy, France and Belgium, and more distant places such as Brazil, Peru, Chile and South Africa.

On the first evening there was a fanfare of trumpets as a great stream of bishops and other dignitaries entered the cathedral. Seven cardinals were present in the sanctuary, and the nave began to fill as fourteen archbishops, seventy bishops and many hundreds of priests took their places there. The rest of the cathedral was soon filled to overflowing with laity from all over the United Kingdom, and the number arriving was so great that many were left standing in the aisles. Addressing the gathering, Cardinal Vannutelli reflected in anticipation on the Pre-Reformation days when the Holy Eucharist was carried in solemn procession along the public ways, but as it happened, on the following day, Thursday 10 September, an attempt was made to ban any such public procession, through representations made by Protestants to the Prime Minister, Herbert Asquith, who supported them.[53]

Archbishop Bourne telegraphed Mr Asquith immediately saying he could not alter the public arrangements unless he was authorized to state that he did so at the request of the Prime Minister.[54] At a meeting in the Albert Hall that evening, the Archbishop told the gathering of twenty thousand that he had made a stand over this restriction, and that a procession could legally go ahead through the streets as planned. He explained that Benediction would take place on the balcony of the cathedral and the ceremonial procession was to be inside its walls, instead of through the streets. The public were opposed to Asquith's intervention, and although the carrying of the Blessed Sacrament outside had to be abandoned, the public procession which took place first was joined by thousands more people, both non-Catholics and Catholics, when they walked through the streets of Westminster.

The scene that day was described in *The Times*: 'The enthusiasm of the people was extraordinary. Such cheering! It was a continuous roar of applause from the moment we left the Cathedral to the moment we returned to it again.' On returning to the cathedral Cardinal Gibbons from America preached a sermon that day that proved to be a sequel to John Henry Newman's 'Second Spring'. He said that 'Newman's prophesy for the future had now come true. Five thousand Catholics witnessed the procession as well as others.' The public widely condemned the repressive attitude of the Government, and the incident was to have far-reaching effects of a kind that had not been anticipated by those in power – newspapers differing widely in political outlook joined in and denounced the stand they had made, and the whole incident appeared in many ways to mark a distinct turning-point in the attitude towards the devotional life of the Catholic Church in Britain.[55]

## Notes

1  P. O'Toole 'Archbishop Ilsley, A Memoir', *The Tablet*, 11 December 1926.
2  *The Oscotian*, 1932, and also July 1912. John McIntyre had followed in Ilsley's footsteps by attending Sedgley Park School between 1869 and 1873.
3  D.B., p. 21.
4  *Ibid.*, p. 23.
5  Correspondent for *The Universe*, 3 December 1926.
6  He blessed the statue of the Sacred Heart on this visit. Details of the occasion are contained in a letter from Richard Manners, SJ, 15 July 1985. See also a photograph and description of an ordination by Archbishop Ilsley in Father Brian Doolan, *St George's Worcester, 1590–1999*, pp. 21, 22.
7  Percy M. Young, *Letters of Edward Elgar and Other Writings*, Letter to Charles Buck, 13 October 1888, p. 38. Edward Elgar became assistant organist to his father Mr William Elgar in 1873 at the age of 14. William Elgar was a non-Catholic who was appointed to the position in St George's from 1842 until 1883.
8  Hereford and Worcester archives. Letter from Bishop Ilsley to Edward Elgar, 10 October 1900. Also: 'The first performance of *The Dream* was handicapped by the fact that the chorus only had the parts for a few weeks, and the orchestra had only one orchestral rehearsal before the performance. Hans Richter, the conductor, saw the score only ten days

before the first performance. The one rehearsal with everybody was a disaster, and matters were not improved by Elgar's angry intervention. While at the performance it was clear that the chorus in particular, could not stay in tune!' Letter from Percy Young, 20 November 1992.

9   D.B., p. 23.

10  B.A., B11574, Letter to Alfred Austin, 6 January 1896. Alfred Austin was a lay student at Oscott for the year 1852–3. Ilsley wrote: 'It may interest you to know that out of the number of your contemporaries the names of Souter, Duckett, Davies & Hawksford are on the roll of our Cathedral Chapter.'

11  B. A., B10679, 12 March 1892.

12  B.A., B10126, Letter to Father Joseph Parker, 10 September 1889. Joseph Parker had completed his work as secretary to Bishop Ullathorne.

13  D.B., pp. 15, 18.

14  Pastoral letter given February 1891. He had a translation of the encyclical made and distributed among his clergy to be read to their congregations. Although the use of slaves no longer existed in the Western world, the practice was still carried on in the Middle East.

15  'Given at St Mary's, Oscott this first day of August, the Feast of St Peter's Chains, 1892'. See D.B., p. 16.

16  B.A., Pastoral letter for Mid-Lent Sunday describing the English pilgrimage to Rome.

17  Chadwick, p. 411.

18  *The Birmingham Mail*, 2 December 1926.

19  Pastoral letter, 'Given at Rome, outside the Flaminian Gate, this 17th February 1900'.

20  Schobel, pp. 7, 8.

21  These were *Lamentabili Sane*, given in July 1907, and *Pascendi Dominici Gregis*, in September 1907. Those who were condemned in this movement 'fell into the trap of putting scientific method ahead of our faith'. Clifton, p. 23.

22  The movements of Modernism, Liberalism and Scepticism were a matter of debate at this time. The Biblical Commission dealing with recent questions raised in the world of science had taken place in 1890. See also, Clifton, ch. 4.

23  Such subjects as, LXXVII 1897, 'Inspiration of Scripture'; XCVII 1899, 'The Origins of Man'; and CVI 1900, 'Eternity of Hell. Sacred Scripture'.

24  Barry, pp. 263–6.

25  O.C.A., Letter written jointly to Henry Parkinson and John McIntyre, to congratulate them on their ordinations and the completion of their studies at the English College in Rome, 26 May 1877.

26  *The Universe*, 10 December 1926

27  Catholics were termed as the newer 'Liberal' or 'Oratory Catholics', and

those older in outlook were known as 'Garden of the Soul Catholics'.

28  F.R., p.7.

29  Chadwick, vol. ii, pp. 407–8.

30  Henry Edward Manning, *The Reunion of Christendom*, 1867 p. 12.

31  Chadwick, vol. ii, pp. 406–7. Edward VII also objected to it and only reluctantly spoke the words at his coronation.

32  See also, Snead-Cox, vol. ii, ch. 7.

33  Chadwick, vol. ii,p. 406.

34  Letter from Bishop Ilsley to Abbess Laurentia Ward, 1 October 1900. Queen Victoria died on 23 January 1901.

35  Fitzgerald, pp. 272–3.

36  Snead-Cox, vol. ii, p. 80.

37  O'Neil, p. 407.

38  Father Nugent had brought the idea back from America. It had been organized by a group of social workers who founded Newman House in Kennington.

39  Letter from Bishop Ilsley to Sydney Parry, *The Tablet*, 5 June 1894.

40  H. O. Evenett, 'Catholics and Universities', in Beck, p. 307.

41  Letter from Bishop Ilsley to Sidney Parry, 5 June 1894.

42  Westminster Archives and also Beck, p. 307.

43  O'Neil, pp. 409–10.

44  O'Neil, p. 405.

45  Westminster, Vaughan Papers, Vaughan to Cardinal Prefect, 19 May 1896.

46  Beck, p. 309.

47  Chadwick, vol. ii, p. 410. Also Bellenger, p. 331, describing how things were in Ullathorne's time – 'The liturgy was to be conducted with dignity and the Gregorian Chant used "exlusively".'

48  *St Chad's*, p. 65.

49  Michael Hodgetts, *A Guide to The Metropolitan Cathedral Church of Saint Chad, Birmingham*, p. 14. The redecoration was carried out by Hardman's, a firm serving the cathedral since it was built.

50  He wore the new robes he had for this occasion for the first time two months later, in October, at the formal opening of the church erected at the Oratory to the memory of John Henry Newman.

51  B.A., Scrapbooks, 'Pulpit Sketch', St Thomas, Erdington, 8 November 1906.

52  The Bishops of Shrewsbury, Northampton, Portsmouth, Salford, Southwark, Hexham and Newcastle, Clifton, Menevia, Middlesborough, Newport, Birmingham, Liverpool, and Nottingham, and the Archbishop of Westminster.

53  'The Protestant Alliance', in Oldmeadow, p. 398.

54  *The Daily Telegraph*, 11 September 1908.

55  Thomas M. Schwertner, *The International Eucharistic Congresses*, p. 273.

## CHAPTER FIFTEEN

# *Cotton College*

Although Edward Ilsley could be held mainly responsible for steering through the unfortunate events concerning Cotton College during the years between 1900 and 1903, an examination of the circumstances reveals that so many others were playing major roles in the affair that in the end it falls quite naturally into the mould of a 'grand diocesan squabble', in which everyone was the loser, rather than a purely personal involvement for the Bishop.

## James Dey

Father James Dey was one of the men who played a leading part in this episode. He had been trained at Oscott and was ordained there in 1894. That year he joined the staff at Cotton College, where he remained until 1900 and then transferred temporarily to St Edmund's, to work under Monsignor Bernard Ward, until 1902. By then he was 31. Forty years later, it was James Dey who published an analytical article for *The Cottonian* entitled 'The Presidency of Dr Hopwood', in defence of what was by then diocesan history. He was prompted to do this when Canon Willibrord Buscot's *History of Cotton College* was published. Buscot was on the staff at Cotton for thirteen years, from 1889 till 1902, working with the Revd Walter Ireland, who became President of the college in 1897. Buscot served Ireland amicably as his vice president for two years from 1899, and the account in his book of what had happened at that time at Cotton was naturally biased in Ireland's favour. He did admit, however, that as President, Ireland had 'never caught its spirit' when he was in charge of the college, because not having attended Sedgley Park as a boy he did not appreciate its traditions. Dey's summary of the events in his *Cottonian* article was written in order to clarify certain points, and he also suggested where Bishop Ilsley might have gone wrong in dealing with the matter. He wanted justice done to the memory of John Hopwood and wrote, 'my duty to a former beloved chief, now dead for many years, obliges me to join issue with Canon Buscot over certain passages in this book'.

'In matters of policy', wrote Canon Buscot, 'it is inevitable that differences arise from time to time.' He was describing difficulties that had arisen in connection with the running of Cotton College during the years 1902–3. The staffing of such colleges came directly under the jurisdiction of the bishop in those days, in contrast to later years when such decisions would also be in the hands of a board of governors or a committee. So when a series of incidents directly involving the administration of Cotton led on to a most unsatisfactory conclusion, it was Bishop Ilsley's handling of the affair that was ultimately questioned, and as far as many of his critics were concerned, the blame came to rest squarely on his shoulders. A careful examination of the facts, as far as we know them, still leaves a number of questions unanswered, and given this distance in time, it is difficult to discern exactly why things went so wrong, or who may have been chiefly responsible for the final sad outcome, particularly with so many of the participants presenting differing views.

## Walter Ireland

The problems first began to accumulate when Henry Parkinson, then Rector of Oscott College, reported in 1900 to Bishop Ilsley that he was not satisfied with the quality of some of the students Cotton was sending them. Father Walter Ireland, who was then President of the college, had taken over from Canon Hawksford three years previously. He had worked at Cotton for 24 years altogether, having first come there as a lay master at the age of 23 when the college first opened under Joseph Souter in 1873. Two years later he went to Yvetôt in Normandy, where he trained for the priesthood. After he was ordained he returned in 1879 to work with Joseph Souter once more as his prefect of discipline. On Souter's retirement in 1885 he became Vice President under Canon Hawksford until 1897, and he then became President at the age of 47.[1] So it would seem from this that his service as Vice President had brought no undue criticism from Canon Hawksford. But according to James Dey's article in *The Cottonian* written in 1940, standards of work dropped noticeably when Ireland took over. Quoting from Canon Buscot's *History of Cotton College* published that year, he said: 'After I have read on page 209 that Cotton under Canon Hawksford surpassed all the other Catholic Colleges in success at the London Matriculation, I am not impressed when I read on page 272 that Cotton under Ireland gained certificates in handwriting.'[2]

Dey's article did not give a fair picture of the circumstances that had brought about the drop in standards which occurred in the years 1898 and 1899. When Ireland took over a year earlier he had been given an undertaking from the Bishop that all the senior church students should from then on remain at Cotton until they were ready to move on to Oscott, providing the college could prove it was giving them as good an education as the other colleges. In previous years their best students had been transferred to St Edmund's to finish their education, which meant that their numbers never exceeded 120 and their examination successes were not as high as they could otherwise have been.

Spurred on by the Bishop's promise, the Cotton staff not only proved within the first year of Ireland's presidency in 1897 that they could succeed in competition with the leading Catholic Schools, but they also came top in the Oxford Locals next to Stonyhurst. After this time the school was designated as the centre for the local Oxford examinations. But in spite of this very promising start, Walter Ireland was dismayed to discover in September, at the beginning of the new school year, that four of the boys who had brought honour to the college by their examination results had been transferred to St Edmund's in the system of 'poaching' that had prevailed in previous years. He complained bitterly to Bishop Ilsley that in spite of the hard work on the part of his staff which had brought the college into the position of taking the lead among the other Catholic colleges, 'now the very students who won this brilliant success have either been removed to other colleges or are being so, in order that these colleges may reap what they have not sown. St. Wilfrid's must go on as in the past ... a mere preparatory school for colleges engaged with less success in the same work.'

Frank Roberts suggests at this point that the sense of frustration so obvious in Ireland's letter may have contributed to the fall in standards in the year 1898–9. But there were obvious practical reasons for this as well, not the least being the decline in Walter Ireland's health that caused him to go to Rome after Easter, on 23 April 1899, for a 'much needed holiday' until 9 June. Six months later, in January 1900, Henry Parkinson reported to Bishop Ilsley about his dissatisfaction with the Cotton students, and in order to follow up Parkinson's report, the Bishop made an exploratory visit to the college that year and was not satisfied with the facts that emerged concerning Father Ireland's management.

On discovering considerable friction between Ireland and several members of his staff who had serious differences of opinion with him, namely Fathers Dey and Hofler and Mgr Price, Ilsley decided that the time had come to appoint a new president for the following year, with a view to introducing some basic reorganization. So in preparation for the future, he arranged for James Dey to transfer temporarily from Cotton to St Edmund's College in order to study Monsignor Ward's methods of education, and Hofler and Price were also removed at the same time. Bernard Ward had left the staff of Oscott in 1890, and became President of St Edmund's College in 1893.

On the face of it, Ilsley's decision to replace Ireland seems unnecessarily drastic, particularly when all the facts about the drawbacks Ireland was facing are reasonably taken into consideration. But as it happened the news of the Bishop's proposed plans for changes at Cotton somehow leaked out and soon became common knowledge all round the diocese, amid a great deal of gossip and speculation. At this juncture, possibly realizing he had not been altogether fair, Ilsley showed some consideration towards Walter Ireland, because, having every wish to spare the President's reputation, he decided to postpone any further move in that direction for the time being, allowing some time to elapse between 1900 and 1902 for the rumours to die down before attempting to act again. Ilsley had been unwell during the winters of 1899 and 1900, suffering from attacks of bronchitis, and as he needed to spend some time abroad it would not be a good time for making such decisions. But because of the removal of his members of staff, Ireland had to take over the duties of prefect of studies himself, and as he was already acting as procurator he was for some of this time doing the work of three men.

## Appointment of John Hopwood

Cotton College, 'the new Sedgley Park', was already playing a prominent part in the educational system of the Birmingham diocese, and in December 1901, having a view to its further development, Ilsley proceeded to appoint Father John Hopwood from the staff of Oscott College to the position of President at Cotton, and James Dey was to be his prefect of studies. They were to be ready to take up their appointments in September 1902, and all this was unofficially arranged between themselves, without Walter Ireland's knowledge. So if Ilsley had made a wrong move earlier over his treatment of Ireland, he now seemed to be following it up with another. Hopwood was also given

Figure 15.1 *James Dey, who was an army chaplain between 1903 and 1829. From the archives of the Roman Catholic Bishopric of the Forces.*

permission to prepare to select his own staff in the new year of 1902, with a view to them taking up their posts with him in the autumn of that year. This was all done on the understanding that they would maintain the utmost secrecy for the time being, which also did not seem a very wise course for Ilsley to take.

By coincidence, at about the same time, in December 1901, Walter Ireland, then aged 51, had decided to resign his presidency. He wrote in the College Annals that he had 'tendered his resignation to the Bishop, Dr Ilsley, who did not acknowledge his letter'. He recorded his reasons as being that his health had broken down through pressure of hard work. This was more than likely the case, but it was also inevitable that the rumours regarding forthcoming changes at the college would come to his ears, and these must also have unsettled him, causing him to consider the move. There was some uncertainty regarding his letter of resignation as the Bishop appears to have received no such missive from Ireland. Indeed, if he had, he surely would have welcomed the opportunity given him and would most certainly have accepted the resignation without delay, thus sparing himself any further trouble on that account. A story developed later, that the boy entrusted to post the letter left it in his pocket and it was subsequently lost. It was just as likely Ireland decided not to send it after all.[3]

At the time of their secret appointments, Father Dey, knowing that Father Ireland was already contemplating some extensive alterations to the buildings, urged the Bishop that the time was now ripe to inform Ireland of his intentions for the future organization of the college, before his plans were too far advanced. But Ilsley still preferred to hold his hand for a further space of time, wishing to steer the matter through as smoothly as possible without risking any disruption to the working of the school, which he felt might easily result should an announcement of this kind be made in the middle of the academic year. He probably also had in mind the fact that owing to the length of time he had served the college Walter Ireland had a group of influential friends in the diocese, including Michael Glancey, Joseph Souter and John Hawksford. Ilsley would have no wish to stir up any criticism against himself just then, nor would he risk starting the rumours flying again, particularly as Joseph Souter would by no means have forgotten his own sudden dismissal from the presidency of Oscott College. But wisely enough Dey repeated his caution on two further occasions, saying that 'Father Ireland had the right to know his fate before it actually came upon him'.[4]

## Hopwood Chooses his Staff

Later on, in July 1902, just before he was about officially to take over the presidency, Hopwood wrote warmly to the Bishop, 'Let me here thank you my Lord, very sincerely, for allowing Father Dey and myself to have the men we chose. That choice, as you know, was no hazardous one, but was the result of careful and serious consideration. And I am convinced that the staff will be not only a suitable but a devoted one, and one with which I shall have a perfect understanding.'[5] He chose Father Augustine Emery as procurator and Father Leonard Emery as prefect of discipline. Fathers Edmund Philips, Bernard Swift and Francis de Capitain were also on the teaching staff, and Father James Dey was to be his vice president. There were five lay masters already on the staff: George Wilson, Joe Moran, James Morgan, Sydney Clay and P. W. Thackeray. Canon Buscot was later to observe in his history of the college that Hopwood had made what was generally considered 'a very efficient selection, and great things were expected of it'. It was later jokingly termed, 'The Cabinet of All the Talents', which was a reference to the Grenville-Fox administration of 1806.[6]

Figure 15.2 *A drawing of John Hopwood made from a photograph in the Oscott College albums.*

In appointing John Hopwood, Ilsley appears to have chosen a man after his own heart. He was described by his contemporaries at Oscott as a studious man, always ready to help both staff and students. He was appointed secretary to the Board of Bishops of the Central Seminary in 1897, was a popular choirmaster, and took a special interest in music. The locality of Oscott suited him, as 'his walks and recreation generally took him to his home, which was not far away'.[7] He had been one of the first boys to come to Cotton in 1873 and as he had been a student at St Bernard's during Ilsley's term of office as 'Father Rector', the Bishop knew him well.

Hopwood was 41 at this time and had been a professor at Oscott for the past thirteen years, living what was later described by Dey as a quiet and peaceful existence. He felt gratified when the Bishop chose him to direct the new order at Cotton – it seemed to him a special mark of trust from his ecclesiastical superior, especially when he had not sought such promotion. The fact that he had been educated at Cotton meant that he was familiar with the workings of the school, and James Dey's recent experience at St Edmund's would be of considerable assistance to both of them. From the outset, Bishop Ilsley appeared to have the utmost confidence in Hopwood's ability to carry the college forward successfully as part of his future plan for the system of ecclesiastical education in the diocese, and he was prepared to allow him a great deal of freedom and initiative.

Ilsley made another visit to Cotton in May 1902, to discuss plans with Father Ireland for what he termed 'the betterment of the College'. He still did not mention on this occasion that he had already appointed a new president for the coming academic year, but as he was almost about to leave he told Ireland he had appointed James Dey to return to the college the following September to act as prefect of studies. Probably shocked at the prospect, although Ireland appeared to acquiesce at the time, he wrote to Ilsley the next day on 27 May, strongly objecting to the appointment on the grounds that as president, he should have been first consulted on the matter.[8] He questioned Dey's ability to fill the post adequately anyway and gave a list of his reasons for this, saying, 'during his higher studies at Olton and Oscott, he gave trouble to his superiors, and was a great source of anxiety to them. On the day of his ordination as priest he set you at defiance by refusing certain terms which you wished him to accept. In consequence of his insubordination he had to leave Oscott, and came to St Wilfrid's where for three months he taught in the last class in the College. He then became Prefect of Discipline, and turned out to be a failure because he could never manage boys or men.' He finished by saying he now refused to have him back. Ireland's attitude stemmed from the fact that the two men had considerable antipathy towards one another dating back to their previous association before Dey went to St Edmund's, so this *impasse* presented itself as soon as the Bishop made this announcement, and any mention of Dey seemed destined to stir up trouble.

In his reply to Ireland, Ilsley at first appeared to be conciliatory. Looking at the best side of Ireland's motives and recognizing the fact that they were both putting the school first, he said that although his decision regarding James Dey still stood, 'I believe that you are actuated by as strong a desire for the good of the college in objecting to and declining my proposal, as I am in making it.' The tone of the letter then altered, saying that any proposals they had discussed 'lost their immediate importance in the face of the serious question raised by your letter.' He then went on to say that he alone had the right to appoint or discharge members of staff and that Ireland's protestations on that score touched on the inalienable rights and responsibilities of the diocesan bishop in his own diocesan college. He made it clear that he would under no circumstances tolerate any challenge to his power of control. However sympathetic Edward Ilsley was in dealing with others, he was known to be 'a keen disciplinarian' and would tolerate no encroachment on his position as bishop, especially from one of his own clergy. This reproach was followed by a solemn note of warning as he concluded, 'I cannot as Bishop of the Diocese, accept your contention. I must now consider what step I am bound to take.'[9] It would now seem that Ilsley had chosen to make a major issue out of a reasonable protest on Ireland's part over the reappointment of an insubordinate member of staff. Through this means Ilsley evidently hoped Ireland would resign his presidency.

Meanwhile, on hearing of his supposed appointment as prefect of studies, and having already been offered a permanent post at St Edmund's by Mgr Ward, James Dey wrote to Bishop Ilsley on 4 June respectfully requesting him that he should not have to go to St Wilfrid's in September and work again under Father Ireland's regime.[10] Dey said, 'In my interviews with you two years ago, I tried to explain my attitude towards the present government of St Wilfrid's – how that in the opinion of others besides myself who had experienced it, it failed in many ways to provide a good training for boys aspiring to the priesthood. Hence I was surprised that you should have suggested me as one likely to co-operate with Father Ireland in his peculiar methods of management.' He continued by pointing out that Ireland would probably make him his prime reason for leaving the college and he said he naturally had no desire to become a major scapegoat in the matter. Ilsley replied the following day in a characteristically protective and fatherly manner, reminding him that nothing they originally planned had been altered, and 'a radical change of management' had already been decided on, and that 'no pretext will be afforded to anyone of accusing you of being instrumental in ousting Father Ireland'.[11] His tone was reassuring. 'As regards your reputation, if only you will trust it to the safekeeping of your Bishop, who will see that it shall in no way suffer from compliance with his wishes.'

## Problems Increase

Ilsley may have told Ireland of Dey's new position only as a prelude to explaining to him about John Hopwood's appointment. On the other hand it may have been simply a strategy on Ilsley's part to provoke a reaction from Ireland leading to his resignation. It is difficult to discern what the motives were behind the tactics Ilsley employed over these months. But by delaying too long over the final outcome, and

Figure 15.3 *Walter Ireland, Vice President of Cotton College (1884–97), President (1897–1902). Oscott College albums.*

not being direct with Walter Ireland over his dismissal, he only succeeded in stirring up a lot of justifiable resentment on Ireland's part over the manner in which he had been treated. So by trying to avoid one set of difficulties Ilsley simply multiplied others for himself.

He continued to delay matters as the weeks slipped by, but as the end of the school year approached he had to act decisively, and he finally summoned Ireland to Bishop's House on 23 June and told him of his intentions, saying that 'he was convinced that the changes he intended making were for the good of the school'.[12] The phrase he used here was particularly significant because Ilsley had plans for making far-reaching changes at Cotton which entailed an injection of fresh talent to carry them out. Aware of the importance of these changes he had moved cautiously, and it may have been that right up until this time Ilsley had been hoping Ireland would resign of his own volition, and so avoid the humiliation of a direct dismissal, or he may have been trying to avoid a confrontation with Ireland particularly as he had the strong backing of his friends. Nevertheless, he now had to tell him that he wished him to transfer to a mission. From this time on it was Ireland who embarked on a course of procrastination, first regarding the clearing up of his affairs at the college, and then by not making any immediate decisions regarding his future work, and always by excusing himself as being unfit at the time. And so the matter rested.

A month later, on 23 July John Hopwood arrived at Cotton ready to take over as the new president, only to find Walter Ireland still in the process of 'winding up the business', which, he later explained to the Bishop, took him some time. Fortunately Hopwood had brought Father Parker with him as auditor to go through the college accounts, and although he appeared to resent this, Ireland signed a document in the presence of these two men, authorizing Hopwood to draw on both the deposit and current accounts of the college at the bank. A few days after this, Ireland appeared to be willing to leave quite reasonably to take his holiday abroad, so although Hopwood had been anxious at first about their encounter, and had actually come armed with a formal letter from the Bishop to use if necessary to persuade Ireland that he must leave, he was able to write to the Bishop on 27 July saying, 'I have had no real difficulty with Fr. Ireland at all, his going was entirely his own choice.'[13]

Regarding Ireland's position, James Dey later commented, 'certainly in the weeks that followed, Dr Ilsley showed him the greatest forbearance and consideration, but unfortunately this clemency entailed a real injustice to Dr Hopwood. He should not have been asked to enter the scene at Cotton till the stage was cleared of the presence of his predecessor and ready for him. In reality he had to take on the unpleasant task of clearing the stage himself. He had to go to Cotton and convince Father Ireland that the Archbishop really wanted him to go, and that he was to take control at once.'[14]

Already having the Bishop's permission to take a holiday, Ireland, having settled up his affairs at Cotton College and taken his leave of John Hopwood, wrote to the Bishop immediately after, on 27 July, telling him that his doctor had ordered him to take three months' rest.[15] He astutely established a salient point in this letter by reminding Ilsley that he had previously said, 'considering your long service at St Wilfrid's you have every right to have your wishes consulted in this matter. My own feeling would be to offer you what would be considered a post of importance.' He then left for the Continent.

It was only after Ireland had gone, however, that some apparently devious behaviour on his part was revealed, as Hopwood was to discover that although all the college finances originally appeared to have been made over to himself on both the current and deposit accounts, he had no power to draw any money from the deposit account until it was officially transferred to him, and this still had not been done. Instead it would seem that Ireland had sent off a letter to the bank manager just before going abroad, instructing him that no money could be drawn from that particular account without his signature. He then left promptly for his holiday on the Continent, and a space of four months intervened before his return.

## Financial Help for Cotton

At this time it was of course assumed by both Hopwood and Ilsley that Ireland still had the sole trusteeship of all the college funds, but they were to discover later that this was not so. Meanwhile Ireland's unwarranted behaviour left Hopwood virtually penniless apart from routine current expenses, and as he had immediate plans for making considerable improvements to the school straight away, he now found his hands tied. Fortunately the Bishop came to his aid by arranging for a draft of a thousand pounds to be put at his disposal, so he was able to go ahead without further delay, and the new designs that he drew up followed in essence some that Father Ireland had submitted to the diocese the previous year which had met with the Bishop's full approval. Certain additional features were incorporated by Hopwood, such as a tower to be constructed as part of the main entrance to give it a more imposing appearance, and there were several internal additions to the layout. All this would have brought the college in line with, or surpassing, the other leading colleges of the time. Frank Roberts wrote later, 'The Bishop professed himself ready and willing to find the money for all this,'[16] so the problems to do with finance and any alterations to the buildings seemed to be overcome.

During the latter part of the year of 1902 Hopwood, who was by then President, arranged for a number of improvements to the buildings to be carried out, most of which were completed by Christmas: all the masters' rooms were redecorated, cloakrooms were installed on the two upper floors and washbasins put in the dormitories. The cloisters and all the corridors were repainted, new desks were installed, replacing the old Sedgley Park ones, and extra classrooms were made by the use of glass partitions. He also introduced a more modern approach to the organization of the curriculum and the general running of the school, and appointed senior boys as prefects to help with the discipline. On the spiritual side, Dr Hopwood began the new term with a three-day retreat given by himself. 'The college flourished exceedingly in numbers and there were at one time one hundred and thirty boys under its roof' – there had been only 87 boys at the beginning of the year when Hopwood took over. It was later written of him that 'he endeared himself to his staff and was really loved by the boys', and 'in that short time he compressed a work of organisation that many would have been glad to accomplish after several years of effort'.[17] It certainly seemed Bishop Ilsley's reputation for placing a well-chosen man in the right position was about to prove itself to be true once more.

## Ireland Seeks Advice from Friends

Walter Ireland remained abroad for several weeks longer than was expected – from the end of July to the first week in December – and he was then contacted by Bishop Ilsley, writing to enquire after his health and 'matters of business' immediately on his return early in December. One matter that the Bishop requested very positively was that Ireland should resign his trusteeship of the college finances immediately. Ireland's reply two days later on 8 December showed that he was now adopting an ultra-cautious approach. Reminding Ilsley that he was still in the hands of his doctor, he said that he would deal with these things 'as soon as I can see my way to do so prudently. To leap without looking is very dangerous: to take a leap in the dark is folly and madness. Within the next few days I shall, I hope, be well enough to consult in person those most competent to advise me how to act. By following their advice I shall not run the risk of doing in haste what I might have reason to repent of at leisure for many a long day to come.' [18] This letter of Ireland's indicated that he was carefully planning how to proceed and that he was about to entrench himself in 'the opposite encampment', with his friends in the diocese to help and advise him.

Ireland followed up this letter a fortnight later on 21 December by answering Ilsley's letter of 6 December in full. He first of all most surprisingly revealed that 'I beg to inform you that I am neither, as far as I know, a trustee of St Wilfrid's nor am I a trustee of the Bank nor of any money in the Bank and that, therefore, I have no trusteeship to resign.' He then said that the deposit account could not be made over to John Hopwood until the deposit receipt endorsed by Canons Hawksford and Souter and the Revd W. Ireland had been handed into the bank. He expressed astonishment that the missing document still had not been found. Referring to a letter he had received from

Hopwood about it, he said that he had found his accusation that he was travelling with it on the Continent quite absurd, and the fact that Hopwood was 'impudent enough to threaten me with I know not what should I fail to act in compliance with his orders, just as if he has it in his power to make or move me – nothing short of nonsense'. He continued, 'What a pity it is after all, that my well-meant offer made to Dr Hopwood to remain at St. Wilfrid's long enough to wind everything up satisfactorily was rejected with scorn and contempt.' He ended by saying that by that time his former ardour to be of service was reduced to 'a mere spark now, if not indeed extinct'. The danger for Bishop Ilsley was that this difficult situation for which, in fairness, he had only himself to blame, was beginning to spread out in ever-widening circles throughout the diocese, and Walter Ireland's last letter suggested that there were influential members of the clergy siding with him because of the way he had been treated. Most of his supporters represented 'the old guard', who would not anyway be particularly in favour of the Bishop's policies for the improvement of the college. So it would seem that all the pitfalls Ilsley had tried so carefully to avoid were now beginning to open up rather menacingly before him.

Ilsley replied to Ireland's letter immediately, saying that even if he were not a sole trustee, urgent matters still needed to be cleared up. He suggested that the signed document they required had probably been accidentally left in his desk, as it could not be found in the safe where he said it had been originally placed. He put his point clearly and directly and showed his sympathies were decidedly with John Hopwood: 'You showed it to Dr Hopwood on the eve of your departure and locked it up again in the safe. The following morning soon after you left Dr Hopwood looked for it in the safe – and it was gone. If you had handed him the receipt or the key he would have been responsible for the receipt. But as the key did not come into his possession till after you left, the responsibility rests with you.' He was referring to the fact that Ireland had left the safe key with the housekeeper who passed it over to Hopwood the next day. 'It is for you therefore to find it, or else to come to some understanding with the Bank to pay over the amount to Dr Hopwood.'

The desk in question was in Hopwood's room at Cotton, but Ireland had taken away that particular key, and in October Hopwood wrote scathingly to the Bishop saying he would refuse to allow Ireland into the college to look in the desk while he still had the trusteeship of the college funds. This statement appears to be rather high-handed, but by that time John Hopwood was showing signs of being upset and annoyed at the constant distraction caused by the long-drawn-out business continuing while he was engaged in the initial stages of organizing his quite considerable new programme of work for the college. It was obvious he needed every opportunity to be able to concentrate on the business in hand, and writing to Ilsley that October he spoke plainly: 'It matters little now whether the document is found or not. What does matter is that I, and those with me here, have a right to be made, once and for all, perfectly secure from his interference.'

## Hopwood Under Pressure

The postscript to a letter Hopwood wrote to Monsignor Parkinson at Oscott in November 1902, two months after he had taken over at Cotton, gives an idea of his busy life and the pressures he had imposed on himself during those first few months as he settled into his new appointment: 'Ps. Father Brown of Stonyhurst wrote to me concerning "Exchange Lectures", I was obliged to decline. I have only just escaped being "knocked up", altogether; I feel I have no right to undertake anything at present beyond what I have in hand.'[19]

In January 1903 there was a further argument over Ireland's desk key and the key to the safe, and the Bishop must have felt entrapped in the difficult position of 'having to judge between two conflicting stories', with Ireland saying that he had handed the keys over at a certain time, and Hopwood denying that he was even at Cotton at that time.[20] Hopwood's letters to the Bishop over this period were intent on persuading him that Ireland was a sick man, and he was beginning to try to induce Ilsley to see the scale of Ireland's short-comings: 'If he cannot see, even now, that he has acted towards me in an utterly shameful manner, he must be hopelessly incapable indeed,' Hopwood wrote to Ilsley in October 1902 while Ireland was still away.[21] The Bishop, still trying to assist Hopwood, was now no longer prepared to tolerate any further delay created by Ireland. He confessed he was at a loss to comprehend Ireland's motives, and aptly termed the whole business as being 'still shrouded in mystery'. In early January 1903 Bishop Ilsley ordered Ireland to recall his instruction to the bank, and at this point Ireland finally complied.[22] Just why, long before this time, the Bishop as trustee of the diocese, or his treasurer, did not take steps to override this financial tangle created by Ireland seems strange to say the least. But at last the vexed financial problems appeared finally to be ended.

# Notes

1 Buscot, p. 272.
2 Dey, p. 91.
3 Roberts, pp. 151–2.
4 Dey, p. 91.
5 B.A., Letter from Hopwood to Ilsley, 21 July 1902.
6 Buscot, p. 274.
7 Obituary, *The Oscotian*, 3rd Series 13 (July 1913), p. 141. His home was in Handsworth.
8 B.A., Letter from Ireland to Ilsley, 27 May 1902, from St Wilfrid's.
9 *Ibid.*, Rough notes of a letter from Ilsley to Ireland, 27 May 1902. Also *The Birmingham Owl*, 28 February 1908. Ilsley was presented with a gift 'by the clergy by whom he was considered a keen disciplinarian but extremely popular'.
10 *Ibid.*, From Dey to Ilsley, 4 June 1902, from St Edmund's College, Ware. The word 'regime' was a term commonly used at the time to describe the system used by the president.
11 *Ibid.*, Ilsley to Dey, 5 June 1902.
12 Roberts, p. 152.
13 B.A., Letter from Hopwood to Ilsley, from St Wilfrid's, 27 July 1902.
14 Dey, pp. 91–2. There is some validity in Dey's suggestion, although Hopwood did have the assistance of Father Joseph Parker, who accompanied him as his auditor at the time.
15 B.A., Letters from Ireland to Ilsley, from The Presbytery, Burton-on-Trent, 27 July and 29 July 1902.
16 Roberts, pp. 155, 143.
17 Obituary, *The Oscotian*, 3rd Series, 13 (July 1913), p. 142.
18 B.A., Letter from Walter Ireland to Bishop Ilsley, from The Presbytery, Burton-on-Trent, 8 December 1902.
19 *Ibid.*, From Hopwood to Mgr Parkinson, 3 November 1902. These lectures were introduced between Oscott and Stonyhurst that year. John McIntyre had delivered two of them earlier, on 17 and 18 March.
20 Roberts, p. 157.
21 B.A., Letter from Hopwood to Bishop Ilsley, 23 October 1902.
22 *Ibid.*, Bishop Ilsley, rough notes, 23 December 1902 and 6 January 1903.

## CHAPTER SIXTEEN

# A Transformation Scene

At the beginning of 1903 everything appeared to be in place at Cotton for the college to move forward and take up its position beside the other leading Catholic colleges of its day. With its mellow stone buildings well situated in open country, and considerable promise shown by the newly appointed staff, the future looked secure. Looking back over the events that occurred at this crucial period, James Dey observed that John Hopwood had soon been made to feel by his staff 'that he could count on them for loyalty and heartfelt co-operation in all his plans. With their support he felt he could overcome all the petty annoyances that beset him at the outset of his new career, provided only that he could retain the confidence and trust of his ecclesiastical superiors.'[1]

## Ireland's Just Grievance

Unfortunately the situation suddenly became very volatile, with problems still centring on Walter Ireland, because by that time he had gained the sympathy of influential friends in the diocese who considered he had been unjustly removed from his presidency. His personal complaint to the Bishop was that 'I was hustled out after twenty-four years' service like a bad and faithless servant.'[2] On the face of it, this seemed a just grievance, because he was given extremely short notice of his dismissal, and the manner in which it had finally been done seemed unkind to say the least, particularly considering the long years of service he had previously given to the college.

The fact that a change of administration was desirable at Cotton was either being ignored or just not accepted by Ireland's friends, so instead of the future becoming more settled and secure for John Hopwood and his staff at this time, the opposite began to happen, as the tide of opinion began to run against them. Ireland's supporters meanwhile, to their discredit, continued to make it their business unfairly to run down and criticize the 'modernised administration' of the college. Their attitude was to defend the old ways, and disapprove of any changes that were being brought in, their argument being that it should not be necessary to introduce any imitations of the public school system into Catholic schools, because they already had adequate traditions of their own. Ireland's group of friends also tended to look upon Hopwood's team as being young and cocksure, and running too far ahead of themselves, while they patronizingly maintained their own standards were best, and 'it was apparently the appointment of monitors that aroused the greatest scorn among the critics'.[3] This was an absurd assumption on their part, as both Hopwood and Dey were mature and experienced men with a good staff who appeared to be steering things through in the right direction. But unfortunately, within eight short months of Hopwood's taking over, the situation which at first seemed so full of promise suddenly began to deteriorate and collapse in the most unexpected manner.

## Canon Michael Glancey

One of Hopwood's chief opponents was Canon Glancey, a long-standing friend of Walter Ireland. He was an experienced and influential man, and having served as a professor at Oscott College for four years, he was then appointed inspector for schools. Now aged 48, he was the Vicar General *Oeconomus*, and was also responsible for compiling the chronicle in the Diocesan Year Book, and both of these positions gave him an ample lever to use against John Hopwood. He began to prepare notes to be inserted into the Year Books, making disparaging references to the forward-looking policies of the new government of Cotton.[4] He likened Hopwood's innovations, and the changes he had brought about, to 'a most wonderful Transformation scene at St Wilfrid's College'. He portrayed the process of reorganization throughout the college as though it was a charade being acted out on a stage, being witnessed by an audience, and he gave a most elaborate description of how the new order had overtaken the old. It would seem, the 'transformation' he was alluding to was meant as a description of the changing images projected by the new-style magic lantern that had recently been acquired by the college.

But if these assertions of Glancey's were meant as a snide joke, they were ill-timed and overstepped the mark in such a sensitive situation.[5] Canon Hymers protested to the Bishop about the effect they were having generally, at which point Ilsley rebuked the culprit and insisted that in the future the chronicle was to be looked over by himself before going to print. But in the meantime the feelings of Dr Hopwood and his staff had not been spared, and the criticisms spread still further as Michael Glancey now used his second strong arm, this time over finances, and he raised a general alarm by drawing attention to 'the increasing amounts that were being spent at Cotton'. The outcry ought not to have been considered to have any real significance because the changes being made already had the seal of approval from the diocese, and as far as expenses were concerned, 'the money was available'.[6] It was the fact that a considerable amount of work had been done in a relatively short time that probably gave a false impression of high expenditure.

Until the spring of 1903 Ilsley had always seemed ready strongly to defend Hopwood's position, but something evidently occurred about that time that must have caused him to shift to a different way of thinking. On his part Hopwood must have instinctively felt that Ilsley's confidence in him was beginning to drain away, and he could not understand why – possibly Ireland's friends may have finally convinced Ilsley of their case. The effect that this change, for whatever reason, had on Hopwood is described by James Dey: 'We on the staff who loved and revered him were shocked and dismayed at the change we noted daily in his gentle and happy nature, and we realised the injustice that was gradually destroying him.'

## The Bishop's Change of Attitude

Ilsley's change of attitude could have come about because the tone of some of Hopwood's letters to him had recently become very demanding, and certainly one of his proposals that the Bishop did not wish to sanction (although not a major issue) was that the front of the building should in any way be altered as suggested in Hopwood's new plans. He felt that this would be causing a break with some of the old venerable traditions of the place dating back to the time when Father Faber lived there with his group of fellow converts in the 1840s,[7] and as a result of Ilsley's intervention the old building still retained its original appearance. Regarding this apparent change on the Bishop's part, James Dey later asserted that 'Neither the building or any material or financial question had anything to do with it.' But this may not have been entirely so, because although plans had been approved in Father Ireland's time, Canon Buscot stated, 'but when the new plans involved the rebuilding of the whole brick front including the old Hall and the Faber extension, then opposition was met'.

The storm clouds now seemed to be gathering fast, and this was particularly so in the March of 1903 when Hopwood discovered that Father Ireland had been appointed to take over the mission at Handsworth. This was where John Hopwood's own parents and relatives lived and where he always spent his holidays. It was indeed an extraordinary choice and showed an unusual lack of foresight on Ilsley's part under the circumstances. Not surprisingly it seemed too much for Hopwood to accept, and he wrote to the Bishop on 29 March complaining bitterly about it. Taking it as a personal blow directed towards himself, he said: 'Your Lordship's appointments as such are no concern of mine; but your recent appointment at Handsworth is, I venture to say one which concerns me deeply indeed. If your Lordship had wished to make it clear to everyone that, I was unworthy to be considered, to ignore the work I have done for you here, to take the heart out of the work yet to be done, and make me seriously doubt whether my appointment here has been genuine at all, I think you could hardly have chosen better means for the purpose.'

The manner that Hopwood adopted in certain letters from this time on is described by Frank Roberts as 'tactless though justifiable'.[8] Reading through them, it can be seen that for some reason Hopwood seemed quite unable to curb his feelings sufficiently to prevent his mood of indignation interfering with his professional life at this time, and in the end he allowed Ireland's appointment to Handsworth to become a major distraction to him. So it finally came about that he was even willing to set aside his important work as President at Cotton simply because he was unable to rise above his bitter personal resentment against Walter Ireland. His whole approach seemed to have become rather presumptuous, suggesting to Ilsley in the same letter concerning Ireland: 'If I had urged my strict rights, he ought to have made a humble apology to me long ago – your Lordship's action in appointing him to that mission has practically made it impossible that he will ever do me justice. You have made capital, on his unworthy behalf, out of my generosity to him.'

The style of this letter, and of others written during this closing period of 'the Cotton affair', do not show Hopwood as being entirely the gentle and reserved person he was always described to be by James Dey, although these particular characteristics might have been part of what Dey described as 'tremendous earnestness'.[9] One could only suppose that this attitude emanated from the considerable strain

Hopwood was under at the time, causing this over-assertive side of his personality to react in this way, and this in turn led on to the inevitable withdrawal of support by the Bishop. Indeed the whole tone he was adopting towards Edward Ilsley in the written word is astounding to say the least, and especially so, considering all the time and trouble the Bishop had expended on him during the previous months. He finished his letter about Ireland's appointment with, 'Why such indignity should have been thrust upon me passes my comprehension. Has your Lordship disbelieved me and believed him? So please tell me at once. Has your Lordship believed me? Then, what evil have I done to deserve such public punishment, and I will add, such cruel punishment as this?'[10]

## The Handsworth Appointment

The Bishop on his part was naturally not willing to be coerced, nor to have his appointment of one priest criticized by another. He could be most sympathetic toward those in his care, but Hopwood's attitude was now threatening his authority, and Ilsley had to show that his decisions stood firm and could not be reversed. But even in the face of all these difficulties, he went some way in attempting once more to pour oil on very troubled waters, by writing and fully explaining his motives to Hopwood in a letter, the contents of which were so highly sensitive that he requested him to burn it as soon as he had finished reading it. He explained that he had made a promise to Walter Ireland previously regarding his choice of an appointment, and that Hopwood should understand that this particular position was only conditional, and should Ireland prove unsuitable, he would remove him from Handsworth. This was not exactly a retreat on Ilsley's part, but the door was left open generously enough, and it was a great pity that Hopwood did not come into line with Ilsley at this stage, while the situation might well still have been recovered.

The Handsworth appointment was a most unfortunate decision on Ilsley's part. Ireland had been offered several other positions, but he had given as many excuses each time for not accepting them. This last choice seems almost strangely contrived, and it would seem that it was not Ilsley's decision alone. But it was the deciding factor in the breakdown of relations between the Bishop and John Hopwood and his clerical staff, and the resulting chasm which opened up between them as a result of this, sadly enough brought Ilsley's vision for the advancement of the college to an abrupt end.

The outcome of the whole situation pivoted on Hopwood's reaction to Ilsley's approach at this crucial stage, but unfortunately he was in no mood to listen to any of the Bishop's proposals in the highly charged atmosphere.[11] Writing again on 4 April to Bishop Ilsley, he opened his letter with, 'I beg to acknowledge your letter of yesterday and beg to thank your Lordship at any rate for making my course of action clear to me at last. I think your Lordship has managed effectually to destroy a personal devotion of well-nigh thirty years,' and he continued by saying he would give the Bishop a last opportunity of 'retrieving the fatal situation you have created', and that unless Ireland's appointment was altered, 'I will resign my presidency forthwith' and that 'should I resign, my resignation will be absolutely decisive and final'.

Admittedly Hopwood had cause for complaint, but he now seemed ready to destroy all the good work he had done as President, for his narrow personal reasons. This fact is borne out by the last sentence in this last letter to Ilsley on the subject, which runs: 'I never asked to come here: as things are I have no wish to stay. If things cannot be changed I will thankfully go, without the smallest hesitation. I shall, at any rate, have kept my honour and self-respect: and I would rather have those than all the presidencies in the world.' James Dey was later to describe Hopwood as previously being 'quite happy in the quiet usefulness of his life at Oscott and in the close neighbourhood of his family life to whom he was devotedly attached'. He now seemed ready to return to this former background. Mentioning the confidence that Hopwood's superiors had in him, Dey also says significantly, 'as time went on he was made to feel, rightly or wrongly that this trust was being withdrawn, not through his own fault'.[12] It was on the debatable point as to who was most at fault, that the whole case seems to hinge.

## Resignation of Rector and Staff

Unfortunately the Bishop received another letter on the same day as Hopwood's resignation which complicated the whole business still further. It was jointly written by all the priests on the Cotton staff and was signed by James Dey, Augustine Emery, Leonard Emery, Edmund Philips, Bernard Swift and Francis de Capitain. They stated that should Hopwood's resignation be accepted, they would all resign as well. They wrote rather dramatically: 'With Dr Hopwood's departure, the great tie binding us to St Wilfrid's would be broken and we fear the fortunes of the new work we hoped to co-operate in, doomed to failure.'[13] It was immediately pointed out to the Bishop by the 'Opposition' in the name of Canon Glancey that he had been presented with nothing short of an ultimatum, which pointed 'a pistol at your head'. Glancey went on: 'His threat to act in this way, and thus as far as in him lies, to irretrievably ruin the College, shews him to be utterly unreliable, and shews the necessity of accepting his resignation forthwith.'[14]

Glancey was of course right in his conclusion that Hopwood had proved himself unreliable on this occasion inasmuch as he was willing to sacrifice the position of the college in order to satisfy his own personal views, and it does seem extraordinary that he was now quite ready to throw in his position as President of the college as a pawn to be played one way or another in his struggle against Walter Ireland. Bishop Ilsley must have seen this, and hedged round as he was by many self-styled advisers, and because the whole affair had now taken on the proportions of a bitter public row, he now had finally to concede. He therefore accepted Hopwood's resignation on the understanding that he would work on to the end of the summer term, and Father Dey, 'who was considered to be the instigator of the whole business', was to be recalled immediately. But Dey himself pointed out that his departure would not look good, and Hopwood also took up the cudgels on his behalf, saying that he would close down the school early if any change was made in the staffing.[15]

Canon Glancey now attempted to influence things further by trying to organize the immediate removal of Hopwood from the scene and

Figure 16.1 *Revd Michael Glancey as a professor at Oscott in 1880. Oscott albums.*

bringing in Father Hymers, who by that time had been appointed to take over at the end of term. But here the intervention of Canon O'Hanlon and Canon Hawksford prevailed – they pointed out that Father Hymer's immediate entrance would look like 'a public disbelief and little short of defamation of character' toward Hopwood.[16] So it was decided that he and his staff should remain as arranged, until the end of the academic year, and as the five lay masters on the staff were unaffected by the resignation, they would stay on and continued to work with Father Hymers when he took over.

## James O'Hanlon

James O'Hanlon made a suggestion at this stage to attempt to ease the situation. He wrote to Ilsley in early May, 'At risk of wearying you with my suggestions in reference to Cotton I will venture respectfully to add one more: viz. that Dr McIntyre should be appointed President. He will save the situation if anyone can; and dear good Fr Hymers will, I feel sure, be overjoyed at being "let off". If this suggestion were adopted Dr McIntyre might, I should think, go to St Wilfrid's at once as President-elect, not as acting President.' It may have been that Ilsley was reluctant to lose a good secretary at the time, so nothing came of the suggestion. Having been asked by the Bishop to look into the affair, Canon O'Hanlon visited the college later on that term, 'to see how the land lay'. It was his aim to try to persuade the priests on the staff to remain there, especially if ordered by their bishop to do so. So it would seem that an effort was still being made by Ilsley to at least partially retrieve the situation. He visited the college in early June to address the staff, and sought to drive a lesson home by disciplining them for their action in their relation as priests of the diocese to their Ordinary. He then invited them to think over his words and put their conclusions in writing to him.

But Ilsley's admonitions, rather than bringing the staff round to his way of thinking, were to have the opposite effect. A fortnight after his visit he received an angry letter from Hopwood defending the rights of the priests on his staff. His message was that if others criticized him, it was his turn to do the same to them, and he continued, 'I cannot stand idly by and see in silence men stigmatised.' He then began in a very confrontational manner to take the whole question of the resignation a step further by putting himself in the position of instructing Ilsley how he should or should not proceed in the matter: 'To contend that the resigning of an office in the diocese is in itself a violation of the Ordination promise, would be I submit, a straining of that promise beyond all legitimate bounds. The history of any diocese in the land would shew that that promise is not the vow that some religious take, to go or remain anywhere, under all circumstances, merely at the wish of the superior, and without having a voice in the matter.' His letter, in the guise of being coolly logical, overstepped the mark as before. Almost presuming to reprimand Ilsley for the manner in which he had spoken to the staff, he said: 'your Lordship spoke to them not on your own initiative at all, but as urged on by others – others who are near at hand and have the ear of your Lordship, while we are far away, and unable to meet them'.[17] The breadth of the arguments that Hopwood was now using seemed to indicate that he was taking his advice from some other quarter. Were these caustic letters delivered by him entirely his own handiwork, or were they written simply because he, like the Bishop, was also 'urged on by others'?

When the priests on the staff wrote to Ilsley, their words echoed those of Hopwood. They claimed that under the present circumstances their appointments were, strictly speaking, only voluntary, and would be binding only if they were working on the mission or in a seminary. Their replies to the Bishop were all similar in substance, and on the major points they hung together, and so the resignation stood. Although this 'Great Resignation', as it was later termed, would appear to be the most devastating aspect of the business, Hopwood seemed quite clear in his mind that he was the injured party, and he concluded his final letter to the Bishop by stipulating, 'we have done nothing disgraceful. We leave this College with honour and not with shame, and those who seek to cast shame upon us will be answerable for the result.' It seems a pity that this great unity between himself and his staff could not have been put to far better use at the time, and focused on the good of the college.

Hopwood sent out a letter to the Cotton parents in July, telling them, 'It is my painful duty to announce to you the retirement of the present staff of clergy at St Wilfrid's.' When the news of what had occurred broke, the whole affair caused considerable shock round the diocese. One of the most regrettable aspects of the incident was the sad aftermath, mainly caused by Ilsley appointing Edward Hymers in Hopwood's place – a man whose personality and outlook were in absolute contrast to his predecessor. He was reluctant to take over 'but accepted in duty bound'. In time, the selection of Edward Hymers came to be considered 'a tragedy for himself and for the school', but as

Frank Roberts pointed out, 'fate and the machinations of others were far more responsible for this than Father Hymers himself'.[18] Many of John Hopwood's innovations still lingered on in practice after he had left, but standards dropped once more, causing the fortunes of the college to go into a state of temporary eclipse, and twenty years were to pass before any real recovery took place. 'It was just the time when the diocese should have put all it could into the school,' was the observation of Frank Roberts, who had taught there from 1931: 'Whatever the reason, the opportunity was lost, just when bold expansion was needed, and so the school stayed in the 19th century.'[19]

## Frank Roberts's Opinion

Frank Roberts could be direct in his opinions. His summing-up of the case was as follows: 'The Bishop was all for a quiet life, and though he could be firm enough when sufficiently goaded, he hesitated to oppose men of stronger will than himself, and was too easily swayed by those who constituted themselves as his advisers. Most prominent among these were the Rector of Oscott and Canon Glancey.' James Dey put his point more kindly, saying that in this case the Bishop had exercised 'the greatest forbearance and consideration' towards Walter Ireland, and that was where his fault lay. Ilsley may have considered it better to handle an outspoken man like Michael Glancey with a certain amount of discretion rather than to make a direct stand against him, because this was his way of handling people. The suggestion that he could be ruled by others does not ring entirely true, even though Roberts liked to dub Glancey as 'the power behind the throne'.

Henry Parkinson, the rector of Oscott, was described by Leslie Toke, the first secretary of the Catholic Social Guild, as 'so diffident, so over-anxious to please all parties, so fussily alarmed over any policy that might offend the good and the great',[20] which makes it difficult to imagine that Ilsley would in any serious way have been ruled by a man of Parkinson's temperament. So even though Ilsley relied on him to take a lead in academic affairs and the general overseeing of the seminary, that would seem to be the extent of Parkinson's influence, although it is possible that he may have entertained some personal prejudice against Hopwood which has not hitherto come to light. Father Bernard Miller, who was on the staff of Oscott from 1903 until 1923, and was Vice Rector from 1914 until 1923, noted the effect the dissolution of the Central Seminary had on Henry Parkinson: 'In his way of bearing it I saw the first of a long series of striking illustrations of two virtues which, I think, were among his most outstanding characteristics, namely, his loyal submission to authority and whole-hearted devotion to duty.'[21] If this was the case, Parkinson would surely not be likely to attempt to throw his weight to any extent against Ilsley's authority.

The irony of the situation was that those who had been so ready to criticize John Hopwood's methods with such determined energy soon lost any interest in the college altogether, and detached themselves from the situation once John Hopwood and his staff were gone. At the Birmingham dinner held at the school in 1912 Canon Hymers made his 'Cinderella speech', in which he made just this point. As for the loyal staff of priests who had surrounded Father Hopwood, the dio-cese under Thomas Leighton Williams, who was Archbishop from 1929 till 1946, gave them due recognition in the future for their talents, and to his credit and theirs, nothing was held against them in the years to come. From their ranks came a bishop, two rectors of Oscott College, two canons, and two monsignors.[22]

James Dey, who was considered to be the black sheep among those concerned in the affair, joined the Royal Army Chaplains Department, and for the following ten years did a tour of duty in South Africa. He later distinguished himself during the First World War as an army chaplain and then returned again to Africa to continue what would appear to have been a self-imposed exile from the Birmingham dio-cese for another ten years, only returning when his life-long friend Thomas Leighton Williams became Archbishop in July 1929. On leaving the service that year, when he was 60, Dey was appointed Rector of Oscott by Archbishop Williams. He retired six years later from what had proved to be a successful rectorship and became Bishop-in-Ordinary to the Forces in 1935, serving in that office throughout the Second World War. He died a year after the war ended in 1946 when he was 76. He wrote of his experiences with the army in two books: the first published in 1922 was entitled *A Cavalry Chaplain*, and the second in 1937, *An Army Chaplain's War Memories*.[23] From Dey's exceptional record over the years, it seems Walter Ireland's opinion that he 'could never manage boys or men' was entirely misjudged!

The circumstances were to prove particularly unhappy for John Hopwood, who reaped no reward for his months of dedicated hard work, finally suffering a rejection brought about as much through his own over-sensitive attitude as anything else, and the reason for which, from the tone of some of his letters, it is obvious he could not com-prehend. When he died in his early fifties in 1913 at Wolverhampton, where he was serving the mission at St Peter and Paul's, the whole matter was, no doubt, brought to mind again.

## Death of Walter Ireland 1907

As for Walter Ireland, he was only to remain at Handsworth for just over a year when, due to his increasingly poor health, he moved first to Burton and then on to Tamworth, where he died early in 1907 at the age of 56, of heart failure. The Bishop's sympathetic handling of Ireland in this case can be well appreciated, as he probably foresaw what might happen and in the end would be reluctant to go against him further. Ireland was already far from well at the time three years earlier when Ilsley first started looking into the case, and this was certainly one of his reasons for seeking to replace him with Hopwood. The shortness of Ireland's stay at Handsworth had almost been predicted by Ilsley to Hopwood, who at the time was unfortunately not ready to listen to him.

There are some difficulties involved in understanding Bishop Ilsley's handling of the final stages of this unfortunate episode. Trying to shield John Hopwood and those loyal to him from the criticisms of Walter Ireland and his associates was no easy task for him, and he finally found himself faced with further developments in the situation due to Hopwood's reaction which made it entirely too difficult for him to save. Ilsley's apparent change of attitude toward Hopwood, and the consequent turn of events, is only partly explained. His concern for the fate of Oscott College once Francis Bourne became Archbishop of Westminster in 1903 may have begun to outweigh his interest in Cotton for the time being, and his forward-looking plans for St Wilfrid's may have been temporarily lost to view with the threatened drop in status of Oscott he was grappling with at the time. Unfortunately much of the evidence in the case was destroyed, as 'after Hopwood's death, his brother burnt all relevant documents' and the available information does not seem complete as it stands.

In September 1903 the new staff consisted of Father Edward Hymers, Father Michael Hamlin who had been a lay master from 1855 to 1891 and who was his vice president and prefect of discipline, Father Joseph Upton, an old boy and a Doctor of the Roman University, Father Edward Godwin, who had been on the staff of Oscott College from 1898, and Father Thomas Williams. In addition there was Father Ernest Wilks and Canon Hawksford (who still occasionally took classes) and the lay masters from 1902–3. Just why Ilsley made the selection of Edward Hymers, after having made the promising choice of John Hopwood, is not clear. If it was to 'damp things down' by putting a 'safe man' in, it was a sad miscalculation, and it was bound to put an end to any immediate vision for the future. However, there are indications from the consistent support he gave Father Thomas Williams that Ilsley planned to appoint him to take over as President in due time, once things had settled down. He was an old boy and had just come down from Christ's College, Cambridge, with an MA degree and a teaching diploma and was then 27. Unfortunately he was dismissed at the end of the first term by Father Hymers, and 'both the Bishop and Father Williams were surprised, and the former unsuccessfully asked Father Hymers to reconsider his decision. The trouble was that Father Hymers thought Thomas Williams to be a disruptive element, lacking in co-operation and likely to damage the cordial relations of the staff', and although Williams gave good reasons for wishing to remain at Cotton, Father Hymers remained adamant over his decision,[24] so Williams finally transferred to St Edmund's.

In 1907 Ilsley made another attempt to reinstate him when he wrote to Canon Hymers, saying, 'I fancy Father Williams is pretty tired of his occupation of Prefect of Discipline at St Edmund's. Would you like him back?'[25] On this occasion Canon Hymers said he personally would be very glad to have Father Williams back, 'but he feared that the rest of the staff would not be equally pleased. But he promised to sound them on the subject and notify the Bishop if he thought that things were likely to work smoothly.' Unfortunately the clerical staff employed the same argument as had been used in Hopwood's time. They did not feel their bishop had any jurisdiction over them in this particular matter. Ilsley had condemned the reasoning of the staff in Hopwood's time but must have decided not to make a stand over it just then and so the consensus of opinion prevailed. The war years intervened and Father Williams was an army chaplain from 1916 until 1920, after which time he became the principal of St Charles House, the Catholic house of studies at Oxford, finally returning in 1922 to become headmaster of Cotton College for the following seven years.

## A Bone of Contention

The business of Cotton remained a bone of contention throughout Ilsley's long term of office. In 1908 Canon Hymers publicly stated at the Old Boys' Meeting that he still sensed there was an underground movement in the diocese against the college. The overriding problem was to do with the constant shortage of money brought about through a system of uneconomic fees imposed by the diocese, through charging the same level of money from the parents of the lay pupils as it did for its own church students. As it could not pay its way, the school had to borrow from the diocese and consequently got deeper and deeper into debt.[26] The comment that Frank Roberts made about this system was, 'It sounds completely mad but that baldly is what happened.' In 1911 there was some question of the school being sold off to Douai Abbey as testified by a draft letter of Ilsley's in the Birmingham archives, but no final decisions were arrived at. For some years its fortunes remained at a continually low ebb, with Hymers even suggesting in 1916, the extreme measure of bringing the boys back to Oscott, 'like Ushaw and St Edmund's'.

Roberts defends the part Bishop Ilsley played in the history of the college: 'It has often been said,' he wrote, 'that the Archbishop took no interest in Cotton, which is manifestly untrue. He and Canon Hymers had a great esteem for each other, but as the Archbishop grew older he tended to entrust more and more to men of lesser stamp, and as a result the school very nearly foundered. In the Canon's estimation, three subordinates were the real culprits, and the Finance Board were the arch villains, complete with horns and cloven hoofs.' Hymers named no names, so one can only surmise who the three main culprits would be.

In the summer of 1919 Archbishop Ilsley wrote to Dr Upton, who was then Edward Hymer's prefect of studies, about plans for a science room. Roberts remarked: 'It is sad to notice in this letter from the Archbishop how his writing, which up to this time had been beautifully clear, was at last beginning to show signs of his great age.'[27] He was then 81. In the last few months before Ilsley retired in 1921, in spite of gloomy forecasts, the examination results were excellent, and *The Cottonian* paid a generous tribute to the Archbishop: 'On several occasions, when the affairs of the college seemed to have reached a crisis, when candid friends were offering up Job's comfort, his steady and consistent support, backed by the weight of his authority, has silenced idle tongues and comforted those who were engaged in the arduous task of keeping the work of the college at full pressure.'[28]

## Thomas Leighton Williams Headmaster in 1922

After John McIntyre took over from Ilsley as Archbishop of Birmingham, Father Thomas Leighton Williams replaced Canon

Hymers as headmaster in the winter of 1922. He at long last succeeded in pulling things round by introducing the drastic changes that were needed, and by the time of the jubilee celebrations in 1924, it was generally recognized that things were well 'on the move' for the college after all the wasted years. Sadly Cotton closed its doors for the last time on 10 July 1987. It was the oldest Catholic school in the country.

# Notes

1  Roberts, p. 158. Neil Henshaw edited and completed Frank Roberts's *The History of Sedgley Park and Cotton College*, which was published in 1986. He was a lay master at Cotton in 1975–6 and moved to Stonyhurst in 1987.

2  B.A., Letter from Walter Ireland to Bishop Ilsley, 21 December 1902, from The Presbytery, Burton-on-Trent.

3  Frank Roberts's original manuscript, ch. 14.

4  *Ibid.*, ch. 15.

5  This Year Book came out in July 1903. In his manuscript, Frank Roberts counters this with a note saying, 'It is only fair to Canon Glancey that he later proved to be a friend to the school in many ways.' See Frank Roberts, *A History of Sedgley Park and Cotton College*, ch. 15.

6  Roberts, pp. 155–7.

7  Dey, p. 92.

8  Roberts, p. 157.

9  Obituary, *The Oscotian*, 3rd Series, 13 (July 1913), p. 143.

10  B.A., Letter from John Hopwood to Bishop Ilsley, 29 March 1903.

11  *Ibid.*, The letter from John Hopwood to Henry Parkinson written on 3 November 1902 showed Hopwood already to be under considerable pressure.

12  Dey, p. 92.

13  B.A., Letter of resignation from Hopwood, and a letter from the priests on the Cotton staff to Bishop Ilsley, both dated 4 April 1903. In his letter Hopwood said that he had burnt Ilsley's letter as requested.

14  *Ibid.*, Letter to Bishop Ilsley from Michael Glancey, 12 April 1903.

15  Roberts, p. 158.

16  B.A., Letter from Canon O'Hanlon to Bishop Ilsley, from St Peter's, Bromsgrove, 20 April 1903.

17  *Ibid.*, Letter from John Hopwood to Bishop Ilsley, 22 June 1903.

18  Roberts, pp. 61, 159.

19  Frank Roberts's original manuscript, ch. 15. Frank Roberts taught on the staff for 43 years, until 1974 – leaving aside war service.

20  'Monsignor Parkinson, President of the Catholic Social Guild', *Oscotian* 24, p. 187.

21  'Mgr Parkinson, Rector of Birmingham Diocesan Seminary', *Oscotian* 24, p. 178.

22  James Dey: Domestic Prelate 1928, Rector of Oscott 1929–35, Bishop of the Forces 1935–46.

Augustine Emery: Domestic Prelate 1932, i.e. Monsignor.

Leonard S. Emery: Rector of Oscott 1935–61, Domestic Prelate 1941.

Francis de Capitain: Diocesan Treasurer 1918–40, Canon 1937.

Bernard Swift: Hon. Canon 1956.

Many of these promotions took place when Thomas L. Williams was Archbishop (1929–47). He was headmaster of Cotton in 1922–9, and during that time continued the work initiated by John Hopwood.

23  James Dey, *A Cavalry Chaplain*, London, Heath Cranton, 1922, and *An Army Chaplain's War Memories*, London, Burns & Oates, 1937.

24  Roberts, p. 164.

25  *Ibid.*, p. 169

26  *Ibid.*, p. 194. The diocese charged interest on their loan to the college. Repairs to the buildings suffered as a result of this, and educational resources were inadequate.

27  *Ibid.*, p. 191.

28  *Ibid.*, pp. 193–4.

Figure 17.1 *Edward Ilsley at the time of his investiture as first Archbishop of Birmingham (1911). Private collection.*

## CHAPTER SEVENTEEN

# Archbishop and Metropolitan

## Three Ecclesiastical Provinces – Westminster, Birmingham and Liverpool

In October 1911 a document, *Si Qua Est*, was drawn up in Rome by Pope Pius X announcing, 'If there is any Church in Christendom which deserves special care or forethought from the Apostolic See it is surely the Church of the English.'[1] Since the restoration of the hierarchy, in 1850, England was created one ecclesiastical province consisting of the Metropolitan See of Westminster and the remaining thirteen dioceses as suffragan sees; but the growth of the Church now made it necessary to introduce three ecclesiastical provinces instead, to cover England and Wales, namely Westminster, Liverpool and Birmingham. The Province of Birmingham would now comprise the Archdiocese of Birmingham with the suffragan sees of Clifton, Plymouth and Shrewsbury.[2]

The size of these new divisions was considerable. The Birmingham province stretched down to the southernmost parts of the country, running along the coasts of the Bristol and English Channels, and out along the South-West Peninsula, extending as far as Land's End. Archbishop Bourne's own words were, 'The two new provinces each possess more churches and larger bodies of clergy than were contained in the whole country in 1850.' In 1850 there were 82 churches in the four counties of Staffordshire, Worcestershire, Warwickshire and Oxfordshire which together formed the Diocese of Birmingham, and now they numbered 144. Since Edward Ilsley became Bishop of the diocese nearly 24 years earlier in 1888, more than one new church had been built there every year. The number of priests in the diocese had risen from 124 in 1850 to well over 300 by 1911, and there were now 27,600 children in Catholic schools, all but 1,000 in elementary education. The Catholic lay population over the four counties had swelled to over 85,000 from 36,000 in 1850.

Bishop Ilsley of Birmingham and Bishop Whiteside of Liverpool were created Archbishops, and were granted the rights of metropolitans, having authority in certain matters over the dioceses in their respective provinces. The cardinalate of Archbishop Bourne was also announced at this time, and certain special privileges were accorded to the See of Westminster, the Archbishop taking precedence over the other archbishops in order 'to preserve the unity of Government and Action'. The cardinalate normally went with the Archbishopric of Westminster, beginning with Wiseman in 1850, but in this particular case Archbishop Bourne had to wait eight years before the honour was bestowed on him.[3]

It also happened that on 29 June 1911 Edward Ilsley completed 50 years of his priesthood, and on that day of his golden jubilee all the clergy of the diocese offered their Masses for their Bishop, while he sang his jubilee Mass in St Chad's Cathedral, with the students from Oscott College rendering the chant, and the cathedral choir the polyphony. During a special luncheon later held at Bishop's House, a letter from Pope Pius X was read out by Provost McIntyre, which concluded with an obvious reference to his work on behalf of Oscott and Cotton, 'We are pleased to commend among other things your eminent service for the education of the clergy and the religious training of the young and most willingly send you our Apostolic Blessing.'[4]

Figure 17.2 *Dioceses in England and Wales*

It had previously been decided to postpone any public celebrations of the golden jubilee until the Bishop's feast day, the feast of St Edward the Confessor, on 13 October, but there was a further postponement of these arrangements when the news of the forthcoming investiture was made known. At this ceremony Edward Ilsley was to be invested with the sacred *pallium*, on the occasion of his elevation to the rank of Archbishop and Metropolitan, and it was finally decided that it would be most suitable for that important event and the golden jubilee to be linked together, making one magnificent joint celebration. The date finally chosen for both was the feast of the Immaculate Conception of Our Lady, to whom the diocese was dedicated, on 8 December.

## Elevation of Ilsley to Archbishop in 1911

The elevation of Bishop Ilsley to the position of Archbishop in his jubilee year was a landmark in the history of Roman Catholicism in the Midlands.[5] But it was more than just a focal point of local interest, because the rare historical character of the event made it of national importance too. He had the option of going to Rome to be invested with the *pallium* by the Pope himself, or to send a deputy to petition the Holy Father for authority for a prelate to perform the investiture in Birmingham. Characteristically it was Ilsley's wish to receive this honour among his own clergy and his own people, particularly as he wanted them to have the opportunity of witnessing such a rare ceremony. It had taken place only once before in Britain since the sixteenth century, when Herbert Vaughan became Archbishop of Westminster. He received it in London to provide an ecclesiastical pageant that would remind the people of the past history of the Church and its links with Rome.[6] Writing to Bishop Amigo on 11 November, Ilsley was not in agreement with Archbishop Bourne over the matter: 'The Cardinal-Elect says it would be very suitable for me to receive it in Rome. But our people would like to see the interesting ceremony.'

Final decisions had already been made concerning a suitable presentation to Bishop Ilsley for the occasion of his golden jubilee; everything had been kept in the deepest secrecy, and preparations had already been well in hand for several months when the news of the division of the provinces become known. The very special event was an opportunity for the diocese to express their love and veneration for their Bishop. By now 'the quiet, dignified Ilsley was known to two generations of Catholics, confirming both fathers and children, and appearing at functions everywhere in the region'.[7] To their great satisfaction, just as the Bishop's jubilee blended in with the inauguration of his archbishopric, so the idea of the gift they had already chosen was suited to both occasions.

It had been decided some months before, to present him with a set of vestments made from cloth of gold, and woven to a special design of pomegranates and *fleur-de-lys*, interspersed with the martlets of St Edward and the cross of St Chad. Suitable looms had to be made large enough to take the cloth, some of the gold thread having to be specially dispatched from the Far East.[8] The embroidery, which was brocaded on the gold cloth in the finest silk threads, was carried out by twelve different religious communities in the diocese.[9]

There was to be a presentation ceremony in the Birmingham Town Hall on the evening of the investiture, and because of the nature of the double celebration, it happened on this occasion that the Archbishop was formally presented with some of the vestments he had actually been wearing earlier, but under the circumstances this was considered to be perfectly acceptable. These vestments have continued in use throughout the years for special ceremonies, with the colour and detail remarkably preserved.[10]

## The Ceremony of the Investiture

The ceremony of the investiture, during which the Archbishop was first attired with these robes, and later received the sacred *pallium*, was impressive. The press described the large crowds that had gathered outside the cathedral to watch members of the hierarchy and the important dignitaries arriving 'to the clash and clang of a joyous peal of bells'. Those fortunate enough to have managed to get their seats by ticket had a good view of the historic scene from the moment they saw the first procession making its way from the sacristy and slowly moving down the south aisle and round the dimly lit church, finally proceeding up toward the high altar to the accompaniment of the organ.

It was like a pageant of the whole diocese, the vestments reflecting the glow from the candles and seeming to light up their surroundings as they passed. The choir, headed by the cross-bearer, was followed by the seminarians from Oscott. Then came the regular clergy, the Franciscans, the Dominicans, the Passionists, the Fathers of Charity, the Jesuits and Benedictines, lending contrast to their surroundings by the simplicity of their habit.[11] More colour was added to the scene by the distinctive dress, light purple in shade, of the canons of the metropolitan chapter. After these came the seven Bishops of Plymouth, Shrewsbury, Northampton, Southwark, Clifton, Newport and Menevia, in full canonicals and each attended by a chaplain. They moved to their assigned places beyond Pugin's richly carved and ornamented rood screen, and there was a moment's pause while the members of the Metropolitan Chapter proceeded to the west door to receive the Archbishop who was accompanied by Bishop Mostyn of Menevia, and then they conducted him to the sanctuary, the choir meanwhile singing the *Ecce Sacerdos Magnus*.[12] 'The second procession which the congregation now saw moving up the centre aisle was much smaller than the first, but it was nevertheless more striking in its composition.'[13] The macebearer came forward followed by the papal knights resplendent in their uniforms trimmed with gold, who were ready to escort the Archbishop to his throne. The celebration of Palestrina's *Missa Brevis*, sung by the combined choirs of the cathedral and the Oratory church, now began.

'One fold and one shepherd'[14] was the text appropriately taken from the day's Gospel. The Bishop of Newport, John Hedley, used these words in his discourse to sum up the occasion. He said they were

INVESTITURE
OF THE
Archbishop of Birmingham
WITH THE
Sacred Pallium,
ST. CHAD'S CATHEDRAL,
Feast of the Immaculate Conception.
December 8th, 1911.

Figure 17.3 *A cover for a booklet brought out for the investiture. Archidiocesan archives.*

of the deepest significance – prophetic, creative, historical and living. 'They might well be recalled on a day like this' he said 'when celebrating the feast of the pastor of a flock. Of the Archbishop of a newly-formed ecclesiastical province, a teacher and judge of that Christian faith, who bore on his shoulders that day for the first time the historic *Pallium* brought from the tomb of St Peter, sent by the Pontiff who sat in St Peter's chair.'

The ceremony of investiture followed the sermon, and those sitting towards the front of the cathedral could see the full splendour of the occasion. In his magnificent robes Edward Ilsley knelt in front of the altar and read the oath of fealty, which was accepted by Bishop Francis Mostyn, delegate for the Holy Father, in the name of the Holy See. He then received the *pallium* from the hands of the bishop. In contrast to the richness of his robes, this simple encircling band made in plain white wool about three inches wide and with six black crosses embroidered on it, was now placed round his shoulders. Having received it, Archbishop Ilsley rose and solemnly blessed the assembly.

## A Congratulatory Banquet

A congratulatory banquet was arranged that evening at the Great Western Hotel, and afterwards everyone went to the town hall for the formal presentation of the jubilee vestments. There was a large gathering of both clergy and laity, and as soon as the Archbishop came into the hall 'his appearance was a signal for an outburst of the most enthusiastic cheering that was renewed again and again'. The speech he made later, thanking the people of his diocese, was typically honest and very human. He was now 73, and the natural, open way in which he spoke reflected a lifetime's experience with them. He said that when the first whisper reached him of this celebration of the golden jubilee of his ordination, he felt it was inflicting too great a burden on the diocese, especially as only a few years ago they had shown their kind feelings toward him on the occasion of the silver jubilee of his episcopate. But he realized that they felt they were not doing themselves justice unless they found some means of expressing themselves and they had taken advantage of a great occasion to express their feelings toward him. He added, perhaps giving them a rare hint of the loneliness imposed on him by his position: 'Though at times it seemed almost too good to be true, you have gone a great way in the matter of giving me that encouragement which even bishops require from time to time to help in the anxieties with which their lives and work are beset, and I appreciate it most fully and deeply.' He also took the opportunity to convey to them what was in his mind after the day's ceremony by saying that 'something more was expected of them now that the diocese was a metropolitan one'.[15]

The changed status of the diocese did have one noticeable effect – from that time on Cardinal Bourne gave it his special attention regarding the possible alteration of its boundaries. When the Holy See brought about the new division of the provinces, the Constitution gave a hint that new dioceses, as well as new provinces, were contemplated. But matters were delayed, and apprehension mounted whenever Archbishop Bourne attempted to bring about such changes. While the celebrations for the jubilee and the formation of the provinces were in progress in the Birmingham diocese, Francis Bourne was in Rome simultaneously being created Cardinal. His letter of congratulation sent from Rome to Archbishop Ilsley which arrived on 4 December, four days before the ceremony, made the assumption that it was his special influence that had been brought to bear in Rome's decision. It ran, 'May I offer you again all my good wishes and prayers on the happy anniversary that you are to keep so solemnly on Friday and also my heartfelt congratulations on your reception of the Sacred *Pallium*. It is a joy to me to have had some part in obtaining for your Grace and for Birmingham the enhanced dignity of Metropolitan rank.'[16] He now regarded the formation of new dioceses as the next step to be taken, and had very clear ideas in his mind of just how he would proceed.

## Need for Oxford to Remain in Diocese

Anticipating Archbishop Bourne's intentions as soon as the archdiocese was formed, Edward Ilsley sent a letter to Cardinal Lepicier, who was a member of the Consistorial Congregation in Rome, both clearly and strongly giving his reasons why Oxford should never be torn away from the diocese: 'The severance of Oxford from Birmingham would be deeply regretted, not because of the financial lack to the diocese, but because it would be felt as carrying away from the diocese the centre of events that make perhaps the most glorious pages in our diocesan history. The two names of Oscott and Oxford were so closely linked during the whole of that most important period of ecclesiastical history, now known as the time of Tractarianism, that they were almost looked upon as one combined force in the struggle against Anglicanism. If Oxford goes what will become of that History of which the new Archdiocese is justly proud. Gratified for the great honour conferred on the diocese by its elevation in the hierarchical order, it could itself feel a pang of regret that that elevation should be accompanied by the loss of so many deeply cherished memories.'[17]

It was one of Ilsley's chief priorities that Oxford should continue to be an essential part of the diocese, especially now that permission had been granted by the Holy See for Catholic clerics to attend the university, and he had in mind a scheme linked with the training of his priests that he wished to implement. After some negotiations, he set up St Charles House at Oxford in 1920, as the Diocesan Centre for Advanced Studies, with Father Thomas Leighton Williams as its first principal. To ensure that some priests should be sent for higher studies, he made provision for them to take advantage of a university course: 'The excellence of the Christian priesthood is the glory of the Christian people,' the Archbishop wrote in his mid-Lent pastoral that year, adding this far-sighted statement, 'That is why the enemies of the Christian name always direct their fiercest efforts to lower the priesthood in the eyes of man.'

Peter Amigo was consecrated Bishop of Southwark by Cardinal Bourne in 1904. He and Francis Bourne had originally been close friends, having spent some of the years of their youth together at St Edmund's College. At a luncheon given at the time of Amigo's consecration Bourne said 'he desired Amigo to be his successor in Southwark because he believed that he of all men would continue and develop his work'.[18] But it would seem Bourne made a wrong judgement in that regard because the years ahead were chequered with matters over which the two men did not see eye to eye. A break came early in their association, in 1907. It was over the appointment Amigo made of Arthur Doubleday to be Rector at Wonersh, against Bourne's expressed wishes, and for some years after this, until 1924, Bourne dealt with Amigo in a formal and distant manner.[19]

## Ilsley and Amigo Close Friends

Amigo and Ilsley maintained a close, almost daily, correspondence at this time, which continued over the years. The volume of these letters suggests a greater friendship between the two men than either of them had with the other bishops. Bourne disapproved of their friendship, but as it happened many of the problems they shared were directly brought about by his plans which threatened their dioceses. Referring to the difficulties Amigo was experiencing with Bourne,

Figure 17.4  *The Right Reverend Peter E. Amigo (1864–1949), Bishop of Southwark.*
*From a photograph in* A Bishop and His People: Pronouncements by the Rt
Rev Peter Amigo, *selected by H. Rochford. Burns & Oates, 1934.*

Ilsley commented to him on 12 April 1912, 'I have intended asking your Lordship to receive me as your guest next week and I mean to come on Monday evening even though it may be late when I arrive. The differences between your Lordship & the Cardinal need not interfere with our fraternal relations and if you honour me with your confidence, he has no right to resent it. If the day ever comes when I can in any way promote a settlement of those differences I shall be only too happy to seize the opportunity.'[20] During these years Ilsley kept as vigilant an eye on his own diocesan boundaries as he had in the past over Oscott College, as far as Archbishop Bourne was concerned.

One of the proposals Bourne put forward that was to become a major worry for Bishop Amigo was that the Diocese of Southwark, which was south of the river, would be united with Westminster on the north side. This became termed 'The Unification of London' and Bourne sought the title of 'Bishop of London' to go with it. Although the idea originated in the Vatican (who consistently showed themselves ignorant of the English scene), it was Cardinal Bourne who endorsed it and persistently pursued it over the years, rather than Rome. He had valid arguments in favour of wanting to see that area formed into one diocese, reasoning that as London was administered as one large unit by the London County Council, so the diocese would fit conveniently into the same unit as regards administration. Through this move he would also have incidentally gained Surrey, which would have given him the control he would have liked to have over Wonersh again. Amigo had very real reasons for holding out against these proposals because Southwark had been in considerable debt since the allocation of funds had entirely favoured Portsmouth when it was divided off from Southwark. His argument was that when the debt was cleared, and should the Catholic population increase in his area, then he would be willing for a further division to be made.[21]

Ilsley gave his friend constant practical guidance over the years. In March 1912 he advised Amigo, 'I think you would do well to approach the H. Father again as he graciously invited you to & remind him of his promise that you should not be disturbed & that the question about the partition of your diocese may be set at rest for some years so that public confidence may be restored & that you may work with your people to wipe out the huge debt with which the diocese is burdened & that you may be delivered from interference in the management of your diocese.'[22] The staunch attitude held by the two bishops, for right or wrong, to block these schemes, seemed to pay off, and the following December 1912 Ilsley wrote to congratulate him 'that the anxiety and suspense which has weighed upon you so long has been dispelled forever & that you are at last to be left in peace'. Francis Bourne failed to implement the plans he had in mind for Southwark, nor was he able to wrest Oxford from the Diocese of Birmingham, which he also had in mind and which Ilsley strongly opposed. So the Birmingham boundaries remained intact.

Of all the men that Edward Ilsley came across in his long administration, Francis Bourne was probably the least easy he had to deal with, and he admitted to Bishop Amigo on one occasion, 'I don't understand the mentality of H. E.' Commenting on a letter Cardinal Bourne sent to Michael Glancey regarding a Commission to consider the Southwark accounts in 1912, Ilsley wrote to Bishop Amigo: 'I have read the correspondence – it makes painful reading – H .E cannot deal with a case on its merits but must always make a personal matter out of it. You could not condone that insulting letter – in the correspondence you have taken up just the points of H. E.'s letters which jarred on my feelings.'[23] He was very much in sympathy with Amigo over his difficulties with Bourne, and in 1917 wrote again, 'So if H. E. is to have his way you are to be victimised again – It looks like a monomania he has got for crippling Southwark – he can't go to Rome without stirring that up again, altho' you have been given to understand that you are to be left in peace to pay off the diocesan debts.'[24]

## Cardinal Bourne – His Personality

In his position as Cardinal-Archbishop of Westminster, Bourne was at his best when dealing with the broad spectrum of government departments and officials. But more generally he became known as 'The Quiet Cardinal', and was also dubbed 'The Cold Cardinal', because of 'the impersonal carrying out of his high position' on public occasions. This gave the impression that he was austere and distant; and because he was also undemonstrative in his everyday dealing with people, he caused some of his priests in their turn 'to keep aloof when they would have been gladly welcomed'.[25] His first biographer, Ernest Oldmeadow, does not on the whole give a happy picture of him, right from his earliest youth at the age of nine years when the early death of his father made life hard for him: 'The truth is that Francis Bourne, after the premature death of his father, had to tread stony and thorny ways to the very end, but speaking broadly, the student, the seminarian, the priest, the Rector, the Bishop, the Cardinal was called to struggle by dark ways.' He was talking about the opponents of

Bourne's policies, who accumulated among his bishops as time went on. Bourne once summed up the outcome of this side of his life, when he said to one of his suffragans, 'Hardly ever have I planned a useful bit of work without the Devil putting it into the head of some good man to spoil it.'[26]

Although Edward Ilsley was 26 years older than Amigo, the two men had a lot in common. Like Ilsley, Amigo took the same detailed interest in his own diocese, taking on the task of visiting each mission at least once every three years, and keeping in touch with his people by meeting as many of them as possible on these occasions. He also enjoyed visiting the schools, and took a genuine interest in the welfare of the children, having a humorous and natural way with them. He maintained a simple lifestyle, preferring to use public transport to being driven in a private car, a habit he kept up until his later years, feeling that he was keeping more in line with the lives of his people in this way.

When the new provinces were created, the Constitution granted Archbishop Bourne certain prerogatives. It was decreed that the Archbishop of Westminster should preside over the episcopal meetings for the whole of England and Wales. He also had precedence over the other two archbishops, and represented the entire body of bishops in England and Wales in all dealings with the supreme civil authority. But he was disappointed to discover that the right to the title 'Primate' had been omitted from this list of privileges, and in 1912 he sought permission to use the title 'Primate of England and Wales', by inviting his bishops to sign a petition to this effect to be sent to Rome. The argument he used in favour of its use, was that he did not wish this ancient title to be 'abandoned to the Anglicans', a point he made in a letter to Bishop Hedley, saying he sought it 'not for himself but for his successors'.[27] But knowing Bourne's temperament, this last statement hardly rings true!

A meeting with Cardinal Lepicier had been held in London in August 1911, between Archbishop Bourne, Bishop Whiteside of Liverpool and Bishop Ilsley, which took place before the public announcement of the division of the provinces was made known. At this meeting Ilsley agreed to the suggestion that the title of Primate should be accorded to Archbishop Bourne, not knowing that he was also soon to become a cardinal. When Bishop Hedley wrote to him a year later in December 1912, assuming that he was still in favour of the title being conferred, he discovered that Archbishop Ilsley now held the opposite view. 'I replied that when the other two provinces were created I was in favour of it,' he wrote to Bishop Amigo, 'but now I shall certainly not give my vote to it. There were other reasons I did not name, why I should not give my vote for the primacy,' he continued. 'The reasons were the policy he has persistently pursued grasping at the control of the diocese of Southwark, harassing its Bishop and endeavouring to force his own views upon everyone else.'[28]

## The Question of the Primacy

The question of the primacy continued to be a major issue during the following year, and Ilsley expressed his fears to Bishop Amigo regarding the outcome, should Cardinal Bourne get his way in the matter. He finally decided in the January of 1913 to write a very frank and explicit letter to Cardinal Merry del Val, which began, 'I have learned on excellent authority that some 9 Bishops of the English Hierarchy have given their names to a petition to be presented to the Holy See that the title of Primate may be conferred on our Cardinal Archbishop of Westminster. But considering the arbitrary line of action he has taken up and displayed so notably in his recent contentions with the Bishop of Southwark, I fear that his nomination as Primate would only open the door further to more arbitrary action and further friction. On this account far from supporting the petition I feel constrained to oppose it.'[29]

Writing to Amigo a day or two later, he appeared to be torn between a sympathetic impulse towards Bourne, and his stern sense of duty. In his time Ilsley's judgement had been broadened by the experience of working, not only with Bishop Ullathorne, but also under Cardinal Manning and closely with Herbert Vaughan, and now, like others, he had come to consider Francis Bourne as a man needing to be held in check by his bishops. 'There were 9 bishops who assented to a petition for H. E. to be named primate. When I heard this I thought it was only right to declare my sentiments to Cardl. Merry. It was hard for me to write this, but duty impelled me,' he wrote. 'The request re the Primacy came from himself and the Bishops gave their names, I fancy, because they were asked to do so.'[30]

We are told of 'a certain unfriendly voice which for nearly thirty years murmured objections to the Cardinal's most cherished schemes and made itself heard in Rome'.[31] The suggestion made by the voice at this time was that the primacy was resented by a number of bishops in England and Wales. How far Ilsley's words, or those of this particular 'voice' moved Rome to act on their suggestions may never be known, but Francis Bourne did not succeed in his quest for the primacy, and the matter came to rest for the foreseeable future.

## Bourne's Schemes for Oxfordshire

Bourne had various schemes for Oxfordshire which involved its removal from Birmingham. In 1912 he proposed handing over Oxfordshire to Northampton as part of his plan. Another idea he considered in 1913 was to create one joint diocese of Oxford and Cambridge, to be called 'the Diocese of Oxbridge'. He proposed placing Dom Bede Jarrett, who was then 31, in the position of bishop of the diocese. On yet another occasion he considered joining it on to the Diocese of Portsmouth. On 7 January 1912, Ilsley gave his practical reasons to Amigo as to why another of Francis Bourne's schemes would not work out: 'It is currently reported', he wrote, 'that it is the intention of the Sacred Congregation to partition off Oxfordshire from the Diocese of Birmingham & add it to Northampton. Personally I know that the scheme is unworkable owing to the lack of direct railway communication between Northampton and Oxfordshire One would think that, before coming to a decision on that matter, I might have been consulted as one likely to have practical knowledge of the district in question.'[32] But on 11 January Amigo wrote urgently to Ilsley from Rome that Bourne was planning to have both universities in his province: 'Last night I saw Card' Merry del Val,' he wrote. 'He had a Catholic Dir. Map on his table, & he pointed out to me the absurdity of having Oxfordshire in Birmingham. He certainly would be in favour of yielding to our Cardinal in this. The best course would be if you could present yourself here now & we could support one another.'

It was at this time Archbishop Bourne was also trying to gain control of the English Colleges in Rome, Lisbon and Valladolid. On 18 January Amigo wrote again from Rome, 'I think that I have stopped our Cardinal becoming Protector of the English College & having a preponderating voice in matters there.' At the same time he warned Ilsley that because Cardinal Bourne had put forward John McIntyre's name as Rector of the English College it would be as well for Ilsley to secure him as auxiliary bishop. He added this afterthought 'Would McIntyre be willing? He would do splendidly. My only fear is that you would lose a valuable man, who ought to be your Auxiliary.'[33] By then Ilsley was feeling the need of extra help in administering the archdiocese with its widely increased responsibilities, and concerned at the possibility of losing McIntyre to Rome he acted on Amigo's warning and applied to the Holy See for an auxiliary, and the choice he made of his secretary, John McIntyre, was a popular one generally among clergy and people alike. The request to Rome was granted, 'and his consecration took place in St Chad's Cathedral on July 30 1912'. (He was given the titular See of Lamus – 'lame 'oss', as his old friend Canon Glancey, who was never slow to make a quip, termed it.)[34]

Being the older of the two, Edward Ilsley was in a position occasionally to give Amigo the benefit of some special advice. A letter that he wrote in January 1912 has a direct bearing on the difficulties they were both experiencing through Cardinal Bourne, and it is written in anticipation of the worst that could arise if Amigo did not continue to put his case forward in Rome: 'Most great questions have several aspects,' he wrote. 'The testimony of one witness, even though he be an expert, will give one aspect only and that is probably a biased opinion – for the best of us is not free from bias – unless other evidence is heard and examined, we have no security that a momentous decision may not be arrived at which may prove disastrous. Of course whatever may be the decision arrived at by the Authority we must do our best to carry it out loyally and with whatever enthusiasm we can summon up.' He concluded: 'Make what use you like of this.'[35]

At the start of 1912 the Bishops of Westminster, Southwark, Liverpool, Northampton and Newport were appointed to a commission to look into the issue of the formation of three new dioceses of London, Brighton and Cambridge, and towards the end of the year they voted on it. Bishop Amigo had already warned the authorities in Rome of the bishops' opposition to this move, but in 1913 Cardinal Bourne was so sure that he had won his case in favour of the changes that he had a map printed for the *Catholic Directory* showing London as all one diocese. Archbishop Ilsley saw the map in his advance copy of the directory, and straight away got in touch with Bishop Amigo. Amigo wasted no time, it is said, in going straight to the publishers to order them to delete all the maps from the copies that were for distribution to the public, and this was duly carried out.[36] The decision of the bishops meanwhile was in favour of no division, with only the Bishop of Liverpool siding with Bourne, so Amigo's action was vindicated. The outbreak of war the following year, and the death of Pope Pius X, meant Bourne's whole scheme had to be postponed indefinitely.

## A Special Directory for the Newly Formed Province

Meanwhile the recent reorganization of the Catholic hierarchy in 1911 had given Canon Glancey the idea of publishing a special directory for the newly formed Province of Birmingham. The bishops of the province gave it their approval, and Bishop Hedley expressed the hope that it would 'help bind us together'. Archbishop Ilsley agreed that it should be styled 'official' and asked Canon Caswell to compile the *ordo*. Unfortunately things did not go entirely smoothly before publication, partly because Archbishop Bourne objected to the whole idea on the grounds that it showed 'Provincial Independence', also Burns & Oates, who printed the *Catholic Directory*, were concerned that their profits would fall off with a rival publication being produced. In order to keep up their sales they decided to make a special gesture by issuing their directory for the first time ever in a neat cloth binding without increasing the price. As it happened the editor of the *Catholic Directory* was, unfortunately for Birmingham, a secretary at Archbishop's House, Westminster. He was described as 'a little Jack-in-the-box' who 'sent out letters of remonstrance to the Archbishop and Bishops' on behalf of his own publication, and against the provincial publication!

To add to all this, other objections were raised that certain additions had been made to the provincial directory without consultation with the other bishops, and Michael Glancey refused to take any of the blame for Ilsley's oversight or to be used in any way as a scapegoat in the matter by the Archbishop, who, he said, would have liked to have passed the responsibility of this particular venture on to him: 'But I had no mind to be sacrificed on the altar of episcopal opportunism, & consequently was never forgiven,' Glancey wrote. However, once the new directory came out, it was seen that the reaction by Burns & Oates had been quite groundless, especially as only the Province of Birmingham was involved, so there was no real rivalry with the *Catholic Directory*, which was a national publication. Canon Glancey observed that this fact was of course quite lost on those 'who were bent on crushing the freedom of the Dioceses'.[37]

## 150th Anniversary of Cotton

In 1913 Bishops Ilsley and McIntyre attended the celebrations for the 150th anniversary of the foundation of Cotton College. The Annals recorded that 'on Whitsunday the Bishop celebrated Pontifical High Mass at the opening ceremony of the Jubilee', and 'in the evening

Figure 17.5 *Cover of the* Official Catholic Directory of the Province of Birmingham 1920. *Birmingham Archdiocesan Archives.*

Archbishop Ilsley came and held a reception in the Study Place at 7 o'clock, at which guests, masters and senior boys were presented'. That evening there was a dinner in the refectory and the Archbishop was principal speaker. On the same evening, 'after dinner there was a grand firework display in front of the house at which a thousand rockets went up'. The festivities continued a whole week, the first half for the visitors, and the second for the boys, with Bishop Keating, Bishop Mostyn and Bishop Amigo among the important guests. In a group photograph taken for the occasion the dignified figure of Archbishop Ilsley is immediately discernible, as he usually stood nearly a head taller than any of those around him.

Cotton College was described at this time to be in 'an era of peaceful progress',[38] and it was evident that the unfortunate incidents of ten years ago over the administration were fading well into the past in most minds, although John Hopwood's sudden and untimely death, from cerebral haemorrhage, only a month earlier, must have stirred painful memories for some. Edward Ilsley sang the Requiem Mass on that sad occasion, and John McIntyre delivered the funeral panegyric.[39] In his funeral notices in *The Cottonian* and *The Oscotian*, James Dey seemed to be gently raking over the smouldering ashes of a fire that would now perhaps be allowed at last to die down, and the act of John Hopwood's brother, in burning all the letters and documents concerning an episode which in his opinion was best forgotten, had an air of finality about it.

The celebrations for the jubilee encouraged a great deal of optimism regarding the future of the college, and Canon Hymers was able to declare at the old boys' dinner in the January of 1914, that the year of 1913 had been a glorious one. It seemed at last that the old prejudices which had arisen through the set of involved circumstances, which Father Patrick O'Toole was later to describe as, 'turbulent events of a transitory nature',[40] were now finally coming to rest. But within six months, the outbreak of the First World War was effectively to dash the hopes of any real progress for the college yet once again, while the nations of Europe prepared themselves for the bitter struggle extending over the following four years.

## National Catholic Congress at Plymouth 1913

In the first week of July 1913, the Archbishop attended the National Catholic Congress at Plymouth, and at the final meeting, which was held at the Guildhall, under the presidency of Cardinal Bourne, the subject chosen was 'Religion in Modern England'. Although there was unanimous agreement that Roman Catholicism was not only holding its own, but progressing, the picture drawn of religion in England generally was rather a gloomy one, and one speaker maintained the country could no longer be described as Christian. Several speakers insisted on the absolute necessity of preserving the religious education of their children, as they regarded that as the only hope of a Christian country. This drew loud applause from the audience. To Edward Ilsley this must have come to him as familiar ground, as one of his absolute priorities: 'Priests are reminded that catechising is one of their chief duties and ought to be performed by them with regularity and exactitude,' he had announced at his synod in 1900. At the same time, firmly discouraging the frequenting by Catholic children of non-Catholic schools, he said that the catechism was to be taught once a week at least, 'and that by the Rector himself or his assistant priest, and not left entirely to the teachers, no matter how capable or zealous they may be'.[41]

Cardinal Bourne in his final speech to the congress agreed with their conclusions, saying they now had unique opportunities of spreading the Roman Catholic faith, as thousands were ready to hear what they had to say.[42] Unfortunately these 'unique opportunities' mentioned by the Cardinal had not been grasped by him and used as they might have been, in the building of much-needed Catholic primary schools. Bishop Gordon Wheeler wrote in 1950, 'Cardinal Bourne has been criticised for his concentration on St. Edmund's to the detriment of provision for primary education in the suburbs.' He continued: 'There seems to be some justification for this. Before Cardinal Hinsley's time there was no Diocesan Schools Commission, and educational enterprise was left entirely to parish priests who received little or no direction in the matter.' So sadly enough the schools which so urgently needed to be built in his own diocese at the time had to wait, in some cases for many years, long after his time in office.[43]

## Notes

1   *Si Qua Est*, Rome, 1911.
2   The See of Plymouth containing Devon, Cornwall and Dorset, the Diocese of Clifton consisting of Somerset, Gloucestershire and Wiltshire, while Shropshire and Cheshire comprise the Diocese of Shrewsbury.
3   Clifton, pp. 24–7. The cause of this delay was said to be through a rumour that had been spread about Archbishop Bourne being in some

way linked with Modernist ideas supposed to be prevailing at Wonersh. The matter was finally altogether refuted towards the end of 1909.

4 *The Birmingham Post*, 30 June 1911.

5 William Ullathorne was made Archbishop on his retirement. The special significance of Ilsley's appointment was that he became Archbishop and Metropolitan.

6 Archbishops Wiseman, Manning and Bourne received the sacred *pallium* in Rome, but Vaughan thought an investiture by an apostolic delegate sent to London as 'too good a trump-card against the Anglicans to throw away'. *The Letters of Cardinal Herbert Vaughan to Lady Herbert of Lea* (London, Burns and Oates, Shane Leslie, 1942), p. 405. Also: *The Birmingham Catholic Magazine*, 1911: 'Cardinal Pole received the Pallium on Lady Day, 1556 in Bow Church, London'. This was when he was consecrated Archbishop of Canterbury in the reign of Mary I. See also, Southwark, Letter from Ilsley to Amigo, 1 November 1911 and *The Birmingham Mail*, 1 December 1926.

7 Kiernan, p. 46, and Myerscough. Also B.A., Box p1–d. The President of the Roman Catholic Schools Association commented regarding Ilsley: 'His urbanity & geniality have secured to him the affections of all who have met him.'

8 The linings, in pale blue silk brocade, were woven to the same design as the cloth of gold, and the fringes, borders and cords were all made from special patterns. The gold fabric was hand-woven by the Essex weavers who had settled there in medieval times, and the blue silk was woven in Spitalfields by the descendants of the Huguenots.

9 *The Birmingham Archdiocesan Directory*, 1911.

10 Vestments presented to the Archbishop were also made for the deacon, subdeacon and assistant priest. The Archbishop's vestments consisted of chasuble, stole, maniple, burse also chalice veil, cope and humeral veil. They are still in use on special occasions: e.g. for the ceremony during which a priest is created a canon of the cathedral chapter – 'I was at St Chad's today as there was a special Mass there for the installation of a new canon ... the Archbishop wore your vestments – the new canon was Denis Toplass.' Letter from Father Peter Dennison, 3 December 1985.

11 When Ilsley was ordained in 1861 there were three religious houses of men established in the diocese: the Passionists at Broadway, the Fathers of the Oratory and the Fathers of the Institute of Charity at Rugby. By 1911 there were twenty religious orders or congregations of men.

12 The metropolitan chapter consisted of: Provost O'Hanlon and Canons Frances Hopkins, John McIntyre, Michael Glancey, Edward Hymers, John Caswell, Joseph Robinson, George Williams, William Barry, James Rigby, Charles Wheatley and James Keating. Joseph Souter and Henry Davies were honorary canons.

13 *The Birmingham Daily Post*, 9 December 1911.

14 John 10.16.

15 *The Birmingham Catholic Magazine*, 1911, Birmingham Central Library.

16 O.C.A., From Archbishop Bourne, congratulating Ilsley on his Golden Jubilee and receiving the sacred *pallium*. The English College, Rome, 4 December 1911.

17 B.A., Draft letter from Archbishop Ilsley to Cardinal Lepicier, 18 October 1911.

18 *The Times*, 26 March 1904.

19 Clifton, pp. 37–8.

20 Southwark, Archbishop Ilsley to Bishop Amigo, 10 April 1912.

21 Clifton, pp. 11–15 and 38–45. All these matters are dealt with in detail by Michael Clifton, 'such a division was made in 1966 when the Diocese of Arundel & Brighton was created by cutting off Surrey and Sussex from Southwark'.

22 Southwark, Ilsley to Amigo, 28 March and 20 December 1912. Ilsley was referring to Pope Pius X.

23 *Ibid.*, Letters from Bishop Ilsley, 28 August 1917 and 7 September 1912.

24 *Ibid.*, From Ilsley to Amigo, 4 March 1917.

25 Oldmeadow, vol. ii, p. 346.

26 *Ibid.*, vol. i, pp. 235–6. When he was Bishop of Southwark he had been unpopular with his chapter. See Clifton, pp. 11–12.

27 Oldmeadow, vol. ii, p. 85. Letter from Archbishop Bourne to Bishop Hedley.

28 Southwark, Letter from Archbishop Ilsley to Bishop Amigo, 15 December 1912.

29 B.A., Rough draft of a letter from Archbishop Ilsley to Cardinal Merry del Val, 8 January 1913.

30 Southwark, Letter from Ilsley to Amigo, 10 January 1913.

31 Oldmeadow, vol. ii, p. 87.

32 B.A., Archbishop Ilsley to Bishop Amigo, 7 January 1912.

33 Southwark, Amigo to Ilsley, 18 January 1912.

34 D.B., p. 23. Also Kiernan, p. 47.

35 Southwark, Archbishop Ilsley to Bishop Amigo, Epiphany 1912.

36 Clifton, p. 46. Bourne's reaction is not recorded. There is one of these maps in the Southwark archives.

37 B.A., Uncatalogued papers. *The Provincial Directory* continued to be published until 1921. It did not rival *The Catholic Directory.*

38 Frank Roberts, original manuscript, ch. 15, pp. 27–8.

39 Buscot, p. 274.

40 D.B., p. 25.

41 *Synodus Diocesana Birminghamiensis Duodecima. Anno 1900. Decr. XXII.*

42 *The Western Weekly News*, 12 July 1913.

43 Beck, G. Wheeler, 'The Archdiocese of Westminster,' p. 173.

## CHAPTER EIGHTEEN

# *The Great War*

## The Archbishop's Illness in 1913

In early September 1913 when he was 75, Edward Ilsley became ser-iously ill, and his condition was suddenly so grave that Bishop McIntyre administered the Last Sacraments to him.[1] A few days later, on 15 September, 'after giving his blessing to all', Ilsley entered a pri-vate nursing home, where he underwent an operation on 18 September. He soon appeared to be making a good recovery, and McIntyre was able to describe to Bishop Amigo how 'He bounded at once from the effects of the operation, was able not only to dress and sit up but also to go out for drives.'[2] Just over a month later, on 25 October, he returned to Oscott, with the thought of taking a holiday, but his promising recovery did not last for long, and 'his strength gave way',[3] and he was soon so overcome with tiredness and exhaustion that he had to take to his bed once more, and could see no-one. Writing from Oscott a week later, John McIntyre described to Bishop Amigo, 'I think that a reaction has set in and he must resign himself to perfect quiet for a while.' Finally, even the effort of signing papers became too much for him, and a period of complete rest was ordered.

In the first week in November Ilsley suffered a further severe relapse, and on the 11th, McIntyre wrote to Bishop Amigo: 'The Archbishop has had a somewhat serious heart failure. The doctor had to be hurriedly summoned and gave the Archbishop an injection of strychnine. Things can hardly remain in the same state many days longer.' His strength seemed to be failing and those closest to him were concerned for his life. It was then that he made this very final-sounding statement, 'In the course of a long reign such as I have had, I must have been, however unwittingly, the cause of offence to many. I ask their forgiveness for any injury I have done them, but more earn-estly than their forgiveness, I ask their prayers.'[4]

Ten days later, on 21 November, John McIntyre wrote to Bishop Amigo, 'A most uncanny thing happened yesterday,' and he went on to describe how the nurse asked him to go in and talk with Ilsley. When he went in, 'he looked uneasy and his face was clouded . . . and then the Archbishop said to me, "Did you not promise to stay with me to the end?" I said yes. "And you were willing to do this in any capacity?" I again replied yes. Thereupon he now settled again.'

McIntyre then told Bishop Amigo that he had received a letter that morning from Cardinal Vannutelli, requesting the recommendation of a candidate for the rectorship of the English College in Rome. 'I had made no mention of it to his face,' he wrote, 'He must have had some intimation of the contents of the letter by telepathy.' McIntyre let a day pass before he told Ilsley of the Cardinal's letter, and he then only mentioned that Charles Cronin's name was submitted. 'The Archbishop does not know the enquiry was about me,' he said, 'I ventured to add a bit of my own to Card. Vannutelli. I felt it necessary to say that my name ought to be expunged from the list of candidates because I could not leave the Archbishop, with whom I had thrice promised to stay till the end.'

Four days later, on 15 November, McIntyre sent another bulletin to Amigo saying that the Archbishop 'had taken a decided turn for the better'. He said 'H. E. keeps *altum silentium*. If my secret machinations have been in progress I trust that the Archbishop's recovery will frustrate them. Think of the situation his death would have created! McIntyre in Rome – Amigo in Birmingham and Southwark – ?' Fortunately over the following weeks 'the bulletins became more hopeful' and in a pastoral letter he gave on 1 December McIntyre announced 'the Archbishop's health continues to show a marked improvement'. Two months later, by the new year of 1914, Ilsley was gradually able to begin his administration again with support of his devoted auxiliary. McIntyre remained uncertain over the appointment at the Venerabile and again wrote to Amigo, 'Nothing has come hither from Rome or Westminster. That W should be silent I can understand, but the silence of Rome perplexes me.' Asking Amigo if he could make an investigative visit to the Continent he wrote humorously to him, 'I suppose you did not forget anything when you left Rome last, that would be sufficient excuse for you going back to fetch it?'

## The English College, Rome – McIntyre's Appointment

Then in mid-January 1914 came the somewhat unwelcome news that Bishop McIntyre had been appointed by the Holy See to the rectorship of the English College in Rome. Archbishop Ilsley confessed at the time that 'he felt as though he had lost his right hand,'[5] and this was understandable because John McIntyre had been his secretary for 24 years, as well as his auxiliary for the last two. The thought of his having to leave so suddenly caused a sense of regret throughout the diocese, and the question must also have been in many minds as to why the Archbishop should have to lose his assistant bishop just at a time when he appeared to need him most. But the authorities in Rome had decided that he should not continue in Birmingham, because the time had come for him to broaden his experience. Amigo warned Ilsley two years previously that Archbishop Bourne had submitted McIntyre's name to Rome, and his proposal had now been taken up. Bourne's motives for proposing McIntyre seem questionable when he was obviously so much needed in Birmingham. At his farewell banquet the day before his departure expressions of genuine sadness at the loss of their much-loved auxiliary bishop were joined with the congratulations given to him on his important appointment.[6]

A footnote to a letter written to Bishop Amigo on 22 January conveys Edward Ilsley's sense of loss: 'My dear friend Bishop McIntyre

Figure 18.1 *John McIntyre, Rector of the English College, Rome (1913–17),*
*Archbishop of Birmingham (1921–8). Oscott College Archives.*

leaves this afternoon.' He made no further comment, but in the same letter he wrote, 'My Chapter have met again with the result that they have advised me to apply for a coadjutor.' Although it seemed particularly expedient just then, after his serious illness, for Archbishop Ilsley to have the help of an auxiliary to take the place of Bishop McIntyre, the fact that he had such hopes of McIntyre one day becoming his successor proved an insurmountable obstacle to such an appointment. Earlier in the month he had confided to Amigo about his concern over just that point, 'Choosing a coadjutor now', he wrote, 'would mean that Bishop McIntyre will have no chance of becoming Archbishop, and in my opinion he would be an excellent one. We hope that he will not be wanted for many years, and meantime he will be making a reputation in Rome.' It was about this time that Father Percy Styche took over as the Archbishop's secretary. He was a young man of 26, who had been ordained two years earlier, 'and he continued at the task until 1922, under Archbishop McIntyre'.[7]

The question of his resignation must have been a consideration in Ilsley's mind during those months following the time when he had been so gravely ill. The probability of it may have caused the authorities not to press for the appointment of a coadjutor, and the matter was left open for the time being. When Ilsley first lost McIntyre, he briefly considered asking for Charles Cronin as his auxiliary. Cronin had just returned from the English College in Rome, having been Vice Rector there for the past sixteen years, since 1898. But John McIntyre wrote to Amigo in early February, two weeks after his arrival in Rome, to say it would not be practical for Ilsley to have a coadjutor but that it might be the best time for his resignation if he wished to be relieved of the responsibilities of the new province. He said this was 'because there was sympathy for him and the Holy Father, who expressed much affection for him, would do anything to meet his wishes. Moreover now would be the best time for his resignation as everyone would understand his position; it would not be so if he resigned later.' He said he had written a similar letter to Ilsley by the same post.[8] The question of the appointment of a coadjutor was alluded to in Ilsley's letters from time to time. He wrote to Amigo a month later on 8 March telling him, 'Bp. McIntyre told me the Card. decidedly would not grant one because at my death he would be a burden on the diocese', so it would appear that by then he had decided against such a move, and the idea certainly seemed to be quite forgotten six months later with the onset of the Great War during early August.

## A Remarkable Recovery

Father Patrick O'Toole, writing in *The Oscotian*, observed that 'During the crucial period of the war, the Archbishop who had recovered from his serious illness, seemed to have his strength renewed like the eagle's and was enabled to carry on single-handed.'[9] As Monsignor Cronin was teaching at Oscott College for the following three years, he was conveniently on hand to serve the Archbishop in any way necessary, and Ilsley appeared to manage quite well by using this method of working with him and with the help of his new secretary Father Styche. Cronin, then aged 42, had some exceptional points in his favour – he was capable of making concise decisions on any point in canon law, and was also able to make sound legal judgements, and his years of experience in Rome meant that he was of considerable help to Ilsley with his official letters.[10] The Archbishop also had the help and support of his chapter, which included James O'Hanlon, who was Provost and his vicar general.

Although he was now 76, the Archbishop's energy and enthusiasm seemed remarkably undiminished in spite of what he had been through in the previous months. It would of course be natural for a man of his outlook and temperament to assume that he had been spared from his illness in order to continue with whatever was required of him, and now without further question he seemed prepared to give the spiritual lead and necessary guidance to his people throughout the demanding war years, and beyond. Official portraits at this time give the impression of a man at peace with himself, whose face is full of kindness and good humour. It was later said of him that 'his piety was not of a kind to prevent his seeing the humorous side, even of matters ecclesiastical'.[11] An anecdote told about him bears this out, showing the Archbishop was quite ready to permit a small joke at his own expense: During a procession in the cathedral, an altar boy trod on the hem of the *cappa parva*, the cloak he was wearing for that particular ceremony, causing a seam to tear as a result. On returning to the sacristy, as he was disrobing he was heard to joke as the cape was removed from his shoulders: 'The High Priest rent his garments!'[12]

## War Declared in 1914

On 24 February 1914 Ilsley was feeling sufficiently strong again to be planning a visit to Rome, 'When the weather takes up say at the beginning of May, it will be very pleasant and beneficial, besides making oneself more at home with the H. Father & the Cardinals, & getting to know more distinctly what they want one to do,' he wrote to Amigo. But within a few months things on the Continent had drastically changed, with Germany declaring war on France on 3 August. On 7 August he wrote to Canon Glancey, 'The authorities are commandeering right and left – horses, motor cars etc. They have taken over Birmingham University as a hospital with 500 beds – suppose we get an order one of these days to put up 50 or 60 wounded here? I fear we shall have to send our students to their homes.' On 9 August Father Hudson received a request from the Red Cross to hand over St Gerard's Hospital to them for their use. It had been built a year earlier at Coleshill. He made an arrangement instead to take in 36 war wounded. By 1917 the number had grown to about 50 and the recreation room had to be extended to accommodate them.[13]

On 16 September, even as the storm clouds gathered more threateningly over Europe, Ilsley was still able to consider the progress at Oscott and Cotton with obvious pleasure. In his correspondence with Bishop Amigo the impression is given that he had set aside any disappointment over the disestablishment of the Central Seminary five years earlier. He was probably more than contented with the fact that as the diocesan seminary it was again within his own jurisdiction, and he realized the benefits this situation brought with it! He wrote enthusiastically about the record number of students at Oscott, and in his customary manner showed a practical interest in the general improvement and upkeep of the buildings in his care: 'We have 52 students on our books today. We are installing hot water in St. Wilfrid's – electric light was done last year. Twenty-five years today since Oscott became the diocesan seminary. *Jubilate!*'[14] But only a month later the effects of the war on the Continent were being felt in Britain, and Ilsley was soon organizing help for a flood of refugees from Belgium, who had many nuns and priests among them.

By November he wrote again pressing Amigo over the question of insufficient chaplains in both the army and the navy at this time – 'It seems to me that we ought to bring it up at our next meeting,' he said, 'and we should elicit information if we can't do more effective work. Our University buildings are being utilised as a Hospital & there are many Belgian wounded soldiers there – when it was first opened I called to see the Catholic patients & at the suggestion of the Colonel in charge I asked for War Office recognition for Father Keating, the priest of the local mission who was attending the Catholic soldiers. In a few days I received notice of his appointment.' The business of setting-up army chaplains to be nominated as a permanent and regular institution for the future had been negotiated by Bishop Grant as early as 1858, but the pressing need now was to increase the numbers to suit the present situation.[15] They served as officers although they maintained their ecclesiastical titles, coming under the Roman Catholic Ordinary of the Forces, and were of course non-combatant.

## James Dey an Army Chaplain

James Dey joined the Royal Army Chaplains Department in 1903 at the age of 34, and after a tour of duty in South Africa returned home in 1913. He saw service in France during the war and was at the battle of Mons administering to the soldiers in the trenches and at the base hospitals at Wimereux. He was mentioned in dispatches and for his service was awarded the DSO and later even found it in himself to joke that Mons was the best retreat he had ever made! In 1916 at the age of 46 he was sent as Senior Chaplain to the Forces to East Africa, where he supervised Catholic chaplains in General Smut's army.[16] About thirty Oscotian priests served at the front as chaplains, but only one, Herbert Collins, was killed during the war. He was one of Cardinal Vaughan's students who came to Oscott from Westminster in 1902 and was ordained there in 1908, the year before it ceased to be the Central Seminary.

In his Advent Pastoral Archbishop Ilsley gratefully encouraged his people for their efforts in helping the refugees in different ways: 'It has given great consolation to us, dear children in Jesus Christ, to know how warm has been the welcome which you have accorded to the exiled, homeless fugitives from Belgium, who have lost their all because they refused to betray the truth and the right.' One positive aspect of the war situation was that it caused much closer connections between England and the Catholic countries of Europe to be established than had ever existed before.

A letter the Archbishop sent out to his clergy at the beginning of hostilities seemed to forecast the horror the future would bring: 'Within the past few days war has been declared involving this nation and nearly all the nations of Europe. The conflagration thus ignited is one of unparalleled magnitude involving loss of innumerable lives and inflicting untold suffering. Who can fail to see that such a war as this is a scourge in the hand of the Almighty for the chastisement of our sins? It behoves us therefore to humble ourselves before God, and accept with patient and willing submission the ordinances of His justice.'[17]

Figure 18.2  *Bishop James Dey, Senior Chaplain to the Forces.*

## Oscott During the War

The war soon began to present its hardships and difficulties, with many students leaving the seminary to join up. But the numbers at Oscott actually increased at that time because the college took in a number of Belgian refugee seminarians. It fell on the shoulders of Bernard Miller as Vice Rector to try to make any necessary adjustments as best he could by dealing with the shortages of staff and insufficient supplies of food. The food situation became acute in 1916 until the government introduced a proper rationing system, which then eased things a little. One austerity affecting everyone in the college was brought about through the shortage of coke for the boilers, and this meant little or no hot water was available. The students also had to help out by making their own beds, and it was impressed upon them that their only reason for not 'joining up' at this time could be because God had called them to a higher warfare in the service of the Church.[18] In 1916 a blackout was imposed nationwide because of the danger of air attacks and bombing from zeppelins, which were by then occuring in different parts of the British Isles. The airships met with little opposition and travelled as far as Edinburgh, where a bomb hit the castle mound! When writing to Bishop Amigo in February 1916, Ilsley described an 'invasion of Zeppelins on Monday night last. We had indulged the feeling that in the Midlands we were safe from enemy aircraft. Vain delusion! We must keep to our prayers very earnestly & trust in Divine protection.' William Barry graphically described a similar experience when he was in Milverton Terrace in Leamington Spa: 'The night was dark, we had retired to our rooms, when a peculiar whirring in the air told us that mischief was abroad. My younger colleagues rushed out and beheld an airship of which we could hear the engines at work. Had it sailed close to our bell tower 120 feet high we had all been surely destroyed. Whilst I lay awake listening, my windows were violently rattled by vibration from the airship, but nothing ensued.' He later mentioned his deep sympathy 'for Mr Snead-Cox who lost two sons in the Great War'. He was well-acquainted with him through *The Tablet*.[19]

In a footnote to one of his letters to Bishop Amigo in March 1916, Ilsley said, 'I fear I have made a blunder – ask Bishop McIntyre to tell you of it – you will be sorry for me.' There was no further explanation, but whatever had happened appeared to cause a distinct setback for Ilsley, and for the first time in all the years he seemed to be filled with uncertainty. He was 77 at the time, and he wrote again a few weeks later: 'Of course I don't get any younger & of late I have found the memory failing, & I experience a difficulty in putting my thoughts together & perhaps I have blundered in matters of administration of late. I am hoping to go into retreat on Friday evening for a few days & may get some light on the subject – But if you tell me I ought to resign it would weigh with me – I suppose the Holy See would make some provision for me.'[20]

Bishop Amigo, obviously very touched by the tone of Ilsley's letter, replied the following day saying that although he was perhaps feeling the weight of his years, people had been astonished by the amount of work he had accomplished, but now it was all too much for him. He advised him to ask Cardinal de Lai if there was any chance of having John McIntyre back as his Auxiliary. 'I hope that by having Bp. McIntyre by your side you will be able to go on without resigning,' he wrote. A week or so later Ilsley was still not settled in his mind, 'I am thankful for your prayers,' he wrote, 'but I did not obtain any decisive light during the course of the retreat. Perhaps you may be able to spare me a quarter of an hour in Low Week to talk it over.'[21] Ilsley usually stayed with Amigo during the Low Week meetings, so the two would have ample time for discussion. They appear to have settled the problem, because it was not mentioned again, and the question of Ilsley retiring seemed to be set aside.

## 'Lawnside'

It was about this time he procured a large house in Norfolk Road, Edgbaston, called 'Lawnside', for the new Archbishop's House. It had long been felt that the official residence built by A. W. Pugin and situated in the rather drab, narrow streets near St Chad's Cathedral was inadequate for the general needs of the archdiocese, and in November 1915 when the bishops of the province met in Birmingham, Ilsley reported to Amigo: 'The new Archiepiscopal residence served very well for the accommodation of the suffragans at their meeting & that is a comfort.' During that year he went to stay at Lawnside for a trial period. Bishop Amigo had suggested a move from Oscott some months earlier when he wrote, 'I wish it were possible for you to live away from Oscott quietly with Monsignor Cronin, you would have the comforts which you ought to have, but which cannot be obtained in College life.'[22] Ilsley acted on his advice, but the move to Lawnside was apparently not successful, and proved to be only a temporary one because he obviously came to realize that Oscott was the background he really had no wish to relinquish. If the idea had been for him to prepare to retire there at this time, it came to nothing, and he finally returned to Oscott and remained permanently in residence there until the end of his days. Archbishop Keating later said that Ilsley remained at Oscott because 'he loved the seminary life with its religious atmosphere, its restrictions and its opportunities for self-denial ... by the spirituality of his life he impressed us all'.[23] But apart from Frederick Keating's description, Ilsley must have felt drawn to it for many other reasons, not the least of which would have been his liking for the simple everyday routine that he would follow there among his friends and colleagues as the months and years passed by.

## Edward Ilsley – Samuel Myerscough's Description

A description of Edward's later years spent there is given by Samuel Myerscough, who was a student at the college between 1905 and 1912: 'The heart of His Grace was undoubtedly in his seminary at Oscott. It was his home in more senses than one; not only did he return to its quiet seclusion from the labours of the episcopate, but it was the centre of his hopes and affections. He delighted in the peace of its hallowed walls, and the presence of his family of students round him. Every Oscotian will recall with pleasure his daily presence among us in the chapel at our ceremonies and functions, and in the general life of the house. That venerable figure passing erect to and fro in the cloisters; or kneeling erect at his place in the chapel with eyes on the tabernacle, throughout meditation or night prayers, was an encouragement in difficulty and an incentive in time of slackness or fatigue: a consolation in sadness, an edification always; for we knew how he worked and never spared himself or rested at the oar; we sensed the paternal care with which he regarded us and the constant prayer he uttered in our welfare.'[24]

The religious revival that war brings, while it lasts, caused Ilsley to write in one of his letters to Bishop Amigo on 29 December 1916 about the effect the dreadful upheaval of the war was having on the spiritual life of his people. The appalling Battle of the Somme had begun at the beginning of July that year and after five months' fighting there had been nearly 500,000 casualties. 'Our people have been very devout this Christmas, thronging the Altar in greater numbers than ever,' he wrote. His sympathies would have been very much with them at this sad time when the war was entering its darkest stages. Many families throughout the land had suffered the loss of their loved ones and everyone lived in constant fear of receiving some dreaded news from the front. The war gave a sudden impetus to Catholic life during these years and the total Catholic population in Britain had risen considerably from 1.3 million at the beginning of the century, to 1.9 million by the end of the conflict in 1918, and the priests, secular and religious, from 3,000 to 4,000 during those years. This was partly because of the closer connections that had been established between England and Catholic countries on the Continent through the influx of refugees. Although nearly 80, the Archbishop still had the most remarkable energy – 'I sang the 11 o'clock Mass on Xmas Day', he wrote to Amigo, 'after saying the other two.'

In September 1916 his cab was involved in an accident with a private car: 'I don't mind telling you, because you won't repeat it, that my taxi cab last Monday week collided with a private motor car that was coming at right angles in Selly Park,' he wrote to Amigo. 'Both cars,' he wrote, 'were seriously damaged but the occupants escaped miraculously. I phoned for another car and drove all the way to Oscott.' When ordered to rest a badly bruised leg, he put the matter to good use, because his letter continues; 'So far I am enjoying the enforced rest which gives me time to think.'[25]

John McIntyre continued working at the English College from January 1914 until August 1917, and although his presence was very much missed in Birmingham, the fact that he was in Rome during this time proved to be of great value, because it placed him in a strong position to be of assistance to both Ilsley and Amigo with regard to their vexed 'boundary questions'. Cardinal Bourne was still seeking tirelessly to bring about the division of the dioceses to his own satisfaction, and continued to introduce various schemes, even against the background of the war, which brought most other considerations of that kind to a halt. McIntyre's office of Rector of the English College 'proved to be one of the most trying periods of his life; the big depreciation in Italian currency made his position very embarrassing, and he found it well nigh impossible to maintain the *Venerabile* in a proper state of efficiency'. But he had the pleasure of being able to renew his past friendship with the Holy Father, Benedict XV, with whom he had been a student in his old Roman days, and this contact proved to be of considerable benefit to them both because 'from time to time the Holy Father sent for his old friend to assist in tracing prisoners of war ... as a token of his worth he was appointed by the Pope a Consultor of the Biblical Commission'.[26]

## Liaison between Ilsley, Amigo and McIntyre

Bishop Amigo found it necessary to travel to Rome frequently in order to defend the position of his diocese during those years. It would seem that the liaison between the three men, Ilsley, McIntyre and Amigo, formed an impregnable triangle in defence of their boundaries, which preserved them against the changes they feared might otherwise come about. Because of their resistance a number of Bourne's plans either did not come to fruition or were delayed until later years. The merits of some of their opposition to him is debatable, but he also met with similar resistance from a number of his bishops increasingly through the years.[27]

Between 1916 and 1917 when Europe was in turmoil, instead of remaining with his people, Cardinal Bourne had a long absence from Westminster which he spent in Rome, where he was engaged in an all-out attempt to push his various schemes through. As he stayed there from the previous November until April 1917, rumours began to spread that he was to remain there permanently, and an article was published in *The Westminster Gazette* on 19 March 1917 entitled 'Another English Cardinal?' It ran 'According to these rumours Cardinal Bourne is to remain in Rome permanently; the Archbishop of Liverpool is to replace him at Westminster – probably to become Cardinal in due course – and the Bishop of Menevia will be translated to Liverpool.' But a letter written on 9 February from McIntyre to Amigo had already made the position clear regarding just how things stood at the time: 'The item in *The Tablet* that the Holy Father had asked H. E. to stay in Rome and help with his counsel is all moonshine. The authorities here would be glad to see his back, and are beginning to think that he has not much to do with his diocese. He asked the authorities to put him on the Consistorial hoping thereby to pilot his schemes through. But he has been sadly deceived. We were too active for him; and just before the general meeting on Thursday last, some friend must have given a hint that there would be no thoroughfare, for he withdrew his little bill to avoid rejection.'[28]

On 20 February Cardinal de Lai wrote to Bishop Amigo suggesting that the Congregation were going to assist Bourne in putting through his schemes, but McIntyre took the view that, for one reason or another, Bourne was not very likely to succeed. He enumerated his reasons to Bishop Amigo in a letter written on 25 March 1917, saying, 'That Westminster had succeeded in bringing about a wonderful unity among the Bishops but against himself, and that the financial condition of England would prevent the success of the proposed schemes.' He added that there was little need of worry on this account because the authorities in Rome only considered the proposals to be of a theoretical nature.

Although Archbishop Bourne might not have been successful in interfering with the dioceses of the other bishops, he succeeded in devising a scheme of narrowing the limits of his own by releasing that part of the Westminster diocese lying in Essex which was to become the new Diocese of Brentwood, and Monsignor Ward was translated to the diocese on 20 July 1917. All the rumours about Bourne's activities were soon quenched when on 5 April *The Universe* gave an account of the Cardinal's return, together with a translation of Pope Benedict's letter praising him for his proposal. The Pope's message, which suggested that the time had come for certain changes to be made, would have given Bishop Amigo little comfort at the time, in spite of what McIntyre had written to him. It ran: 'Would that others also of the English Episcopate might see their way to imitate the excellent example which you have set! For the size of the territory assigned to them is so great that the strength of one man is hardly equal to the task of governing it.'[29]

## Meeting Called in Bourne's Absence

While Archbishop Bourne was still away in Rome, Bishop Amigo called an unofficial meeting on 7 March 1917 of the suffragan bishops of Westminster, to discuss the ongoing question of the dioceses, and they firmly agreed that they wished to be consulted before any action was taken. Amigo then extended this to a special meeting of the other bishops to be held the following week, and it was Archbishop Ilsley who, in the continued absence of Cardinal Bourne, called for it to be held at Oscott College, and as the senior member, took the chair. On this occasion they decided to send a letter to Archbishop Bourne in Rome to announce their conclusions, and when he received it Bourne replied by sending Archbishop Ilsley a letter of protest saying: 'My absence does not transfer to anyone else either my rights as Metropolitan, or the special privileges accorded to the Archbishop of Westminster.'[30] In this case Edward Ilsley stood firm, sending a reply drawn up by Monsignor Cronin, which was also approved by the Archbishop of Liverpool. In it he said that he considered at the time, and still considered now, that he was quite within his rights in calling the meeting on 15 March.[31]

Cardinal Bourne made a similar protest to the Westminster bishops about their meeting, and on his return from Rome attempted to thrash the matter out. His only measure of success was that all the bishops said that they accepted that 'no formal meeting of the whole hierarchy could be called except by the Archbishop of Westminster'. The Cardinal always kept notes of what had occurred, and he completed his note on this particular matter by adding, 'All asserted emphatically however, that the meetings held were absolutely private, informal and unofficial. Therefore the matter is closed.'[32] It would appear that the bishops had closed ranks on this occasion, in a determination to protect their venerable Brother in Christ, Edward Ilsley, and themselves, from any further reprimand.

Meanwhile, just before the Low Week Meeting at which Bourne presided, an article appeared in *The Tablet* at this time which created a scare among the bishops. It was supposedly a translation of a document received from Pope Benedict by Archbishop Bourne, and in it the Pope appealed for the bishops' consent to the division of dioceses. Although the matter now seemed final, Amigo did not trust the wording of the article, and on contacting Cardinal Gasquet in Rome, he was assured by him that the translation was not correct, and that the Pope meant this to apply only if such divisions were 'useful and possible'. He said that the Holy See would not proceed to dismember dioceses in opposition to the wishes of the bishops. So, once more Francis Bourne failed to reach his goal, and he published an apology in *The Tablet*. The Low Week meeting of 1917 went decisively against him.

## The Return of McIntyre in 1917

In the summer of 1917 the workload that Archbishop Ilsley had been carrying was at last eased by the return of John McIntyre, after he had served for three and a half years as Rector of the English College. Much to Ilsley's satisfaction, he again assumed the role of his auxiliary, and he was also appointed Vicar General, and was raised to the office of Titular Archbishop, in order to maintain the prestige he had gained during his time in Rome.[33] Ilsley had recently put forward the suggestion that McIntyre should be elevated to this position, and it would seem that his years of patience were at last being rewarded. On the following 22 November he wrote to Bishop Amigo, 'I find the Archbishop is quite vigorous and has developed in a marked manner during his three years' sojourn in Rome. He has written a beautiful

Pastoral which you will receive probably tomorrow and from that you will judge how useful he is.' At the annual reunion of Birmingham Catholics the following January, McIntyre staunchly defended Pope Benedict against the pro-German accusations that had been made against him in the English press by reporting that he had remained silent over the invasion of Belgium and other violations of international law. He refuted the charges, saying that of all the neutral powers of the world the Holy See was the only one to publicly protest against such German actions as their attacks upon open towns, as was done in air raids. Speaking later Bishop Bagshaw of Nottingham deprecated the fact that the Pope had been excluded from the Hague Conference.

Notes in *The Oscotian* for 22 December 1917 announced, 'For the first time for many years the students did not remain at Oscott for Christmas Festivities but commenced their vacation upon this date.' This was due to the influenza epidemic that was sweeping the country, it was a pandemic and many millions died throughout the world. It was later reported that both the Archbishop and the Rector 'had fallen victim to its ravages'.[34] It had already begun to spread the previous year and Ilsley had written to Amigo: 'We have had Mgr Parkinson on his back with a severe attack of influenza followed by pneumonia – Two days ago I was really anxious about him. But he is now progressing altho' slowly.' Writing a year later in January 1918 to Bishop Amigo when there were air raids in the southern part of the country, there was a hint of weariness and hopeful expectation in Ilsley's letter when he added, 'When will it all end? In the New Year?' When hostilities finally ceased the following autumn, Archbishop Ilsley's letter to the clergy opens like a fanfare of trumpets: 'The war is ended, *Deo Gratias*! He has heard our cry: He has given us the victory we asked for.' He concluded typically, 'There will be ample need of the divine assistance in the days that are before us.'

## The Formation of the Church after the War

The formation of the Catholic Church that emerged at the end of the war was very different from the one that Ilsley was dealing with thirty years earlier at the beginning of his administration. By now 'the general fusion of the diverse elements in the Catholic community was largely complete'. In her book *The Great Hunger*, Cecil Woodham-Smith describes part of this development: 'It was not until the second or third generation that Irish intelligence, quickness of apprehension and wit asserted themselves, and the children and the grandchildren of the

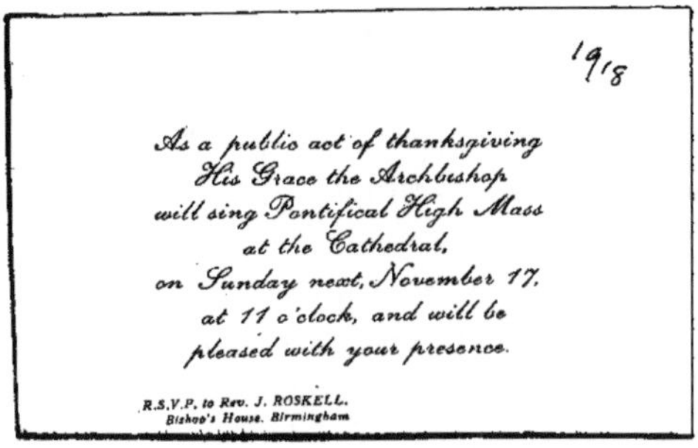
1918

As a public act of thanksgiving
His Grace the Archbishop
will sing Pontifical High Mass
at the Cathedral,
on Sunday next, November 17,
at 11 o'clock, and will be
pleased with your presence.

R.S.V.P. to Rev. J. ROSKELL.
Bishoo's House. Birmingham

Figure 18.3 *Invitation to a Pontifical High Mass celebrated by Archbishop Ilsley in thanksgiving for the termination of the Great War, 17 November 1918. Birmingham Archidiocesan Archives.*

poor famine emigrants became successful and powerful in the countries of their adoption.'[35] Some of the blending had been brought about by the general assimilation of the Irish immigrant community and the converts with 'the definitely English tradition', which in its turn had been greatly modified since the first years of the revival. Cardinal Bourne was a typical representative of this change as the son of a convert English father and an Irish Catholic mother. In spite of all these social developments, there were still to be no relaxations of any previous regulations regarding religious practices, and Ilsley followed the firm traditions set by Manning and Vaughan in opposing mixed marriages. Constantly urging his clergy to persuade opinion against these marriages as a danger to the Catholic religion, he made it clear that they were to be avoided wherever possible. At his synod in 1900 he stipulated that: 'By occasional sermons, in house to house visitations and whenever favourable opportunity offers, our people ought to be made to realise how much the Church holds these unions in abhorrence.'[36] But although his directions had the backing of the new Code of Canon Law laid down in 1917, the sweeping social changes brought about by the war were altogether against such regulations succeeding, and within two generations the requirements had largely given way.

Edward Ilsley's awareness of the resulting chaos existing in Europe, and the uncertainty and general disillusionment concerning the future, were only too apparent in a letter written on Armistice Day 1918 to the Abbess of Stone. Surveying the unprecedented events of the past four years, he questioned a changed world which in many ways was questioning itself, and he strove in his own way to find solutions: 'But what big events are happening! They fairly bewilder us.

And what is going to become of the nations of Europe, we shall see sometime, but just now it is all topsy-turvy. Who will be able to restore order out of chaos? God will raise up someone, no doubt; but we must pray meantime.'[37]

He later expressed his belief in and support of the newly formed League of Nations as his hope for the future years. The Covenant of the League of Nations came into being when the Treaty of Versailles was signed on 28 June 1919, and when addressing a meeting held at the Birmingham Town Hall in October 1921, he said, 'The claim of the League of Nations to a fair trial is borne in upon the conscience of every right-thinking man by the strongest moral arguments. It is in our hands whether it succeeds or fails.'[38]

## Notes

1   *The Universe*, 3 December 1926 and *The Oscotian*, 3rd series, 14, no. 1 (1913).

2   Southwark, Letter from John McIntyre to Bishop Amigo, 30 October 1913. He was operated on by Mr Leedham-Green, *The Birmingham Post*, 19 September 1913. He was thought to have had an appendix operation.

3   *The Oscotian*, 3rd Series, 14, no. 1 (1913).

4   *The Universe*, 3 December 1926. This message was reminiscent of Cardinal Manning's phonograph message which he recorded in 1891: 'To all who may come after me: I hope that no word of mine, written or spoken in my life, will be found to have done harm to anyone after I am dead.' *The Times*, 17 February 1894.

5   D.B., p. 24.

6   *The Catholic Times*, 23 January 1914.

7   *The Catholic Directory*, Obituary notice, 1963.

8   Southwark, McIntyre to Amigo, 8 February 1914.

9   D.B., p. 24.

10   *The Cottonian*, Obituary (Spring 1942). Charles Cronin was appointed Rector of Oscott by Bishop McIntyre in 1924 on the death of Henry Parkinson, having become his vice rector the previous year.

11   Obituary, *The Times*, 2 December 1926.

12   His great-nephew Francis Ilsley told me this.

13   These details are included by Sylvia Pinches in her history of *Father Hudson and His Society*. She also describes how the soldiers were included in the life of the homes as much as possible: 'The boys put on entertainments for them, and at Christmas 1916 a banquet was held, which was attended by Fathers Hudson and Connor,' pp. 15, 16.

14   Southwark, Mentioned in a letter to Bishop Amigo on 16 September 1914. See also *The Oscotian* (1914), pp. 54–5.

15 Southwark, Letter from Ilsley to Amigo, 10 November 1914. Owing to his special experience brought about through his father's army service, Bishop Grant's authority in these matters was recognized during the Crimean War of 1854 to 1856. Charged with the welfare of Catholic soldiers in that war, he insisted that chaplains be appointed and made arrangements through the government for a permanent body of them to be set up in 1858. See Norman, *The English Church in the Nineteenth Century*, pp. 184–6.

16 Obituary, *The Tablet*, 15 June 1946. As a senior chaplain his title would have been 'Senior Chaplain to the Forces' – so he would have been described as 'SCF'. General Smuts commanded the South African Forces in East Africa in 1916–17 in his drive to eject the Germans from German East Africa. In 1935 at the age of 65 James Dey was appointed Bishop-in-Ordinary for Catholics in all branches of the Forces. He served in this office throughout the Second World War and died a year after it ended at the age of 76 in 1946. See also Chapter 16.

17 *The Tablet*, 15 August 1914.

18 'Monsignor Parkinson Rector of the Birmingham Diocesan Seminary'. *The Oscotian*, 3rd Series, 22, no. 66 (Autumn 1922), p. 181. See also Judith Champ's *Oscott*, pp. 23–4.

19 Southwark, Ilsley to Amigo, 3 February 1916. Barry describes such raids 'as the War was drawing to a close'. Barry, pp. 274–5, 250.

20 *Ibid.*, Letter from Ilsley to Amigo, 8 March 1916.

21 *Ibid.*, Ilsley to Amigo, 24 March 1916.

22 B.A., Letter from Bishop Amigo to Archbishop Ilsley, 27 April 1914.

23 D.B., p. 24. Also *The Birmingham Mail*, 26 December 1926, and Obituary, *The Oscotian* (1926), p. 196.

24 *Birmingham Catholic Directory*, 1927, Obituary Notice.

25 Southwark, Letter from Ilsley to Amigo, 6 September 1916. Incident recorded in the 'Provincial & Diocesan notes'.

26 McIntyre Obituary, p. 5.

27 *Ibid.*, pp. 11–12: 'It seems Bishop Bourne was none too popular with his Chapter.' Also Oldmeadow, pp. 235–7.

28 Southwark, Letter from McIntyre to Amigo, 9 February 1917, from the Collegio Inglese, Roma.

29 Letter from Pope Benedict XV to Cardinal Bourne, 22 March 1917.

30 Oldmeadow, Cardinal Bourne's letter to Archbishop Ilsley, March 1917, vol. ii, p. 86.

31 Southwark, Letter from Ilsley to Amigo, Good Friday 1917.

32 Oldmeadow, vol. ii, p. 87.

33 Letters of Archbishop Ilsley and Bishop Amigo, June, July and August 1917. McIntyre was promoted Archbishop of Oxyrhinchus.

34 *The Oscotian*, 22 December 1917. More than 20 million died world-wide – more than those killed in the whole of World War I.

35   Beck, p. 423. Also, Cecil Woodham-Smith, *The Great Hunger* (New English Library, London, 1974), p. 202.

36   B.A., Synod, *anno* 1900.

37   Oulton Abbey Archives, Stone. Letter from Archbishop Ilsley to the Abbess of Stone, Dame Laurentia Ward, 11 November 1918.

38   A meeting called by the League of Nations Union on 25 October 1921. *The Oscotian*, 3rd Series, 21/3, no. 63 (Autumn 1921). Also, *The Birmingham Post*, 26 October 1921.

CHAPTER NINETEEN

# *Besford Court*

## A Home for Mentally Handicapped Children

In 1915 the Archbishop planned to set up a central home for mentally handicapped children. The idea came from Father Hudson, who, seeing the need for special education among some of the children admitted into his homes, persuaded Father Thomas Newsome, then 35, to take on the work in a new home that would be modelled on much that was already in use at Coleshill. Father Newsome was ordained in 1905 after training at Oscott, and had recently been in charge of a mission at Chasetown, in Wallsall. After the bringing in of the Mental Deficiency Act of 1913, and with the return of some of the men from the war front who were disturbed in their minds, the mentally ill were treated with more sympathy generally as individuals with certain rights, and came under medical care, instead of being shut away and tending to be forgotten, as they often were formerly. Under this Act suitable education had to be provided for the less able children and at this time about two hundred children in the diocese came under this requirement.

Archbishop Ilsley chose an ideal property for his purpose which was set out in the Worcestershire countryside. It consisted of an ancient Tudor manor house with outbuildings, which had once been part of the neighbouring abbey of Pershore. Adjacent to this was the shell of another building, reminiscent of one of the old colleges in a university town, as it was designed to stand round an open court. This building, called 'Besford Court', had been left in an unfinished state by the previous owner, Sir George Noble. The rooms were spacious, and had the potential to provide airy dormitories, a large refectory and the type of classrooms needed for such an establishment. So the Archbishop arranged for work to begin to put it in order, and although the alterations were not fully completed by then, the home was opened on 1 October 1917.

Father Newsome was appointed administrator, and it is interesting to observe how Ilsley guided and helped him by making suggestions to him on various matters, particularly when the scheme was first being launched. This watchfulness continued over the years, not so much through any reluctance on Ilsley's part to delegate final authority, as through Newsome's need for advice and support, which he sought from George Hudson as well. The buildings were surrounded by well laid out grounds, beyond which stretched several acres of farmland, and Father Hudson's father, Charles Hudson, moved there at this time. He was appointed to the board of management and undertook control of the estate and the farm,[1] and in this ideal environment the children were able to learn naturally about their surroundings. They were looked after by the Sisters of Charity of St Paul, the same order as those who worked under Father Hudson at Coleshill. In one of his letters to Father Newsome, written in February 1918, Ilsley shows a sensitive understanding of just how these children needed to be treated by his helpers, if any positive relationship between adult and child was to be established: 'I have written to Mother General what I told you I would, about the need of some of the sisters being trained: the necessity for winning by unstinted kindness the affection and confidence of the children; no punishing or threatening or harsh words,' he wrote.[2] The first headmistress was Sister Philip Neri, and her staff were later specially trained for the work.

The Home was placed under the patronage of 'Sister Theresa, the Little Flower of Jesus', who was canonized in 1925. Ten years before this, in August 1915, Edward Ilsley was encouraging Newsome – 'The Novena you are promoting to obtain the Beatification of the Carmelite Nun known as Sister Theresa of the Infant Jesus has my hearty approval. If you can help make this servant of God better known to our people you will be doing a service to religion for which we will be ever grateful. She lived her short life, and died in an odour of sanctity ... so may we hope that with the sanction and encouragement of the Holy See the odour of her life and virtues may be diffused throughout the world to the edification and profit of thousands of souls.'

An interesting illustrated booklet brought out in 1916, so aptly called *Gather up the Fragments*, with the subtitle *The Besford Book for 1916*, was produced by Father Newsome to help lodge an appeal towards the building fund. William Barry wrote the prologue, and contributions made by Father Rickaby SJ, Hilaire Belloc, Sir Bertram Windle and Father Bernard Vaughan give a valuable insight into the initial stages of the task in hand. Line drawings signed 'E. Coffin', accompany descriptions given by Thomas Newsome of the fine buildings and how they were being completed. He also gives an outline of the work to be undertaken on behalf of the handicapped children in an article entitled 'A Great Catholic Charity'.

## Mounting Costs at Besford Court

Costs had mounted considerably by the time the opening of the home was approaching in 1917, particularly as Besford was an independent venture on the part of the Archbishop, with no established funds to draw upon. He was only too aware of the situation, but was optimistic in a letter to Father Newsome when he mentioned that 'The initial outlay required to satisfy the demands of the Government has been considerable, I may say enormous. But once we have established it, the burden of maintenance will be comparatively light thanks to the generous assistance afforded from public funds.'[3] Keeping a practised eye on things at this stage, he advised Newsome, on 18 March 1916, how to proceed carefully and with consummate tact: 'Let me repeat the caution I gave you not to publish nor speak about the amount of our liabilities. To do so would shock people and alienate their sympathy and support, because of the recklessness of our expenditure.' Apparently some £10,000 had already been borrowed, and a further £8,000 was required to finish the work, but the need was there as far as Ilsley was concerned and it must be met. He looked for support among wealthy patrons, and told Newsome he had written to Madame de Navarro, who lived in the district and was wife of the papal chamberlain, Tony de Navarro. He said he had told her about the work in progress – 'She will speak of it to the leading people of the neighbourhood and get you friends to interest themselves in your work,'[4] he wrote.

Ilsley did not solely concern himself with financial matters, but devoted his interest to every aspect of life surrounding the little community at Besford Court. On 26 February 1918 he wrote to Father Newsome, displaying his ever-watchful eye for detail: 'As I was coming along in the train yesterday I observed orchards in which the fruit trees had their trunks coated with lime. I thought it might be as serviceable for your trees as for these in preserving them from blight.' Characteristically, he was taking time and trouble to help Newsome with advice on all levels. He always took a particular interest in people's state of health, and throughout his correspondence with him

Ilsley showed particular concern for Newsome's physical and mental well-being, from the small footnote at the end of a letter in August 1915 saying, 'Don't forget the warning I gave you about overwork,' to the use of helpful maxims a year later which hold good for all time: 'Dr Ullathorne was very insistent on our repressing overeagerness in business of all kinds, especially in matters concerning the spiritual life – doing everything with due deliberation. Make not haste in time of clouds (Eccles. ii. 2). Wait till the light comes. Second thoughts are often better than the first. Take counsel with the wise. "*Festina Lente*" must be your motto.'[5]

## Newsome's Difficulties

A letter from Thomas Newsome to the Archbishop, written on 2 December 1917, a month after the opening of the home, gives a picture of how things were for him at that time. He was having difficulties to do with the contractor, a man named Grant, who was employed to complete the building of Besford Court. He had overcharged for his work, and when he did not receive the full payment he asked for, had taken to spreading rumours locally against Newsome and his management of the Court. Among other things, he made accusations that the farm animals were being neglected, that servants would not stay, and that his workmen had been plied with drink. What was more serious was that Grant questioned Newsome's methods of fundraising, and some of the man's associates had also become involved; the stories had spread to members of the Birmingham Catenian Association and the local council, and so the matter had soon got quite out of hand. In his letter to Ilsley, Newsome listed all the various duties he had been called upon to carry out in his present capacity, such as the administration of the estate, his efforts at fundraising, the training of staff, as well as his office as chaplain to the nuns, all of which he claimed to be 'the work of several men'. He told Ilsley that through the effort of dealing with this extra burden to do with the contractor, he was now 'in the hands of a doctor who was anxious to avert a nervous breakdown'.

Ilsley replied the following day, 'You quite understand that I may not anticipate judgement before completing such enquiry as is called for in the painful circumstances.' He continued with obvious concern: 'I cannot forbear telling you that my feeling is one of deep sorrow after what you have disclosed to me that you should have been subjected to such an ordeal, & of admiration for the marvellous way you have

Figure 19.1 *Thomas Newsome standing outside the stables at Besford Court.*
*Birmingham Archdiocesan Archives.*

borne up under it … It will be my duty to vindicate you after the odious charges with which you have been assailed.' The matter was taken up by Canon Villiers and Father Hudson, and they discovered no foundation for what had been said. 'I have many faults,' Thomas Newsome said later, 'but he has not hit on the right ones, and I am able to meet all the accusations with either complete denial, or else an explanation which will show that in these respects there is nothing worthy of condemnation.'

The chapter at this time consisted of the Provost James O'Hanlon, who was also Vicar General, Henry Parkinson, Michael Glancey, Edward Hymers, Charles Wheatley, Joseph Robinson, John Caswell, William Barry, Walter Hanley and James Keating. Alarmed by the recent gossip and the rumours they heard that were circulating in the diocese, they sent Ilsley a memorandum on 8 November 1917 requesting a full clarification of the financial affairs to do with Besford Court.[6]

## The Chapter Sends Ilsley a Memorandum

The main charge in their memorandum was that the Archbishop had embarked on a considerable undertaking such as Besford Court without previous consultation with his chapter. The document stated: 'Canon Law clearly lays down that a bishop may neither undertake nor decide upon any work *gravis momenti, inconsulto capitulo*.' They went on to say that Besford Court was a matter of *gravis momenti* and that although two-and a-half years had passed since the decision was taken, they were 'still groping in the dark for such information as it seeks'.

It would seem that although Ilsley was initially under this grave obligation to consult the chapter, that obligation became still graver 'when the work was perceived to be largely exceeding in scope and cost anything originally contemplated'. They also complained that instead of taking counsel with his *consiliarii nati*, he had allowed the control to pass into the hands of men who were 'for the most part untried, not known to be steady or safe and in whom neither clergy nor laity have confidence'.

They mentioned that Ilsley had sent out an appeal to the clergy asking for the sum of £20,000 to be raised, and then later in a circular to the general public the amount was given as 'some £25,000'. They feared that any failure to repay the annual instalments on these large sums would involve the diocese in coming to the rescue – 'In this view the Chapter agrees, and therefore respectfully asks His Grace to institute an enquiry by a Catholic chartered accountant into the funds and liabilities of Besford Court.' It would seem that Ilsley had gone about setting-up Besford Court as though it was almost a private venture, but at the same time it was being carried out in the name of the diocese, so his chapter were more than justified in calling for this inquiry.

The matter did not end there as the chapter did not see eye-to eye with the Archbishop about the home being open to children of all denominations. Ilsley had taken this path, to stretch out a helping hand to all concerned, as there was so little special help of this kind generally available. He also saw it as a way of ensuring financial support on a broader basis as far as the local council authorities were concerned. The chapter said in their memorandum that they considered 'this abandonment of Catholic principle unnecessary and uncalled for', and they felt it meant abandoning the Catholic character of the school. This was of course not true, as the home was to be set up solely as a Catholic establishment.

Three days after receiving the memorandum, Ilsley wrote to Canon Wheatley telling him: 'It may interest you and the Chapter to know that as soon as it came home to me that people were talking unfavourably about B. Court I instituted an inquiry and asked Mr King to look into accounts and report to me about them and the financial situation – When the report has been handed in I hope we shall find it all satisfactory.'[7]

On 6 December after having an interview with his chapter, Ilsley sent a copy of the notes of this interview to Canon Wheatley, which began: 'Referring to the Memorandum of 6th Novr. His Grace said that with regard to the main charge he had no defence to offer.' He continued, 'At the same time it was only fair to say in extenuation that as no diocesan money was being sunk in the scheme, not even for the initial outlay on the purchase of the estate, he was perhaps on that account the less sensitive as to the obligation of consulting the Chapter.' In his recording of these notes he attempted to prove to them that he had not lost his touch but had handled the undertaking in his usual businesslike way.

## An Over-Ambitious Scheme

But in spite of Ilsley's seeming optimism over the outcome of the financial inquiry, the auditors' accounts and detailed report drawn up by Mr King, which he had ready for the chapter meeting in March

1918, did not go in the Bishop's favour. In his final statement King gave the total sum borrowed for setting-up Besford Court as £22,000, and his summary of the situation was: 'The Diocese has been uncanonically committed to an undertaking of a magnitude and costliness quite uncalled for ... a large capital debt has been contracted and a heavy annual maintenance charge must be faced.' But King's final words, 'Thus diocesan money though not actually sunk, stands imperilled,' although forbidding, certainly bear out Ilsley's previous argument that he had not actually sunk diocesan money in the scheme and therefore the situation was viable. The history of Besford Court over the past eighty years bears testimony to Edward Ilsley's courage and undoubted vision when embarking on what was then quite rightly described as an over-ambitious scheme.

Having received Mr King's report the chapter communicated to Ilsley again after their meeting on 5 March 1918. They said that they could not 'in conscience pass over the violation of the obligation to consult them in a matter of such magnitude', with the added complaint, 'especially as this is not the first time'. They asked him therefore to submit to them any further consideration that might obviate the necessity of laying the matter before the Holy See. They were in fact requesting positive proof from Ilsley that the interests of the diocese were safe in his hands.

Accordingly, on the following day Ilsley wrote to Wheatley, 'I have a feeling that the Chapter has been under a misapprehension as to the facts connected with the history and financial state of Besford Court. And I have asked a Priest in whose experience and judgement the Chapter will have confidence, to draw up for me a sound, impartial and businesslike statement. That statement I now offer for the consideration of the Chapter; and I trust it will reassure them.' The priest Ilsley mentioned was George Hudson, and he replied to Ilsley's request a month later on 5 April: 'I send you my notes re Besford Court,' he wrote. 'I have arranged them under definite headings so that your Grace and those seeing them would pick out what they require. I can give fuller information on any point should it be wanted.'

## George Hudson's Assistance

George Hudson's notes were set out in a clear and concise manner. He dealt first with the need for such a home and went on to describe how the purchase of the property had come about in January 1914 because 'an endeavour was made to find a suitable house to serve as a Home for Mentally Defective Catholic Children'. He then outlined his negotiations for the purchase of the Court with its 54 acres of gardens and additional farmland and said that although £30,000 had recently been spent on the property by the owner, and it was originally offered for sale at £8,000 by the auctioneers, the sum of £6,077 was the final agreed purchase price.

He continued: 'The building as bought was merely an empty shell,' and he then went into the details of what had been required for its completion, the whole sum, including the cost of the original purchase, amounting to £28,841. His letter was courageous and showed he had no wish to hide anything. In loyal support of Ilsley he said, 'The whole of the arrangements for completion were left in my hands', and added, 'I am alone responsible for the decision as to what works should be done for completion, and as to the manner in which they should be carried out.' He concluded, 'I consider this to be a very low cost for an Institution completed in war time.'

In his final paragraph George Hudson faced up to the criticism of the chapter regarding the home's acceptance of non-Catholic children by pointing out that the same policy was approved by the Cardinal-Archbishop for the special residential schools in his own Diocese of Westminster – and he added, 'At present there are only three – two sent by Local Authorities and the third by a Protestant gentleman who is a subscriber to the Home.'

At their next meeting on 4 June the chapter appeared to have toned down their approach, saying, 'it was resolved that the Chapter should not pursue the matter of Besford Court or make it the subject of an appeal to Rome'. Nevertheless, one thing seemed to have led to another, and some among them must have felt that the time had come for the Archbishop to leave the scene. At the same meeting it was resolved that a report should be drawn up by Canons William Barry, Charles Wheatley and Henry Parkinson stating reasons for and against the advisability of recommending His Grace the Archbishop to resign, to be presented at the following meeting on 2 July.

They commenced the report by listing the many positions Edward Ilsley had held over the years and enumerating his honours and distinctions, including the fact that he was now in his eighty-first year and was the oldest bishop in the English hierarchy.

They continued: 'The Holy See is accustomed to treat aged prelates very tenderly, as the spirit of religion demands.' They then acknowledged that as the Archbishop had an auxiliary of his own choosing, the Holy See had provided for him all that the clergy and laity could ask. They also had to admit that although Archbishop McIntyre had rare qualities, 'he was not formed to be an administrator', so there was even some doubt as to whether his succession would bring an improvement in this respect. They also had to acknowledge that the proposal that he should resign would surely seem to Archbishop Ilsley 'wanting in kindness and courtesy from a Chapter which is altogether his own creation'.

'Thus far some of the reasons against action.' They now began to deal with the other side of the question by pointing out that the metropolitan chapter 'has duties towards the Diocese and the Province. It ought not to shirk them in deference to personal consideration.' Then came the rather momentous statement reminiscent of Ilsley's earlier days, that it must be borne in mind that: 'The Bishop is for the Church, not the Church for the Bishop.' They said that revision and reconstruction were imperative, but after listing a number 'of matters of prime importance' needing urgent consideration, they seemed to retreat a little, saying that certain reforms could well wait, and 'the lead of the Metropolitan may wait; the other Bishops of the Province do not seem to want any interference'. They also questioned, 'Besides what were the other Provinces doing?'

## McIntyre Appointed Vicar General 1918

Their final conclusion was that, 'taking the whole of these considerations into account, the present writers would not advise a proposal in terms that His Grace should be called upon to resign'. They suggested the best solution to a number of their present problems lay in the hope of the appointment of a young and vigorous man as Vicar General, 'to whom the office should be entrusted without restriction', and they finished the report by cautiously suggesting that 'If the Archbishop intimated any thought of resigning himself, it might well be encouraged in a respectful way'. The following year, in 1918, McIntyre was appointed Vicar General to assist James O'Hanlon, who was then aged 78 and had failing sight. This situation continued until O'Hanlon died in 1921. When McIntyre became Archbishop in Ilsley's place the following year, instead of appointing someone 'young and vigorous' to be Vicar General as had been suggested four years earlier, Michael Glancey took over from him at the age of 67 and he was also appointed Provost in 1923. Thus the action on this occasion taken by his chapter would seem to have amounted to a reprimand mingled with kindness, and a solemn warning for the future. Although the Archbishop's spending was undoubtedly excessive, it did not appear to have hindered the future progress of the undertaking in any way!

Newsome was 37 in 1917, and George Hudson 44. There were times when Ilsley appeared to be particularly concerned over Newsome's state of mind and general health. In June 1918 he wrote, 'I was hoping you would be able to send us a more favourable report of your progress. But Abp. McIntyre is strongly of the opinion that things will go better as soon as you are able to occupy yourself with congenial business – a life of inaction is not what you are accustomed to and it is depressing you.' It would seem, from Newsome's correspondence, that he worked fairly closely with Father Hudson and followed his ideas in the general running of Besford, with 'certain modifications which naturally arise from the nature of the institution'.[8] His work never appeared easy for him, and three years later on 27 February 1920 he was again writing to Ilsley: 'The work of the last six months has been very strenuous and I should have taken a rest before. Consequently, I had on Sexagesima Sunday a rather silly breakdown in health, but from which I have now nearly entirely recovered. For the time being I am working only up to luncheon and am spending the afternoons digging in the garden and in simple forms of exercise.'

## Neville Chamberlain Supports Besford

There may have been some thought in the Archbishop's mind at times of the need to relieve Thomas Newsome of the considerable task he had in hand, but his advice to him was always to take things at a steadier pace, and the trust must have been there on Ilsley's part, and the belief that Newsome could carry things through, in spite of these setbacks. As it happened Newsome brought the work successfully forward, for a period of twenty years altogether, until his retirement in 1933. He saw the work at Besford Court as representing 'a centre for information and research upon the whole question of the treatment of the feeble minded. A new and modern department of national work – the first great Home founded after the passing of the Mental Deficiency Act. Above all,' he wrote, 'they will cease to be the butts of ridicule, or the objects of deplorable neglect.' Neville Chamberlain, the younger son of Joseph Chamberlain, was a notable non-Catholic politician who gave his support to Besford, and Archbishop Ilsley joined him there, in September 1918, when he gave out the prizes to the children.

Right up until two years before he died in 1926, Ilsley continued writing personally to Thomas Newsome. One of the last letters he wrote to him in February 1923 opened with this simple statement: 'There will be great rejoicing today in Rome & in countless places of the whole world on the occasion of the Beatification of the Little Flower.' His final message was written on a small postcard on 15 February 1924, 'A short visit such as you propose will be very delightful. Meantime may God preserve you and the Court from all harm.' His prayers were answered. Like his many other undertakings, so soundly established at the initial stages, Besford Court continued to progress for the following eighty years, always taking a lead in its field. One of its main aims was in rebuilding the lives of those in its care, in order to provide a better future for them. Unfortunately, through financial cuts, the school had to be closed on 31 August 1996.

## Notes

1   Details about the life of George Hudson's father Charles, and his work at Besford Court, are given by Sylvia Pinches, in *Father Hudson and His Society*, p. 3.
2   O.C.A., Letter from Archbishop Ilsley to Father Newsome, 26 February 1918.
3   Letter printed in Thomas Newsome, *Gather Up the Fragments: The Besford Court Book for 1916*. Board of Education standards had to be met.
4   O.C.A., Letter from Ilsley to Newsome, 6 May 1915.
5   *Ibid.*, Letters from Ilsley to Newsome, 15 August 1916 and 27 September 1916.
6   B.A., Document no. 197 Besford Court papers.
7   *Ibid.*, Letter from Ilsley to Canon Wheatley, 11 November 1917. Mr King was an accountant working for the firm of Bates Neal & Co., 110 Edmund Street, Birmingham.
8   Letter from Ilsley to Newsome, 15 July 1916.

## CHAPTER TWENTY

# *Retirement*

## The Feast of St Chad

A new calendar came into force for the Archdiocese of Birmingham during the war years in 1916, and among the local feasts restored was that of the Translation of St Chad, which was appointed to be held on the fifth Sunday after Easter. From then on the relics of the saint, who died on 2 March 672, were carried in procession round the cathedral during the evening service. On the first occasion in 1916, Father Docherty, who was one of the cathedral clergy from 1912 to 1917, expressed the hope that when peace returned there would once more be an annual pilgrimage to the cathedral on that special day, just as there had been at Lichfield in pre-Reformation times.

The festival originally took place at the cathedral shrine of St Chad at Lichfield in the early fifteenth century, where the relics of the saint were revered by the people as being among its chief treasures. With the coming of the Reformation they were removed from the cathedral for safe keeping, and after passing through several hands, were lost sight of after 1790. On being rediscovered in 1839 under the altar in the chapel at Aston Hall, they were investigated there and identified as those of St Chad by Bishop Walsh and his coadjutor Bishop Wiseman. Wiseman then solemnly translated them to Oscott and placed them for veneration in the choir of the college chapel.

Having obtained permission from Pope Gregory to expose the relics for public veneration, Bishop Walsh had them taken, on 20 June 1841, to the newly built cathedral in Birmingham, standing on the site of a former chapel dedicated to St Chad. Here they were placed in an oak casket before the Lady Altar, and a vigil was kept by members of the Holy Guild of St Chad, a confraternity that had been founded the previous year. During the consecration ceremony which took place the following day, the relics, now placed in a new gilded outer-casket,

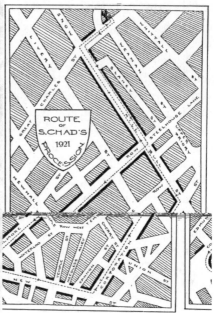

Figure 20.1 *Souvenir programme cover of the first procession of St Chad. Archdiocesan Archives.*

Figure 20.2 *Published route of the procession of St Chad, 1921. Birmingham Archdiocesan Archives.*

Figure 20.3 *The gilded casket containing the relics of St Chad being carried in the procession in 1920. Drawing made from a photograph in* The Birmingham Post.

Figure 20.4 *Archbishop Ilsley walking in the procession of St Chad.* The Universe, *14 May 1920.*

were carried out of the west door and returned in procession into the cathedral, where their final resting-place was on top of the stone reredos above the high altar.[1]

During the two years following the restoration of the feast, the numbers of people attracted to the evening service for its celebration had increased to such an extent that the procession had difficulty in moving round inside the cathedral. In 1919, with the war ended, a decision was made by Archbishop Ilsley, then in his eighty-second year, that the procession inside the cathedral would join a larger one outside presented by the people themselves. This would then move along some of the streets in the vicinity, thus giving the opportunity to many more worshippers to venerate the relics and to receive the Archbishop's blessing. In this way the annual pilgrimage was restored and the final links were forged with the ancient festival of the saint dating back to pre-Reformation times.

The festival began with the exposing of the relics inside St Chad's by the Archbishop, who then celebrated Pontifical High Mass at 11am. The assistant priest was Canon Wheatley, and Archbishop McIntyre was present in the sanctuary. The Archbishop and the officiating clergy wore the vestments presented to him on his golden jubilee. As the relics were exposed for veneration 'they were guarded in relays by members of the Catholic Young Men's Society' from the conclusion of the service until vespers were sung at six o'clock.[2] Meanwhile a luncheon was held at Archbishop's House for the clergy and special guests.

## The Procession

At the end of vespers at 6.30pm, a procession was seen to emerge from the cathedral led by the crossbearer, the Revd P. Styche, followed by the thurifer, to join a larger procession that had formed itself outside in readiness to pass through the streets in the surrounding area. Many of the children were from nearby parishes. First came the youngest ones wearing garlands of spring flowers, then the older children, who presented a series of tableaux, each mounted on a lorry and depicting the life of the child Jesus. 'My youngest brother Joseph was the child Jesus in the carpenter's shop,' one of them wrote in later years. 'A young man in the parish was St Joseph, and Our Lady was one of the teachers in St Chad's Infant School.'[3] The cathedral choir, the students from Oscott College, and the church unions and confraternities followed, bringing the numbers of men, women and children up to at least a thousand. The 'kaleidoscopic display of colour' they presented as they passed by was described afterwards by the onlookers, who said how much the unmistakable devotional fervour of all those taking part had impressed itself on them. The pavements were crowded with people lining the whole route as the procession moved through Bath Street into Whittall Street, proceeding down Steelhouse Lane and turning into Snow Hill. Even those who came purely for the spectacle found themselves drawn by admiration and respect for what they were witnessing.

The most solemn part of the procession now came into view. The gilded casket, in which were enshrined the precious relics of St Chad, was borne aloft on a wooden carrier, hung with a richly embroidered cover, the supports at each end resting on the shoulders of four students from Oscott College in major orders, moving slowly forward past the waiting crowds. The bearers were Louis Maxwell, Joseph Dunne, Edward McHugh and Patrick Moore. *The Universe* gave a graphic description of the scene: 'and so the whole sinuous line, in the mellow radiance of the evening sun, wound its way along some of the principal streets in the vicinity of the Cathedral ... And now came into view the stately figure of the successor of St Chad, wearing his richly ornamented mitre and cope – the picturesque centre of a picturesque pageant, the cynosure of all the eyes of the vast crowds that lined the route six deep, receiving the affectionate homage of his people ... It was a touching sight as the aged prelate bestowed the episcopal blessing, to see the crowds of the faithful fall to their knees and rise again as he passed along, so that surveying the procession from the top of Snow Hill, it looked like a river of colour flowing slowly between the banks, which seemed to rise and fall with almost rhythmical precision.'[4] When the procession returned to the cathedral, it filled once more to overflowing, and Pontifical Benediction brought the festival to a close.

The following year, in 1920, the Catholic Young Men's Society planned a more ambitious route leading right into the heart of the city, but it had to be changed at short notice from the one published because several road repairs were being done. They now had to go down Weaman Street instead of using Snow Hill, and then they passed through Upper Priory into Corporation Street, and after moving past the town hall they continued along New Street, going round Victoria Square and into Colmore Row. Here again they left the planned itinerary by turning into Church Street, and from there finally made their way back to the cathedral.[5]

Because of the added length to the route, Edward Ilsley had been cautioned by his doctor not to walk the full length of it. But characteristically he decided to ignore this advice, and knowing what his presence in the procession meant to the people, went ahead on foot as planned. Somewhere, well in the background, a car moved slowly forward, as those responsible were taking precautions lest the strain of the day's events should prove too great for their Archbishop. But fortunately it was not needed, and the account in *The Universe* mentioned that on returning he 'showed no obvious sign of fatigue'.

## Resignation of the Archbishop 1921

Thousands took part that day, many coming from parishes outside the city – notably Lichfield. Those who were unable to get inside the cathedral for the final part of the service followed it outside, where it was relayed to them by wireless loudspeaker. But it was to be the Archbishop's last procession, because eight months later on 18 January 1921, when he was 82, he sent a letter to the clergy of the diocese announcing his resignation. It ran, 'No-one will be surprised to receive the announcement I have now to make. After due consideration and consultation, I felt it my duty owing to my increasing infirmities, to beg the Holy See to accept my resignation of this important diocese.'[6] It was to be read in all the churches on the following Sunday, and even if it contained no great element of surprise, many people would have been touched with a sense of sadness at the news. Father Samuel Myerscough expressed the same feelings when he later wrote: 'Through the long years of our childhood, and on to adolescence and manhood, he was always "the Bishop", the revered supreme spiritual authority ... There are tens of thousands who as long as they live, will cherish the pleasant recollections of their venerable father in God, through their personal contact with him on some occasion and the gentle dignity of his manner when among them.'[7]

Ilsley wrote to Bishop Amigo on 10 January, 'My eye has just caught the statement in *The Tablet* that you have gone to Rome. You will probably be hearing news about me, and you will wonder why, as your friend, I did not consult you before taking the step you will have heard of. It seemed to me that I had indication enough that it was God's will I should retire, in the simple fact that my health was not restored.' 'His retirement', Mgr T. E. Bird later explained, 'was due to loss of memory at the laying of the foundation stone of the new church of the Sacred

Heart at Aston; he did not know where he was or what it was all about; so he decided to ask the Holy See to accept his resignation.'[8]

Michael Glancey wrote to Bishop Amigo in Rome a fortnight later on 23 January, in his usual inimitable style, on notepaper with an engraving of St Michael on the heading. His habit of wrapping up important matters in an almost facetious manner is apparent here: 'You will doubtless have heard that the Great Renunciation has come at last. As an experienced meteorologist could you give us some idea which way the wind is blowing? Or about to blow? Is there any evidence of a gale from the West ... or an anti-cyclone from S. W.? We hope you are staying in Rome till the gale blows over, to protect Birmingham from being wrecked. If you are not able to stay, can you suggest someone in Rome to look after our interests?'[9] He was anxious that Birmingham should be kept on an even keel at this time, being only too aware that Cardinal Bourne might try to use the present opportunity to take an advantage for himself by personally influencing the choice of a future archbishop for the province.

As the Archbishop of Liverpool lay seriously ill, Amigo's fears over the present situation had been foremost in his mind for some time, and when the news of Archbishop Whiteside's death came through on 28 January he wrote to Glancey: 'H. E. never had such a good chance as now when Birmingham and Liverpool are vacant.' It seemed things were hanging on a knife-edge. The question of whether he himself might be appointed to either Liverpool or Birmingham was actually being debated in Rome. If Amigo could have been persuaded to leave Southwark his absence would have greatly assisted Cardinal Bourne in bringing in some of his schemes. One of these included the setting-up of the Brighton vicariate in the southern section, which would have absorbed a large part of the Southwark diocese. But Amigo knew the value of working with the priests with whom he was familiar in his own diocese, and had no wish to be moved into a different situation where he would be considered 'a complete outsider'. He also knew that Southwark was not yet ready for any such changes to be made, and that any moves in this direction would be premature.[10]

## Amigo Preserves Boundaries

Once more Amigo managed to ward off any immediate changes by giving detailed reasons to Rome why the scheme was unsuitable at the time because there was insufficient population growth in his diocese.

As Frederick William Keating was translated to Liverpool in the June of that year Amigo was able to hold on to his position in his own diocese, and also helped to preserve the situation for Birmingham. This he continued to do until after Archbishop Bourne died fourteen years later. He notified Glancey, who was liaising with him at this time, that there had been a recent suggestion 'to take off Oxfordshire'. 'It comes from a desire of a certain eminent person to have two universities in his Province. A letter which I sent to Cardinal de Lai will probably dispose of this absurd proposal.'[11] He also said that the Bishop of Cardiff, who would be in Rome for some time, had undertaken to keep Glancey informed until things were more settled.

Ilsley wrote to Bishop Amigo on 25 February with sad news: 'I have lost my dear old Provost O'Hanlon & best friend & support all through my life – R. I. P. but I must not grudge him a day of his reward.' Ilsley himself had been too ill to attend the funeral in the cathedral, at which Archbishop McIntyre preached the panegyric. Writing to Amigo three months later, on 7 June, Ilsley said, 'The death of Mgr. O'Hanlon was a great blow to me, although for months he was blind – The poor man dared not face the ordeal of an operation for it – He tried very hard to dissuade me from resigning – and when I did he lamented grievously – but he did share the burden of the work most loyally as long as he had any strength in him.' James O'Hanlon and John McIntyre were both vicars general, and they had worked together since the year after McIntyre's return from Rome in 1917.

Archbishop Ilsley gave a final word to his people in his Mid-Lent Pastoral, thanking them for their unfailing kindness and loyalty. This was to be his last message of this kind, and he allowed himself to deviate a little, 'And now, dear brethren in Christ, perhaps I may be allowed to make a personal reference. When on December 4th 1879 I received episcopal consecration at the hands of the then Bishop of the diocese, the Right Reverend William Bernard Ullathorne, that venerable prelate, and the assembled company expressed to me a hope and wish that I might carry on the work of my episcopate till the end of the century. We were then twenty-one years from the end of the century, and my work has continued for twenty-one years beyond.' Ilsley was now in the sixtieth year of his priesthood, and had been caring for the diocese for the past forty-two years as bishop and archbishop.

The impression given by Father Patrick O'Toole in his memoir of Ilsley as 'Diocesan Bishop' was that he was a reserved man, disliking 'the limelight', particularly on public platforms. The main reason for this was that Ilsley felt such occasions often lacked sincerity. But it was equally said of him in the local publication *Birmingham Faces and Places*,[12] two years after he became bishop of the diocese: 'Like many of the Catholic dignitaries of the present day, he takes a great interest in the social life of the people, not only of his own community, but of the people generally, and he is always willing to take part in those local functions which mark the public life of Birmingham and other populous places of the Diocese.' When the further observation is added to this that 'his was a great personality in those quiet and useful circles where educational and social questions were prominently dis-cussed in the interest of the working classes',[13] a clearer view of him comes into focus of how he liked to spend his time profitably for the good of his people. This last observation was of course referring to the time he was always willing to give to the committees looking after the interests of poor and destitute children. Drawing on his considerable reserves of energy he would urgently follow up whatever had been discussed, seeing to it that the necessary changes were set in motion to help to improve their lives.

He wrote to Bishop Amigo in April 1921, regretting he would be unable to be with his fellow bishops at Westminster during the Low Week meeting, because he was still unwell. His letter shows that even though he may have been retiring by nature, avoiding ostentation, he always sought to keep contact with his friends: 'It was kind of you to write to me after the Low Week meeting that I had the sympathy of the Bishops to cheer me in my loneliness. One could not but feel out in the cold on the recurrence of the annual meeting in which I could not take part.' These were the words of a man missing the company of his friends and associates, at what would have been his last official meeting at Westminster, rather than one who was in any way distant or stand-offish in his personal disposition.[14]

Canon Toplass explained that Ilsley's outstanding virtue was his genuine humility. This came about, he said, through a very complete awareness of his own limitations and his relative unimportance in God's scheme of things. 'He was, in consequence obedient and ever willing to pursue a task which he clearly understood to be the will of God.' This, he said, made him appear to be almost a contradictory character because although he was basically gentle and unpretentious (and even hesitant in his speech at times), he would at the same time work with unswerving strength of will and determination to carry any task in hand through to the end, 'no matter how difficult the com-pletion', once he was convinced of its 'Divine sanction'.[15]

## McIntyre to Succeed Ilsley

In early May 1921 the news came through from Rome that Archbishop McIntyre was appointed to succeed Edward Ilsley as the new Archbishop of Birmingham. A letter McIntyre wrote to Bishop Amigo on 6 May gives a very clear indication of how Ilsley felt on hearing the news: 'I am struggling to answer a mass of felicitative messages, of which, to my surprise, a large amount has come from London. I cannot answer your warm and friendly letter in the same brief fashion as that in which I am compelled to reply to most. Yesterday I went over to Oscott to see the Archbishop. (By the way, his telegram of congratulation was the very first message that reached me.) He was beaming and seemed to have grown suddenly younger. He had been oppressed by the fear that a stranger might have been set over us; but now his anxiety is at an end, and he feels that he has an unquestioned home in Oscott. His delicate sensitiveness would have made him feel as though his possession of the *Episcopium* at Oscott were an intrusion and he would never have been at ease with a stranger at the head of the diocese.'[16] John McIntyre's letter goes back to Bishop Ullathorne's concept of life at the seminary being 'a common life and a family life' – the way Ilsley had always lived at Oscott – but there had obviously been decided reservations in Ilsley's mind that his time there could have come to an abrupt end.

McIntyre went on to say that 'the Chapter has a number of capable and friendly men who will be a great support'. This was a picture of a situation that had prevailed in Birmingham over the years, in many ways this closeness had always remained among them. McIntyre had an excellent group of men to help him, with Michael Glancey appointed as Provost and Vicar General, Charles Cronin and Francis de Capitain, and the other members of his chapter, which included Henry Parkinson, William Barry, Arthur Villiers, Edward Hymers and Charles Wheatley – all men of considerable experience and absolute loyalty. Ilsley's great 'staying power' must have been sustained, particularly in his later years, by such loyal support, and his hope of securing the appointment of the familiar figure of John McIntyre, through his own long stay in office, had now finally been achieved.

Even so, one questions why Ilsley did not retire four years earlier when McIntyre returned from Rome, or when his hard work was over at the end of the war? An active man by temperament, he possibly felt, even at that late stage, there were still 'things to be done', and the attitude of some of his chapter may have been to protect his position in those final years rather than gently leading him in the right direction towards retirement. Even at the time of the difficulties over Besford Court, when it was stated in the report to the chapter of July 1918 that it was considered that the Archbishop 'has come to an end of his ideas – no forward policy can be expected of him', doubts were still expressed among them as to whether the administration under McIntyre would be any better.

Ilsley may also have been influenced by James O'Hanlon's and Henry Parkinson's persuasive philosophy of 'holding on'. Those sitting at table on one occasion at Oscott College, shortly after his retirement, hoped that his deafness had prevented him from hearing Parkinson's *faux pas*, uttered when he heard there was a rumour going about that he also was about to retire. Parkinson could be blunt at times, and to quash the rumour, he announced to the table in general, with Ilsley sitting there, 'The man who retires, when he could still go on, is a fool!'

## Glancey as Vicar General

Speaking of Ilsley's retirement, Mgr Bird said that although he was 83 at the time, 'hardly had he done so than he regretted it'.[17] That statement can be qualified by the fact that Bishop Whiteside's death came just two weeks after Ilsley's resignation, and this meant Bourne had a unique opportunity to work his will in the question of two important new appointments – one at Birmingham, and the other at Liverpool. This must have filled Ilsley with anxiety and regret about the situation his resignation had created, hence his relief at McIntyre's appointment. Ilsley was not well at the time, and added to this he was suffering from increasing deafness, so the time was more than right for his departure. Even the faithful McIntyre confided to Amigo that Michael Glancey had been hammering at the point for years that 'I was wasting my life in mere routine and little things.' Noted for being patient and gentle, he was now sadly to reflect: 'I fear we have drifted away somewhat from the true course; a V. G. sinks into a parish priest, a bishop sinks into a V. G. – and where is the true Bishop? Mgr Glancey will be on the alert now to help in genuine effort and reform.' He was referring to the fact that he had persuaded Canon Glancey to come out of retirement and take over the now vacant position of vicar general, which he himself had just relinquished. His old friend was prepared staunchly to assist him, and share the task before them, and had even sold up his home in Wolverhampton and moved into

Archbishop's House in Norfolk Road so that he could give more time to the task in hand. But the situation was by no means ideal as McIntyre was already aged 57 when he became Auxiliary Bishop in 1912, and he was now 66, and had never been strong.[18] Glancey, the same age, had already retired three years previously in 1918, on account of ill-health.

In fairness to Ilsley there were indications that he would have retired some years earlier had McIntyre, who he hoped would succeed him, not suddenly been removed from the scene to go to Rome in 1914. McIntyre was always anxious Ilsley should not be hurt by any suggestion that he should go, and Ilsley always had it in his mind to wait for McIntyre's return. So time slipped away, and the Archbishop had grown old in many years of service. Michael Hodgetts makes the observation in his *Guide to the Metropolitan Cathedral Church of St Chad, Birmingham* that 'Ilsley and Ullathorne between them ruled for seventy-two years, a record which is likely to stand for a long time.'[19] Possibly Ilsley finally lacked the clear mind to make the necessary decision to go, hence McIntyre's rather poignant comment, 'I fear we have drifted away somewhat from the true course.' In spite of these obvious shortcomings on Ilsley's part, Canon Toplass, in his short biographical sketch of him, described the genuine and honest attitude he had about himself. He finally had no doubts about going, and really made no bones about it: 'I don't regret my resignation,' he wrote to Amigo, 'the See required and deserved better service than I could give & my duty was, so it seemed, to clear out of the way.'[20]

## A Letter from Monsignor Barry

As soon as the news of the Archbishop's retirement became known, a great number of letters came from all quarters. Monsignor Barry looked back over the years: 'As the earliest and thus the oldest of those clergy surviving who have been associated with you – for I became your Vice-Rector at Olton in August 1873 – I cannot allow the event of which you gave intimation yesterday to pass in silence.

'Looking back on forty-eight years and more, I have to thank your Grace, and do so heartily, that in our dealings there is kindness to remember, and freedom was given me, and trust yielded during my long course of writing, teaching, working. My paths were often unexplored; I had to judge as best I could, and you relied on my judgement. Eventide has come. I hope it will be for your Grace a time of rest, when the burden of the day is at length off your shoulders.

Prayers will not be wanting to you from many hearts.'[21] It would seem from this letter that the Archbishop and William Barry, who was an exceptionally gifted man, had developed a considerable mutual understanding and appreciation of one another over the years.

There is a note at the top of this letter written in Ilsley's hand, 'I delayed replying, hoping to do so in my own hand.' He was just beginning to have difficulty with his sight, because of an incipient cataract, but nevertheless he continued writing letters for the next four years in a clear, if not strong, hand. That he managed to overcome his difficulty is evident in a letter from Tony de Navarro in 1924: 'What always remains a wonder, is your persistent habit of writing your letters and never having recourse to typing. A welcome and distinguished survival of an old custom in which I discover courtesy. God bless you, for preserving to all your friends something of that priceless but fast disappearing refinement.'[22] The de Navarros lived in the lovely Cotswold village of Broadway, and Mary de Navarro took a great interest in the work of Besford Court, and was active in fundraising for them. Ilsley would sometimes stay with them when visiting the Passionist Monastery there: 'Oh! Now I shall feel lost without

Figure 20.5 *Antonio and Mary de Navarro. Private collection.*

you as our dear Archbishop,' Mary wrote to him on 21 January as soon as she heard of his retirement, 'But we must pray that you will be happy with your successor. If Archbishop McIntyre is elected you will be happy ... Needless to say we will be delighted to see you ... We can make you more comfortable than at the Monastery – the rooms are cold there. "Labours that are over are very sweet" – You will be relieved of much hard work and can come and have a peaceful rest now.'

Cardinal Bourne's reply, on receiving Ilsley's communication telling him of his resignation through pressures of ill health, was also dispatched on 21 January. It was a cold brief note barely filling one small page: 'I am grieved to have your letter, and do trust that you are not suffering. I will beg Our Lord to give you every grace and much consolation as you rest from the burden that you have borne so valiantly and so long.'

## The Announcement in *The Universe*

*The Universe* devoted a central portion on its front page to the announcement of his resignation: 'As we go to press we received official news that his Grace the Archbishop of Birmingham has resigned. The Holy Father has accepted the resignation, and has directed His Grace to act as Administrator Apostolic pending an appointment.' *The Times* made their announcement under the heading 'A friend of Cardinal Newman' and there was mention that 'a close friendship existed between them'. By now many of those who had been Ilsley's friends or associates in earlier years had been long since dead, and had become almost legendary figures. As time moved on, the precise nature of how things had once been had already passed into the realms of 'historical inexactitudes'. Ilsley's position in relation to Cardinal Newman could not be termed as 'a close friendship', even though something more special appeared to have existed between them than just the mutual respect due to each, through their relative positions as Cardinal and Bishop.

Ilsley was not well enough to attend John McIntyre's enthronement, which took place on Tuesday 5 July. The diamond jubilee of his priesthood occurred a week earlier, on the feast of Saints Peter and Paul, but no public mention was made of this in the Catholic press, or any periodicals. The college diary was also silent on the matter, only mentioning a concert in the Northcote Hall taking place after supper on that day. With his typical courtesy it would seem most likely that he would have wanted no attention drawn to the occasion, but that it was his wish to spend the time quietly in his apartments at Oscott College in deference to McIntyre's important day.

The speech that the newly appointed Archbishop of Birmingham made at his celebration luncheon projected more than one meaning: 'I concluded that my vocation in life was to be that of a quiet, retired, inoffensive pedagogue; but Providence probably foresaw that I should have degenerated into a mere lover of peace and contentment; so gradually I was ousted from my position & forced to meet the rough glances of the outer world, and things have gone for me from bad to worse, & today the very worst that could possibly happen in the diocese of Birmingham has come upon me.'[23]

The words that John McIntyre took for his motto, *Fide et Lenitate*, meaning 'By Faith and Mildness', seemed particularly appropriate for him. Some of the clergy expressed their opposition to McIntyre's succession – Bishop Ullathorne's experience in these matters is called to mind, as he used to say that 'there was always backstairs influence in Rome which comes to the front, especially in the appointment of bishops'. In spite of a rule of secrecy regarding these matters, William Barry announced at the luncheon that the choice of the chapter had been unanimous over the appointment, which, he said, usually seals the case.[24] Ilsley's title at this time was transferred to 'The Titular Bishop of Macre'.

## Notes

1   The relics were rediscovered at Aston-by-Stone by Benjamin Hulme. According to the registers and his own word, he arrived there after 1839. William Barry gives a full account of the history of the relics in chapter 7 of *The History of St Chad's Cathedral 1841–1904*, entitled 'The Relics of St Chad'. The narrative by Michael Hodgetts, in his *St Chad's Cathedral, Birmingham*, is accompanied by some very fine illustrations describing their history which is depicted in the stained-glass windows in the cathedral. Further details are given by Michael Greenslade in *Saint Chad of Lichfield and Birmingham*. These last two being publications 4 and 10 of the Archdiocese of Birmingham Historical Commission.

2   *The Birmingham Weekly Post*, 30 May 1919.

3   Mary and Joseph Ilsley, 14 and 12, both at St Chad's School. They were the great-niece and -nephew of the Archbishop. Letter, June 1986, from their cousin Cecilia Ilsley.

4   *The Universe*, May 1919.

5   The Catholic press, Archdiocesan scrapbooks. The changed route is mentioned in *The Universe*, 14 May 1920.

6 B.A., Letter to all the churches in the Archdiocese, 'Given at St. Mary's College Oscott, this 18th day of January, 1921'.

7 *Ibid.*,Obituary in *The Official Catholic Directory of the Archdiocese of Birmingham, 1927.* This was written by Samuel Myerscough.

8 T. E. Bird, 'An Archbishop in Retirement', *The Clergy Review* (May 1955), p. 277.

9 B.A., Letter from Canon Glancey to Bishop Amigo, 23 January 1921.

10 Clifton, ch. 5, 'Differences with Bourne', p. 49.

11 B.A., Letter from Amigo to Canon Glancey, 10 February 1921. Rome had no wish to go against the interests of the bishops concerned when such changes were proposed. Clifton, p. 48 and Oldmeadow, vol. ii, p. 137.

12 *Birmingham Faces and Places*, vol. iii, 2 February 1891.

13 D.B., p. 22. Also *The Birmingham Mail*, 2 December 1926. He presided over conferences of the Catholic Truth Society, the St Vincent de Paul Society and the Catholic Poor Law Guardians. He had wider interests such as the Housing Reform Association to which he was elected in 1908.

14 Southwark, Letter from Archbishop Ilsley to Bishop Amigo, 12 April 1921.

15 Toplass, p. 124.

16 Southwark, Letter from John McIntyre to Bishop Amigo, 6 May 1921.

17 Toplass, p. 277.

18 Obituary, Archbishop McIntyre, *The Oscotian*, 5th series, vol. 5, no. 1, Shrovetide 1935, p. 5, 'His constitution had been impaired since his Sedgley Park days.'

19 Michael Hodgetts, *A Guide to the Metropolitan Cathedral Church of Saint Chad, Birmingham*, p. 15.

20 Toplass, p. 134. Also, Southwark, Letter from Ilsley to Amigo, 12 April 1921.

21 B.A., Letter from Monsignor William Barry to Archbishop Ilsley, Leamington, 21 January 1921. In a letter to William Barry on his golden jubilee, Pope Pius XI described him as one of 'the illustrious Catholic authors who combat writing by writing, and have long defended the Truth and the sacred rights of the Church'. The Vatican, May 1923.

22 *Ibid.*, Letter from Tony de Navarro, February 1924. Antonio de Navarro was Papal Chamberlain. Having given up a successful stage career to marry in 1890, Mary Anderson de Navarro returned to the stage in 1915, acting only to raise money for war charities. *A Few Memories* (1896) and *A Few More Memories* (1936) were her memoirs. Also Fitzgerald, vol. ii, p. 431.

23 *The Universe*, Friday 8 July 1921.

24 McIntyre Obituary, *The Oscotian* (Shrovetide 1935), pp. 5, 6.

## CHAPTER TWENTY-ONE

# *Final Years*

## Harvington Hall

As the weeks passed, the Archbishop gradually regained his strength, and later in that first summer of his retirement he stayed for six weeks at Harvington Hall in some rooms in the North Tower, where he was looked after by a maidservant from Coughton Hall and his sister Anne. In spite of the decayed state of the rest of the building it was still possible to stay there because 'a set of apartments in the North Tower was well maintained so that members of the family or friends could visit from time to time'.[1] Writing about his own stay there, William Barry remembered when he was in charge of the mission at Harvington some forty years earlier in 1880, 'it had been so long deserted that the highest roofs and attics were in a state of ruin'.[2] He described his room there as 'my moated chamber'.

Ilsley was familiar with the house. He knew all the different rooms and greatly revered the secret hiding-places. His knowledge of the place was due to the visits he had made from the earliest years of his childhood to see his aunt Isabella and uncle Joseph Ilsley, who had lived there when his uncle was the schoolmaster of the little village school housed in a former chapel in the grounds. Joseph Ilsley and his family lived in rooms in the Hall from the time of the setting-up of the school in 1825 until he died there in 1874.

Father Brownlow was the priest at the nearby church of St Mary's in those early years. He came to Harvington in 1824 as a young man at the age of 29 from nearby Stourbridge when the church was being built, and he opened it in 1825. A year later Joseph Ilsley took over the school, and he retired 51 years later in 1874. John Brownlow wrote a great deal about the history and traditions of Harvington Hall throughout his time there, and must have had very close contact with the Ilsley family throughout all those years, especially as the presbytery was not built until twelve years after his arrival, so he would also have been living in the Hall at that time. It was most likely through his influence that Edward developed his considerable interest in all that had happened there in times past, particularly as it was mentioned in Father Brownlow's obituary that he had known Edward Ilsley 'from a boy'. This would also explain Ilsley's lifelong concern for what might happen to it in future years. Father Brownlow died on 4 March 1888 in his ninety-third year, and Bishop Ilsley sang the *Requiem* Mass on 8 March in the Harvington Church. He was Auxiliary Bishop at that time and he became Bishop of Birmingham a fortnight later.

In 1896 Ilsley received a set of photographs from Benjamin Stone, who lived in Erdington. Enclosed was a letter saying, 'herewith the photographs of Harvington Hall, I recently promised. I think it is possible you will find them of interest.'[3] Ilsley must have been saddened to see the dilapidated state the of the old place revealed in these pictures. Although still owned by the Throckmorton family, it had been badly neglected for over a century, and by the time of his visit in 1921 'the greater part was little better than a ruin smothered with ivy, with stems as thick as tree-trunks, and the moat choked with vegetation and debris'.[4]

## A Child's Memory

Memories of the Archbishop and his sister while on this visit, as seen through the eyes of a ten-year-old local child called Rosie Martin, are recaptured by her in her book *My Lord and the Angel: An Encounter at Harvington Hall*. She describes how, having found her way into the building, she used to explore there: 'It seemed to me such a queer house; so many winding staircases and passages with odd steps in unexpected places because the floor levels differed from room to room.'

On one of her frequent visits there she met the Archbishop in the grounds, and she described how 'he was wearing a long black kind of dress with hundreds of scarlet buttons running in a straight line from his neck to the hem. Round his neck he wore a beautiful chain with a crucifix hanging from it. In one hand he held a black leather book with gilt edges to the pages; the other hand he raised to beckon me closer had a large ring on one of the fingers that glinted in the sunshine.' She returned there on several occasions: 'More often than not my Lord would be sitting on his tree trunk saying his office when I paid Harvington one of my frequent visits,' she said. 'Sometimes on

Figure 21.1 *Archbishop Ilsley in his later years. Oscott College archives.*

his quiet tired days, we did not go into the house but spent an hour or two in the grounds.' Describing him as 'a dear kind teacher', Rosie said he told her many things and 'above all else, he taught me many things which I have stored away in my mind'.

He always called his sister 'My dear', and Rosie continues: 'Sometimes My Dear would come out and join us.' On these occasions she would often bring with her a packed luncheon basket, her maid following her laden with a pile of rugs and cushions. Rosie describes another meal they had together inside the Hall (in a handsome room where the sun danced on the polished walls), and this showed the Archbishop obviously enjoyed his food: 'We had a splendid lunch. My Lord settled for a piece of cold pie with a considerable amount of greenery livened up with bright splashes of tomato and long thick whiskers of pickled cabbage – he washed his food down with a glass of beer and I politely accepted a glass of lemonade . . .'

She gives personal descriptions of Ilsley in her narrative not to be found elsewhere. Apparently he explained to her that the old place had been neglected so long that it was not safe for her to explore there any more, and he asked her to promise not to go inside the building by herself again. She said, 'Although his voice was gentle enough, there was an undertone of firmness attached to it and I knew I could never break a promise made to him.' He suggested instead that she should accompany him on a tour round, and afterwards she said, 'Seeing the house with him that afternoon, I noticed many details about the building hitherto unobserved by me.'

Among other things Rosie remembered about him was his hearty laugh and what she called his 'one-eyebrow-raised-grin'. She also described 'his steady blue eyes twinkling' as he stood on the bridge that spanned the moat and how if he said 'Amen' during a discussion it meant the subject was closed. On leaving Harvington at the end of his visit, his kindness and concern were shown in a letter he wrote to her aunt Mary, who looked after her at that time, which contained money for a new pair of shoes for Rosie. As a result of this meeting Rosie was received into the Church after she had moved away to London to be with her mother again 'two or three years later'. On leaving school she trained as a teacher with the *Notre Dame* Sisters in Liverpool. Her memories of Harvington always remained with her.

In 1879 a stone crucifix was erected in the grounds of the church of St Mary in memory of Father John Wall to mark the bicentenary of his martyrdom in Worcester. After this time private pilgrimages were made to Harvington by individuals from time to time, and some of them were fortunate enough to be able to go inside the house as this was made possible by an old lady living there who was 'very obliging to the visitor who would look over the old place'.[5] While on his visit in 1921 Edward Ilsley said he always prayed that Harvington, as a place of refuge in penal times, would one day be restored so that people could come in their numbers to visit it once more as a shrine. But he said he realized, 'my day's work is nearly done', so it was to be the devotion and tenacity of others that must continue the quest.[6]

## The Hall Presented to the Archdiocese

Three years later, in 1923, he had the comfort of knowing that the house had been bought from the Throckmorton family and presented to the Archdiocese by Mrs Ellen Ryan Ferris of Kings Norton (mother of the present Lord Harvington). Some urgent restoration was begun in 1929 in Archbishop William's time, three years after Edward Ilsley died. This came about because it was decided the hall 'must not be allowed to perish'. Careful restoration continued over the years, and when Harvington Hall officially became the centre of pilgrimage to the English Martyrs in about 1932–3, Ilsley's quest was safely fulfilled.

The following March 1922, when he was nearly 84, Ilsley requested Archbishop McIntyre to allow him to administer confirmation again from time to time. John McIntyre's reply was very much in the affirmative: 'It was very welcome news to me to learn that you are so well and hungry for work. You spoke to me when I visited you at Oscott about giving Confirmation. I said then and I now repeat, that you may do whatever you please as long as I am alive and have care of the diocese.' There is a little humorous quip at the end of his letter: 'After my death you must make fresh arrangements with my successor.'[7] Sadly enough, his joke was to prove to be not so far from the truth when, two years later, in March 1924, Archbishop McIntyre suffered a stroke which compelled him to remain a virtual invalid for the rest of his life, and he retired four years later. This must have come as a great personal blow to Ilsley, and it would have been an anxious and worrying time for him. He endeavoured to do whatever he could to help out by continuing to make good use of the Archbishop's previous sanction, because in a letter from his sister Anne, written four months after McIntyre's illness, she wrote: 'I heard you had been doing a stroke of business before you went away, confirming some boys. I am proud of you.'[8]

That summer, she wrote to her brother on 28 June, offering him

Figure 21.2 *A distant view across the fields.*

her sympathy over the death of his lifelong friend Henry Parkinson. 'I thank you for bringing him to see me a short time ago, but how ill he looked. It took me the few minutes you stayed to get over my agreeable surprise, and my deafness prevented my hearing what you said as your voice was weak.' Knowing the sadness his death must have brought her brother, she offered him comfort with startling simplicity, 'I feel nearer to him now, for after all isn't heaven very near to earth? Now I can intercede with him for you and those he has left behind. He will not forget you.'[9]

The loneliness of old age must have fairly enveloped Edward Ilsley at this time, because on 13 July 1924 his niece Philomena, a nun in a Belgian order in Bruges, wrote telling him of his brother Charles's death. 'You know well that nothing but the "cloister" would prevent me from coming in person to comfort you in your great sorrow . . . I wish to let you know as soon as possible how sorry I feel for you and assure you of my fervent prayers, but especially in these days, when Our Lord allows the weight of the cross to weigh more heavily on you.'[10] This news must have stirred some memories of the past for Edward, and brought to mind his brother's lifelong regret for having given up his vocation to the religious life. He wrote a letter of sympathy to his brother's wife, who replied saying, 'For the last four years his health had been very indifferent, in fact he never really recovered from his operation a little over four months ago.'[11]

## Deaths of Charles and Anne

This rather suggests that the two brothers had not communicated recently, or his sister Anne, who wrote to Edward, 'I had no idea he was so ill or I would have written to him.'[12] This would appear to be one of the last remaining letters that Edward received from her, because six months later, his sister, who had always addressed him as 'My very dear brother', also died. She was probably the person who had been closest to Edward throughout his life, and more especially so as she had received the habit during the same year as his ordination. With her death, a door on a very special part of his life must have closed. But he was not without the support of others in his family, for although his elder sister Ellen Brindley had died during the first year of the war, her husband John, and their family of two sons and eight daughters, still lived nearby at Erdington, where he was a regular visitor over the years.

Having been 'in harness' for so long, the old Archbishop must have found it difficult to slacken his pace after he had retired and to adjust to the inevitable changes in his everyday life. It was noticeable, for instance, that the amount of his morning post was lessening, and the story was told by Mgr Thomas Bird, a professor at the college, that when Ilsley came in to breakfast one morning, on passing the long table in the hall where the letters were always laid out, he discovered nothing addressed to himself. 'It was his custom to glance through these at table, sort them out, then take them to his room, where he would read them carefully, answering most of them by his own hand,' Dr Bird said. 'But the day came when there were no letters for the Archbishop – the first time, I suppose, for some sixty years! His face fell, and after a silent breakfast, crestfallen, he went to his room.'[13]

Archbishop McIntyre petitioned for the assistance of an auxiliary after his stroke, and in the September of 1924 Canon Glancey was appointed to the position. He chose a very apt motto on this occasion, *Non recuso laborem* – 'I do not shirk the burden' – which seemed to indicate that he was aware of the heavy task he was about to take on, because under the circumstances a great deal of the government of the archdiocese was bound to fall on his shoulders. Only a year was to pass when the shock of Glancey's sudden death meant that John McIntyre was once more without the help and support he so very much needed. In 1927 John Barrett was appointed his auxiliary, and McIntyre retired the following year and went to live in a house near the Oratory.[14] It was not surprising that R. H. Kiernan, when later writing about McIntyre's successor, Thomas Leighton Williams, in *The Story of the Archdiocese of Birmingham*, commented: 'After the long illnesses and great age of recent Archbishops, his drive and administrative experience were needed.'

Found among Edward Ilsley's notes and papers is a list he wrote out of all the positions he had held over the years, which he put under the heading 'Posts occupied by me'. This suggests he was about to embark on writing a memoir. There are some other sheets with the heading, 'Notes relating to Archbishop Ullathorne. Stories for which I can vouch the truth', as though someone may have suggested to him that his memories should not be lost. But these notes look as though they were written with some difficulty in an old, frail hand, and none of his attempts at writing things down were to get very much further than a few lines written on small pieces of half-foolscap paper. Philip Hughes, in his essay 'The Bishops of the Century', listed the many calls that bishops have upon their time, and added, 'It is perhaps not surprising that writers have been rare among the bishops, although those who wrote before finding themselves *in altissimis* seem also to have found a means to continue this apostolate.' He listed Wiseman, Manning, Ullathorne and Hedley as the few exceptions to the 'common run of non-writing bishops', and continued, 'If to the bishops just named we add the mid-Victorian convert, Brownlow of Clifton, we have told the tale of writing bishops.'[15]

It had probably never occurred earlier to Edward Ilsley to record anything about himself for future use in the writing of a biography, in spite of the example given him by his predecessor William Ullathorne, who had documented his own life so fully. It was Ilsley's intention, as his assistant bishop, to spare Ullathorne as far as possible from much of the heavier work of the diocese, and this undoubtedly freed the old Bishop to devote so much time to his writing. But as far as Ilsley was concerned, fortunately the many letters he wrote and received were destined to become a fairly close record of his own life.

## Plans for a Memorial Chapel

Those who came after him planned a different way of preserving his memory. Six months after he died, plans were drawn up for a memorial chapel to be built 'to perpetuate his memory among us'. A central committee was formed 'for the furtherance of the scheme', and to raise money to defray the cost. Six years later, in 1933, 'The Chapel of St Edward' was built on the north-west corner of St Chad's Cathedral, thus completing A. W. Pugin's plan which originally included a side-chapel, but this had to be omitted through lack of money when the cathedral was completed nearly a hundred years earlier in 1841. Seen from the outside, the structure of this chapel is rather like the character of the man for whom it was erected. It gives a feeling of stability, strongly buttressing the main building against the slope of the land which runs steeply away from it on that side. Inside the chapel the Archbishop's arms can be seen in the panelling in the centre of the oak stalls mounted on the west wall. Carved quite vigorously in low-relief, and most effectively gilded and coloured, they are placed under a raised pediment with a brass memorial plaque below. The stained-glass in five tall Gothic windows tells the history of St Chad's relics, and in one of them, Archbishop Ilsley is seen taking part in the Procession of St Chad, which he promoted and brought to the people again.[16]

Looking into the chapel, immediately to the right of the altar and placed high up in the wall, is another window of some significance.

Figure 21.3 *The original designs by Donald B. Taunton for the stained-glass window depicting Archbishop Ilsley and St Edward the Confessor. To be found in the St Edward Memorial Chapel. John Hardman and Sons, Birmingham.*

Divided into two lights, on the left side Archbishop Ilsley is seen enrobed and kneeling in prayer, while on the other side Saint Edward is shown standing, with his right hand raised in blessing. His tunic of azure blue displays a gold heraldic cross between four martlets, which was the device Edward Ilsley incorporated into his arms on becoming Bishop of Birmingham.[17] It is taken from the arms of Westminster, and this is explained by the fact that he had taken Edward the Confessor as his patron.[18] Designed by Hardman's, these windows are very fine. Beautifully drawn and crafted, their clear colouring lends an almost jewel-like quality to them.[19]

Figure 21.4 *Drawing of front view of St Chad's Cathedral showing St Edward's Chapel.*

Ilsley had a weekly visit from Mgr Bird, whose parish was at Sutton Coldfield. Thomas Bird came to the college to give lectures every Friday morning, and during the last two of Ilsley's life was his confessor. After his lecture Father Bird went up to the Archbishop's room to hear his confession, and they would then sit and discuss the news of the day. Now in his mid-eighties, the Archbishop liked at times to reminisce, and he sometimes let his mind go back to the 'old days' when he was a young boy in Stafford. One story he told Mgr Bird would have been about an incident that happened between 1847 and 1848 when Ilsley was nine or ten years old before he went to school at Sedgley Park. Father Dominic Barberi had come from Italy to give missions in Britain, and was in Stafford at the time. Did I know Stafford? Ilsley asked Father Bird. Did I know the Wolverhampton Road? Did I know a street leading out of a road, where there now is a lamp-post? 'Well I was a boy serving on the sanctuary at St Austin's when Father Dominic was giving a mission there. I met him at that corner where now is the lamp-post; I looked up at his face and said "You do speak funny"'!' It was said by a contemporary witness that there were difficulties for Barberi's listeners because, although the missionary's basic language was good – 'his pronunciation is defective, so it is hard to understand him'.[20] So the young Ilsley was not the only one who would have found the Italian priest's delivery strange. The Italian missionaries were not readily accepted or understood by the old Catholics, who regarded them with suspicion, and like them, Edward must have found the unfamiliar black habit which Dominic Barberi was wearing quite dramatic, emblazoned as it was with a heart surmounted by a cross.[21]

## Recollections

The old Archbishop would also give his recollections of Bishop Ullathorne displaying his dry humour. Ullathorne hoped that when he resigned, Edward Ilsley would succeed him, but there was another candidate who was highly favoured by many of the clergy – namely John Caswell, then Vice Rector of Oscott. When Ilsley was chosen instead of Caswell, Ullathorne quietly remarked: 'Ah well! Caswell will be just as well without the C!'

'Archbishop Ullathorne was unwilling to yield a point in an argument where his antagonist was a convert,' Ilsley had written among his notes. He described how on one occasion Ullathorne was pressed so far that he exclaimed, 'You will allow me to say that I taught the Catechism with a mitre on my 'ead when you were an 'eritic.' He was referring to a brush Ullathorne once had with Cardinal Manning, and was also underlining the fact that the Bishop was noted for heavily dropping his aitches as well!

The story to do with Ullathorne that amused Ilsley most was the one he told about Father Daniel Haigh, who built the church at Erdington. Father Haigh had a special devotion to Saint Francis of Assisi and was anxious that his church should go to the Franciscans after his death. One day he described to Bishop Ullathorne a vision that he thought he had in a dream, of Saint Francis standing by the main door. He was hoping this would finally persuade the Bishop to agree to his request for the future of his church. But Bishop Ullathorne, OSB, had other ideas, and his reply to this was: 'Father 'aigh, the next time Saint Francis appears to you, tell 'im that I'm bishop of this diocese, not 'im!'[22]

Mgr Bird described how during the last year before his death the Archbishop 'suffered mental agony for some two or three months from what appeared to be diabolical obsessions'. He continued, 'It was painful to witness his distress; he begged me to help him, to suggest some prayer or ejaculation that would comfort him.' Thomas Bird brought him the life of the Blessed Gemma Galgani, whose sufferings closely resembled his, and 'he was much consoled by what was written there. Then for a prayer I suggested Psalm XXVI, 1 & 2: "The Lord is my light and my salvation; whom shall I fear? The Lord is the protector of my life; Of whom shall I be afraid?" He told me he found the repetition of these lines most helpful, and the obsessions ceased as suddenly as they had begun; the last months of the dying archbishop were full of spiritual peace.'[23]

One day Thomas Bird asked Edward Ilsley what he considered to be the greatest change he had noticed during the long years of his priesthood. 'Vividly do I remember his immediate and emphatic reply as he turned his head to me: "The attitude of the laity towards the clergy," he said at once. He explained that when he was a young priest there was far more reverence for the clergy; what they said was received with respect even if there was not agreement; nowadays, he said, that old-time reverence was greatly diminished; what the clergy said and did was freely criticised; the layman thought he was equal to the priest. To what he attributed the change I did not ask,' said Mgr Bird. But he later questioned in his own mind – 'Was it the clergy's fault? Or the growth of democracy? Or "education"? Certain it is that this loss of respect and reverence have been harmful to clergy and laity alike.' His conjecture was right, education was the prime cause – which the bishops themselves had so zealously promoted.

## The Last Months of Ilsley's Life

There is a final glimpse into the last months of Edward Ilsley's life at Oscott College in *The Oscotian* – 'He lived among us, walked and talked with us, ate with us and made himself in all things a member of our community, until advancing age and growing infirmity compelled him to withdraw himself more and more into his apartments.' Difficulties with his eyesight caused him to write to Archbishop McIntyre on 9 June 1921, 'Shall I be in order if I ask you to present to the H. Father that I have difficulties in getting through my breviary, especially when the daylight or the artificial light is dull, and it would be a relief to me if at those times I could substitute the Rosary for Divine Office. If you think this would be in order I will ask your Grace to present my petition orally when you have an audience.' There was of course no need for the old Archbishop to have a dispensation as far as this difficulty was concerned, but nevertheless after McIntyre had a private audience with Pope Benedict on 26 June, he wrote the following note to Ilsley: 'The Holy Father was pleased to grant the foregoing Petition of the Most Rev. Edward Ilsley, adding that one third part of the Rosary should be said in lieu of Matins and Lauds, one third in lieu of the Little Hours and one third in lieu of Vespers and Compline.' From his later letters, it could be seen that his field of vision was narrowing, causing him gradually to write fewer words on each line. In spite of this he managed to continue to correspond regularly with his friends and family right up to a few months before he died, the handwriting and the message conveyed retaining their clarity to the end. On New Year's Day 1925, he wrote to Bishop Amigo, 'I have said Mass nearly every day, but I fear the sight will hardly last out.'

During those last months the students would come up to his room and read to him. One of his favourite books was Marmion's *Christ the Life of the Soul*, which he liked to have read over to him, time and again.[24] Father David Ford was an altar boy at St Chad's in 1910, and he went to Cotton College in 1911. In 1917 he did war service in the navy and on returning in 1919 he entered Oscott and was ordained in 1927. He said the Archbishop's sense of humour was very much still alive on the occasions when the students went up to read to him, because if a word was mispronounced by one of them it would be corrected by the old Bishop amid peals of laughter. David Ford remembered one of his friends saying he had read out 'mizzled' instead of 'misled' on one occasion, which caused the old man great amusement. 'He hardly ever

Figure 21.5 *A portrait of Alice Holden taken from a photograph in the Oscott College albums.*

left his room,' David Ford remembered 'and to the best of my memory I never spoke to him personally but only observed him as it were, from a distance. But to me he was all a Bishop should be, perhaps in an old-fashioned way, very stately, almost majestic, rather remote but much loved and admired; perhaps Victorian in many ways, and in the best sense of the word, a gentleman.'

The old Archbishop would take his daily exercise walking slowly up and down the length of the first-floor gallery on the arm of his nurse, Alice Holden, who obviously cared for him with great devotion in these last years. 'I hope you have recovered from your cold,' Sister Josephine wrote to him in 1924, 'This morning I received a letter from dear old Alice telling me how ill you have been, which I am sorry to hear. I must put extra steam on in my prayers for you.'[25] Later that year she wrote, 'I hope dear Alice is keeping well. Will you give her my grateful love.' Alice would sometimes write out letters for the Archbishop at this time, if he was not feeling quite up to it himself. Writing to Monsignor Newsome in the spring of 1925, she says, 'His Grace, I am sorry to say, is very poorly. I shall be glad when he is able to get out. The only two things he desires most to do are saying Mass and going outside.'[26] She was counted with the family among the chief mourners at his funeral.[27]

A year after Ilsley retired, Father Roskell, who was administrator among the cathedral clergy, received a letter from Father Styche on 26 November 1922, enquiring on behalf of the Archbishop, 'how the matter stands concerning burials in the Cathedral'. He concluded, 'Of course you will see the drift of this matter – but I suppose the civil authorities will not allow it.' There had been few interments in the crypt since the turn of the century, but special permission was granted to the Archbishop on this occasion.

Whenever he felt able, he would appear in the organ loft for Benediction. He could do this by going through a door at the end of the upper corridor, which spared him the difficulty of having to go down the main stairs, and through to Pugin's chapel. He still managed to go outside though, and throughout that last summer of 1926 could be seen, whenever the weather was fine enough, on the front terrace in his wheelchair.[28] He liked to be wheeled by one or other of the students, while engaging in conversation with them. A snapshot in one of the family albums shows him sitting in his wheelchair wearing his broad-brimmed Roman hat, contentedly surveying all the activity around him.

## Death of the Archbishop

By the autumn of 1926, he had become very frail and needed special nursing.[29] His end came gently on Wednesday 1 December. That day *The Birmingham Dispatch* printed the following: 'We regret to announce the death of the Most Reverend Edward Ilsley, the former Archbishop of the Roman Catholic Diocese, which occurred today at Oscott College. Dr Ilsley who was in his 89th year had been in infirm health for a considerable time, but was able to get about until Friday last, when he was taken ill and death took place at 8 am today.' An article in *The Oscotian* tells us: 'It was of course well known that His Grace was gradually growing physically weaker as old age grew upon him and his 89th year was now approaching completion. Still there was no apprehension of imminent danger till a few days before death actually took place. The Archbishop's weakness slowly but steadily increased, till at last the tired heart ceased to beat ... His Grace was anointed on Sunday night the 28th of November, and received the Holy Viaticum and Last Blessing on the following morning. From that time he was practically unconscious until he breathed his last breath on Wednesday, the first of December.'

Understandably a keen sense of almost personal bereavement was felt among many at Oscott College, and this was very simply conveyed in the last paragraph of *The Oscotian*: 'It remains only to express our deep sense of the loss we have sustained. It is difficult to visualise Oscott College without Archbishop Ilsley. If we add eight and a half years during which he was a student at Oscott before his ordination to the priesthood, to the thirty-seven years he was there as Rector, Bishop and Archbishop, we find he had lived at Oscott during half the life-time of the present College. No wonder Oscott feels that she has lost part of herself.'

*The Dispatch* reflected further: 'To know Archbishop Ilsley was to love him, and to love him was to be spiritually educated, so genuine was his character, so magic the influence that radiated from him.' An obituary in *The Times* had something more to say of Ilsley's public image: 'Dr Ilsley long enjoyed the reputation of being one of the best organisers and administrators among the Roman Catholic Bishops in England, as befitted the disciple of the essentially practical Ullathorne.'

The late Archbishop : A deathbed sketch from life, made for the UNIVERSE by Fr. Jerome Esser, C.R.P.

Figure 21.6 *A last sketch of Archbishop Ilsley made by Father Jerome Esser, CRP.* The Universe, *10 December 1926.*

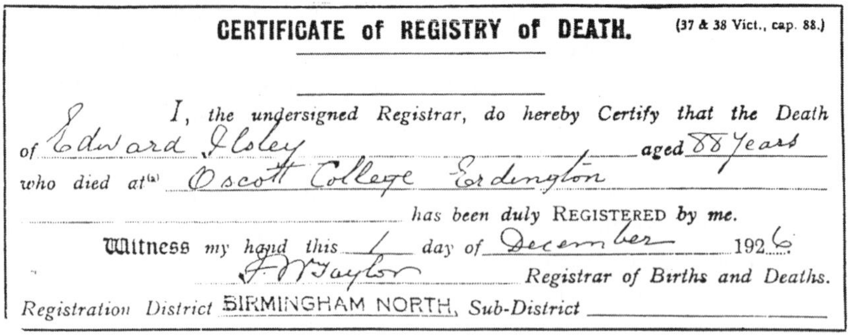

---

**CERTIFICATE of REGISTRY of DEATH.**   (37 & 38 Vict., cap. 88.)

*I, the undersigned Registrar, do hereby Certify that the Death*
of *Edward Ilsley* _____ aged *88 Years*
who died at⁽ᵃ⁾ *Oscott College Erdington*

_____ *has been duly* REGISTERED *by me.*

Witness *my hand this* _1_ *day of* December 192*6*
*F. W. Taylor* _____ *Registrar of Births and Deaths.*

*Registration District* BIRMINGHAM NORTH, *Sub-District* _____

---

Figure 21.7  *Death certificate.*

# Notes

1   Rosie Martin, *My Lord and the Angel: An Encounter at Harvington Hall*, p. 10. Also, Letter from Rosie Martin, 1 March 1998: 'My Lord spent six weeks at Harvington Hall in the North Tower. I myself knew him for a short forty days because he said not to visit when it was raining and when he spoke in a certain tone of voice you always did as he told you without question.'

2   Barry, pp. 138–9. He commented, 'It should have been treated in England as a public monument; but of course until recently, our monuments were left to take care of themselves.'

3   Benjamin Stone was a well-known photographer of his time. Some of his photographs were used in Dom Bede Camm's book *Forgotten Shrines* (1910).

4   Christopher Hussey, *Harvington Hall*, p. 3.

5   The architect W. Niven, *Illustrations of Old Worcester Houses*, p.6.

6   *My Lord and the Angel*, pp. 36, 54. The most urgent repairs were completed in 1931 and a great deal of further structural work and restoration has been done in recent years.

7   O.C.A., Letter from John McIntyre, 20 March 1922.

8   B.A., Letter from Sister Josephine, 29 July 1924.

9   Charles Cronin succeeded Henry Parkinson as Rector of Oscott College, and he also became Vicar General.

10   B.A., Charles's eldest daughter Sr Francisca in *Les Dames de Saint André*, Bruges, 13 July 1924. The Order was then semi-closed, no visits were permitted to home or family. She had special permission to come to England in 1938 to see her mother, then 81. The rule was finally relaxed in 1968.

11   B.A., An undated letter signed 'Elizabeth' from 18 St Albans Road, Woodford Green, Essex. She was called 'Aunt Liz' by his sister's family in Erdington, and 'Sal', a shortened version of Sarah, by Charles.

12  *Ibid.*, Letter from Sister Josephine, 29 July 1924.

13  Told by Mgr Bird, who was Scripture professor at Oscott and who was there between 1915 and 1932. He was Vice Rector between 1919 and 1932.

14  Obituary, *The Oscotian* (Shrovetide 1935), 'The Oratorian Fathers nearby, true to the tradition of their founder, ministered to the stricken prelate, with tender and constant care, and he was well served for eleven years by his faithful nurse.'

15  Beck, p. 192.

16  Pictures of these windows are reproduced in Michael Hodgett's *St Chad's Cathedral, Birmingham*, accompanied with the story they depict. They were designed by the artist Donald B. Taunton. The traditional annual procession was discontinued during the late 1960s. This may have been because the urban motorway running so close to the Cathedral required a network of subways to be installed in order to give access to the centre of the city.

17  The design on the left side of the shield is described as follows: 'Argent, on a chevron azure between three crosses potent quadrate gules as many broom cods proper.' The broom cods represent Our Lady.

18  On the Archbishop's Memorial Card, Edward the Confessor is shown as both saint and king. The arms appear prominently at the top of the card, and St Chad's Cathedral rises up at the foot of it.

19  St Chad's, p. 71: 'In recognition of the services which the Hardman firm had rendered to Catholic art in this country, Leo XIII created John B. Hardman a Knight of St. Gregory.' This was in 1901.

20  Denis Gwynn, *Father Dominic Barberi*, p. 178. Also Fitzgerald, vol. i, p. 174: 'It is extraordinary that this poor, obscure monk should in a strange country force the language as it were, into his knowledge, train himself to think, speak, and preach in the new tongue.'

21  This is the heart of the wearer. It is intended as a reminder, as St Paul of the Cross said, 'How pure & spotless that heart should be that bears the Name of Jesus engraven upon it.' Also Chadwick, vol. i, pp. 276–7.

22  *The Clergy Review* (May 1955), p. 278.

23  *Ibid.*, '*Dominus illuminatio mea, et salus mea: quem timebo? Dominus protector vitae meae: a quo trepidabo?*'

24  Monsignor James Crichton, who was a student at Oscott College in 1925, gave me these recollections. Letter, 2 April 1984.

25  B.A., Letter from Sister Josephine to Edward Ilsley, 22 April 1924.

26  O.C.A., Letter from Alice Holden to Monsignor Newsome, 9 April 1925.

27  *The Tablet*, Saturday 11 December 1926. The family mourners were Misses J., L., M. and S. Brindley, nieces of the late Archbishop; Mr C. A. Brindley (nephew); and Mr W. Wardle and Miss M. Wardle (cousins).

28  Obituary, *The Oscotian.*

29  Executors' account, 14 January 1927. Nurse Baines came to assist.

# *Epilogue*

## Coffin placed in the Cathedral

The Archbishop's body remained at Oscott College for two days from Wednesday until noon on Friday. It was then placed in the coffin and conveyed to St Chad's Cathedral, where it was carried up the centre aisle to the intonation of the *De Profundis* and was laid on a catafalque in the Lady Chapel until Sunday evening. Then it was removed to the centre aisle and placed before the high altar for the solemn dirge which was recited by the assembled clergy. Here it rested until the funeral service the following morning on 6 December.

Eight members of his family attended the funeral that day. They were his nephew Charles and his nieces Elizabeth, Mary-Ellen and Juliana from among the Brindleys, and his nephew Wilfred and niece Lilian, who represented the Ashfords. There were two cousins Mr W. Wardle and Miss M. Wardle. Also among the chief mourners were Alice Holden who had looked after him to the end, his nurse Miss Baines and Mrs Richardson, matron of Oscott College.

The *Requiem* Mass was celebrated by Francis Mostyn, the Archbishop of Cardiff, and 'upwards of three hundred' clergy were present in the body of the church. In the sanctuary were Bishop Amigo representing Archbishop Bourne,[1] Archbishop John McIntyre, Bishop Charles Carey-Elwes of Northampton, Bishop Hugh Singleton of Shrewsbury and Archbishop Frederick William Keating of Liverpool, who gave the panegyric.

A description of the scene inside St Chad's was given by *The Birmingham Mail:* 'The congregation was very large, and when the service was started the side aisles were also thronged, testifying to the love and respect in which Dr Ilsley was held. The high altar was draped in black, and on a large bright red cross was placed a golden crucifix. The great screen was covered with black hangings in the

Figure E.1 *Archbishop Ilsley's coffin lying before the high altar in St Chad's Cathedral. Taken from a sketch for the* The Universe *by William Wainwright, 17 December 1926.*

centre of which were the late Archbishop's arms, and the pillars of the church were draped in black and gold. Three tall candelabra each holding seven lights were arranged on either side of the coffin. Upon the pall reposed the Archbishop's mitre of plain white.'[2]

When he preached, the Archbishop of Liverpool took the words, 'Learn from me because I am meek and humble of heart.'[3] *The Universe* printed a personal study that took up the same theme: 'To us who knew him only as a Bishop, his extraordinary equanimity, his unruffled calm, his gentleness, the balanced wisdom of his counsel, his interior as well as his exterior quiet – all of these were accepted because they were his and he was our Bishop.'[4] The article continues: 'Another quality that endeared him to his clergy and his people was his accessibility. I do not mean merely that it was easy to see him, but what is more, it was easy to talk to him. He knew from his own experiences the difficulties and trials of parish life, and a long episcopacy had taught him how to face and solve them. Newman once whimsically remarked that "Rome had a knack of being right", Archbishop Ilsley's judgements were usually right in the long run.'

## A Man of Profound Simplicity

Much that was said in that study of Edward Ilsley in *The Universe* rings true. A man of profound simplicity in his everyday life, he was invariably calm and unruffled. Much of his wisdom lay in thinking things over carefully before embarking on any undertaking. He would then see the matter through with a great deal of thoroughness. Mgr Bird, who knew him so well, said of him: 'His career as bishop and archbishop, while not spectacular, was steady, thorough, fruitful and far-seeing.'[5]

He also made himself accessible to all and knew those who worked round him well, and used them well. Generous of his time and interest on behalf of others, he was ready to give assistance whenever he was needed. Many of his achievements have stood the test of time. He made his mistakes, and being human, some of these were considerable – but who would question that in many ways his judgements were usually right in the long run?

Archbishop Keating did not neglect to mention another side of Edward Ilsley's character – 'Though it was far from him to set himself up against the opinions of others, he was as inflexible as steel when he knew he had to make a stand for a principle,' he said. The writer in *The Universe* commented further in this respect: 'Bishops have the privilege of choosing their own motto. Happy are they who carry it through life so unsullied that it can be placed on their tombstone as Archbishop Ilsley's may surely bear his, *"Justus et Tenax Propositi"* – "Just and Firm of Purpose".'

Increasingly loved and venerated to the last, much was written in his obituaries of his widespread work, especially on behalf of the poor. When he retired, over 1500 children were being cared for in residential institutions and orphanages, or special schools, throughout the diocese,[6] and some 300 children were being sent out annually from Coleshill to Canada, through the Catholic Emigration Society, to make new lives for themselves out there. The welfare of children in need had been one of his main priorities since his earliest days.

The description of the ceremony continues: 'At the end of the Funeral Mass the body was taken from the front of the High Altar which was draped with black hangings, and carried down the aisle. The ten massive pillars were enclosed in sheaths of sombre cloth. An avenue of people awaited the cortège outside the church from where the remains were taken to their resting place in a grave beneath the floor of the crypt chapel of St Peter at the side entrance to the Cathedral.'[7] There the coffin was placed in a vault and the Archbishop of Birmingham, John McIntyre, recited the final prayers.

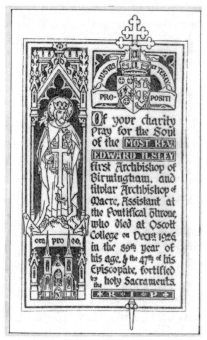

Figure E.2 *Edward Ilsley's memorial card.*

In his funeral oration Archbishop Keating described Edward Ilsley as a man 'whose saintly example had been a rock of faith unmoved by the transient feet of time'.[8] How well those words concerning his spiritual tenacity must have been understood by those listening who had worked with him over the years, or who had the good fortune to pass through his hands as students!

'The second of the Bishops of Birmingham, the successor of Dr Ullathorne, the contemporary of Manning, the diocesan of Newman. Memories of these great names and the battles in which they were champions clustered round the coffin.' The question was then asked: 'What was his place in the later Catholic history of England?'[9]

When his early achievements were recalled it was realized that a great deal of Ilsley's work as a young man had begun nearly forty years before the turn of the century, and that he had the unique experience of having worked with many of those great churchmen of his time who had been instrumental in re-establishing the restored Catholic Church. The part he played was in consolidating and holding on to what they had won – in some cases by courageously readjusting their undertakings. His transfer of the diocesan seminary established by his predecessor William Ullathorne, away from Olton and back to Oscott, is an example of this, and the work he undertook towards the creation of the Central Seminary is another. His subsequent care and protection of Oscott when it reverted to the diocesan seminary once more is also to his credit.

## His Work through Many Years

His strength lay in his consistency and quiet staying-power, and the many years he was able to continue his work and see it through to full fruition. He acted as a reliable cornerstone, securing the past with what was to come, and he was able 'to crown in peaceful days the work of his valiant predecessors' long after many of his contemporaries had left the scene.

To those who knew him well, Edward Ilsley's character was a blend of those qualities that were predominately priestly, and this is how he would chiefly be remembered. A tribute in *The Universe* published two days after his death succinctly summarizes his long life's work and catches something of the truth about him that we are after: 'One is accustomed to read of Bishops who have passed to their reward, that such a one was a great orator or another a great theologian, or another was a great administrator. When we look back on the career of Dr.

Edward Ilsley, a simpler, and perhaps in some ways, a grander epitaph rises in our minds – he was a great Bishop.'[10]

## Notes

1 Archbishop Bourne was absent that day. His failure to attend Edward Ilsley's funeral was unavoidable because he was in Rome for a consistory meeting from 3 to 12 December. One of the subjects coming under discussion with Cardinal de Lai at that time, which was considered a matter of some urgency, was the question of a coadjutor for Archbishop McIntyre who had not been at all well since his stroke in March 1924. Bishop Amigo was probably elected to stand in for Cardinal Bourne because of his long-standing friendship with Archbishop Ilsley.

2 The velvet pall covering the coffin was the Shrewsbury Pall, which had been presented to the Cathedral after the first anniversary of the death of Earl John, the 16th Earl of Shrewsbury in 1853. A description is given in *St Chad's*, p. 152.

3 Reported in *The Universe*, 10 December 1926.

4 *Ibid.*, 3 December 1926. This article was signed S. J. G.

5 *The Clergy Review* (May 1955), p. 280.

6 *The Catholic Directory* for 1888 and 1921.

7 It was Edward's wish that he should be buried in the cathedral crypt, and special permission had been granted by the local authorities and leave given by the Home Secretary, when preparations had been made by his secretary some five years earlier. Archbishops John McIntyre and Thomas Leighton Williams have also been buried in the crypt since then.

8 *The Birmingham Post*, 7 December 1926.

9 *The Universe*, 10 December 1926.

10 *Ibid.*, 3 December 1926.

# Bibliography

Anderson de Navarro, Mary, *A Few More Memories*, London, Hutchinson, 1936.

Atterbury, Paul, and Clive Wainwright, *Pugin as a Gothic Passion*, London and New Haven, Yale University Press, 1994.

Barry, William, *Memories and Opinions*, London and New York, G. P. Putnams Sons Ltd, 1926.

Beck, George Andrew (ed.), *The English Catholics 1850–1950*, London, Burns & Oates, 1950.

Bird, Vivian, *Staffordshire*, London, Batsford, 1974.

Briggs, J. H., *A History of Longton*, University of Keele, 1983.

Buscot, Canon W., *The History of Cotton College*, London, Burns & Oates, 1940.

Butler, Dom Cuthbert, *The Life and Times of Bp Ullathorne, 1806–1889*, London, Burns & Oates, 1926.

Camm, Dom Bede, *Forgotten Shrines*, London, Burns & Oates, 1910.

Chadwick, Owen, *The Victorian Church*, 2 vols, London, Adam & Charles Black, 1970.

Champ, J. F. (ed.), *Oscott College, 1838–1988. A Volume.of Commemorative Essays*, Stafford, George Street Press, 1988.

Champ, J. F., *Oscott*, The Archdiocese of Birmingham Historical Commission, 1987.

Cleary, J. M., *Catholic Social Action in Britain 1909–1959*, Oxford, Catholic Social Guild, 1960.

Clifton, Michael, *Amigo: Friend of the Poor*, Leominster, Fowler Wright Books Ltd, 1987.

Clifton, Michael, *A Victorian Convert Quintet*, London, The Saint Austin Press, 1998.

Couve de Murville, Maurice, *John Milner*, Archdiocese of Birmingham Historical Commission, 1986.

Denvir, John, *The Irish in Britain, From the Earliest Times to the Fall and Death of Parnell*, London, Kegan Paul, Trench, Trubner & Co, 1892.

Doolan, Brian, *St. George's Worcester, 1590–1999*, The Archdiocese of Birmingham Historical Commission, 1999.

Drane, Sister Raphael, *The Life of Mother Margaret Hallahan*, London, Longmans, Green & Co Ltd, 1929.

Engels, Friedrich, *The Condition of the Working Classes in England*, London, Sonnenschien & Co, 1892.

Fitzgerald, Percy, *Fifty Years of Catholic Life and Social Progress*, London, T. Fisher and Unwin, 1901.

Gillow, Joseph, *Bibliographical Dictionary of the English Catholics*, London and New York, Burns & Oates, 1885.

Glancey, Michael, *Characteristics from the Writings of Archbishop Ullathorne*, London, Burns & Oates, 1889.

Gray, Robert, *Cardinal Manning*, London, Weidenfeld & Nicolson, 1985.

Greenslade, Michael, *St Austin's, Stafford*, Stafford, Greengate Press, 1962.

Greenslade, Michael, *Saint Chad of Lichfield and Birmingham*, The Archdiocese of Birmingham Historical Commission, 1996.

Greenslade, Michael (county ed.), *The Victoria History of the County of Stafford*, Oxford, Oxford University Press, vols iii, vi and viii.

Gwynn, Denis, *Father Dominic Barberi*, London, Burns & Oates, 1947.

Hill, C. P., *British Economic and Social History, 1700–1964*, London, Edward Arnold, 1957.

Hillier, Bevis, *Master Potters of the Industrial Revolution. The Turners of Lane End*, Cory, Adams & McKay, 1965.

*A History of St Chad's Cathedral, Birmingham, 1841–1904*, compiled by the Cathedral Clergy, Birmingham, Cornish Brothers, 1904.

Hodgetts, Michael, *St Chad's Cathedral, Birmingham*, The Archdiocese of Birmingham Historical Commission, 1987.

Hodgetts, Michael, *A Guide to the Metropolitan Cathedral Church of St Chad, Birmingham*, Gloucester, British Publishing Co., 1978.

Hussey, Christopher, *Harvington Hall near Kidderminster Worcestershire*, revised by Michael Hodgetts, Exeter, The Catholic Records Press, 1981.

Kelly, Bernard William, *Historical Notes on English Catholic Missions*, London, Kegan Paul, 1907.

Lewis, Roy, and Joan Anslow, *Stafford in Old Picture Postcards*, Netherlands, European Library, 1984.

Lewis, Roy, and Joan Anslow, *Stafford as it Was*, Keighley, Hendon Publishing Company, 1980.

McClelland, Vincent Alan, *English Roman Catholics and Higher Education, 1830–1903*, Oxford, Clarendon Press, 1973.

McCormack, Arthur, *Cardinal Vaughan*, London, Burns & Oates, 1966.

McEvoy, Frederick J., 'These Treasures of the Church of God: Catholic Child Immigration to Canada', a paper published by the Canadian Catholic Historical Association, 1999.

Martin, Rosie, *My Lord and the Angel: An Encounter at Harvington Hall*, Droitwich, Grant Books, 1997.

Mee, Arthur, *Staffordshire*, London, Hodder & Stoughton, 1971.

*Meir Remembered*, Meir Local History Group, 1986.

Napier, Michael, and Alistair Laing (eds), *The London Oratory Centenary 1884–1984*, London, Trefoil, 1984.

Neville, William Payne, *Addresses to Cardinal Newman*, London, Longmans, Green & Co., 1905.

Newman, John Henry, *The Idea of a University*, London and New York, Longmans, Green and Co. Ltd, 1927.

Newman, John Henry, *Letters and Diaries of J. H. Newman*, Oxford, Oxford University Press, 1977

Newman, John Henry, *Sermons Preached on Various Occasions*, London, Burns & Oates, 1857.

Niven, W., *Illustrations of Old Worcester Houses*, London, John Strangeways, 1873.

Norman, Edward, *The English Catholic Church in the Nineteenth Century*, Oxford, Clarendon Press, 1984.

Oldmeadow, Ernest, *Francis Cardinal Bourne*, 2 vols, London, Burns & Oates, 1940.

O'Neil, Robert, *Cardinal Herbert Vaughan*, Tunbridge Wells, Burns & Oates, 1995.

O'Toole, P., 'Archbishop Ilsley, A Memoir', *The Tablet*, 11 December 1926.

*The Oscotian, Literary Gazette of St Mary's College, Oscott. The Jubilee of Oscott. 1888*, Birmingham, Hall & English, 1888.

Parkinson, Henry, *A Primer of Social Science*, Oxford, The Catholic Social Guild, 1913.

Parry, David, *Scholastic Century: St. Augustine's Abbey School, Ramsgate, 1865–1965*, Tenbury Wells, Fowler Wright, 1965.

Penny, Beth, *Maryvale*, The Archdiocese of Birmingham Historical Commission, 1985.

Pinches, Sylvia, *Father Hudson and His Society: A History 1898–1998*, The Archdiocese of Birmingham Historical Commission, 1998.

Purcell, Edmund Sheridan, *The Life of Cardinal Manning Archbishop of Westminster*, London, Macmillan & Co. Ltd., 1896.

Roberts, Frank, *A History of Sedgley Park and Cotton College*, ed. Neil Henshaw, Preston, T. Snape & Co. Ltd., 1985. ('Roberts' in the abbreviations; 'Frank Roberts' refers to the original manuscript, 1960.)

Roskell, Mary, *Francis Kerrill Amherst D.D.*, London, Art Book Company, 1903.

Schwertner, Thomas M., *The International Eucharistic Congresses*, London, Burns & Oates, 1926.

Snead-Cox, J. G., *The Life of Cardinal Vaughan*, 2 vols, London, Burns & Oates, 1912.

Strickland, Gillian, *Policy-Making in Elementary Education 1870–1895*, Oxford, Oxford University Press, 1973.

Trevor, Meriol, *Newman: Light in Winter*, London, Macmillan, 1962.

Ullathorne, Archbishop, *Letters*, 2 vols, edited by the nuns of St Dominic's Convent, Stone, London, Burns & Oates, 1891–2.

Vaughan, Robert, *The Age of Great Cities*, London, Jackson & Walford, 1843.

Wagner, Gillian, *Children of the Empire*, London, Weidenfeld & Nicolson, 1982.

Walsh, Michael, *An Illustrated History of the Popes*, London, Marshall Cavendish Editions, 1980.

Ward, Wilfrid Philip, *Life and Times of Cardinal Wiseman*, London, Longmans, Green & Co, 1897.

White, William, *History, Gazetteer and Directory of Staffordshire*, Sheffield, printed for the author, 1851.

Woodham-Smith, Cecil, *The Great Hunger: Ireland 1845–9*, London, Hamish Hamilton, 1962.

Young, Percy Marshall, *Letters of Edward Elgar and Other Writings*, London, Geoffrey Bles, 1956.

# Index

Acton, Canon 146
Alexian Brothers 32
Allen Hall 189, 200–1
Amherst, Francis Kerril, Bishop of
    Northampton 40, 90
Amigo, Peter, Bishop of
    Southwark 200, 259, 311, 316,
    318, 320, 326, 339, 368, 396
Appleyard Court 1
Armistice Day 346
Arms 385, 398
Arnold, Dr Thomas 11
Articles of Agreement 167
Arundel, Earl of 232
Austin, Alfred 146, 253

Bagshawe, Edward, Bishop of
    Nottingham 132, 345
Barberi, Father Dominic 388
Barnardo's Homes 216
Barry, Canon Michael 166
Barry, Monsignor William 6, 8, 44,
    69–70, 131, 210, 224, 259, 338,
    372, 375, 377
Benedict, Pope 341, 343, 345, 390
Besford Court 169, 350
Bird, Father Thomas 366, 371, 384,
    387, 398
Birmingham
    Diocese and Archdiocese 200,
    208, 309
    Diocesan Rescue Society 216, 218

industry 211, 235
oratory 108, 113, 384
oratory school 146, 147
Province 309, 324
town hall 269, 312
university 142
Bishop, Rev George 149, 174
Bishop's and Archbishop's
    House 91, 99, 158, 167, 285,
    310, 372
Black Country 6
Board of Bishops 38, 160, 165, 189,
    190, 196, 199
Bourne, Francis, Cardinal
    Archbishop of Westminster
    Amigo and the Unification of
    London 318
    becomes Cardinal 310
    Bishops' meeting 343–344
    boundary questions 315, 322,
    342, 367
    characteristics 319
    education 187
    enthronement 189
    policy changed 201
    reversal of Vaughan's policy 198
    seminary policy 154, 189,
    198–199, 303
    translation to Westminster 187
Brathwaite, Sarah 17, 37 n.5
Brindleys, the 17, 18, 72, 271, 383,
    396

Brookes, D. 22, 30
Brompton Oratory 114
Brown, James, Bishop of
	Shrewsbury 7, 40
Brownlow, Rev John 3, 231, 377–8
Burton, George Ambrose, Bishop
	of Clifton 197
Buscot, Canon Willibrord 11, 276,
	277, 294
Butler, Dom Cuthbert 43, 145
Butt, John Baptist, Bishop of
	Southwark 154, 187, 191–2

Cahill, John Baptist, Bishop of
	Portsmouth 190, 191, 197
Canada 399
Canon Law 81, 346, 355
Capuchin Fathers 133
Caswell, John 82, 85, 113, 137
Catechism 8, 28, 327
Catenian Association 353
Cathedral Chapter
	Birmingham 66, 67, 105, 128, 129,
		313, 333, 355, 370
	Westminster 189, 190
Catholic
	emancipation 230
	Emigration Association 209,
		219, 221, 222, 223, 399
	Poor Schools Committee 231,
		232
	Relief Act 6
	reunion 108, 269, 345
	schools 230–45
	Social Guild 142
	Truth Society 142, 216, 224
	Young Men's Society 364, 365
Central Seminary, 151–86, 187, 190,
	197, 202, 269, 400
Challoner, Bishop Richard 4, 48,
	261
Chamberlain, Joseph 243
Chamberlain, Neville 360
Chaplains 302, 304, 335, 336

Christmas 8, 56–58
Clergy
	addressed as 'Father' 10
	dress 10, 32
	preaching 65, 260
	training 48–50, 53, 56, 121, 144,
		173, 253, 260
Clifford, William, Bishop of
	Clifton 114, 132, 313
Cobridge 28, 245
Coleshill
	St Paul's Home 212
	St Vincent's Home 217
	St Edward's Home 216, 217
	St Gerard's Hospital 218, 335
	St George's Home 209
Confirmation 250, 271, 381
Conversion of England 158, 170,
	255, 256
Cotton College 148, 276–307, 324
Couve de Murville, Maurice,
	Archbishop of
	Birmingham 250
Crewe, Frederick 74–5, 113
Crichton, Monsignor James 84,
	200
Cronin, Mgr Charles 252, 331, 333,
	334

Daniel, Rev Edward 18, 32, 35 n.
	40
Darwin, Charles 142, 261
de Capitaine, Francis 110, 267, 281,
	297
de Lai, Cardinal 339, 342, 368
de Lisle, Edwin (M.P.) 129
de Navarro, Mary and Tony 352,
	373–4
Deed of Foundation 162
Dey, James 276, 281, 292, 295, 302
Divines 37, 39, 118, 119, 125, 138, 189
Division of Dioceses 309
Douai 5, 37, 121, 230
Downside 40, 45

Ducket, Canon   224
Duhamel, Archbishop of
    Ottawa   221

Education Acts
    1870   27, 233, 236
    1897   239
    1899   239
    1902   240, 242
Edward the Confessor   53, 311, 386
Elgar, Sir Edward   250, 273–4 n. 8
Elizabeth I   5
emigration   220
Emigration Association see Catholic
    Emigration Association
English College, Rome   63, 331
Estcourt, Canon Edgar
    Edmund   43, 44, 77, 82
Eucharistic Congress, London   272
Eucharistic Congress,
    Montreal   209

Faber, Rev Frederick William   294
Fabian Society   142
Fenn, Canon   163
Flanagan, Rev Thomas   7–8
Fort Augustus   268
French Revolution   6
Fund Raising and Donations
    238–9

Gasquet, Dom Aidan   193
Gladstone   236, 237
Glancey, Canon Michael   216
    Auxiliary Bishop   384
    Cotton College   281, 293
    death   384
    Letter to Amigo   367
    Letter from Bourne   319
    Provincial Directory   324
    Provost and Vicar General   359

Godwin, Canon Edward
    Henry   137–8, 165, 181, 303

Grace Cup   66–7
Grant, Thomas, Bishop of
    Southwark   37, 77, 144, 336
Gregorian Chant   202, 268
Gregory, Pope   362

Hammersmith   153
Hansom, Edward   41, 59 n. 12, 119
Hardman, Mother Juliana   54
Hardmans   67, 386
Harvington Hall   3, 231, 239, 377
Hawksford, Canon   147, 277, 281,
    288, 299
Hedley, John, Bishop of
    Newport   81, 190, 193, 195, 197,
    313, 320, 385
Henfield   187
Holcroft, Rev Vincent   100, 133, 137
holidays   8–9, 57
Holden, Alice   391, 392
Holy See   123, 187, 191, 207, 254,
    264, 339, 358, 396
Hopwood, Dr John   137, 179, 279,
    292, 302, 326
Horarium   45
Hudson, Rev George Vincent   169,
    209, 213, 215, 220–4, 229 n. 31,
    335, 350, 355, 357
Hughes, Mgr Philip   77, 185, 187, 384
Hyde Lea   1
Hymers, Rev Edward   74–75, 293,
    299, 303, 306, 326

Ilsley, Edward, Archbishop of
    Birmingham
    appointed Canon   66, 67
    assistant to the Pontifical
        Throne   271
    audiences with Pope Leo   167,
        257
    auxiliary Bishop   84–85, 106
    becomes Archbishop   310
    birthday   1, 53–54
    car accident   341

Cecilia (niece) 97 n. 21
character 10, 47, 49, 51, 52, 84,
    103, 107, 156, 159, 249, 260, 334,
    352, 366, 368–9, 388, 390, 393,
    398–9
Charles (father) 1, 72–3, 87–8
Charles (brother) 1, 17, 72, 383
consecration 88–89, 110
curate at Longton 21, 23
death 392
Diamond Jubilee 374
Ellen Brindley (sister) 1, 383
family and childhood 1–6
feast day 53
Francis (great nephew) 347 n. 12
funeral 396–9
Golden Jubilee 310–12
illness 256, 279, 330
investiture 210, 312
Joseph (uncle) 3, 231, 377
letters 63–65, 69, 109, 126, 137,
    167, 195, 251, 253, 260, 283, 318,
    366
Mary Bryan (mother) 1
music 7, 11, 26, 27, 30, 48, 49, 202
ordained 16
pastoral letters 118, 207, 238,
    241, 249, 257, 336
portrait 207, 208
preaching 58, 65
Rector of St Bernard's 29, 43, 96,
    261
Rector of Oscott 138, 158, 169
resignation 366
school 6–9
school manager 27
seminary policy 121–2, 127–8
Silver Jubilee 103, 267
Sr Francisca, (niece,
    Philomena) 72, 383
Sr Josephine, (sister, Anne) 1, 2,
    16, 54, 377, 381–3
training at Oscott 10–12
visitations 207–8

William (uncle) 4, 33 n. 6
Inauguration ceremony 53
Industrialists 18, 21
International Congress 209
Ireland, Rev Walter 276, 278, 280,
    288, 292, 303
Irish Immigrants 1, 211, 233

Jen's Shoe Factors 12 n.7
James II 6

Keating, Frederick William,
    Archbishop of
    Liverpool 202, 216, 326, 340,
    368, 396
Kidderminster 4
Kiernan, R. H. 258, 384
Knight, Edmund, Bishop of
    Shrewsbury 40, 81, 113, 132

Lane End 18, 22
Lawnside 339
League of Nations 347
Lepicier, Cardinal 315, 320
Leo XIII 66, 142, 144, 155, 158–9,
    187, 214, 226, 254, 257
Liberal Catholics 275 n. 27
Lichfield 362, 366
Lilly, W. S. 254
Liturgy 267–268
Lloyd, Rev Francis 165, 178, 180
Longman, Canon 86–7, 102, 129
Longton 18–21
Loretto 69

Mackinlay, Rev Boniface 208
McCave, Canon James 96, 100, 102,
    103, 157
McIntyre, John
    Archbishop of Birmingham 305,
    370, 375, 399
    Auxiliary Bishop 249, 323
    Bishop's secretary 138, 249, 332
    Central Seminary staff 165, 179

Cotton College 290, 299
   letters 195, 330–331, 333, 370
   Rector of the English
      College 322, 332, 341
   St Bernard's 101
   Titular Archbishop 344
Manning, Edward, Cardinal
      Archbishop of Westminster
   created cardinal 65
   death and funeral 114
   letters 102, 106
   Newman, (comparison
      with) 76–77
   policies reversed 121, 198
   preaches on Newman 114
   schools 234, 235, 239
   Seminary policy 38, 144, 192
   Ullathorne's retirement 104, 105
   universities 263, 266
   visits St Bernard's 54
marl pits 19
Marsh Lane 27
Martin, Rosie 378
Mason's College 142
Massam, Rev James 16, 22, 30, 32,
   237
Maynooth 100, 196, 203 n. 14
Memorial Chapel 385
Mental Deficiency Act 350
Merry del Val, Cardinal 321
Messiah, the 58
Metropolitan 189, 311
Midnight Mass 57
Milner, Bishop John 6, 22
Minute Books 200
Mission Schools 27, 28, 237
Mivart, St George 257, 260, 267
modernism 140, 258, 259
monasteries 7, 13 n. 27
Montreal 209
Morris, Rev John SJ 154
Mostyn, Francis, Archbishop of
      Cardiff 190, 197, 313, 326,
   396

Myerscough, Rev Samuel 11, 21,
   340, 366

Newman, John Henry
   becomes Cardinal 73
   Bishop Ullathorne 77
   Canon Estcourt 44
   comparison with Manning 76, 77
   congratulatory address 73–75
   illness and death 113
   influence of 11
   preaches 10, 53
   support for Ilsley 109
   visits St Bernard's 53, 75
Newsome, Rev Thomas 169, 350,
   360, 391
Norfolk, Duke of 244, 245, 263,
   265
Northcote, James Spencer 11, 49,
   56, 105, 124, 145, 146

O'Hanlon, Canon James 101, 104,
   167, 299, 334, 359, 368
O'Keeffe, Mother Evangelist 222
O'Leary, Rev James 138, 166, 179
O'Neil, Rev Robert 163, 238, 266
O'Sullivan, Canon 110, 129
O'Toole, Rev Patrick 27, 28, 207,
   326, 334, 368
Old Catholics 261
Olton Seminary, see St Bernard's
Operettas 56
Oratory, see Birmingham Oratory
   and Brompton Oratory
Oscott College 37, 39, 91, 100, 118,
   121, 127, 154, 258, 261, 310, 338,
   362, 396, 400
Oscotian Society 132–3, 174
Oulton Abbey 175, 256, 257
Oxford/Oxfordshire 315, 322, 368

Pallium, Sacred 189, 311, 314
Parker, Rev Joseph 99, 113, 120, 137,
   253, 286

Parkinson, Henry
audience with Pope Leo    167
character    72, 301
contribution made    139–142, 259
difference with Ilsley    93
illness and death    381–383
letter from Bourne    190
letters from Ilsley    63–65
Rector of Oscott College    165,
    177, 201–202, 277, 290, 371
resignation as Vice Rector    92
Vice Rector of St Bernard's    71
Vice Rector of Oscott    137
war conditions    345
Pectoral Cross    86–7
Pius IX    65
Pius X    187, 259, 309, 310
Plainchant    7, 49
Plater, Rev Charles SJ    142
Plymouth, National
    Congress    326–7
Poor, the    211, 218, 231, 233
Poor Law Committee    212
Pope, Rev Thomas    108, 113
Potteries    19, 24, 210
Priests, Priesthood    126,127
Primate    320, 321
Propaganda    39, 157, 193, 194–5, 269
Protestants and non-Catholics    29
Pugin, Augustus Welby    39, 313,
    339, 385, 392
Pugin, Edward Welby    3, 25,
    34 n. 29

Rednal    114
Reformation, The    362
Relief Act, Catholic    6
Rerum Novarum    226
Rescue Society    216, 218
Restoration of the Hierarchy    120,
    309
Riddell, Arthur, Bishop of
    Northampton    157, 177, 190,
    191, 197, 267, 313

Roberts, Frank    278, 295, 303, 305
Romanizing    10, 48, 261
Rome    65, 157, 161
Roskell, Rev John W.    40, 392
Rosminians    17, 72
Ross Monsignor Francis    141
Royal Declaration    262
Rugby School    11

St Aloysius, Feast of    66–7, 119
St Augustine's College    130
St Austin's, Stafford    1, 16, 231
St Bernard's Seminary    29, 94–5,
    101, 118, 121, 199
St Chad's Cathedral    110, 269, 385,
    389
St Chad, Church of (Stafford)    2
St Chad, Feast of and
    Procession    362, 365, 385
St Chad's Grammar School    232
St Charles House    304, 316
St Edmund's, Old Hall    37, 47, 143,
    151, 153, 158, 184, 187, 189, 192,
    198, 200, 279, 304
St Etheldreda's    17
St George's, Worcester    250–251
St George's Home, Ottawa    209,
    223
St Gregory's, Longton    18, 22, 24,
    30
St Mary's, Stafford    2
St Mary's, Harvington    3, 377
St Sulpice    187
St Theresa of Lisieux    351, 361
St Thomas, Erdington    389
St Thomas, Hammersmith    155
St Wilfrid's    7, 118, 278
Sacred Heart    58, 250, 273 n. 6
Salford Grammar School    234
Salvation Army    225
Sandy, Rev Frederick    166, 179
Sandy, Rev Hubert    215, 219
Satelli, Cardinal    195–196

Schobel, Dr Victor Januarius
  Cecilian society   140
  contribution made   139, 140
  *De Seminario Centrali*   161
  letter to Canon Estcourt   94
  letters to Ilsley   125, 164
  Oscott appointment   137, 175
  poor health   176
  programmes of study   46, 55, 140
  St Bernard's Seminary   44
  Vice Rector of St Bernard's   96, 101
scholarships   4
schools   27, 237
school boards   27, 236, 238
secularisation   39, 118
Sedgley Park School   3, 4, 6, 7, 230, 279, 287
Seminary diary   44
Seminary fund   41–2, 59 n. 13
Seminaries, organisation of   37
Seminarians
  dress   47
  journals   55
  Oscott College   138, 312, 364
  recreation   52, 68
  vacations   57
Shrewsbury, James Brown, Bishop of   7, 156
Shrewsbury, Lord   232
Simeoni, Cardinal   106, 113
Sisters of Charity of St Paul   209, 223, 245, 351
Sisters of Mercy, Handsworth   2, 16, 54, 212
Snead-Cox J. G.   153, 164, 174, 176, 184, 338
Souter, Canon Joseph   101, 113, 124–6, 130, 137, 234, 277, 281, 288
Stafford   3
Standon Lordship   5, 230
Statistics   210–11, 223, 231, 234, 235, 236, 240, 270, 309, 341, 399

Stonyhurst   278
Stringfellow, Rev John   21
Styche, Rev Percy   252, 333, 364, 392
Sutherland, William   55, 113
Synods   37, 143, 199

*Tablet, The*   131, 153, 254, 344
Tams Pottery   26
Throckmorton, Sir George   3, 231, 239
Toplass, Canon Denis   149, 369, 372
Tractarianism   44
Training Colleges
  Hammersmith   235
  Liverpool   235, 380
  Roehampton   236
Trent, Council of   37, 121, 154, 161
Tyrell, Rev George SJ   258, 259

Ullathorne, William
  Australia   9
  character   77, 107
  consecrates Ilsley   78
  death   111
  moves into Oscott   91
  opposes 'dual system'   39
  ordains Ilsley   16
  petitions for auxiliary   81
  recommendation of Ilsley   43, 59, 82–84
  relations with Manning   77
  resignation   109
  seeks seclusion   91
  St Bernard's Seminary   40–42
  St Gregory's, Longton   22–24
  trains Ilsley   78
  Vicar Apostolic   77
  writing   111, 385
universities
  Birmingham   142, 202, 335
  Cambridge   263, 264
  Durham   202, 263

Gregorian   44
Kensington   263
London   278
Louvain   187, 202
Manchester   263
Oxford   148, 263, 264
Southampton   202
university question   148, 263–7
Ushaw   37, 143, 187, 194

Vaughan, Herbert
    Archbishop of Westminster   153,
        311
    attitude toward clergy   166–167,
        177, 183
    Bishop of Salford   151, 224, 238
    Cardinal   155
    death   187
    education   234, 236, 238,
        240–241
    health   166
    ownership of *The Tablet*   131
    personal attitude   156, 263, 266
    policies reversed   189, 196
    portrait   161
    Seminary policy   151
Valladolid   322
Vannutelli, Cardinal   272, 331
Verres, Dr   57, 85
Victoria, Queen   1, 262

Villiers, Canon Arthur   47, 48, 50,
    92, 261, 355

Walsh, Bishop Thomas   145, 362
War, First World   223, 252, 326, 333,
    340, 345
Ward, Bernard   137, 189, 195, 276,
    279, 343
Ward, Dame Laurentia   256, 257,
    262, 346
Warwickshire   54
Waterford   1
Weedall, Henry   11, 30, 49,
    124, 146
Welman, Charles J.P.   132
Westminster Cathedral   159, 189
Wheatley, Rev Charles   69, 212, 356,
    364
Whiteside, Thomas Archbishop of
        Liverpool   310, 343, 367
Williams, Thomas, Leighton,
        Archbishop of
        Birmingham   302, 304, 305,
        381, 384
Wiseman, Nicholas, Cardinal   10,
        38, 49, 124, 144, 148, 151, 235,
        310, 362, 383
Wolverhampton   6, 7
Wonersh   153, 184, 187, 193, 316, 318
Worcester   252, 380